D1593853

The Logical Basis of Metaphysics

The William James Lectures, 1976

The Logical Basis of Metaphysics

Michael Dummett

Harvard University Press   Cambridge, Massachusetts   1991

Library of Congress Cataloging-in-Publication Data

Dummett, Michael A. E.
　The logical basis of metaphysics / Michael Dummett.
　　p.　cm. — (The William James lectures : 1976)
　Includes index.
　ISBN 0-674-53785-8
　1. Metaphysics.　2. Logic.　I. Title.　II. Series.
BC51.D85　1991　　　　　　　　90-39999
121'.68—dc20　　　　　　　　　　CIP

To Christopher, Maggie, Louis, and Michael Orlando

Contents

Preface   ix

Introduction: Metaphysical Disputes over Realism   1

1 Semantic Values   20

2 Inference and Truth   40

3 Theories of Truth   61

4 Meaning, Knowledge, and Understanding   83

5 Ingredients of Meaning   107

6 Truth and Meaning-Theories   141

7 The Origin and Role of the Concept of Truth   165

8 The Justification of Deduction   184

9 Circularity, Consistency, and Harmony   200

10 Holism   221

11 Proof-Theoretic Justifications of Logical Laws   245

12 The Fundamental Assumption   265

13 Stability   280

14 Truth-Conditional Meaning-Theories   301

15 Realism and the Theory of Meaning   322

Index   353

Preface

I was honoured to be invited by Harvard University to give the 1976 William James Lectures, which are, in alternate years, in philosophy and psychology. When the invitation was issued, I was informed that a condition of acceptance was that I allow the lectures to be published by Harvard University Press, a condition to which I naturally agreed. Accordingly, I typed out the text of my lectures, which I should not otherwise have done, preferring normally to lecture without a script, and usually without notes, for the sake of greater spontaneity and rapport with the audience. Unlike Hilary Putnam, who was simultaneously giving the John Locke Lectures at Oxford, I did not arrive with texts of the lectures already written, but, living from hand to mouth as always, composed them at Harvard as I went along. Before I returned, via Jerusalem, to England at the beginning of May, I left the typewritten text with Harvard University Press and deposited another copy in the Harvard Philosophy Department library. Asked by the Press how soon they might expect a revised version for publication, I replied, 'By Christmas'.

I tried to keep my promise. I worked on the revision throughout the summer but had not completed it by November, when other obligations, including conducting the Wardenship election at All Souls' College, of which I was then Sub-Warden, forced me to set it aside. My revised text subsequently went astray, but the original sat untouched, in mute reproach, upon my shelves for years. The Press was wonderfully tolerant, sending, at long intervals, letters that politely enquired, but never chivied. In about 1978, I gave a course of lectures called 'The Justification and Criticism of Logical Laws', which elaborated in great detail, and with new ideas, a small part of the lectures; from that point on, I knew that any final revision of them would necessarily be very heavy. Other things always seemed to have a valid claim to priority. After I became a professor in 1979, and increasingly after Mrs. Thatcher's assault on the universities began, teaching and administrative duties have piled so high as to make work on any long-term project unfeasible; I nevertheless maintained a steady resolve to redeem my promise to Harvard. A year's sabbatical leave, spent at the Center for Advanced Study in the Behavioral Sciences at Stanford, an ideal environment in which to work, has enabled me at last to do so, and I am deeply grateful to the Center for electing me a Fellow and providing that environment, and to the Andrew W. Mellon Foundation for financial support.

It is not an easy task to revise something written thirteen years before. These are not the William James Lectures, as delivered; but they are not exactly what I should write now if I were starting afresh to write a book upon this subject. They are a compromise between these. I have tried to retain the plan, and as much of the substance as possible, of the original lectures; but the revision is nevertheless very heavy. Many passages I found inadequate, or simply wrong, and have thoroughly rewritten. Remarks like 'There is no time to go into this here' could not stand in a version published after so long a time, and I have tried to fill the lacunas. I hope the resulting book, of which extensive parts are newly written, and equally extensive parts are no more than stylistic emendations of material composed in 1976, is nonetheless coherent. Although I have attempted to acknowledge the source of ideas I have derived from others, I found a few passages saying things I have not said elsewhere, but which others have subsequently said independently: I decided to let these stand without citing the corroborations. Also problematic were passages whose substance I *have* subsequently put in print; but I likewise decided that to excise them would mar the flow of the argument. In the course of revision, the book has become about two-thirds as long again as the lectures. There are normally eight William James lectures, but I had difficulty in cramming my material into that space, and the Harvard Philosophy Department kindly permitted me to give nine. For reasons of the kind already indicated, their revision has caused a further expansion. There is little here, however, that does not correspond to something in the original text, if only to a remark that an adequate treatment would require discussion of a topic left untouched. The Introduction is an integral part of the whole, representing the substance of the first lecture.

My aim was to achieve a prolegomenon to the work I still hoped to do in philosophy, and regard as one of its major tasks, to resolve the problems concerning realism in its various specific manifestations. I have not yet made substantial progress with this task, and now probably never shall; I shall be content if I have persuaded sufficiently many people of its importance, and of the correctness of my strategy for tackling it, to make it likely that others will achieve what I once hoped to. The prolegomenon was intended to clarify the nature of a meaning-theory and its relation to the semantic theories employed by logicians, and to explain why a meaning-theory need not be subservient to existing practice, but could criticise it and propose revisions to it, and, in particular, how it can serve either to justify or to call in question generally accepted forms of reasoning. I am aware how anti-Wittgensteinian this programme is. We all stand, or should stand, in the shadow of Wittgenstein, in the same way that much earlier generations once stood in the shadow of Kant; and one of my complaints about many contemporary American philosophers is that they appear never to have read Wittgenstein. Some things in his philosophy, however, I cannot see any reason for accepting: and one is the belief that philosophy, as such, must never criticise but only describe. This belief was fundamental in the sense that it determined the whole manner in which, in his later writings, he discussed philosophical problems; not sharing it, I could not respect his work as I do if I regarded his arguments and insights as depending on the truth of that belief.

When I had finished the lectures, I felt a deep satisfaction that I had achieved what seemed to me a definitive prolegomenon, and could now advance to the main task. Naturally, upon my re-reading them thirteen years later, that satisfaction has waned somewhat: I am more aware of the diversity of philosophical opinion, less optimistic about the probability of persuading others, and doubtless less certain of the correctness of my own views. I hope, however, to have succeeded in presenting a clear and even persuasive conception of a methodology for the theory of meaning and a case for the underlying importance of that branch of philosophy for its more glamorous relative, metaphysics.

Michael Dummett
Stanford, California, 1989

The Logical Basis of Metaphysics

Metaphysical Disputes over Realism

The layman or non-professional expects philosophers to answer deep questions of great import for an understanding of the world. Do we have free will? Can the soul, or the mind, exist apart from the body? How can we tell what is right and what is wrong? *Is* there any right and wrong, or do we just make it up? Could we know the future or affect the past? Is there a God? And the layman is quite right: if philosophy does not aim at answering such questions, it is worth nothing. Yet he finds most writing by philosophers of the analytical school disconcertingly remote from these concerns. Their writing treats, often with a battery of technical devices, of matters, like the meanings of proper names and the logical form of a sentence ascribing a belief to someone, that apparently have no bearing on the great questions with which philosophy ought to deal. The complaint, though unjustified, is understandable; and there are various causes for the situation that prompts it. One is that analytical philosophy passed, comparatively recently, through a destructive phase; a few, indeed, have not yet emerged from it. During that phase, it appeared as though demolition was the principal legitimate task of philosophy. Now most of us believe once more that philosophy has a constructive task; but, so thoroughly was the demolition accomplished, that the rebuilding is of necessity slow. Secondly, although we no longer regard the traditional questions of philosophy as pseudo-questions to which no meaningful answer can be given, we have not returned to the belief that a priori reasoning can afford us substantive knowledge of fundamental features of the world. Philosophy can take us no further than enabling us to command a clear view of the concepts by means of which we think about the world, and, by so doing, to attain a firmer grasp of the way we represent the world in our thought. It is for this reason and in this sense that philosophy is about the world. Frege said of the laws of logic that they are not laws of nature but laws of the laws of nature. It makes no sense to try to observe the world to discover whether or not it obeys some given logical law. Reality cannot be said to obey a law of logic; it is our thinking about reality that obeys such a law or flouts it. What goes for the laws of logic goes more generally for the principles of philosophy. The optician cannot tell us what we are going to see when we look about us: he provides us with spectacles that bring all that we see into sharper focus. The philosopher aims to perform a similar service in respect of our thinking about reality. This means, however, that the starting point of philosophy has to be an analysis of the fundamental structure of our thoughts. What may be called the philosophy of thought underlies all the rest.

That brings us to the third reason why contemporary analytical philosophy appears so dissatisfying to the layman. To a large extent, the philosophy of thought has always been acknowledged as the starting point of philosophy. Aristotle's philosophy begins with the *Categories;* even Hegel wrote a *Logic* to serve as the foundation of his system. Where modern analytical philosophy differs is that it is founded upon a far more penetrating analysis of the general structure of our thoughts than was ever available in past ages, that which lies at the base of modern mathematical logic and was initiated by Frege in 1879. The central concern of logic is with inference, which lies somewhat off centre in the philosophy of thought. But there can be no analysis of inferences without a prior analysis of the structure of statements that can serve as premisses and conclusion. An advance in logic is therefore also an advance in the philosophy of thought; and the advance first achieved by Frege was immense. It was difficult to achieve because it involved refusing to be guided by the surface forms of sentences. Frege regarded his notation of quantifiers and variables less as a means of analysing language as we have it than as a device for *replacing* it by a symbolism better designed for carrying out rigorous deductive reasoning, insisting that he had provided not merely a means of representing thoughts but a language in which they could be expressed. It has proved to serve this purpose well. Mathematicians now as a matter of course use logical notation to give more perspicuous expression to their propositions, although their reasoning remains as informal as ever.

Logic, before Frege, was powerless to account for even quite simple forms of reasoning employed in mathematics. Once the breakthrough had taken place, the subject rapidly made advances incomparably greater than those previously made in its whole history. To enquire how much mathematical logic has contributed to philosophy is to ask the wrong question: analytical philosophy is written by people to whom the basic principles of the representation of propositions in the quantificational form that is the language of mathematical logic are as familiar as the alphabet, however little many of them may know of the technical results or even concepts of modern logical theory. In large part, therefore, they take for granted the principles of semantic analysis embodied in this notation; whether or not they make use of technical vocabulary, this often renders their approach opaque to the layman.

It has until recently been a basic tenet of analytical philosophy, in its various manifestations, that the philosophy of thought can be approached only through the philosophy of language. That is to say, there can be no account of what thought is, independently of its means of expression; but the purpose of the philosophy of thought can be achieved by an explanation of what it is for the words and sentences of a language to have the meanings that they bear, an explanation making no appeal to an antecedent conception of the thoughts those sentences express. This approach to thought via language has certainly contributed to the alienation from analytical philosophy of the lay public, which superstitiously stigmatises all discussion of linguistic matters as trivial, through a psychological association as tenacious and irrational as that which causes all interest in playing cards or card games to be stigmatised as frivolous. The thesis of the priority of language over thought in the order of explanation is, obviously, important in itself; but its acceptance or rejection makes comparatively little difference to overall philosophical strategy, because doctrines concerning meaning can be fairly readily transposed into doctrines concerning thought, and vice versa. An analysis of the logical structure of sentences can be converted into a parallel analysis of the structure of thoughts, because by 'logical structure' is meant a representation of the relation of the parts of the sentence to one another that is adequate for the purposes of a semantic, or rather meaning-theoretical, treatment; it is that syntactic analysis in terms of which we may explain the sentence's having the meaning that constitutes it an expression of a certain thought. That is why Frege was able to claim that the structure of the sentence reflects the structure of the thought. Thus the thesis, in the philosophy of language, that the meaning of a sentence is determined by the condition for it to be true, can be at once transposed into the thesis, in the philosophy of thought, that the content of a thought is determined by the condition for *it* to be true: in either mode, arguments for and against the thesis are to a large extent the same. In recent years, a number of analytical philosophers, prominent among them the late Gareth Evans, have rejected the assumption of the priority of language over thought and have attempted to explain thought independently of its expression and then to found an account of language upon such a prior philosophical theory of thought. On the face of it, they are overturning the fundamental axiom of all analytical philosophy and hence have ceased to be analytical philosophers. In practice, the change makes a difference only at the very beginning: once their basic philosophy of thought is in place, all proceeds much as before. This is because, although they challenge the traditional strategy of explanation in analytical philosophy, they accept and make use of the same general doctrines concerning the structure of thoughts and sentences; they differ only about which is to be explained in terms of the other.

The shift of perspective characteristic of analytical philosophy brings about a partitioning of that part of philosophy known as metaphysics. Enquiries into the concepts of space, time, and matter belong to the philosophy of physics, which need not be focused exclusively on the theories of the physicists but equally cannot be pursued in disregard of them. Philosophical investigations of the concepts of objectivity and reality are of a different order, however. These grow directly out of the philosophy of thought; if they cannot be assigned a place within it, they belong to a part of philosophy contiguous to it.

Among them is a cluster of problems traditionally classified as typically metaphysical, problems bearing a structural similarity to one another but differing in subject matter. These are problems about whether or not we should take a realist attitude to this or that class of entity. In any one instance, realism is a definite doctrine. Its denial, by contrast may take any one of numerous possible forms, each of which is a variety of anti-realism concerning the given subject matter: the colourless term 'anti-realism' is apt as a signal that it denotes not a specific philosophical doctrine but the rejection of a doctrine.

The prototypical example is realism concerning the physical world, the world of macroscopic material objects. At least, philosophers usually discuss the physical universe as if it were composed exclusively of discrete objects; but mankind has from the beginning been familiar with matter in gaseous or liquid forms, with the air and the sea, with water, oil, and blood, and with what is not (or not obviously) matter but given off by material bodies, light, heat, sounds, and smells. Nowadays, we have also to reckon into the physical universe electric currents, radio waves, X-rays, and so on, and perhaps also gravitational and magnetic fields; a definition of the word 'physical' is not quite easily come by. Supposing that we know, at least roughly, what the physical universe comprises, there is a metaphysical dispute over whether or not we should assume a realist view of it. Opposed to realism about the physical world are various forms of idealism, of which the empiricist variety—phenomenalism—is the most obvious. Our knowledge of the physical world comes through the senses; but are these channels of information about a reality that exists quite independently of us, as the realist supposes, or are our sense experiences constitutive of that reality, as the phenomenalist believes? John Stuart Mill gave a famous definition of matter as the permanent possibility of sensation. We can deny the objective status of conditional truths about the perceptual experiences of a hypothetical observer at a particular place and time only at the cost of falsifying all our statements about what has not actually been observed: but is there something underlying these conditionals, or are they ultimate truths that rest on nothing? In the former case, most of our statements about physical reality could as well be true in a universe devoid of sentient creatures, because it is not the fact that we do or might make certain observations that makes those statements true; but, in the latter case, there could no more be a physical world without observers than a poem without words.

An analogous controversy relates to a quite different subject matter, that of mathematics. Here the realists are usually known as 'platonists': they believe that a mathematical proposition describes, truly or falsely, a reality that exists as independently of us as the realist supposes the physical world to do. Opposition to platonism takes various forms. On the one hand, formalists say that there are no genuine mathematical propositions at all, only sentences bearing a formal resemblance to propositions, which we manipulate in accordance with rules that mimic deductive operations with ordinary meaningful propositions. Constructivists, on the other hand, do not deny that there are mathematical propositions but hold that they relate to our own mental operations; their truth therefore cannot outstrip our ability to prove them.

Just as some philosophers take a realist view and some an anti-realist view of matter, so some take a realist, and some an anti-realist, view of the mind. For the realist, a person's observable actions and behaviour are *evidence* of his inner states—his beliefs, desires, purposes, and feelings. Anti-realism in this case may take the form of behaviourism, according to which to ascribe to someone a belief or a desire, or even to attribute to him a pain or other sensation, is simply to say something about the pattern of his behaviour.

A similar dispute concerns the theoretical entities of science. Some of these—black holes, quarks, hidden dimensions, anti-matter, superstrings—seem bizarre; but it is difficult to make a sharp demarcation between constituents of the everyday world and those of the physicist's world. Electric currents were not but now are part of the everyday world; presumably radio waves must also be assigned to it. Nevertheless, there remains a controversy between scientific realists and instrumentalists. The realists believe that science progressively uncovers what the world is like in itself, explaining in the process why it appears to us as it does. They are opposed by instrumentalists, who regard theoretical entities as useful fictions enabling us to predict observable events; for them, the content of a theoretical statement is exhausted by its predictive power. This is one case in which the view opposed to realism is made more plausible by empirical results; for a realist interpretation of quantum mechanics appears to lead to intolerable antinomies.

In ethics there is a conflict between moral realists and subjectivists. For a moral realist, an ethical statement is as objectively true or false as one about the height of a mountain; for the subjectivist, it has the same status as a statement to the effect that something is interesting or boring. Something is interesting if it is capable of arousing a certain reaction in us; if we did not exist, or were never either interested or bored, nothing would be interesting and nothing boring. So it is, for the subjectivist, in calling an action cruel or dishonest. It is cruel or dishonest in so far as it is liable to evoke certain kinds of repugnance in those who know of it; there is no objective sense in which it would have been better if that action had not been performed.

The most perplexing of these disputes concern time. The phenomenalist, regarding physical objects as mentally constructed by us out of our sense experiences, must think the same of space, as a system of relations between physical objects; but he usually regards time as objective, since sense experiences themselves occur in time. According to the celebrated view of Kant, however, the temporal character of our experience is itself something imposed upon it by the mind; and post-Kantian idealists have concurred in regarding time as unreal. Augustine already provided a ground for looking on time with suspicion. Our experience is of the present, or, more exactly, of what is now presented to us, like the sound of distant thunder and the light of the stars and even of the Moon and the planets. Our future experience will be of what will be presented to us; our past experience was of what was presented to us. But the present is a mere boundary. We can apprehend a genuine line—not a pencil mark, which is merely a narrow strip, but a line in Euclid's sense—only as the boundary between two regions on a surface or the intersection of two surfaces. If the regions or surfaces did not exist, the line would not exist either. But then, it seems, the present is a mere boundary between two nonexistents, between the past, which is no more, and the future, which is not yet.

This is a deep puzzle: but philosophers who try to solve it by denying the reality of time are now rare. Challenges to realism about one or other temporal region are more common. If statements about the future are now determinately either true or false, how can we affect what is going to happen? How can there be room for choice between different possible courses of action, when it is already the case that one of them will in fact be followed? Why is it, moreover, that we cannot affect the past as we believe we can affect the future? It is not merely that we do not know how to do it: it appears to be nonsensical to suppose that we could do it. There is an inclination to say that the reason is that it *is* now either true or false that some event took place in the past, but not yet either true or false that some other event will occur in the future: the past is *there* in a sense that the future is not; the past is, as it were, part of present reality—of what is now the case—but the future is not. Many philosophers succumb to this inclination. Others resist the idea that there is so profound an ontological distinction between the past and the future: the difference, they hold, is primarily epistemological, residing in the fact that we know about the past in a way that we do not know about the future. These latter are realists about the future, as opposed to the neutralists who believe that there is a strong metaphysical sense in which the future is not yet, but only a weak tautological sense in which the past is no more.

The neutralist view is agreeable to common sense; the converse view, which challenges realism about the past, is grossly repugnant to it. Yet it was adopted by C. I. Lewis and, during his early, positivist, phase, by A. J. Ayer. The motivation for it lies in the inaccessibility of the past. Realism about the past entails that there are numerous true propositions forever in principle unknowable. The effects of a past event may simply dissipate: unless time is closed, so that the recent past is also the remote future, the occurrence of such an event is thereafter irrecoverable. To the realist, this is just part of the human condition; the anti-realist feels unknowability in principle to be intolerable and prefers to view our evidence for and memory of the past as constitutive of it. For him, there cannot be a past fact no evidence for which exists to be discovered, because it is the existence of such evidence that would make it a fact, if it were one.

One may of course combine a realist view of the past with a realist view of the future: both past and future are determinate—though perhaps not causally predetermined—and in some sense exist to render our statements in the past or future tense true or false. All that changes, the realist may say, is the location of our consciousness along the temporal dimension. But then *something* changes—namely, the position of our consciousness. Yet, if there is change in that respect, why not in other respects? Why should the past not change after our consciousness has travelled through it, and why should not the future now be in a different state from that in which it will be when our consciousness arrives at it? That supposition undermines the whole picture. For, if the past can change, what has its condition *now* to do with the truth or falsity of what we say about it? What we wished to speak about was how things were at that past time when our consciousness was at just that temporal location. It is now evident, however, that even the supposition that past and future do not change will not rescue us from the dilemma: for it is not their *present* condition, whether or not liable to change, that we intended to talk about but their condition at the time when our consciousness was or will be at the relevant point in its journey from past to future, so that we were or shall be able to observe the events then taking place. The picture of the enduring past and the awaiting future thus fails to accomplish what it aimed at, namely, to show what makes the statement we now make about past or future determinately true or false. If we eliminate enduring past and awaiting future from the picture, we are left with the ever-changing present, that is, simply the ever-changing world about us, or more exactly the periphery of the backwards light cone. The present, or the presently observed or presently observable, is all there *is*: it is futile to try to invent a sense in which what was is nevertheless *still* there, what will be *already* there. Are we thus committed to being anti-realists about both past and future, to saying that, when nothing that *now* exists renders some past- or future-tense statement true or false, there simply is nothing to make it true or false? Can a proposition be true if there is nothing in virtue of which it is true?

We are swimming in deep waters of metaphysics. How can we attain the shore? These various metaphysical controversies have a wide range of subject matters but a marked resemblance in the forms of argument used by the opposing factions. No doubt, light will be cast upon each of these disputes by studying them comparatively; even so, we need a strategy for resolving them. Our decisions in favour of realism or against it in any one of these instances must certainly make a profound difference to our conception of reality: but what means do we have to arrive at a decision? No observation of ordinary physical objects or processes will tell us whether they exist independently of our observation of them. Admittedly, an unwatched pot will boil as if it absorbs heat as steadily while unobserved as it does while observed; but that was already one of the data of the problem. No mathematical investigation can determine that mathematical statements have truth-values even when beyond the reach of proofs or refutations; no psychologist can determine whether mental states occur independently of their manifestations. The realist thesis is not a possible object of discovery alongside the propositions it proposes to interpret: it is a doctrine concerning the status of those propositions.

It is difficult to avoid noticing that a common characteristic of realist doctrines is an insistence on the principle of bivalence—that every proposition, of the kind under dispute, is determinately either true or false. Because, for the realist, statements about physical reality do not owe their truth-value to our observing that they hold, nor mathematical statements their truth-value to our proving or disproving them, but in both cases the statements' truth-value is owed to a reality that exists independently of our knowledge of it, these statements are true or false according as they agree or not with that reality. Likewise in the other cases: for example, on a realist view of the past, the past event did or did not occur whether or not anyone remembers it or there is any record of it, and whether or not the evidence points in the right direction. What anti-realists were slow to grasp was that, conversely, they had in the most typical cases equally compelling grounds to *reject* bivalence and, with it, the law of excluded middle. The law of excluded middle says that, for every statement **A**, the statement ⌜**A** or not **A**⌝ is logically true. It therefore licenses various forms of argument that will not hold without it, in particular, that known as the dilemma (more exactly the simple constructive dilemma). You wish to prove some proposition **B**, say a mathematical one. You consider some proposition **A**—say the Riemann hypothesis—which no one has succeeded in proving, but which is probably true, and you contrive to prove **B** on the assumption **A**. If, now, you find out how to prove **B** on the contrary assumption ⌜Not **A**⌝, the law of excluded middle allows you to assert **B** outright. When the law of excluded middle is rejected as invalid, this form of argument can no longer be used.

Those who first clearly grasped that rejecting realism entailed rejecting classical logic were the intuitionists, constructivist mathematicians of the school of Brouwer. If a mathematical statement is true only if we are able to prove it, then there is no ground to assume every statement to be either true or false. The validity of the law of excluded middle does not depend absolutely on the principle of bivalence; but in this case, as in many, once we have lost any reason to assume every statement to be either true or false, we have no reason, either, to maintain the law of excluded middle. Being mathematicians, the intuitionists could not rest content with noting that their viewpoint on mathematics rendered certain classical modes of reasoning fallacious: they devised precise canons of valid inference, stricter than the classical ones. Thus was created intuitionistic logic, not the first, but by far the most interesting, non-classical system of logic. The only attempt that is in the least comparable has been the creation, originally instigated by Birkhoff and von Neumann, of quantum logic, which accepts the law of excluded middle but rejects the distributive law that allows us to infer ⌜Either both **A** and **B** or both **A** and **C**⌝ from ⌜**A** and either **B** or **C**⌝; but this is both less developed and far less widely accepted.

For precisely similar reasons, almost all varieties of anti-realism, when thought through, can be seen to entail a rejection of bivalence. No one taking an anti-realist view of the past could suppose every past-tense statement to be true or false, for there might exist no evidence either for its truth or for its falsity; likewise, the phenomenalist could not assume every statement about the physical world to be true or false, since no observational evidence might ever be forthcoming to decide it. In many cases, this ought to have resulted in as firm a repudiation of certain forms of classical argument as that of the intuitionist mathematicians; in practice, the topic was left almost wholly unexplored.

It may, however, provide us with a clue to the correct strategy of investigation. It looks at first glance as though, in these cases, we have a metaphysical doctrine yielding consequences for logic; the difficulty is in seeing how one could decide for or against the metaphysical premiss. We also face another and greater difficulty: to comprehend the content of the metaphysical doctrine. What does it mean to say that natural numbers are mental constructions, or that they are independently existing immutable and immaterial objects? What does it mean to ask whether or not past or future events are *there*? What does it mean to say, or deny, that material objects are logical constructions out of sense-data? In each case, we are presented with alternative *pictures*. The need to choose between these pictures seems very compelling; but the non-pictorial content of the pictures is unclear.

Were the positivists right to say that these are pseudo-questions, all answers to which are senseless? The doctrine was meant to be liberating; but it failed to exorcise the psychological allure exerted by the metaphysical pictures. Its failure is highlighted by the inability of the positivists to refrain from presenting pictures of their own. Phenomenalism is a metaphysical doctrine *par excellence*, being one version of a rejection of realism about the external world; and phenomenalism was strongly supported by the positivists. Their ideal, to engage in philosophy while eschewing all philosophical doctrines, was approached more closely, in his later work, by Wittgenstein. Even he came out, however, as a decided opponent of realism concerning mental states and mathematics. True, he also rejected both behaviourism and formalism; but, if his variety of anti-realism was more subtle than those of his predecessors, he did not succeed in skirting the controversy over realism altogether.

If a decision for or against realism concerning one or another subject matter has practical consequences—namely, the replacement of classical logic by some stricter canons of valid deductive reasoning— neither realism nor anti-realism can be devoid of content. It cannot be a matter of taste whether a form of argument is valid or not; the meanings of the premises and the conclusion must determine whether or not the latter follows from the former. There may be alternative possible interpretations, on one of which the argument is valid and on the other of which it is not; but, the meanings once given, we are bound to be faithful to them in our reasoning. The meaning of a statement determines when we may rightly assert it. It therefore also determines whether our having rightly asserted the premises of a putatively valid form of argument guarantees that we may rightly assert the conclusion. If it does, the argument is valid; if it does not, it is invalid. Hence a disagreement over the validity of certain forms of argument, such as that which marks, or ought to mark, the disagreement between the realist and the anti-realist concerning this or that subject matter, is necessarily also a disagreement about the kinds of meaning possessed by statements of some large range, such as statements about physical reality, mathematical statements, statements in the future tense, or statements of scientific theory.

Such disagreements about meaning must be deep. A superficial disagreement about meaning occurs when the meaning which one party to the dispute assigns to a certain expression is one that the other party accepts as being a perfectly coherent meaning which could be (or perhaps is) assigned to another expression: the dispute relates solely to whether that meaning is as a matter of fact attached to the given expression according to its standard use in the language. A deep disagreement occurs when the meaning assigned by one party is rejected by the other party as incoherent, that is, as not capable of being assigned to any expression whatever. This is often the effect of drawing a conceptual distinction. It is frequently alleged that rationalist philosophers like Spinoza failed to distinguish between a cause of an event and a ground for the truth of a proposition, and that empiricist philosophers like Locke failed to distinguish concepts from mental images. Once these distinctions have been pointed out, it becomes impossible to treat the word 'reason' as unambiguously meaning both 'cause' and 'ground', or the word 'idea' as unambiguously meaning both 'concept' and 'mental image'. A change in our theories may unquestionably have a similar result. Before special relativity, it was surely intrinsic to the meaning of the word 'before' that the question whether one event occurred before another had an answer which it made no sense to qualify as from a particular point of view (frame of reference); once we have accepted the theory, we cannot attach that meaning to the word or any other word. Disagreements over meaning between realists and anti-realists are necessarily of this character but far more wide-ranging. They concern the meaning, not of a specific expression, but of a whole sector of our vocabulary, or else, as in the case of realism about the future and the past, a fundamental linguistic operation such as tense inflection. The divergence is therefore not over how particular expressions are to be explained but over the correct general model for the meaning of a sentence of the kind under dispute. We may also describe it as a divergence about the appropriate notion of truth for statements made by means of such sentences. A constructivist holds, for example, that what renders a mathematical statement true is the existence of a proof; a platonist that it is a certain configuration of mathematical reality. The characterisations in terms of truth and of meaning are not rivals, however. As Frege was the first to recognise explicitly, the concepts of meaning and truth are intimately connected; so intimately that no fruitful philosophical explanation of either can be given that relies on the other's being already understood.

This now provides us with a line of attack upon these problems. Instead of tackling them from the top down, we must do so from the bottom up. An attack from the top down tries to resolve the metaphysical problem first, then to derive from the solution to it the correct model of meaning, and the appropriate notion of truth, for the sentences in dispute, and hence to deduce the logic we ought to accept as governing them. This approach, as we have seen, has twin disadvantages. First, we do not know how to resolve these disputes. The moves and counter-moves are already familiar, having been made repeatedly by philosophers on either side throughout the centuries. The arguments of one side evoke a response in certain of the spectators of the contest, those of the other side sway others of them; but we have no criterion to decide the victors. No knock-out blow has been delivered. The decision must be given on points; and we do not know how to award points. Secondly, even to attempt to evaluate the direct metaphysical arguments, we have to treat the opposing theses as though their content were quite clear and it were solely a matter of deciding which is true; whereas, as we saw, the principal difficulty is that, while one or another of the competing pictures may appear compelling, we have no way to explain in non-pictorial terms what accepting it amounts to.

To approach these problems from the bottom up is to *start* with the disagreement between the realist and the various brands of anti-realist over the correct model of meaning for statements of the disputed class, ignoring the metaphysical problems at the outset. We are dealing, after all, with forms of statement which we actually employ and which, with the exception of the statements of mathematics and scientific theory, are familiar to all human beings. Their meanings are already known to us. No hidden power confers these meanings on them: they mean what they mean in virtue of the way we use them, and of nothing else. Although we know what they mean and have come, in the course of our childhood and our education, to learn what they mean, we do not know how to represent their meanings: that is, we learn to use them but do not know precisely what it is that we learn when we learn that. We do not, in Wittgenstein's phrase, command a clear view of the working of our language. We are able to operate with it in contexts in which we normally find ourselves; but we are like soldiers in a battle, grasping enough to be able to play our assigned parts but completely in the dark about what is happening on any larger scale. Mathematicians certainly understand mathematical statements sufficiently to operate with them, to make conjectures and try to establish or refute them, to follow and devise proofs, often with great insight; but, asked to explain the significance of their enterprise as a whole, to say whether mathematics is a sector in the quest for truth, and, if so, what the truths they establish are about, they usually flounder. Physicists, likewise, know how to use quantum mechanics and, impressed with its success, feel confident that it is true; but their endless discussions on the interpretation of quantum mechanics show that, while they believe it to be true, they do not know what it means.

Perhaps, then, this is true of all of us. Perhaps the flat assertion that we know what our words mean needs qualification: we know what they mean sufficiently well to use them correctly in familiar contexts, but we do not fully understand them. It remains the case that they mean what they do only because of the use to which we put them. To gain a complete understanding, to come to command a clear view of how they function, we need to scrutinise our own linguistic practices with close attention, in order, in the first instance, to become conscious of exactly what they are, but with the eventual aim of attaining a systematic description of them. Such a description will give a representation of what it is for the words and expressions of our language to have the meanings that they do. It must embrace everything that we learn when we first learn language, and hence cannot take as already given any notions a grasp of which is possible only for a language-speaker. In this way, it will lay bare what makes something a *language*, and thus what it is for a word or sentence to have a meaning.

Such a description of how language functions, that is, of all that a child learns during the process of acquiring a language, will constitute a meaning-theory. The task of constructing a meaning-theory can, in principle, be approached without metaphysical presuppositions or *arrière-pensées:* success is to be estimated according as the theory does or does not provide a workable account of a practice that agrees with that which we in fact observe. It thus provides us with a means of resolving the metaphysical disputes about realism; not an indirect means, but one which accords with their true nature, namely as disputes about the kind of meaning to be attached to various types of sentences. The logical laws that ought to be accepted as governing any given fragment of the language depend upon the meanings of the sentences in that fragment, in particular, upon the meanings of the logical constants as used in those sentences. They can therefore be determined from a correct model of the meanings which those sentences have. Specifically, any account of the meanings of the logical constants has to supply a general characterisation of the contribution which a sentence makes to the content of a more complex sentence formed from it. This forces the meaning-theory to frame, for sentences of the language in general, or for subclasses of sentences within it, what has here been called a general model of meaning. In this way the theory will determine the correct logic, either for the language as a whole or, if it is too diverse for there to be such a thing, for each of the various sublanguages that together make it up. It will therefore settle the disagreement between the realist and anti-realist sides in each of the various metaphysical controversies over which logical laws ought to be treated as holding good.

Will it also settle the metaphysical controversies themselves? It is my contention that it will. In the process of constructing a general model of the meaning of a sentence belonging to each sector of the language, the theory will elucidate the concept of truth, as applied to statements belonging to that sector—statements about physical reality, mathematical statements, statements in the past tense, or the like—by setting that concept in its proper place in the characterisation of the meanings of those sentences. It will thus adjudicate between the rival conceptions of truth advocated by realists and anti-realists. For example, it will decide whether, as the realist believes, our understanding of mathematical statements demands to be explained in terms of a grasp of what would render them true, independently of our knowledge of their truth-value, and, if so, in what our grasp of this consists; or whether, as the constructivist supposes, it can be sufficiently explained in terms of our ability to recognise proofs or disproofs of such statements when presented with them. In the latter case, the appropriate notion of truth for mathematical statements is to be explained in terms of their provability. It will therefore resolve the controversy over whether a realist interpretation is tenable or has to be rejected.

It will resolve these controversies without residue: there will be no further, properly metaphysical, question to be determined. The metaphysical character of the controversies derives from their naturally presenting themselves as concerned with deep general questions about the constitution of reality and what it comprises. It is not wrong to say that they do concern such deep general features of reality. The mistake lies in supposing that to resolve these questions we have to study reality, not by the observational and experimental techniques of the scientist, but by applying the reflective insight of the metaphysician. Whichever of the rival metaphysical doctrines we adopt informs our conception of reality by endorsing a particular way of understanding our thought about reality: what the controversy directly concerns is precisely how we ought to understand it. It is therefore to be resolved, if not within logic properly so called, then within that part of philosophy of which logic is a specialised branch: the philosophy of thought, which, when approached via language, becomes the theory of meaning. Once resolved in favour of a particular doctrine, the picture of reality that goes with the doctrine and that gives it its metaphysical expression will automatically force itself upon us; but it has no additional content of its own. Its non-metaphysical content consists in the model of meaning which it suggests; however powerfully the picture impresses itself on us, we have to bear in mind that its content is a thesis in the theory of meaning, and that, beyond that, it is no more than a picture.

The thesis which gave a content to the picture could not be evaluated without constructing an overall theory of meaning; without that, the thesis is merely a proposal for how that part of such a theory ought to go, and we can have at best a hunch that such a proposal is correct. To construct a meaning-theory in the sense explained is obviously a complex task that requires us to make explicit much that we are ordinarily content to leave implicit. It nevertheless provides us with a programme, whose execution will lead, if what I have argued is sound, to a resolution of problems of deep import before which philosophy has for long—in some of the cases, for centuries—been stalled.

I am not aspiring in this book to arrive at a solution to a single one of these metaphysical problems: I am aiming at no more than a prolegomenon to an attempt to tackle them in accordance with the bottom-upwards strategy I have been advocating. The adoption of this strategy does not mean ignoring the traditional arguments for and against realism in the various controversies; it means transposing them from a metaphysical to a meaning-theoretical key. In the process, the different controversies must be laid side by side and treated comparatively. There is little likelihood of a uniform solution to all of them. Realism concerning one subject matter may create a favourable disposition towards realism concerning another but cannot possibly entail it: each case must be judged on its merits. But a comparative treatment can help us to decide what those merits are. Although there is no perfect structural analogy between any two of the controversies, the structural similarities are sufficiently strong that we may hope to develop general criteria for what, in any one instance, a realist needs to establish in order to prove his case. The arguments of the anti-realist often turn on particular features of the subject matter, and there is then no presumption that opting for an anti-realist view in one instance will demand the adoption of such a view in others. It is, however, possible to distil from the arguments that have been used by anti-realists concerning diverse subject matters a general argument against realism in any controversial case, that is, as applicable to any but the most restricted sectors of our language. This argument, if correct, would indeed lead to a kind of global anti-realism; whether such a view would be coherent would have to be tested by applying it to each of the ranges of statement that have generated controversy about the tenability of a realist interpretation. In order to distil such a general argument, a presentation in meaning-theoretical terms is essential: global anti-realism is impossible to frame in any other mode.

To get as far as this in an investigation of these problems, we need a firm base. The base will consist of a set of general principles governing the formulation of a meaning-theory. I have spoken of constructing a meaning-theory as if it were a task we knew how to set about; but of course it is not. The conception of such a theory originates with Frege's theories of sense and reference, or, more exactly, his theory of reference understood in the light of his account of the relation of sense to reference. We are, however, still far from any consensus about the general shape a meaning-theory should take; if we were not, the metaphysical problems I have listed would look much closer to a solution. Just as we do not know how to go about solving those problems, so we do not know how to decide on the correct shape for a meaning-theory; to reach such a decision, we must attain a clear conception of what a meaning-theory can be expected to do. Such a conception will form a base camp for an assault on the metaphysical peaks: I have no greater ambition in this book than to set up a base camp.

In setting it up, we must prejudge no issues. The metaphysical issues we hope eventually to resolve entail a choice concerning the forms of deductive argument that are to be accepted as valid, a choice between classical logic and one or another non-classical logic—intuitionistic logic, quantum logic, or some other logic yet to be devised. A sharp distinction must be made between criticism of a proposed formalisation of the way we are accustomed to reason and a criticism of the way we are accustomed to reason. The controversy, within the traditional

Aristotelian logic, over existential import was of the former kind. The question was whether or not, in enunciating the logical laws, it was best to treat the schematic form ⌜Every **S** is **P**⌝ as implying the existence of at least one object to which the subject-term **S** applied. If one did, certain syllogistic inferences—for instance, Fesapo (EAO in the third figure)—were valid; if one did not, they were not. But no one suggested that anybody had in practice reasoned incorrectly, had, for example, drawn a conclusion of the form ⌜Some **S** is not **P**⌝ from premisses ⌜No **M** is **P**⌝ and ⌜Every **M** is **S**⌝, established only on the basis of the weaker interpretation not involving existential import. By contrast, the intuitionist challenge to the law of excluded middle did concern the right way to reason in mathematics, not merely the right way to formalise our reasoning practice. The intuitionists held, and continue to hold, that certain methods of reasoning actually employed by classical mathematicians in proving theorems are invalid: the premisses do not justify the conclusion. The immediate effect of a challenge to fundamental accustomed modes of reasoning is perplexity: on what basis can we argue the matter, if we are not in agreement about what constitutes a valid argument? In any case, how can such a basic principle of rational thought be rationally put in doubt?

The affront to which the challenge gives rise is quickly allayed by a resolve to take no notice. The challenger *must* mean something different by the logical constants; so he is not really challenging the laws that we have always accepted and may therefore continue to accept. This attempt to brush the challenge aside works no better when the issue concerns logic than in any other case. Perhaps a polytheist cannot mean the same by 'God' as a monotheist; but there is disagreement between them, all the same. Each denies that the other has hold of a coherent meaning; and that is just the charge made by the intuitionist against the classical mathematician. He acknowledges that he attaches meanings to mathematical terms different from those the classical mathematician ascribes to them; but he maintains that the classical meanings are incoherent and arise out of a misconception on the part of the classical mathematician about how mathematical language functions. Thus the answer to the question how it is possible to call a basic logical law in doubt is that, underlying the disagreement about logic, there is a yet more fundamental disagreement about the correct model of meaning, that is, about what we should regard as constituting an understanding of a statement. The answer to the question how the validity of such a law can be rationally discussed is that we have to find some neutral manner of formulating the rival conceptions of meaning so as to be able to argue their merits without prejudging the issue in favour of one or the other.

The logical basis for investigation of the metaphysical disputes, which is what I aim to construct in this book, must therefore allow for all possibilities. It must not assume the correctness of any one logical system but must describe how the choice between different logics arises at the level of the theory of meaning and depends upon the choice of one or another general form of meaning-theory. In trying to construct such a base, we are forced to dig very deep, as solid foundations must necessarily be laid. We must dig below what we normally take for granted, without making explicit, our assumptions, namely, about what our words mean and, above all, about what the logical constants mean.

In the process, we cannot afford to neglect the resources that are at hand. The revolution effected by Frege led to an explosive development of logic; advances in the theory of meaning have proceeded at a far slower pace. Logicians have precisely formulated a variety of non-classical logics; they have explored different ways of formalising classical and non-classical logics; they have employed algebraic methods to characterise those logics, and, by both proof-theoretic and algebraic means, established their general properties; they have converted some of these algebraic characterisations into semantic theories that purport to state the meanings of the logical constants and thereby to provide a standard by which we may judge whether a formalisation is sound, in the sense that all inferences it permits are genuinely valid, or whether it is complete, in the sense that it permits all genuinely valid inferences. What logical theory cannot pretend to do is to adjudicate between these rival logical systems: it can treat them only as objects of investigation. A semantic theory is not a complete meaning-theory but only a preliminary outline sketch of one; and it cannot be judged correct or incorrect until it has been expanded into a meaning-theory which displays the connection between the meanings of the sentences, as represented by the theory, and the practice of using the language. It is obvious, however, that no serious enquiry into these questions is possible if it fails to avail itself of the technical resources that mathematical logic places at its disposal.

This book has been written in the hope of contributing to what I see as the most pressing task of contemporary analytical philosophy, the construction of a satisfactory theory of meaning. On the basis of such a theory, we shall have a clearer grasp of what is required of any piece of conceptual analysis, and hence of how to handle philosophical problems in general; in particular, we shall be well placed to make a direct attack on the metaphysical problems concerning realism which I have been recalling. But, because the contribution it seeks to make is only the construction of a basis, and because, in doing so, I have in places invoked technical concepts of formal logic, it risks arousing the disgust that the layman too readily allows himself to feel towards analytical philosophy. The layman wants the philosopher to give him a reason for believing, or for disbelieving, in God, in free will, or in immortality. In this introduction I have not raised those questions, but I have raised others almost equally profound: yet I am not proposing to answer them. I propose only to try to provide a base from which we might set out to seek for the answers. Worse, I employ, at various stages of the process, technical notions not part of the layman's repertoire.

I make no apology. Philosophical writing of the past, and of the present day as well, supplies answers to the great questions of metaphysics; and the answers usually satisfy no one but their authors. It is because these questions are of an exceptional difficulty that the labours of clever men, over many centuries, have failed to produce answers generally acknowledged as correct. Certainly their combined efforts have brought us somewhat nearer to finding the answers; not, however, as yet any nearer to being able to tell what those answers will be when we find them. This painfully slow pace of advance is also due, I believe, to an underestimation by even the deepest thinkers of the difficulty of the questions they tackle. They consequently take perilous shortcuts in their argumentation and flatter themselves that they have arrived at definitive solutions when much in their reasoning is questionable. I believe that we shall make faster progress only if we go at our task more slowly and methodically, like mountain climbers making sure each foothold is secure before venturing onto the next. Philosophy is, after all, a craft, as plumbing is. Many years ago a plumber who had come to our house to make some urgent repair which my wife had vainly attempted herself said to me, 'You don't want to go at it bald-headed, like your good lady here'. Philosophy would interest me much less if I did not think it possible for us eventually to attain generally agreed answers to the great metaphysical questions; but I should not have written this book unless I also thought that we should do better not to go at them bald-headed.

chapter 1

Semantic Values

How the Theory of Meaning Differs from Logic

Logic and the theory of meaning have two salient differences. First, logic, being concerned with the validity of forms of argument, represented by inference-schemas, must attend to a multiplicity of possible interpretations of a formula or sentence-schema: the notion it requires is that of *truth under an interpretation*. A meaning-theory, by contrast, is concerned only with a single interpretation of a language, the correct or intended one: so its fundamental notion is that of *truth* simpliciter. Secondly, logic, properly so called, is concerned with *inference*, so it can take the notion of truth for granted. It will quite properly analyse what determines a sentence as true or otherwise (or what determines a formula as true, or otherwise, under a given interpretation); but it need not enquire into the point or interest of our having the notion of truth, of our classifying sentences into those that are true and those that are not. We know in advance that what is required of a form of argument, for it to be valid, is that it be truth-preserving, that it carry true premisses into a true conclusion. Whatever point the classification of sentences as true or otherwise may have, that gives the point of classifying arguments as valid or invalid: so it is unnecessary for logic to enquire into the point of either. For the theory of meaning, by contrast, the *significance* of the notion of truth is crucial. It is an evidently correct intuition that the notions of truth and meaning are intimately connected. Obviously, however, the notion of truth has no place in the theory of meaning unless there is such a connection; and it therefore becomes a requirement on the theory of meaning that it make this connection explicit. For instance, when philosophers discuss whether or not the notion of truth can properly be applied to sentences of a given kind—say ethical ones—or, again, whether assertoric sentences containing empty referring expressions should be said to be false or to be neither true nor false, they conceive of themselves not merely as delineating the application of the predicates 'true' and 'false' but as analysing the meanings of the sentences in question. But, if their opinions are to be interpreted as bearing on meaning, we must know what the connection is between the meaning of a sentence and the conditions, if any, under which it is true or false.

That is not to say that the connection is to be stated by some explicit formula relating truth to meaning, such as 'to know the meaning of a sentence is to know the condition for it to be true' or, in a more sophisticated version, 'to know the meanings of all the words of a language is to know a finitely axiomatisable theory of truth for that language'. From such a formula, taken on its own, we learn only how the speaker thinks it proper to use the word 'meaning' or the phrase 'to know the meaning'; it does not tell us the interest which he supposes such a concept of meaning to have. The task of the theory of meaning is to give an account of how language functions, in other words, to explain what, in general, is effected by the utterance of a sentence in the presence of hearers who know the language to which it belongs—an act which is, even in the simplest cases, by far the most complicated of all the things we do. The notion of meaning itself need not, therefore, play any important role in a theory of meaning; if it does, this will be only because a connection is set up between the meaning of a sentence and our employment of it, that is, when we utter it and how we react, verbally and otherwise, to the utterance of it.

Let us now assume that such a connection has been set up. That is to say, we use the word 'meaning' in such a way that any difference in meaning between two expressions involves a difference in effect—the utterance of a sentence containing the one will at least on some possible occasions produce a different effect from an utterance of a sentence containing the other. Now the meaning of a sentence is frequently regarded as correlative with its truth-conditions. Let us assume that this doctrine is intended not as part of a stipulative definition of the word 'meaning' but as a thesis relating to meaning as we are construing 'meaning'. On this understanding, suppose there are two languages which resemble each other in every respect save that in one the meaning of a sentence containing a name is such that an utterance of it is false if the name proves to lack a bearer, and in the other it is such that, in the same case, the utterance is neither true nor false. This difference in meaning must, then, come out in some difference in employment of such sentences in the two languages: a difference that cannot consist merely in a difference in the application to them of the word corresponding, in those languages, to our word 'false'. This shows that, whenever some thesis about the conditions for the truth or falsity of sentences of, say, English is intended to bear on the meanings of those sentences, the criterion for its correctness cannot depend upon the accepted usage, *within* English, of the predicates 'true' and 'false'; rather, the relevant application of the concepts of truth and falsity must be governed by whatever connection it is that these notions are supposed to have with the meanings of sentences, that is, with what is effected by their utterance.

I use the phrase 'the theory of meaning' as coordinate with 'the theory of knowledge' to designate a branch of philosophy, otherwise less happily known as 'the philosophy of language'. To distinguish this from what Davidson and others speak of as '*a* theory of meaning', that is, a complete specification of the meanings of all words and expressions of one particular language, I shall use for the latter the expression 'a meaning-theory'. I am in agreement with Davidson that the correct methodology for the theory of meaning is to enquire into the general principles upon which a meaning-theory is to be constructed.

Now although there exist these two salient differences between logic and the theory of meaning, the two subjects are closely allied, as is evident from the fact that in the work of Frege, from which the modern development of both of them originates, they widely overlap. In fact, throughout the subsequent history of these subjects, the theory of meaning has behaved like the younger brother, borrowing from logic for its own purposes many of the concepts devised by logicians for theirs: Davidson's adaptation of a Tarskian truth-definition is only one such borrowing. Nevertheless, the difference between the respective goals of the two subjects induces very different attitudes to the same concepts. Thus logicians usually take a proof of soundness or of completeness for a logical theory at its face value. A proof-theoretic characterisation of the relation of logical consequence is based on the means whereby we recognise the relation as obtaining. A semantic characterisation of the relation displays the interest that the relation has for us. So regarded, a proof of soundness establishes that certain means of recognising the relation are in fact correct, that is, conform to the purpose for which we want to classify arguments as valid or invalid, while a completeness proof likewise shows that a given proof-theoretic characterisation cannot be improved on, judged by the standards imposed by this purpose. Most logicians are content to regard soundness and completeness proofs in just this light.

Philosophers, however, are usually sceptical about the possibility of justifying any form of argument otherwise than by deducing its conclusion from its premises through a series of arguments of other forms, that is, by showing that it is a derived rule of inference in some system among whose primitive rules it does not figure. That a form of argument may be justified by thus reducing it to other forms of argument already accepted as valid is not open to question: it is equally evident that we cannot, by such means, produce a non-circular system of justifications for all the rules of inference we intuitively accept as valid, that is, are accustomed to treat as such. The standard attitude of philosophers is that no other type of justification is possible. To show that a form of argument is valid in the semantic sense requires some kind of reasoning. If the reasoning itself involves the form of argument to be justified, then, most philosophers suppose, the justification is in effect a *petitio principii;* if it does not, then it amounts to a derivation of that form of argument from others, and its formulation in semantic terms is not significant. On this view, we have no option but to accept as valid certain basic forms of argument without further grounds for doing so. Since few would want to claim that we thereby evince direct insights into the structure of reality, the only alternative account is that, by treating such forms of argument as valid, we impose on the logical constants those meanings which we choose, and are free, to assign to them. We thus come back once more to the theory of meaning, but in a manner which strikingly reveals the different approaches that philosophers and logicians customarily take to concepts they share.

Model Theory

It thus becomes of importance to enquire into the relation between model theory, as practised by logicians, and the theory of meaning. How far can the notions employed by logicians in the semantic treatment of a logical theory be made to serve the different purposes of a meaning-theory for a language?

Logic can begin only when the idea is introduced of a schematic representation of a form of argument: a particular argument is valid only if it is an instance of some valid form. It is a mistake to suppose that, before any genuinely semantic notions have been introduced, only a proof-theoretic characterisation of valid inferences is possible. On the contrary, the use of schematic letters depends, for its intelligibility, upon a conception of a particular interpretation of those schematic letters and, more particularly, upon that of an actual sentence's being an instance of a formula. Hence it lies ready to hand to employ a presemantic notion of an interpretation, that of *an interpretation by replacing* the schematic letters by actual expressions of suitable restricted types, and to characterise a form of argument as valid just in case the conclusion comes out true under every such interpretation under which the premisses come out true. If the formula contains any device for the expression of generality, we must, in specifying such an interpretation, also lay down what the range of generalisation is to be—the 'universe of discourse' in old-fashioned terminology. The principal difference between the notion of an interpretation by replacement and a semantic notion of interpretation, properly so called, is that the former involves no analysis of the way in which a sentence is determined as true or otherwise in accordance with its composition: we simply rely on our ability to recognise certain particular sentences, obtained by replacement from given formulas, as true or as false. A semantic theory requires that we should frame, for each category of expression, a conception of the kind of *semantic value* that an expression of that category possesses. The semantic value of an expression is that feature of it that goes to determine the truth of any sentence in which it occurs: we thus arrive at an account of the determination of a sentence as true or otherwise in accordance with its internal structure. A semantic notion of interpretation is then obtained by bypassing the expressions which might replace the schematic letters: relative to the domain selected as the range of generality, the interpretation directly assigns to the schematic letters semantic values which could be possessed by expressions replacing them.

This notion of semantic value is to be compared with Frege's notion of *reference,* of which it is, indeed, one of the components. Other components are: the identification of the reference of a proper name with its bearer; the intersubstitutability of any expression **t** with the phrase 'what **t** refers to'; and the thesis that the reference of our words is what we talk about. Armed only with the purely programmatic notion of semantic value, we might be inclined at first to take the reference of a singular term as consisting in its having whatever bearer, if any, it has. But since the definition of 'semantic value' entails that the substitution of an expression by any other with the same semantic value cannot convert a true sentence into a false one, the existence of intensional contexts provides prima facie evidence against that view, which can be maintained only by reserving intensional contexts for special treatment, as inducing non-standard semantic values for expressions occurring in them. It cannot be claimed that the truth of an identity-statement is a sufficient condition for the possession of the same semantic value by the terms occurring in it, and hence that we are compelled to treat intensional contexts as non-standard. Rather, a relational expression is recognised as being a sign of identity just in case the truth of an atomic statement containing it guarantees the intersubstitutability of the terms occurring as arguments in all standard contexts. Even if we found reason to reserve intensional contexts for special treatment, we should still not have found a reason to *identify* the semantic value of a name with its bearer, with the consequence that an empty name was devoid of semantic value. The intersubstitutability of an expression **t** and the phrase 'what **t** refers to' is a natural principle when **t** is a name; when **t** is a predicate, it depends on construing the relative clause 'what . . . stands for' predicatively; and when **t** is a sentence, it can only with great difficulty be made to work at all. Similar remarks apply to the principle that the reference of our words is what we talk about; it has little plausibility to say that we use a constituent sentence to talk about its truth-value. For our purposes, the notion of semantic value is not to be taken as having any of *these* features of Frege's notion of reference built into it from the outset.

The provision of a workable semantic theory depends to a very large extent upon the prior adoption of a suitable syntax: since the semantic theory has to explain how a sentence is determined as true or otherwise in accordance with its composition, and since, even to state the formation rules governing natural language, the composition of a sentence is not to be thought of as apparent from a superficial inspection, it is plain that to obtain a successful semantic theory we need first an adequate analysis of the way sentences are to be regarded as constructed out of their component parts. A plausible pattern for the terminus of such a syntactic analysis, that is, for the underlying compositional structure of each sentence, was first provided by Frege, and, so far as I know, it has not been improved on since. Not only do almost all formalised languages conform to this pattern, or some near variant of it; but, even in the case of natural languages, the problems all relate to how the surface forms can be construed as depending upon an underlying structure of this kind. I shall be concerned with the semantics only of languages obeying an essentially Fregean syntax, not because I feel certain that such a syntax is canonical, but because I know of no semantic theory which does not require that the sentences first be mapped on to ones conforming to such a syntax, and I have no counter-proposal to make.

Straightforward Explanations

The importance of the prior syntactic analysis is so great that we must ask whether it is not everything, at least for a language with a classical logic. Once we have a Fregean syntax, are not the details of classical semantics already thereby determined? Is there anything left to do, save to proceed in the obvious way? This does not appear to be the case, indeed, for non-classical semantic theories, since in these the explanations of the logical constants do not take a straightforward form. Classically, for example, we may stipulate that ⌜if **A**, then **B**⌝ is to be true just in case, if **A** is true, then **B** is true; this can be called an *absolutely straightforward* stipulation. A non-classical semantic theory

frequently differs from the classical theory in operating with a relativised notion of truth instead of an absolute notion: truth at a time,
truth in a possible world, or, in the intuitionistic semantics provided
by Beth trees or Kripke trees, truth relative to a state of information. The explanations of the logical constants under a semantic theory
employing a relativised notion of truth cannot be absolutely straightforward; but they may be *relatively straightforward*, as when it is stipulated that ⌐A or B⌐ is to be true in a possible world w just in case
either **A** is true in w or **B** is true in w. If the explanations of *all* the
logical constants are relatively straightforward, we simply obtain a non-
classical semantic theory for a language with a classical underlying
logic. That is not in itself useless, since our meaning-theory may rule
out an appeal to an absolute notion of truth; but the interesting cases
are those in which the logic is non-classical, and hence the explanations of at least some of the logical constants are not even relatively
straightforward. For instance, in the intuitionistic semantics framed in
terms of Beth trees or of Kripke trees, we must make the non-
straightforward stipulation that ⌐if **A**, then **B**⌐ is true at a node p just
in case, for every node $q \leq p$, if **A** is true at q, then **B** is true at q. For
a non-classical semantics of this kind, therefore, it could not be maintained that, given the syntax, the semantic theory followed automatically. Might it not be a distinguishing mark of classical logic, and
explain its preeminence, that for a language with a classical logic the
semantics is trivially determined once the syntax is given?

In order to see the answer to this, we have to look more closely at
the non-classical case. The standard two-valued semantics is so firmly
entrenched for classical logic that it is unnecessary to qualify any proposition concerning the completeness of a fragment of classical logic: if
it be said, of any such fragment, that it is complete or incomplete, we
know with respect to what notion of validity the assertion is meant,
since it is taken for granted that the two-valued semantics is the intended one. In the case of intuitionistic logic, however, the situation is
not so clear: we do not have a *standard* semantics for intuitionistic logic,
and hence any claim concerning the completeness of some fragment
of that logic must specify the notion of validity appealed to, for example, validity on Beth trees. This is not because we are unsure of the
intended meanings of the intuitionistic logical constants. Those meanings were specified long ago in a canonical manner by Heyting, in
terms of the notion of a mathematical construction and of such a construction's being a proof of a statement. The trouble is that the notions
used in Heyting's explanations are not, as they stand, immediately
amenable to mathematical treatment, and hence do not lend themselves to a demonstration of the completeness or incompleteness of

any formalised logical system. Kreisel and Goodman have devoted much effort to devising a mathematical theory concerning the notions of a construction and of a proof. Unfortunately, their efforts have not as yet been fully successful: if they had, then we should undoubtedly have, in the theory of constructions, what all would recognise as being the standard semantics for intuitionistic logic in the same sense as that in which the two-valued semantics is standard for classical logic.

Faced with this situation, we cannot claim, without special argument, that a result concerning the completeness, with respect, say, to Beth trees, of some fragment of intuitionistic logic has the kind of interest that we want such a result to have, namely, one relating to the intended meanings of the logical constants. Partly to obviate this difficulty, some important results in this area have been obtained by appeal to quite a different notion of validity. The relevant notion of an interpretation of a formula of first-order logic is as follows. We first specify some inhabited species as the domain of the individual variables (a species is inhabited if we can find at least one object which we can show to be an element of it). We then interpret each individual constant by assigning to it an element of the domain, each one-place predicate-letter by assigning to it a subspecies of the domain, and so on. The condition for the truth (relative to any assignment to the free variables) of an atomic formula under such an interpretation is then specified in the obvious way, while the condition for the truth of a complex formula is given by means of straightforward stipulations for each of the logical constants; for example, we say that, relative to a given assignment to the free variables, $\ulcorner A \rightarrow B \urcorner$ is true under the interpretation just in case, if A is true under that interpretation (relative to that assignment), then so is B. All that is necessary is that the logical constants that are used in giving these stipulations should themselves be understood intuitionistically. This last requirement restricts the reasoning which we may apply to the notion of validity with respect to such interpretations to reasoning that is intuitionistically correct, and it guarantees that results obtained in terms of it do relate to the intended meanings of the logical constants. It would be a grave mistake to dismiss this notion of validity as unimportant: on the contrary, highly significant results have been obtained by appeal to it, above all the Gödel-Kreisel proof that the completeness of first-order logic implies the validity of a certain form of Markov's principle.

Internal Interpretations

Let us call an interpretation of a formula of intuitionistic logic of this kind an 'internal' interpretation. The conception of such an internal interpretation appears closely analogous to that of an interpretation of a formula of classical logic as it figures in the standard two-valued semantics. Intuitionists are accustomed to speak of species where classical mathematicians speak of sets, and they distinguish saying that a species is non-empty from the stronger assertion that it is inhabited; but, allowing for these expected quirks, everything appears to run on parallel lines in the two cases. So much is this so that in his lectures on intuitionism at Cambridge van Dalen stated categorically that the notion of an internal interpretation is just the intuitionistic analogue of the classical notion. If this is correct, however, it seems difficult to place such a semantic theory as that provided by the Beth trees. It appears that a semantics of this latter kind has no classical analogue at all. How could we explain this? Well, as we have seen, one of the things that distinguishes a semantic theory of the kind provided by the Beth trees is that it gives a non-straightforward account of at least some of the logical constants. So perhaps the situation is this: for classical logic, we can specify the condition for the truth (under an interpretation) of a complex formula *only* by means of absolutely or relatively straightforward stipulations relating to each of the logical constants; whereas, for a non-classical logic, while we *can* proceed in the same manner, we may *also* be able to frame non-straightforward stipulations governing them; for a semantics embodying such stipulations there will be no classical analogue. This would constitute another way of indicating the singularity of classical logic. On this view, it would not of course be true that, whatever the underlying logic, the semantic theory is immediately determined once the syntax is given, since classical and intuitionistic mathematics share a completely Fregean syntax: a Fregean syntax does not guarantee a classical understanding of the logical constants. It would hold, however, that, even when the logic is non-classical, a Fregean syntax taken together with a particular understanding of the logical constants determined one type of semantic theory—that employing internal interpretations— although other types of semantic theory would also be possible; the classical case would be distinguished by the fact that no such other type would be admissible. This would not, however, explain why, in the non-classical case, we were *interested* in arriving at a semantic theory of the kind for which there was no classical analogue.

All this is tempting, but it is quite wrong. We can see that it is wrong as soon as we ask ourselves what happens when a formula which we wish to interpret contains a sentence-letter: what should an internal interpretation assign to a schematic letter that stands proxy for a sentence? The classical interpretation takes the domain to be a non-empty set, the intuitionistic one takes it as an inhabited species; both assign to each individual constant an element of the domain; the classical interpretation assigns to a unary predicate-letter a subset of the domain, the intuitionistic one assigns a subspecies of the domain; the classical interpretation assigns to a sentence-letter a truth-value: what should the intuitionistic interpretation assign to a sentence-letter? The only answer we can give is 'a proposition'. But this answer is quite unspecific; in this context it means only 'whatever is to be taken as being the semantic value of a sentence in an intuitionistic language'. And it is precisely this lack of any specific notion of what the semantic value of a sentence is to be that shows that the notion of an internal interpretation is not a genuinely semantic one at all. The replacement of the word 'set' by the word 'species' was not a mere shift in favoured terminology. Rather, the notion of a species is related to the classical notion of a set precisely as the notion of a proposition, considered as that which is to be assigned by an interpretation to a sentence-letter, is related to that of a truth-value. It is an essential part of the concept of a set that a set is both determinate and extensional: that is, first, for any given set, it is determinate, for every element of the domain, whether or not it is a member of the set, and, secondly, everything that holds good of the set depends only upon which elements of the domain are members of it and which are not. A species is certainly not either determinate or extensional in this sense, but we have no positive characterisation of what a species is, other than that it is the semantic value of a unary predicate. We can say, quite correctly, that a species is an effective mapping of elements of the domain into propositions, just as a set is a mapping of elements of the domain into truth-values. But to make the notion of a species as specific as that of a set we should have to arrive at a more than programmatic notion of a proposition.

It is, indeed, true that by appeal to Heyting's explanations we have a specific account of propositions and of species: a proposition is a decidable classification of constructions (into those that are and those that are not proofs of the statement); a species is an effective association of each element of the domain with such a proposition. But these explanations go along with substantial, non-straightforward, explanations of the logical constants in the same terms. They cannot be incorporated into the notion of an internal interpretation without also incorporating Heyting's stipulations concerning the logical constants and thus altering the whole conception of an interpretation. The notion of an internal interpretation, as we originally framed it, did not appeal to any particular account of the notion of a species nor, therefore, of that of a proposition: it took them for granted as already understood just as it took for granted the intuitionistic meanings of the logical constants.

A Fregean syntax, even when taken in conjunction with a particular understanding of the logical constants, does not, therefore, suffice to determine any semantic theory. But, given a Fregean syntax, virtually only one thing is required in order to determine the general form of a semantic theory: namely, to specify what, in general, is to constitute the semantic value of a sentence. When the theory is to be applied to a natural language, or any language containing indexicals and demonstratives, we should speak of the semantic value, not of a sentence, but of a particular utterance of one; for a formalised language, or the language of a mathematical or physical theory, the qualification is unnecessary. In what follows, I shall not be especially concerned with the complications induced by the presence of indexical and demonstrative expressions, and I shall follow Frege's example in speaking of sentences, where strict accuracy would demand 'utterances of sentences'.

Statement-Values

Given what the semantic value of a sentence is, in general, to be, the corresponding general notion of an interpretation is thereby all but determined, save for the specific explanations of the logical constants. To say that the semantic value of a singular term is, in general, to be an object is, in itself, a purely formal stipulation: it can be taken as a specification of how the word 'object' is to be used, and can accordingly be incorporated into any semantic theory. The same holds good for the requirement that the domain shall consist of objects; and the demand that the object denoted by a term shall be an element of the domain merely reflects the usual idealisation in accordance with which a formalised language is not permitted to contain empty terms. The criterion for two terms' having the same semantic value, and hence for their denoting the same object, will be the truth of the identity-statement connecting them; and, as already remarked, the criterion for a two-place predicate to be the sign of identity is that the truth of atomic statements formed from it shall be a sufficient condition for the intersubstitutability of the two terms. It is different, indeed, if we make the stipulation that the semantic value of a term is to be an object in the context of a background assumption about what objects there are. It then becomes a substantial claim, which may compel special treatment of certain contexts. Frege's conception of the reference of a name as its bearer is precisely such a background assumption, since it tacitly involves that the reference of, say, a personal proper name is to be a human being. Furthermore, given that we know what the semantic value of a sentence is in general to be—let us call it a 'statement-value'—and given that the semantic values of terms are objects, then there is no choice as to what, in general, the semantic value of an n-place predicate is to be: it must simply be a mapping from n-tuples of objects to statement-values. It is true, indeed, that what mappings are admitted will vary from one semantic theory to another. Intuitionists admit only effective mappings; classical semanticists allow arbitrary mappings, including ones that we are unable to specify, even non-effectively. This variation is a consequence of the meaning-theory that lies behind the semantic theory and gives it its rationale; and it was to allow for the variation that I said that we have 'virtually' no choice what the semantic value of a predicate is to be, once we know what the statement-values are. The restriction to effective mappings, in the intuitionistic case, is not a limitation upon the semantic values of predicates, as such: in any context, the only mappings recognised by intuitionists as everywhere defined are effective ones. In all cases, possible semantic values of n-place predicates will consist in mappings, of the most general kind admitted, from n-tuples of objects to statement-values: it is just that theories will differ about what mappings are admissible at all, that is, about what mappings there are. We do not indeed know, from what the statement-values are, precisely how we are to explain the notion of a complex formula's coming out true under an interpretation, that is, what the semantic value of each particular logical constant is: we know only what general form the semantic value of, for example, a binary sentential connective, or, again, of a unary quantifier, should take.

From this it is apparent that the crucial thesis of classical semantics is precisely that which makes it two-valued: the thesis that the semantic value of a sentence consists simply in its being, or in its not being, true. *Every* semantic theory has as its goal an account of the way in which a sentence is determined as true, when it is true, in accordance with its composition. It is the peculiarity of classical semantics that it takes the semantic value of a sentence—its contribution to determining as true or otherwise a more complex sentence of which it is a constituent—as simply consisting in whether it is itself true or not. It is precisely the lack of any specification of what the semantic value of a sentence is to consist in that destroys the parallelism between an internal interpretation of an intuitionistic formula and an interpretation, within two-valued semantics, of a classical formula, and deprives the former of the status of a *semantic* notion properly so called.

What, then, *is* the status of the notion of an internal interpretation? It would be better to view such an interpretation as simply an interpretation by replacement. That is not quite right, however, because, after all, an internal interpretation does associate *objects*, not actual *terms*, with the individual constants, just as a semantic interpretation does.

As already remarked, this does not actually take us any distance towards framing a semantic theory, if all that we know is that **t** and **s** are to stand for the same object just in case ⌜t = s⌝ is true, where '=' is the sign of identity; but it makes a gesture towards a semantic theory. We may call an interpretation of this type a *programmatic* interpretation, because it appeals to purely programmatic notions of the semantic values of sentences and of predicates. When the type of semantic values possessed by sentences is specified, then the programmatic notion of interpretation will have been transformed into a semantic one. We shall then have more to do in order to obtain an actual semantic theory, because we shall have to modify our stipulations concerning when a complex formula is true under a given interpretation. The stipulations relating to the logical constants must show how the semantic value of the complex sentence is determined by the semantic values of its constituents, whereas the programmatic notion of interpretation appeals only to straightforward stipulations in terms of the *truth* of a constituent sentence, and, except in the classical case, the semantic value of a sentence does not simply consist in its being true or not being so.

The Central Notion of a Meaning-Theory

To repeat: just because we know in advance that the notion we need in order to explain the validity of argument-schemas is that of a formula's coming out true under an interpretation, it is the goal of every semantic theory first to frame a suitable general notion of an interpretation and then to arrive at a specification of when a formula is true under such an interpretation. There is no such a priori reason for supposing that, in a meaning-theory, the notion of truth will play such a crucial role; or, if there is, it will be a different reason. But, even if the notion of truth does play a similarly important role in a meaning-theory, it is apparent that a turn of phrase I have sometimes employed in the past is ambiguous. I have sometimes distinguished among meaning-theories according to what they take as their 'central notion', this central notion sometimes being that of truth and sometimes some other notion, such as that of verification, or of falsification, or of a warrant for assertion, and so on. This is ambiguous because it might be taken in the sense in which truth under an interpretation is the central notion for any semantic theory (where by a 'semantic theory' is meant one that subserves the aims of logic); but it might also be taken in a sense in which truth is the central notion only of a classical semantics, namely, one in which the semantic value of a sentence consists in its being true or not being true. Although the goal of every semantic theory is to specify what it is for a formula to be true under an interpretation, not every semantic theory will take the semantic value of a sentence-letter or other constituent formula, under an interpretation, to consist only in one or other of the two truth-values *true* and *false*. Moreover, we have seen that (provided at least that we are operating with a Fregean syntax) the choice of what, in general, is to constitute the semantic value of a sentence (a statement-value) is determinative of the entire notion of an interpretation: hence the general notion of a statement-value that is employed has a good claim to be called the 'central notion' of the semantic theory. On the one hand, to construe the characterisation of a meaning-theory as not taking truth as its central notion in a way analogous to this would be so to classify any meaning-theory according to which a sentence contributes to determining whether or not a more complex sentence of which it forms part is true in virtue of more than just whether or not that constituent sentence is itself true. To construe it as analogous to the sense in which the definition of truth under an interpretation is the goal of every semantic theory, on the other hand, would be so to classify only those meaning-theories under which the way in which a sentence is determined as true is not taken as constitutive of the meaning of the sentence, or of any important ingredient in that meaning, at all. That would amount to denying that truth was the central notion of the meaning-theory only in those cases in which the notion of truth plays no significant part in the theory of meaning. It indeed requires argument to show that the notion of truth does play such a part in an account of language; simply to assume that it does is to take as already known a large sector of what such an account should make explicit.

Types of Semantic Theory

Within *semantic* theories, we have two principles of classification. We have on one side classical semantics, which identifies a statement-value with truth or the lack of it, and, on the other, all other semantic theories, which require some notion other than that of truth to characterise the general conception of a statement-value—some notion, that is, other than that of the possession or non-possession of truth *simpliciter*. We have two familiar models for this. One is that derived from many-valued logics (more accurately expressed, the many-valued semantics proposed for certain logics): we take the statement-values to consist of the elements of some finite or infinite set, of cardinality ≥ 3, of which some non-empty proper subset is singled out as comprising the 'designated' values; it is an underlying assumption of the semantic theory that each sentence will possess a determinate one, and only one, of these values. A formula's coming out true under an interpretation within a semantic theory of this kind is to be identified with its having, under that interpretation, a designated value. The other familiar model, already mentioned, is that of *relativised* truth-values. We consider some space, usually with some kind of structure on it (such as an ordering relation), and assume that each sentence—or at least each atomic sentence—is determinately either true or not true relatively to each point of the space. Examples are the well-known semantic theories for modal logics, where the points of the space intuitively represent possible worlds, and for tense logics, where they represent times. Other examples are the Beth trees and Kripke trees, or more generally Kripke models (partly ordered sets), regarded as yielding semantic theories for intuitionistic logic. Here, if the trees are viewed as sets of nodes, the elements represent states of information: in the case of the Beth trees, it is more convenient to view an interpretation as determining, for each atomic formula (relatively to any assignment to the free variables), whether or not it is 'verified' at each node, and to define from this a notion of truth at a node, which is in general a weaker notion than that of being verified. If we use only intuitionistic reasoning in the metalanguage, we shall not in this case be able to assert that every formula either is or is not true at each node under a given interpretation. On any semantic theory employing relativised truth-values, a formula's coming out true absolutely, under a given interpretation, will be identifiable with its being true relative to some one or more distinguished points of the space, for example, that which represents the actual world, or the present time, or the existing state of information.

There is no need, however, for a semantic theory to assume either of these two familiar forms. Another possible pattern is one whereby the semantic value of a sentence relates it to something that would *make* it true. Heyting's explanation of sentences of an intuitionistic mathematical theory is a simple example of this kind. The semantic value of a sentence is here a principle of classification of constructions into those which do and those which do not prove the sentence; hence the notion of truth is to be arrived at by existential quantification—the sentence is true if there exists a construction which proves it. Another example, more complicated in structure, is Hintikka's semantics in terms of games. The semantic value of a sentence is, in effect, the class of all plays (successions of moves) following a move consisting in the production of that sentence. The notion of truth is then again arrived at by means of existential quantification: a sentence is true if there exists a winning strategy in which the first move is the production of that sentence. No doubt many other patterns are conceivable for semantic theories.

It virtually follows from the way I explained 'semantic value' that the semantic value, under an interpretation, of a formula or other complex expression (term or functor) is determined from the semantic values of its constituents. A semantic theory thus falls into three clearly defined parts: that which lays down in what an interpretation is to consist—what kinds of semantic values are to be associated with each type of schematic letter; that which shows how the semantic value of a formula is determined from those of its components; and, finally, that which defines, in terms of its semantic value, what it is for a formula to come out true under an interpretation. The last step will often be obvious: it will be redundant only for those semantic theories in which truth is one among the possible statement-values, that is, for many-valued logics with only one designated value. We may thus also distinguish between those semantic theories in which the stipulations governing the logical constants are straightforward and those in which they are not. Even though the statement-values do not consist simply in truth and in the lack of it, and perhaps do not even include truth, the stipulation of the semantic value of a complex sentence may still be effected in a (relatively) straightforward manner. Prime examples are the stipulations in the semantics for modal and tense logics that relate to '&', 'v', '→', '¬' and the two quantifiers. Other examples are: the stipulations governing '&' in the semantics given by Beth trees, namely that $\ulcorner$**A** & **B**$\urcorner$ is true at a node p just in case **A** is true at p and **B** is true at p; that governing 'v' in the semantics given by Kripke trees (though not in that given by Beth trees); and, finally, that governing 'v' in Heyting's explanations of the intuitionistic logical constants. This last is that a construction is a proof of $\ulcorner$**A** v **B**$\urcorner$ just in case it is a proof of **A** or of **B**. Even though this is not stated in terms of a relativised notion of truth—or of any notion of truth—we may classify it as a relatively straightforward stipulation; the principle underlying this extension of the notion is obvious. A stipulation may be *circular*, in the sense of using the logical constant to which it relates, without being *straightforward;* thus the stipulation governing '→' on Beth trees and Kripke trees, already cited, is not straightforward but itself uses the connective 'if'; the same holds good for the stipulation governing 'v' on Beth trees, namely that $\ulcorner$**A** v **B**$\urcorner$ is true at a node p if there is a set N of nodes that bars p and such that, for every q in N, either **A** is true at q or **B** is true at q.

Classical Semantics

It was an essential feature of the programmatic notion of an interpretation that the condition for the truth of a complex formula be stated straightforwardly in terms of the truth of its subformulas. This feature is not normally preserved when the programmatic notion is converted into a genuinely semantic one by a specification of what the statement-values are to be. In order to bring out the apparent analogy between a programmatic interpretation for a non-classical logic and an interpretation in classical two-valued semantics, we considered the stipulations governing the classical logical constants as being framed in a similar straightforward manner. Such stipulations of course give an impression of being totally unexplanatory: an understanding of the stipulation governing a logical constant of the object-language depends upon knowing the meaning of the corresponding logical constant in the metalanguage. Whether this is a *criticism* or not, we are not yet in a position to say, since we have not yet enquired whether a semantic theory has, as one of its roles, the *explanation* of the meanings of the logical constants. It is certainly the case, however, that many people, when they first encounter, probably as students, the two-valued truth-tables, experience a sense of illumination, a sense which is by no means imparted by such a stipulation as that $\ulcorner A \to B \urcorner$ is true just in case, if **A** is true, then **B** is true. The reason is, of course, that this stipulation does not *by itself* display the way in which the truth-value of the complex sentence depends solely upon the truth-values of its constituents. Using only the intuitionistic laws as governing the logical constants of the metalanguage, we can indeed show, for each logical constant of the object-language, that each line of the relevant truth-table is correct, for instance that if **A** and **B** are both true, then $\ulcorner A \to B \urcorner$ is true, and that if **A** is true and **B** is not true, then $\ulcorner A \to B \urcorner$ is not true. Using the classical laws for the metalinguistic logical constants, we can also show that the lines of the truth-table exhaust all possibilities, that either both **A** and **B** are true, or **A** is true but **B** not true, or **A** is not true but **B** true, or neither is true. In this way, we can *derive* the two-valued truth-tables from straightforward stipulations, in terms of truth, for the sentential operators; but the derivation depends heavily upon appeal to the classical laws as governing the sentential operators of the metalanguage.

What is important here is that a straightforward stipulation, in terms of truth, will not, of itself, reveal the way in which a complex sentence is determined as true, when it is true, in accordance with its composition. At least it is clear that it does not, in general, display how the semantic value of a sentence is determined from the semantic values of its constituents. Even though we may quite legitimately stipulate, for intuitionistic implication, that $\ulcorner A \to B \urcorner$ is true just in case, if **A** is true, then **B** is true, provided that we understand the metalinguistic 'if' intuitionistically, we cannot, by appeal to the intuitionistic logical laws as holding in the metalanguage, derive from this any account of how the semantic value of ⌜A → B⌝ is determined from those of **A** and of **B**, for any particular choice of a suitable notion of statement-values (say, truth at nodes of a Beth tree, or provability by means of mathematical constructions). This was expressed earlier by saying that, while a programmatic interpretation is automatically converted into a semantic one by a choice of what the statement-values are, this choice does not determine the notion of truth under a semantic interpreta- tion, that is, under the stipulations governing the semantic values of complex sentences formed by means of the logical operators. There is a temptation to say that this does not matter, since the straightforward stipulations in terms of truth show how the *truth* of a sentence is deter- mined in accordance with its composition. That, however, is an illu- sion: if it were not, then, as soon as we had laid down what in general the semantic value of a sentence was to be and how the notion of the truth of a sentence was to be explained in terms of it, we should be able to dispense with the notion of semantic value for all but atomic sentences and, for complex sentences, state everything in terms of the notion of truth. This is quite evident in a concrete case. Suppose we have a tense logic, in which '□' has the intuitive meaning of 'hencefor- ward'. Then we may correctly make the straightforward stipulation that ⌜□A⌝ is true just in case **A** is true henceforward. Now, in a natural way, we take the semantic value of a sentence to consist in its being or not being true at each particular time, and we explain a sentence's being true (absolutely) as its being true at the present time. The stipu- lation determining the semantic value of ⌜□A⌝ is then obvious: ⌜□A⌝ is true at a time *t* just in case **A** is true at *t* and at all subsequent times, from which it follows that ⌜□A⌝ is true absolutely just in case **A** is true absolutely and is also true at all future times. But the form of this stipulation cannot be derived from the mere stipulation that ⌜□A⌝ is true just in case **A** is henceforward true. More exactly, it cannot be so derived unless we conceive of the metalanguage in which the straightforward stipulation is made as already containing quantifica- tion over times and as making the requisite connection between this and the operator 'henceforward', in which case it already in effect em- bodies our semantic theory. We might, indeed, so think of it, but this only shows how much more is involved in the derivation than is em- bodied in the straightforward stipulation itself, which could perfectly well be stated in a metalanguage incapable of quantifying over times save implicitly by means of a few adverbs like 'henceforward'. To think that the straightforward stipulations show how the truth of a complex sentence is determined in accordance with its composition is to confuse stating the condition for its truth *in terms of* the truth of its constituents with showing that its truth, or lack of truth, is *determined by* the truth or otherwise of the constituents. It is just because the truth of ⌜Henceforward **A**⌝ or of ⌜Necessarily **A**⌝ is not determined solely by whether or not **A** is true that we need to take the semantic value of a formula of tense logic or of modal logic to consist in something other than its being or not being true. Likewise, where we take the truth of a sentence of an intuitionistic language as consisting in our presently having a proof of it, the truth of ⌜**A** → **B**⌝ does not depend solely upon **B**'s being true or **A**'s not being true: the condition for the truth of ⌜**A** → **B**⌝ can be *stated* in terms of the truth of **A** and of **B**, but it is not *determined* just by whether or not they are true. It is special to the classical case that the semantic value of a sentence can be taken to consist in its being or not being true—that is the very core of classical semantics—and that therefore, in the presence of sufficiently strong background assumptions, the straightforward stipulations may be made to yield the semantic ones properly so called, namely, the truth-tables considered as governed by the principle that their lines exhaustively represent all possible cases. Even in the classical case, however, the straightforward stipulations do not of themselves display how a sentence is determined as true in accordance with its composition, that is, they do not display the semantic mechanism of the language.

Those who make the mistake that has here been implicitly criticised are often highly sensitive to the charge of triviality, which is not unnaturally provoked by an emphasis on the importance of straightforward stipulations. They often seek to rebut it by stressing the difficulty of arriving at a correct formulation of such stipulations. The difficulty is a genuine one, but it is always a matter of finding a suitable syntax. As was emphasised earlier, a large part of the work needed to frame a satisfactory semantic theory consists in arriving at an analysis of the structure of sentences adequate for semantic purposes. To borrow an example from Wiggins, we shall never arrive at a semantic account of 'most' if we attempt to treat it as a unary quantifier; and this is shown by the failure of such straightforward stipulations as that ⌜Most **F**s are **G**s⌝ is true just in case ⌜if *x* is **F**, then it is **G**⌝ is true of most objects, or that it is true just in case ⌜*x* is **F** and it is **G**⌝ is true of most objects. We shall get somewhere only if we recognise 'most' as being a binary quantifier, like 'more . . . than . . .'. (The traditional logic of course treated 'some' and 'every' as binary quantifiers also: it was due to Frege's genius that he saw that they *could* be treated as unary ones; to think that 'most' can also be so treated is to be unaware of the brilliance of Frege's insight.) A syntactic analysis that is incorrect (for semantic purposes) will be revealed as such by the intuitive failure of the corresponding straightforward stipulation, which is why it is often useful, in semantic discussions, to consider such stipulations. But that does not mean that, by framing such a stipulation correctly, we have as yet done more than find the semantically usable syntactic form.

If this claim is sound, it must *always* be possible to frame a straightforward stipulation with respect to truth. I believe this to be so, indeed to be virtually evident, since it amounts to no more than that we can always have a notion of truth for which Tarski's schema (T) holds, and which, therefore, commutes with or distributes over the logical operations. There are, however, some apparent counter-examples, which all turn, I believe, on construing inappropriately the logical constants of the metalanguage. Here is one example. In Łukasiewicz's three-valued logic, there are three values, 1, ½, and 0, of which only 1 is designated. When 'p' is assigned the value 1, '$\neg(p \rightarrow \neg p)$' receives the value 1 also, and when 'p' is assigned the value 0, it receives the value 0 also; but when 'p' gets the value ½, '$\neg(p \rightarrow \neg p)$' comes out as having the value 0. Since the truth of a sentence must be equated with its having the value 1, this provides an apparent argument against saying that $\ulcorner A \rightarrow B \urcorner$ is true just in case, if A is true, then B is true: for, if B is $\ulcorner \neg(A \rightarrow \neg A) \urcorner$, then, on the sup-position that A is true, B will be true also, whereas, if in fact A has the value ½, $\ulcorner A \rightarrow B \urcorner$ will not be true. The mistake in this argument arises from supposing that, because the truth of B follows from the truth of A, we can assert that, if A is true, then B is true. The straightforward stipulation holds only if the 'if' of the metalanguage obeys the same laws as the '$\rightarrow$' of the object-language; but, in the three-valued logic of Łukasiewicz, the rule of if-introduction does not hold, and so we have no ground for saying that if A is true, so is B. We see here how heavily the understanding of straightforward stipulations for logical constants depends on knowing the laws governing those constants.

chapter 2

Inference and Truth

Is Truth Really the Salient Notion for Logic?

The claim made in Chapter 1 that we know in advance that what is required for the validity of a form of inference is that it preserve truth from premisses to conclusion, and that therefore the crucial notion for logic is that of truth under an interpretation, might be challenged on various grounds, in particular, on those of logical theory. A form of inference is most naturally represented by a sequent, which we may write $\Gamma : \mathbf{A}$, where Γ is a finite set of formulas displaying the structure of the premisses of any inference of that form, and $\mathbf{A}$ is a single formula displaying the structure of the conclusion; Γ is said to be the *antecedent* of the sequent, and $\mathbf{A}$ its *succedent*. We shall simplify our discussion, without losing anything essential, if we restrict ourselves for most of the time to sentential logic. If we have a semantic theory for our logic, incorporating a notion of the truth of a formula under an interpretation, a sequent may naturally be defined to be valid, in accordance with the foregoing claim, just in case the succedent $\mathbf{A}$ is true under every interpretation under which all the formulas in Γ are true. Perhaps we have only an algebraic characterisation of the logic, of a kind formally indistinguishable from a many-valued semantic theory; we may have characterised the logic by means of a single algebraic structure, or by a family of such structures. In either case, the role of an interpretation in a semantic theory will be played by that of an assignment of elements of the algebra, or of one of the algebras, to the sentence-letters; certain operations in the algebra or algebras will be taken to correspond to the sentential operators, so that each assignment to the sentence-letters induces a valuation of the formulas in the algebra; and one, or possibly more, of the elements of each algebra will be picked out as designated. We may then define $\Gamma : \mathbf{A}$ to be valid if $\mathbf{A}$ obtains a designated value under each assignment which gives a designated value to each of the formulas in Γ. The characterisation is algebraic rather than semantic when we lack any means of using the algebra to give the meanings of the logical constants. Gentzen's sequent calculus, which provides a very powerful proof-theoretic technique, requires us to admit sequents of the form $\Gamma : \Delta$ whose succedents are also finite sets of formulas. There is no intuitive notion of an inference to a multiple conclusion; but analogy suggests that we should define a sequent $\Gamma : \Delta$ to be valid if, under every interpretation that brings out true every formula in Γ, at least one of the formulas in Δ is true; algebraically expressed, if every assignment that confers a designated value on all the formulas in Γ confers such a value on at least one of those in Δ.

We may call definitions of validity of this kind definitions *in terms of truth* (or of *designation*). They generate numerous awkwardnesses; and, because of these, it may well be doubted that truth really is the central notion for the characterisation of valid inferences. First, we certainly want all sequents of the forms **A, B : A & B** and **A v B : A, B** to hold in every logic that has operators '&' and 'v', because those sequents will be provable in any ordinary sequent calculus. Any such calculus will have a thinning rule on left and right, enabling us to prove (i) **A, B : A** and **A, B : B**, and (ii) **A : A, B** and **B : A, B**. We may also expect the rules of &-introduction on the right and v-introduction on the left to hold at least in the weakened forms:

$$\frac{\Gamma : A \qquad \Gamma : B}{\Gamma : A \,\&\, B} \qquad\qquad \frac{A : \Delta \qquad B : \Delta}{A \vee B : \Delta}$$

If these laws did not hold, the operators '&' and 'v' could not legitimately be called conjunction and disjunction operators. By means of these laws, **A, B : A & B** must follow from (i), and **A v B : A, B** from (ii).

Now many logics are characterisable by families of finite lattices; and, in a lattice, the join of two elements a and b may be the unit element although neither of a and b is. This difficulty may be readily circumvented in the Kripke semantics for intuitionistic logic, since we can always use Kripke trees rather than general Kripke models; but, on the Beth trees, the difficulty is more serious. If we identify absolute truth on a Beth tree with truth at the vertex, a formula $\ulcorner \mathbf{A} \vee \mathbf{B} \urcorner$ may be true even though neither **A** nor **B** is true, which would render the sequent **A v B : A, B** invalid on the definition in terms of truth. For sentential logic, we can get round this difficulty, clumsily, by artificially restricting the assignments we admit so as to guarantee that a formula $\ulcorner \mathbf{A} \vee \mathbf{B} \urcorner$ is true at a node only if either **A** or **B** is; but this cannot be done for predicate logic, unless we are prepared to follow Kripke in violating the principle of having a single fixed domain for the individual variables.

Much greater trouble arises in quantum logic. As intuitionistic logic can be characterised by finite distributive lattices, so quantum logic is characterised by orthomodular lattices. A lattice with zero and unit is said to be *orthocomplemented* if it admits a unary operation $^-$ which is a complement ($a \cup a^- = 1$ and $a \cap a^- = 0$), satisfies $a^{--} = a$, and is a dual automorphism ($(a \cup b)^- = a^- \cap b^-$) and dually). An orthocomplemented lattice is *orthomodular* if it satisfies the restricted modular law that, if $a \leq b$, $b = a \cup (a^- \cap b)$. Now the law of excluded middle 'p ∨ ¬p' clearly holds in quantum logic, and so the sequent   : p, ¬p, with null antecedent, ought to be valid; if the unit of a lattice is taken to be the sole designated element, it will not be valid on the definition in terms of designation. Moreover, difficulties arise for sequents with only one formula in the succedent, such as p ∨ q, p ∨ r : p ∨ ((p ∨ r) & q). This sequent ought to be invalid, since it is possible to assign elements of an orthomodular lattice to the sentence-letters so as to give the formula in the succedent a lower value than the conjunction of those in the antecedent; but it comes out valid on the definition in terms of designation, since it is not possible to do this so as to give both formulas in the antecedent the value 1. The natural reaction is to suppose that the difficulties can be eliminated by adopting some more sophisticated notion of a designated element; but they are more deep-seated. Given the definition of validity in terms of truth or designation, the logic must have the full cut property, namely, that if $\Gamma : \Delta, C$ and $\Gamma', C : \Delta'$ are both valid, so is $\Gamma, \Gamma' : \Delta, \Delta'$. Granted the hypotheses, any assignment that gives a designated value to all the formulas in Γ and Γ' must give a designated value either to C or to one of the formulas in Δ. If it gives a designated value to C, it must also give a designated value to one of the formulas in Δ'. Hence it must, in any case, give a designated value to one of the formulas in Δ or in Δ', and so $\Gamma, \Gamma' : \Delta, \Delta'$ is valid. Quantum logic, however, cannot have the full cut property. The sequents p ∨ q : p, q and p ∨ r, q : (p ∨ r) & q must both be valid (the latter is a particular case of $A, B : A \& B$). If the logic had the full cut property, p ∨ q, p ∨ r : p, (p ∨ r) & q would be valid, which it cannot be. However we choose the designated elements, validity cannot be defined in terms of designation.

The most general difficulty arises with the Lindenbaum algebra. It is not obvious straight off that all logics can be characterised either by a single algebra, even if infinite, or by a family of algebras. In fact, some atypical logics do lack what Harrop named the 'finite model property', which is to say that they cannot be characterised by any family of *finite* algebras. It is therefore useful to be able to show that every logic can be characterised by a single denumerable algebra. We have only to take the elements of the algebra to be the formulas themselves, where the operation on formulas **A** and **B** corresponding to, say, '∨' is just that which yields ⌜**A** ∨ **B**⌝, and similarly for any other operators; hence the valuation of a formula **A** under an assignment *f* to the sentence-letters is just the result of replacing each sentence-letter p_i in **A** by $f(p_i)$. Then if we take the designated elements to be the provable formulas, the resulting Lindenbaum algebra is obviously characteristic for the logic in the weak sense that a formula is provable if and only if it is valid, that is, if and only if it has a designated value under all assignments. We can usually improve on this by taking the elements as equivalence classes of formulas under the equivalence relation of interderivability; this can be done provided that interderivability is a congruence relation with respect to the sentential operators, as it usually is. (This is to say that if **A** is derivable from **B** and **B** from **A**, and likewise **C** is interderivable with **D**, then ⌜**A** ∨ **C**⌝ is interderivable with ⌜**B** ∨ **D**⌝, and similarly for other operators.) Since all provable formulas are interderivable with one another, we obtain in this way an algebra with a single designated element. However, if the validity of a sequent is defined in terms of designation, the Lindenbaum algebra will not characterise validity for all logics. It will do so for classical logic; but the sequent

$$\neg p \to q \lor r : (\neg p \to q) \lor (\neg p \to r)$$

will be valid in intuitionistic logic under the definition, although the succedent is not derivable from the antecedent, because whenever a formula of the form ⌜¬**A** → **B** ∨ **C**⌝ is provable intuitionistically, so is ⌜(¬**A** → **B**) ∨ (¬**A** → **C**)⌝. Likewise, in quantum logic, if **B** is provable, so is ⌜**A** ∨ (¬**A** & **B**)⌝, and consequently q : p ∨ (¬p & q) is valid on our definition, although, again, the succedent is not derivable from the antecedent.

All these difficulties vanish if we revise our conception of a characterising algebra, and, with it, our definition of the validity of a sequent. In order to characterise a logic, an algebra will now be equipped not with a distinction between designated and undesignated elements but with a quasi-ordering ≤ of the elements; this will usually entail no additional work, since most of the algebras used to characterise logics, such as lattices, are already equipped with a partial ordering. We may then define a sequent Γ : Δ to be valid if, under every assignment, for any element $a \le$ the value of every formula in Γ, and any element $b \ge$ the value of every formula in Δ, $a \le b$. If we say that an actual statement **A** *implies* another statement **B** if the value of **A** ≤ the value of **B**, this is tantamount to regarding a set $\{A_1, \ldots, A_n\}$ as implying a set $\{B_1, \ldots, B_m\}$ if every statement that implies each of the A_i implies every statement that is implied by each of the B_j. Let us call this a definition of validity *in terms of ordering*. When the logic contains the operator 'v', the value of 'p v q' will normally be the least upper bound of the elements assigned to p and to q; and when it contains the operator '&', the value of 'p & q' will normally be the greatest lower bound of those elements. Further, if the logic contains the operator '→', 'p → q' will normally receive the maximal element as value when and only when p is assigned an element ≤ the element assigned to q. In such a logic, therefore, a sequent $A_1, \ldots, A_n : B_1, \ldots, B_m$ will be valid, under a definition in terms of ordering, just in case the formula

$$A_1 \,\&\, \ldots \,\&\, A_n \to B_1 \,\vee\, \ldots \,\vee\, B_m$$

is valid. The result is that, when we adopt this definition, the difficult cases we considered are resolved. In particular, if we take the ordering relation ≤ to hold between formulas **A** and **B** (or their equivalence classes) when **B** is derivable from **A**, the Lindenbaum algebra automatically becomes characteristic in the full sense for the logic to which it relates. Further, a logic for which a notion of validity, defined in terms of ordering, is characteristic, will not in general have the full cut property; but it will have the restricted cut property, namely, (i) that if $\Gamma : \Delta, C$ and $C : \Delta'$ are valid, so is $\Gamma : \Delta, \Delta'$, and (ii) that if $\Gamma : C$ and $\Gamma', C : \Delta$ are valid, so is $\Gamma, \Gamma' : \Delta$. The cut property is important, not merely to establish the strength of a logic formalised by a sequent calculus, but to ensure that the result of conjoining two proofs is still a proof (or, in the cut-free sequent calculus, can be converted into one). Upon this, all mathematical practice depends. Without it every theorem would have to be proved directly from the axioms, whereas with it any previously proved theorem may be invoked in the proof: but the restricted cut property is sufficient to guarantee that this procedure is legitimate. Without question, therefore, the use of a quasi-ordering ≤ between the statement-values is far superior, for the purposes of logic, to that of a classification of them into those that are and are not designated.

Philosophical Consequences

A hasty conclusion from this indisputable fact about logic would be to declare false the claim that what is required for the validity of a form of inference is that it preserve truth from premises to conclusion, and that hence the crucial notion for logic is that of truth under an interpretation: to conclude, in other words, that what logic needs, rather, is a *relation* of being, say, closer to the truth. Such a conclusion would be congenial to a disciple of Austin, who, using examples like 'Sicily is a triangle', insisted that most of the assertions we make are only roughly true. Austin's contention has some substance, indeed; but the logics we have been considering are not adapted to take account of this phenomenon. The conclusion fails, as a general thesis, by not appreciating the significance of the switch from semantic theories with many absolute truth-values to theories with relativised truth-values. In a semantics of this latter kind, relativised truth represents either truth in a world, where a world is the world as it might be, or as it was or will be at a particular time, or else assertibility in a particular state of information. It makes no difference to the validity of any form of inference which is the actual world, or what the present time is, or what information we in fact possess; but the semantic theory is unintelligible unless a sense is accorded to the idea that we might be in one or another possible world, that a certain time is the present, or that we could have any one of the possible stocks of information. To say that the value of a formula **A** under some interpretation is not ≤ the value of **B** is simply to say that there is a world in which **A** would be true but **B** would not, or a stock of information that would render **A**, but not **B**, assertible; this is relevant only because that world might be our world, that stock of information the information we happen to have. That a statement is true, in an absolute sense, if it is true in the actual world or at the present time, or assertible outright if it is assertible on the basis of the information we possess, is already implicit in a semantic theory of this type.

Algebraic characterisations in terms of finite lattices lend themselves particularly readily to the construction of such semantic theories, because in a finite lattice each element is representable as a join of join-irreducible elements, an element being join-irreducible if it is not the join of two elements both less than it. In a distributive lattice, the join-irreducible elements, under the lattice ordering, form the Kripke model whose open subsets correspond to the elements of the lattice. In this case, whether a formula is true, under any assignment, at any one node, depends only on which formulas are true at that node and nodes below it; that is why we need to consider only assignments that make all the formulas in the antecedent of a given sequent true at the vertex.

Somewhat similarly, the points of an orthomodular lattice may be regarded as representing all possible states of information regarding a certain subject matter (such as a quantum-mechanical system). The join-irreducible elements are just the atoms, which represent states of maximal possible information. The unit of the lattice represents the null state of information, and the zero an unattainable state. A proposition is a claim to have at least as much information as is possessed in some one of the possible states; it is therefore assertible in that state and in all states attainable from it, represented by the points below that representing the given state. The disjunction $\ulcorner$A ∨ B$\urcorner$ of the propositions **A** and **B** is a claim to have at least as much information as can be possessed both by someone entitled to assert **A** and by someone entitled to assert **B**. Thus if a and b are maximal states of information, represented by atoms, there will be propositions **A** and **B** claiming, respectively, that we are in states a and b. If there is a possible state of information c such that the only other states attainable from it are a and b, $\ulcorner$A ∨ B$\urcorner$ will be assertible in states c, a, and b. It may be, however, that the state d of greatest information from which a and b are both attainable is one from which other maximal states are also attainable; $\ulcorner$A ∨ B$\urcorner$ will then be assertible in d and in all states attainable from it, and hence will be assertible in certain states from which neither a nor b is attainable. This will happen when the join of the atoms representing a and b has other atoms below it. The conjunction $\ulcorner$A & B$\urcorner$ makes a claim to have at least as much information as can be possessed by someone entitled to assert both **A** and **B**. Since orthocomplementation is not in general unique in an orthomodular lattice, the foregoing sketch of a lattice-based semantics for quantum logic does not determine the interpretation of negation; for this, further considerations must be invoked. The assertibility of a proposition in a given state of information does not depend only on which propositions are assertible in states attainable from it. We therefore cannot confine ourselves to assignments which make the formulas in the antecedent assertible in the null state of information. But this makes no difference: we shall still reject an inference as invalid on the ground that we might be in a state that would justify the assertion of its premises but not of its conclusion. This intuitive justification of a definition of validity in terms of ordering invokes the property of truth or assertibility and explains the ordering relation in terms of it. It therefore cannot support the rejection, in a semantic context, of the use of such a property in favour of a relation of being truer or more assertible.

Many Absolute Truth-Values

Things stand differently for semantic theories of the original kind, in which the several truth-values are all conceived as absolute. Łukasiewicz's three-valued semantics was of this kind. When validity is defined in terms of designation, the sequent p : ¬(p → ¬p) is valid, since the formula in the succedent, which we may write as 'Tp', has the designated value 1 whenever 'p' does. Under the definition in terms of ordering, by contrast, provided that we assume that $0 < ½$ in the quasi-ordering, the sequent is invalid, because 'Tp' has the value 0 when 'p' has the value ½. This cannot be explained on the ground that a statement **A** might be true even though $\ulcorner TA\urcorner$ was not.

What would it be to speak a language for which Łukasiewicz's three-valued semantics was correct, and why should we then resist an inference from **A** to $\ulcorner TA\urcorner$? Would it be reasonable to say that $\ulcorner TA\urcorner$ was further from the truth than **A**? The values 0 and ½ are both undesignated in the semantic theory, but they are not treated alike, since $\ulcorner A \to B\urcorner$ has the value 1 when **A** has the value 0 and **B** the value ½, but the value ½ when **A** has the value ½ and **B** the value 0. $\ulcorner A \to B\urcorner$ is therefore a stronger statement than $\ulcorner TA \to B\urcorner$: if we take a statement to be neither true nor false when it has the value ½, $\ulcorner TA \to B\urcorner$ excludes only the possibility that **A** is true and **B** is not, while $\ulcorner A \to B\urcorner$ excludes also the possibility that **A** is neither true nor false and **B** is false. It is the behaviour of the conditional in this semantics that justifies taking 0 as less than ½ in the quasi-ordering. The assignment of distinct undesignated values, 0 and ½, is merely a device for codifying the different action of negation in different cases in which a sentence fails to be true. Their relative ranking is a device for registering the behaviour of the conditional. The semantic theory thus serves, as it is its task to do, to explain the contribution of the subsentences of a complex sentence to its determination as true or otherwise; but it does not rest on any feature of those subsentences when used on their own as complete sentences. Considered only in the role of a complete sentence, used on its own to make an assertion, a sentence does not fail more grievously to be true when it has the value 0 than when it has the value ½, and so we cannot appeal to any intuitive notion of being less true as a basis for the semantics. Its only basis, in this sense, is the distinction between being true and not being true; the rest serves the sole purpose of systematising the behaviour of the logical constants.

Assertoric Content and Ingredient Sense

The validity of logical inference depends upon the way in which complex sentences are constructed from atomic ones; semantic theories are therefore concerned to represent the manner in which the content of a complex sentence depends on its construction out of simpler ones. To grasp the content of an assertion, one needs to know only what possibilities it rules out, or, positively expressed, under what conditions it is correct. Relatively to any given assertion, a specification of a state of affairs may or may not be sufficiently detailed to determine whether or not the assertion is correct. Let us say that, if it is, the specification is *adequate*. If the assertion is genuinely significant, any inadequate specification must be capable of being expanded to an adequate one. The fact that the content of an assertion is exhausted by the conditions for it to be correct means that we need only a twofold classification of adequate specifications of a state of affairs that may obtain in order to grasp the content of the assertion. Someone who is able, for a given sentence, to classify specifications of possible states of affairs into those that are adequate for an assertion made by uttering it, as a complete sentence, on any given occasion, and then to classify the adequate ones into those that render it correct and those that render it incorrect, may be said to know the *assertoric content* of the sentence. It does not at all follow that he knows enough to determine its contribution to the assertoric content of complex sentences of which it is a subsentence. What one has to know to know that may be called its *ingredient sense;* and that may involve much more than its assertoric content. Ingredient sense is what semantic theories are concerned to explain. In a many-valued semantics, the condition for the correctness of an assertion made by means of a given sentence will be that that sentence have a designated value: so, in terms of a semantic theory of this older kind, its assertoric content is determined by the condition for it to have such a value. The distinction between different undesignated values—and, if there is one, between different designated values—is irrelevant to the assertoric content; it serves solely to characterise the ingredient sense—how the sentence affects the assertoric content of a more complex sentence of which it is part. In Łukasiewicz's semantics, the sentences $\mathbf{A}$ and $\ulcorner T\mathbf{A}\urcorner$ have the same assertoric content; they differ in their ingredient senses.

A failure to observe this point underlies Kripke's thesis concerning unmodalised sentences containing rigid designators. He maintains that even if the name 'St. Joachim' is introduced as denoting the father of the Blessed Virgin, whoever that may have been, the sentences 'St. Joachim had a daughter' and 'The father of Mary had a daughter' have a different modal status, since 'St. Joachim' differs from 'the father of Mary' in being a rigid designator, and we may therefore truly say, 'St. Joachim might not have had a daughter', but not, 'The father of Mary might not have had a daughter'. He infers that 'St. Joachim had a daughter' and 'The father of Mary had a daughter' express different propositions. The word 'proposition' is treacherous. What the two unmodalised sentences share is a common assertoric content; if Kripke is right about the modalised sentences with 'might have', the unmodalised ones differ in ingredient sense, being (logically) subsentences of the modalised ones. The difference between them lies *solely* in their different contributions to the sentences formed from them by modalisation and negation; in a language without modal operators or auxiliaries, no difference could be perceived.

We can use the word 'true' so as to apply to (an actual or possible utterance of) a sentence if an assertion made by it is or would be correct, and we can use 'false' for one for which such an assertion would be incorrect. That is not how the word 'false' is being used when we identify having the value ½ with being neither true nor false. One motive for using 'false' in the latter way is the presence in the language of a negation operator obeying Łukasiewicz's truth-table. We have in the language an operator 'not', which converts a true sentence into a false one and usually converts a false sentence into a true one; but it converts certain sentences which could not be used to make a correct assertion into sentences which still could not be used to make a correct assertion. Since there is a strong impulse to call a statement 'false' only if its negation is true, the sentences of this special class are naturally labelled 'neither true nor false'.

An obvious example is provided by atomic sentences containing empty singular terms. Someone who uses such a sentence to make a serious assertion evidently does not intend to allow for the possibility that the term lacks a reference; its possessing one is part of the condition for the assertion to be correct. But the negation of such a sentence cannot be used to make a correct assertion: the possession of a reference by the term is still part of the condition for the correctness of the assertion made by means of the negation. In calling such sentences 'neither true nor false', we are allowing for an explanation of the negation operator by means of Łukasiewicz's truth-table. Saying something false and saying something neither true nor false are two distinct ways of making an incorrect assertion; but we need to distinguish them only in order to give a systematic explanation of the working of the negation operator and, perhaps, of the other logical constants.

We have in fact no precise practice governing complex sentences containing empty terms, and we do not understand indicative conditionals as Łukasiewicz's truth-table for '→' would require. But what if we did? Someone might have grounds for asserting $\ulcorner T\mathbf{A} \rightarrow \mathbf{B}\urcorner$, without being in a position to assert $\ulcorner \mathbf{A} \rightarrow \mathbf{B}\urcorner$; but why should that rule out an inference from $\mathbf{A}$ to $\ulcorner T\mathbf{A}\urcorner$? If I have grounds for asserting $\mathbf{A}$, I thereby have grounds for asserting $\ulcorner T\mathbf{A}\urcorner$: so how could such an inference lead to error? If we asserted only statements of which we were certain, it could not: assertions of $\mathbf{A}$ and of $\ulcorner T\mathbf{A}\urcorner$, as complete sentences, would be treated as interchangeable. Since we do not, we might exploit the greater strength that the truth-table for '→' confers on $\ulcorner T\mathbf{A}\urcorner$ by reserving its use, in making assertions, for occasions when we had greater certainty, or at least for those in which we are certain that it did not have the value ½. There need be no sense in which we are closer to making a correct assertion when our statement has the value ½ (say because we inadvertently used an empty term) than when it has the value 0; it is the truth-table for '$\rightarrow$' which makes the value 0 further from the value 1 than is the value ½.

Degeneration of Probabilities

The example gives a coarse illustration of a far-reaching concern. In mathematics we do not aim to make assertions save on conclusive grounds; when proofs are defective, they have to be rectified. We cannot claim to be certain of all our results; but our lack of certainty turns on the difficulty of ensuring that a complicated proof is conclusive, not on our acceptance of arguments we know to fall short of being conclusive. Hence it is sufficient, for mathematical purposes, that a principle of inference should guarantee that truth is transmitted from premisses to conclusion. Outside mathematics, we have a motive to demand more, if we could get it. Philosophers discussing the concept of belief sometimes speak of an ideal subject as one who believes all the logical consequences of his beliefs; but, unless we make the further idealisation that he has only true beliefs, there is nothing ideal about him. Most of our beliefs are perforce based on grounds that fall short of being conclusive; but a form of inference guaranteed to preserve truth is not, in general, guaranteed to preserve degree of probability. This is already obvious for the rule of and-introduction: the conjunction of two statements will usually have a lower probability than either. The 'ideal' subject, starting from beliefs whose probability is close to 1, will end up with beliefs with probability negligibly greater than 0; the man of common sense, initially adopting beliefs with a much weaker evidential basis, but reasoning from them only to a meagre extent, will finish with far fewer false beliefs than he. That is why scientific conclusions arrived at by long chains of impeccable reasoning from highly probable initial premisses almost always prove, when a direct test becomes possible, to be wrong. That is not a ground for discouraging scientists from pursuing their chains of inferential reasoning: only so will they discover that, contrary to probability, one or more of their premisses was false. It is a ground only for refusing any credence to the conclusions they reach.

A remedy is not easily come by. One cannot hope to find principles of inference that guarantee to the conclusion a probability higher than that of the conjunction of the premisses; but the probability of the conjunction of all of anyone's beliefs is likely to be extremely low, even when they are not actually inconsistent. Keeping one's beliefs in watertight compartments, however, is not a good policy, either. In science, deductive reasoning is a means to the attainment of truth: for arriving at new truths, if one is lucky, or for uncovering hidden errors, if one is not; but in science, truth is valued for its own sake. In practical life, truth is valued chiefly as a guide to action; and then the principal remedy for the degeneration of probability in the course of inferential reasoning is to employ it sparingly. The Łukasiewicz semantics shows how a semantic property differentiating two sentences with the same assertoric content might be exploited to guard against one possible source of degeneration.

What Is Truth?

A semantic theory, we saw, is an account of how, in general, sentences are determined as true or otherwise in accordance with their composition. Logic being concerned with formulas containing schematic letters standing proxy for expressions of various categories, a semantic theory that subserves the purposes of logic will give an account of how, in general, a formula is determined as true or otherwise under an interpretation. Such a semantic theory has three parts: (i) that which stipulates what, in general, an interpretation consists in, namely, a specification of what the semantic values of each type of schematic letter will be, relative to some domain or domains for the bound variables; (ii) that which lays down how the semantic value of any formula, under any given interpretation, is determined; and (iii) the statement of what it is for a formula to come out true under an interpretation. This third part is otiose only if truth is itself a possible semantic value for a sentence. As thus characterised, it is not part of the semantic theory itself to explain what truth is. As far as the semantic theory itself is concerned, truth might just be the letter T, the number 1, the Moon, former president Nixon, or anything you like. Of course, it will not be a *semantic* theory if the word 'true', as used in part (iii) of the theory, is not used in its proper sense, that is, if the 'truth' of the theory is not genuine truth, since the phrase 'semantic theory' was explained as denoting a theory that gives an account of how a sentence is determined as true or otherwise in accordance with its composition, and the word 'true' was not there being used to mean 'correlated with the letter T'. But it does not belong to the semantic theory to explain what truth is; hence, as far as mathematical results stated in terms of the semantic theory are concerned, truth could as well be the letter T. This is a matter of drawing boundaries, but there is a reason for drawing the boundary in this place. Our initial question was, in what relation does a meaning-theory for an actual language stand to semantic theories as they figure in the study of logic? But logic, as we saw, can take the notion of truth for granted: we know in advance that precisely what is required of an inference, for it to be valid, is that it be truth-preserving, and so, if we have an account of how a formula is determined as true or otherwise under an interpretation in accordance with its composition, we can by appeal to it characterise valid inferences without having to enquire further what truth is.

What does it mean to enquire what truth is? If we are told, for a given language, the conditions under which any sentence of the language is true, do we not know what truth is, for sentences of that language? Well, suppose that you are told this for some language that you previously did not know at all, and now someone says to you, 'There is a group of people who speak that language: go ahead and talk to them'. If your knowledge of the conditions for the sentences of the language to be true enables you to do this—that is, if it provides you with an understanding of the sort of thing to say and how to respond to what is said to you—then that is because you know the connection between the conditions for a sentence to be true and the practice of speaking the language, of engaging in converse in that language. That is to say, the transition between the rules determining the truth-conditions and the practice of speaking the language was mediated by the prior understanding you had of the notion of truth. If, when the rules for determining truth-conditions were stated, some hitherto meaningless word, say 'alby', had been used in place of 'true', you would not have been able to comply with the suggestion that you converse in that language: it would have been no use to say to you, 'Well, go ahead: you know what condition has to hold for any sentence in the language to be alby; so why don't you join their conversation?' You would naturally reply, 'I don't know what to do: I don't know what I shall be saying if I utter a sentence of the language'. To explain what it is you understand about the word 'true', and do not yet understand about the word 'alby', is what I intended by speaking of explaining what truth is.

Actually, an answer can be given to the question, as thus posed, which is not the answer that I want: that is because I have not posed the problem quite correctly. The answer is this. Because of the case we have taken—that of an alien language of which you had no previous knowledge—we cannot here appeal to the Tarski (T) schema for the case in which the metalanguage, the language in which the statement of the truth-conditions is given, is an extension of the object-language; and we do not want, as Tarski does, to appeal to the obscure notion of translation. But what you need to know about truth, in order to go from the truth-conditions of the sentences to the significance of an utterance of a sentence, is the principle which underlies the (T) schema. This principle is that to assert a sentence is tantamount to asserting that the condition for it to be true obtains.

In the statement of this principle, the word 'assert' is used in two different ways: in the construction 'to assert that such-and-such is the case' and in the construction 'to assert a sentence'. 'To assert a sentence' means here 'to utter a sentence assertorically'. We do not have a similar construction with 'ask': we could not supplement the principle by 'To ask a sentence is to ask whether the condition for it to be true obtains'. But we could say a number of things like 'To utter a sentence interrogatively is to ask whether the condition for its truth obtains', 'To utter a sentence imperatively is to command that the condition for its truth be made to obtain', and so on. If we suppose that the rules determining the truth-conditions of sentences are supplemented by a statement of whatever conventions govern the recognition of whether a sentence is uttered assertorically, interrogatively or imperatively, where these adverbs are merely, as yet, labels of which no prior understanding is required, then the proposal is, for the case I imagined, entirely correct: equipped, now, with these various principles, of which the prototype is 'To utter a sentence assertorically is to assert that the condition for it to be true obtains', the student is in principle in a position to engage in converse with speakers of that language.

This answer is some improvement upon a mere appeal either to the statement of the truth-conditions or to the Tarski (T) schema; but, as remarked, it is not what we are after. The trouble is that the case just imagined was one in which the student already knew a language and, in that language, was a master of constructions of the form 'assert that . . .', 'ask whether . . .', 'command that . . .', and so on. But, when what we are interested in is what in general a mastery of a language consists in, what constitutes someone's mastery of his mother tongue, we cannot take a speaker as having an antecedent grasp of what it is to assert that something is the case, ask whether it is the case, or the like. Rather, his understanding of that is part of what makes up his mastery of the language: whether or not his language contains the constructions 'assert that . . .', 'ask whether . . .', and so on, his grasp of what it is to assert something, to ask something, or to command something consists in his knowledge of the *practice* of making assertions, asking questions, and giving commands, that is, of uttering sentences assertorically, interrogatively, or imperatively. Hence what we require is an account of what these practices consist in which is *not* of the form, 'To utter a sentence assertorically is to utter it in such a form and in such a manner as conventionally to indicate that the speaker is asserting that the condition for its truth obtains'—that is, in this instance, an account that does *not* appeal to the notions of asserting that something is the case and the rest. Why will such an account constitute an explanation of what truth is? Well, if such a thing as a *general* account of the practice of, say, assertion is to be possible at all, it must explain the significance of an assertoric utterance of a sentence whose particular content is given: if nothing at all is assumed to be known about the sentence, or only its phonetic and syntactic composition, then we could not possibly give any such account. The account, if it is possible at all, must be uniform over the particular contents of the various sentences that can all be used to make assertions: and so it will have to be stated in terms of whatever it is that determines the assertoric content of the sentence. This whole discussion, however, has been based on the assumption that the assertoric content of a sentence is given by the way that the condition for its truth is determined. To make this assumption, the account of the practice of making assertions (and of asking questions, and so on) will have to be framed in terms of the condition, taken as already known, for a given sentence to be true. It is that account which will display the connection between the truth-conditions of sentences and the practice of speaking the language: and so we may take it as explaining not only what assertions, questions, and commands are but also what truth is.

How to Explain the Logical Constants

One of the tasks of a semantic theory is to explain the meanings of the logical constants; but an explanation may be required for different purposes. We may want it for purely philosophical purposes: that is, when we are satisfied that we *do* understand the logical constants, but are perplexed to say in what our understanding consists, or simply want to find a perspicuous representation of it. The paradigmatic use of explanations, however, is to convey understanding to someone who lacks it. It is especially likely that this will be needed when the fundamental laws of logic are in dispute. It can seem impossible for them ever to come into dispute, since they are constitutive of the very meanings of the logical constants. Someone who rejects the law of excluded middle, for example, cannot mean the same by 'or' and 'not' as one who accepts it, nor one who rejects the distributive law the same by 'or' and 'and'. That is quite correct: a difference over fundamental laws of logic must reflect a difference over the meanings of the logical constants. But if there is to be any fruitful exchange between supporters and opponents of some fundamental law, they must have a means of explaining to one another how each understands the constants. One way to achieve this is by supplying an appropriate semantic theory. How is this to be done?

A thoroughly pernicious principle has gained considerable popularity in recent years. It is that in formulating a semantic theory the metalanguage must have the same underlying logic as the object-language. When this principle is followed, the proponent of a non-classical logic has a perfect counter to an argument in favour of a classical law that he rejects, namely, that the argument assumes the validity of the law in the metalanguage. An advocate of quantum logic may claim to accept the classical truth-tables for 'v' and '&', and hence to give just the same meanings to these operators as is given them in classical logic. An adherent of classical logic thereupon asks him how he can avoid accepting the distributive law and demonstrates that the law follows from the truth-tables; but to this the quantum logician retorts that, in taking the four lines of the truth-table to exhaust all possibilities, the demonstration has assumed the distributive law in the metalanguage. The quantum logician agrees that each statement is either true or false; he does not accept that it follows that either both of two statements are true, or both are false, or one is true and the other false. By this means a complete impasse is produced. The quantum logician has rendered himself invulnerable to any attempt by the other to persuade him of the validity of a law he takes to be inescapable; but he has deprived himself of any power to explain to the other what he is at. The classical logician was baffled to understand from what standpoint it was possible to repudiate the distributive law; simply to be told that he himself has begged the question in his argument in favour of the law provides no enlightenment whatever.

The quantum logician was appealing to a semantic theory highly sensitive to the underlying logic of the metalanguage: if that logic is classical, the distributive law comes out as valid; if it is quantum logic, the law comes out as invalid. What is needed, if the two participants to the discussion are to achieve an understanding of each other, is a semantic theory as insensitive as possible to the logic of the meta-language. Some forms of inference must be agreed to hold in the metalanguage, or no form of inference can be shown to be valid or to be invalid in the object-language; but they had better be ones that both disputants recognise as valid. Furthermore, the admission or rejection in the metalanguage of the laws in dispute between them ought, if possible, to make no difference to which laws come out valid and which invalid in the object-language. Thus, within sentential logic, the semantics of Kripke trees or Beth trees is insensitive to whether the logic of the metalanguage is classical or intuitionistic: exactly the same forms of inference can be shown valid or invalid on that semantic theory. If both disputants propose semantic theories of this kind, there will be some hope that each can come to understand the other; there is even a possibility that they may find a common basis on which to conduct a discussion of which of them is right.

The Significance of Internal Interpretations

An internal interpretation is maximally sensitive to the logic of the metalanguage. Any logical law that holds in the metalanguage can automatically be shown to be valid in the object-language, and no law can be shown to be valid in the object-language unless it holds in the metalanguage. The use of such interpretations is therefore devoid of explanatory power, at least as far as the logical constants are concerned; this is not to say that it serves no other purpose. We considered three notions of an interpretation for intuitionistic formulas. The first was that in terms of Beth trees; the second was that given by Heyting in terms of the general notion of a mathematical construction and of a construction's being a proof of a statement; and the third was what we called an internal interpretation. To specify an internal interpretation, we specify an inhabited species as the domain of the variables and associate elements of the domain with the individual constants, subspecies of the domain with the monadic predicate-letters, and so on. An atomic formula $\ulcorner Fa \urcorner$ is then true under the interpretation if the element associated with 'a' belongs to the species associated with **F**. For the complex formulas, we simply use straightforward stipulations: for example, we say that $\ulcorner \mathbf{A} \to \mathbf{B} \urcorner$ is true under the interpretation just in case, if **A** is true under it, then so is **B**, and so on for the other logical constants. Here it is essential that the logical constants occurring in these stipulations, those of the metalanguage, are understood intuitionistically. If you accept the intelligibility of a classical language, there is no absurdity in your reasoning classically about interpretations on Beth trees of intuitionistic formulas; but it is simply nonsense to reason classically about internal interpretations, because, by using the logical constants in their classical senses, you have prevented yourself from talking any longer about those interpretations.

The use of internal interpretations is by no means to be criticised: important mathematical results can be obtained by this means and, as things stand, by no other. What was criticised was the idea that, in an internal interpretation of an intuitionistic formula, we have the analogue of the standard notion of an interpretation of a classical formula as it appears in two-valued semantic theory. In fact, as we saw, an internal interpretation is not a semantic interpretation at all; we cannot put the theory of internal interpretations alongside that of Beth trees and the theory of constructions as a third type of semantic theory for an intuitionistic language. The reason why the notion of an internal interpretation does not attain the status of a semantic notion is that it does not provide any specific conception of the semantic values of expressions; and it does not do so because it does not say what the semantic values of sentences are to be. I dramatised this by asking what, in giving an internal interpretation, we should assign to the sentence-letters, if any occurred in a formula. But the point is not just one about sentence-letters. In an actual language we are unlikely to have any primitive (non-complex) sentences; and we might do logic without using sentence-letters, or without even separating out sentential logic as a significant fragment. But to fail to specify what the semantic values of sentences are is to fail to specify what the semantic values of predicates are, too. The notion of a species that is appealed to in saying what an internal interpretation is to be is as unspecific as that of a proposition, if we say that the semantic value of a sentence is a proposition. Moreover, in a genuine semantic theory, we must know what should constitute the semantic value of a sentence—of a formula under any one interpretation—in order to frame the second of the three parts of the theory, namely, that which stipulates how the semantic value of any formula, under a given interpretation, is determined. We should not be confused by the fact that by moving to one of the genuine semantic theories for an intuitionistic language, say, to the theory of constructions, we do become able to say specifically what a proposition or a species is. If we make this move, then we are no longer talking about internal interpretations but have moved to a context in which straightforward stipulations, in terms of truth, are no longer those we require for the logical constants. It is essential to the notion of an internal interpretation that what corresponds to the second part of a genuine semantic theory should consist solely of straightforward stipulations in terms of truth. An internal interpretation is not a semantic interpretation at all—that is, not one explainable in terms of any semantic *theory*—but what we called a *programmatic* interpretation, half-sister to an interpretation by replacement.

Although a programmatic interpretation can be converted into a semantic one by a choice of what the semantic values of sentences are to be, this choice does not determine the notion of truth under a semantic interpretation; that is, it does not determine how the semantic values of complex sentences formed by means of the logical operators are to be specified. We saw that the temptation to say that this does not matter—since the straightforward stipulations in terms of truth show how the *truth* of a sentence is determined in accordance with its composition—is an illusion: for if it were not, then, when it had been stipulated what in general the semantic value of a sentence was to be and how the truth of a sentence was to be explained in terms of its semantic value, it would become possible to dispense with the notion of semantic value for all but atomic sentences, stating everything for complex sentences in terms of their being true. But this we cannot in general do. For instance, if we say that a formula is true, absolutely, under an interpretation with respect to a Beth tree if it is true at the vertex (that is, intuitively, if we are entitled to assert it on our present state of information), then it by no means holds good that if it is the case that, if **A** is true absolutely, then **B** is true absolutely, then ⌜**A** → **B**⌝ is true absolutely. For example, we may know that **A** is not true at the vertex, possibly because there is some lower node at which ⌜¬**A**⌝ is true, and it will then be correct, under the intuitionistic understanding of 'if', to say that, if **A** is true at the vertex, so is **B**; but ⌜**A** → **B**⌝ may very well not be true at the vertex, because there is another lower node at which **A** is true but **B** is not. All that this means, of course, is that this notion of (absolute) truth does not distribute over 'if'. The argument depended on the fact that it does not commute with 'not': the fact that **A** is not true at the vertex does not show that ⌜¬**A**⌝ is true at the vertex. But, although it may be the case that we can always introduce some notion of truth which, in this sense, distributes over or commutes with all the logical operators, there is no general reason why such a notion of truth should be explicable for atomic sentences in terms of what we want to take as the semantic values of their components; and, if it is not, then it is not available as a means of framing stipulations governing the logical constants.

Even if the required notion of absolute truth is one which, in this sense, distributes over or commutes with the logical operators, it will not in general satisfy the requirements for a notion in terms of which a semantic theory can be framed. Consider the relation between **A** and ⌜¬¬**A**⌝, intuitionistically understood. When **A** is true, so is ⌜¬¬**A**⌝; and, when **A** is not true, ⌜¬¬**A**⌝ is not true. Is the truth, or otherwise, of ⌜¬¬**A**⌝ therefore determined by the truth, or otherwise, of **A**? By no means: the truth of ⌜¬¬**A**⌝ does not imply that of **A**. But suppose it said that we can easily state the condition for the truth of ⌜¬¬**A**⌝ in terms of the truth of **A**: ⌜¬¬**A**⌝ is true if and only if it is not the case that **A** is not true. We have here to invoke our distinction between stating the condition for the truth of a complex sentence *in terms of* the truth of its constituent sentences, and showing its truth, or lack of truth, *to be determined* by the truth or otherwise of its constituents. What is demanded of a semantic theory is that the semantic value of a sentence should be determined by the semantic values of its components and, in the case of a complex sentence, by those of its subsentences. We cannot in general require that by knowing the semantic value of a sentence we thereby know whether or not it is true. Heyting's sketch of a semantics for an intuitionistic language in terms of constructions is a case in point: by being able to tell, of any given construction, whether or not it is a proof of the sentence, we do not thereby know whether the sentence is true, since we may not know whether there is any construction that satisfies that condition. But we can, and must, require that the semantic value of a sentence is determined by the semantic values of its components, that is, that, in all cases, it follows from a statement of what the semantic value of each component is what the semantic value of the whole is; for this is just what is demanded of a semantic theory, that it show how the semantic value of each expression is determined in accordance with its composition. It follows that whenever the semantic value of a sentence is taken to be such that, from knowing it, we know whether or not the sentence is true, in the absolute sense, the truth or otherwise of a complex sentence must be determined by the semantic values of its subsentences. This means that, if knowing whether or not the subsentences are true does not tell us whether the whole sentence is true, then the semantic values of the subsentences cannot consist merely in whether or not they are true, and so, in general, the semantic value of a sentence cannot so consist. Hence a specification of the condition for the truth of a complex sentence in terms solely of the truth or otherwise of its constituent sentences will not belong to a semantic theory, properly so called. Thus, as we saw, if in a tense logic we interpret the operator '□' as having the intuitive meaning 'henceforward', we may correctly say that ⌜□A⌝ is true just in case **A** is henceforward true, and that is to state the condition for the truth of ⌜□A⌝ *in terms of* the truth of **A**; but it is not a stipulation that has any place in a semantic theory, since the truth of **A** (naturally identified with its *present* truth) does not determine whether or not ⌜□A⌝ is true.

It is only in the special case of a purely classical language that the semantic value of a sentence may be taken to consist simply in its being or not being true. In this case, the straightforward stipulations in terms of truth for the logical constants may be made, in the presence of sufficiently strong background assumptions (namely, as to the validity of the classical logical laws), to yield the semantic ones properly so called, namely, in the case of the sentential operators, the truth-tables considered as governed by the principle that their lines exhaustively represent all possible cases. Even in the classical case, however, the straightforward stipulations do not of themselves display the semantic mechanism of the language, which governs how a sentence is determined as true in accordance with its composition: that requires to be *derived*, by heavy appeal to the classical laws of logic.

An Objection

At this point, the following objection is very natural. I have made out, it may be said, that there is a wide gap between an internal interpretation and a semantic one for a language with a non-classical logic, a gap so wide that the former does not deserve to be called a semantic notion; it may only be called a programmatic one. But a large part of the argument turned on the fact that, in the non-classical case, the truth or otherwise of a complex sentence does not depend solely upon whether its subsentences are true; and precisely this does hold good in the classical case. The rest of the argument turned on the fact that the internal interpretation does not make explicit what the semantic one does: an internal interpretation for a classical formula would assign to a sentence-letter merely a proposition, to a monadic predicate-letter merely a property. All that we should have to know to start with, about propositions, is that they can be said to be true or not to be true; all that we should have to know about a property is that it is something which each element of the domain may be said to have or not to have. But why would that matter? We have allowed it as legitimate, in a formulation of the second part of a two-valued semantic theory, to give straightforward stipulations for the logical constants, since we can derive the truth-tables by appeal to the classical laws assumed as holding in the metalanguage. But if we started with a characterisation of the notion of an interpretation in the so-called programmatic style— one that did not make it explicit that all that mattered about a sentence, for the truth-value of a complex sentence of which it formed part, was whether or not it was true, and that all that mattered about a predicate was of which elements of the domain it was true—if we started with this programmatic style, could we not in just the same way derive these principles by appeal to the classical laws? That is, by construing '**A** is false' to mean either '**A** is not true' or, equivalently, '⌜¬**A**⌝ is true', we can easily prove the principle of bivalence. We can also get the effect of the principle that the semantic value of a sentence is its truth-value by proving, by induction, that sentences that are both true, or both false, can replace one another in any complex sentence without changing the truth-value of the whole. Similarly, we can get the effect of saying that the semantic value of a unary predicate is a set by proving the intersubstitutability of co-extensive predicates. And, if we can do these things, the explicit statements of the principles of two-valued semantics, which I claimed should be present if what is specified is to be taken as a genuinely semantic interpretation, appear to be no more than superfluous flourishes: they can still be derived if we start only with the so-called programmatic interpretation.

This is a highly specious argument; and it is of fundamental importance to see the mistake in it.

chapter 3

Theories of Truth

Meaning-Theories

The question I began by posing was: what is the relation between a meaning-theory for an actual language and a semantic theory of the kind that serves the purposes of logic? I remarked on two salient differences between logic and the theory of meaning: in logic we are concerned with different possible interpretations of formulas, in the theory of meaning with the one correct interpretation of sentences; in logic we can take the notion of truth for granted, in the theory of meaning we cannot, but must say what truth is, that is, expose the connection between truth and meaning. So far, however, we have not attempted to answer the original question. What do we need in order to obtain an answer? Our original characterisation of a semantic theory was as one which displayed the mechanism by which a sentence is determined as true or otherwise in accordance with its composition. Now that we have looked at semantic theories in more detail, we can amend this characterisation slightly. For those semantic theories in which the condition for the truth of a sentence is to be stated, in terms of the semantic value of the sentence, by means of an existential quantification, it will not hold good that to know the semantic value of a sentence is to know whether or not it is true; within semantic theories of other kinds, this will hold. If we want to allow for semantic theories of the former kind, the word 'determine' is too strong; after all, an intuitionist would deny that it is determinate, for every sentence, whether or not it is true. We shall therefore do better to say that the semantic value of an expression is that feature of it on which the truth of any sentence in which it occurs *depends* (rather than that which goes to *determine* the truth or otherwise of any sentence in which it occurs). What a semantic theory is required to do, therefore, is to exhibit the way in which the semantic value of a sentence is determined by the semantic values of its components, and to give the general condition for a sentence to be true, in terms of its semantic value. I shall nevertheless continue to use the briefer phrase 'how a sentence is determined as true or otherwise in accordance with its composition', despite its slight inexactitude in the context of certain semantic theories. In order, therefore, to decide the relation between a meaning-theory and a semantic theory, we have two principal questions to answer. First, what *is* the role of the notion of truth within a meaning-theory? In other words, does an account of how a sentence is determined as true or otherwise in accordance with its composition constitute a part of a meaning-theory, and, if so, is it a central part or a peripheral part? Secondly, how much difference is made by the fact that the meaning-theory is concerned with a single interpretation and the semantic theory with a range of interpretations?

So far, I have said little about meaning-theories, but have been concerned rather with semantic theories, as they figure in formal logic, in particular, with distinguishing a semantic interpretation of logical formulas from what we called a programmatic interpretation. The latter is characterised by the fact that it does not use any notion relating to closed formulas other than that of truth under an interpretation: that is to say, it states the condition for the truth of a complex formula, so interpreted, directly in terms of the truth of its constituent formulas, interpreted likewise. (If, as an auxiliary device alternative to using the notion of the satisfaction of an open formula by a sequence of elements of the domain, we assume the language either to contain a term for every element, or to be expanded so as to do so, we can extend this formulation from sentential to predicate logic, saying that a programmatic interpretation states the condition for the truth of a quantified formula in terms of the truth of its instances.) It is further characterised by the fact that the stipulations governing the various logical constants are all of a straightforward (sometimes called a 'disquotational') form, and that it is therefore essential that the metalinguistic constants be taken as subject to the same laws as those of the object-language. The application of the notion of truth under a programmatic interpretation will then depend crucially upon those laws. It was argued that, for any language subject to a non-classical logic, the use of programmatic interpretations does not constitute a semantic theory at all, because it does not do what a semantic theory is required to do: it fails to show how a formula is determined as true or otherwise under an interpretation in accordance with its composition.

Truth and the (T) Schema

The question what role the notion of truth has in a meaning-theory falls into two parts. First, does that notion have an important role in a meaning-theory at all? Secondly, if it does, does the meaning-theory need to incorporate a semantic theory in our sense—that is, an account of how a sentence is determined as true or otherwise in accordance with its composition—or can it rest content with some characterisation of the condition for a sentence to be true which does not yield such an account? If the notion of truth does have an important role to play, then it seems reasonably clear that the meaning-theory must indeed incorporate a semantic theory. Indeed, it is often claimed as a merit of a Tarski-style theory of truth, presented as comprising the whole or a large part of a meaning-theory for a language, that it does exhibit the way each sentence is determined as true or otherwise in accordance with its composition. We may therefore consider the concomitant claim that a theory of truth framed in the manner of Tarski provides the correct manner of characterising the notion of truth, as this notion is required for a meaning-theory for an actual language, say, a natural language. This claim takes it for granted that the notion of truth *does* play a central role in a meaning-theory. In particular, it is sometimes contended that the claim may be acknowledged to be correct in advance of coming to know whether the language has a classical underlying logic. Now there are three ingredients to a Tarskian truth-definition. First, there is the requirement that the definition yield every instance of the (T) schema

S is true if and only if **A**,

such an instance being obtained by replacing 'S' by the name of a sentence of the object-language, and '**A**' by that very sentence (if the metalanguage is an extension of the object-language) or by a translation of it (if it is not). Secondly, there are the various clauses which, taken as axioms of a theory, will permit such a derivation. Hitherto, the term 'straightforward' has been applied only to stipulations governing logical constants. It may be extended in a natural way to those governing non-logical expressions. Examples are:

'London' denotes London

and

For any object a, the predicate 'x is fragile' is true of a
if and only if a is fragile.

It is characteristic of a Tarskian truth-definition that all of those of its clauses which relate to particular primitive expressions of the object-language, whether logical or non-logical, will have a straightforward form. And, thirdly, there is the device, originating with Frege, for converting these inductive stipulations into an actual explicit definition.

In a sense, the second and third ingredients of such a truth-definition are non-controversial. That is to say, if we start with the idea that we shall arrive at a complete characterisation of the notion of truth, for the purposes for which we require it, by defining it in any way that yields each instance of the (T) schema, then the second and third ingredients of the truth-definition simply show us definitively how to achieve a definition which does just this and no more. What we therefore need to concentrate on is the (T) schema itself; more specifically, the claim that all that is required is a definition or theory of truth that yields each instance of that schema.

To claim that a Tarski-style theory of truth can be seen to be the right characterisation of the condition for a sentence to be true, for the purposes for which we need the notion of truth in a meaning-theory for an actual language (in advance of deciding whether that language has a classical logic), is to claim that such a theory of truth is neutral as between different logics. Now, evidently, what we get by means of such a theory of truth is a specific interpretation of the kind that we have called programmatic. It follows from our conclusions concerning programmatic interpretations that, if the logic of the language should prove to be non-classical, then a theory of truth of this kind will *not* provide us with a characterisation of truth—that is, of the general condition for a sentence to be true—of the sort we need for the purposes of a meaning-theory. In the first place, we have no general guarantee that that notion of truth which we need for these purposes will be one for which each instance of the (T) schema is correct. It will not be correct for any notion of truth with respect to which there are counter-examples to the principle of bivalence, that is, sentences which are neither true nor false. More generally, whether or not we want to identify the falsity of a sentence with the truth of its negation, the (T) schema will fail for any notion of truth which does not commute with all the logical constants, in particular negation, and hence for any under which we have reason to say that a sentence may fail to be true without its negation being true.

It would be wrong to go still further and say that the (T) schema is incorrect for any notion of truth under which the principle of bivalence fails. The principle of bivalence cannot hold in any semantics for an intuitionistic language, but that is not enough to show that under the appropriate notion of truth there will be counter-examples to the (T) schema, since, if a sentence is false just in case its negation is true, and if truth commutes with negation, it would be contradictory to say that there was a sentence which was neither true nor false. What matters is not whether bivalence holds but whether there are sentences that violate it; intuitionistically, however, we cannot go from saying that there are no sentences that are neither true nor false to saying that every sentence is either true or false. The Beth tree semantics reflects a natural inclination to equate the notion of the intuitionistic truth of a sentence with our present entitlement to assert it, in which case we have a notion of truth that does not commute with negation; a sentence may not be true although its negation is not true either.

The point is not merely that the notion of truth we want may not be one for which the (T) schema is correct: that schema may still be correct, for the appropriate notion of truth, even though the logic is non-classical. The principal point is, rather, that, whether or not the (T) schema is correct, a Tarski-style theory of truth will not display the way in which a sentence is determined as true or otherwise in accordance with its composition, when the logic is non-classical, for just the reasons for which we saw that a programmatic interpretation does not do so. That is to say, what we need, for the purposes of a meaning-theory, is *not* just any characterisation of truth that yields each instance of the (T) schema. What we need is a characterisation which shows how each sentence is determined as true or otherwise in accordance with its composition; and, when we have that, we may then enquire, as a matter of interest, whether or not each instance of the (T) schema will hold. For no non-classical language will a Tarski-style theory of truth give us what a semantic theory provides, and what must be demanded of a meaning-theory, if, as we are here assuming, the notion of truth is to play a crucial role in a meaning-theory.

A Non-classical Logic for Natural Language?

How might a natural language, such as English, prove to have a non-classical underlying logic? There are two possibilities. First, it might have a classical fragment but be non-classical as a whole: the logic of the sentential operators 'and', 'or', 'if' (as used in indicative conditionals), and 'not', and that of universal and existential generalisation, might be classical, and yet the language could contain what had to be treated as genuine modes of sentence composition, genuine logical constants, which could not be handled by a two-valued semantics. It would be tendentious to cite sentences ascribing propositional attitudes ('John believes that . . .') in this connection, since there are various suggestions, by Frege, Quine, Davidson, and others, indicating how we might be able to handle these by taking them at something other than their face value. But, apart from these, we have modalities, subjunctive conditionals, the operator 'definitely', whose presence is connected with the existence of vague expressions, and, indeed, the tenses and other means of temporal reference, whose status raises very obscure problems. In the second place, it may be that even the logic of the ordinary sentential operators and the two quantifiers is not uniformly classical, that is, not classical for all kinds of sentence in the language. (It is this question that is connected, in my view, with the deep metaphysical problems which I listed in the Introduction.) And here it is not merely that a Tarski-style theory of truth will not give us what we need a meaning-theory to do: it will also leave us without a means to decide what we should take our logic to be. As we have noted, the logic that can be shown, by appeal to a theory of truth of this kind, to hold in the object-language is directly sensitive to the logical laws assumed to hold in the metalanguage. This hangs together with a view according to which the meanings of the logical constants are fixed by our simply imposing a set of logical laws governing them. But such a view leaves us powerless to discuss the question which laws we *should* take as holding. Hilary Putnam at one time believed that, so long as the language is taken to include statements of quantum mechanics, the distributive law is not in general valid. Intuitionists believe that, at least if it includes mathematical statements, the laws of excluded middle and of double negation fail. The conception of a meaning-theory as embodying a Tarski-style theory of truth leaves us powerless to resolve by appeal to the meaning-theory the disagreement between those who make such proposals and those who resist them, for then a law will hold in the object-language just in case it holds in the metalanguage, and, of course, the question what laws we should take as holding in the metalanguage is no advance on the question what laws we should take as holding in the object-language.

How are we to resolve such disagreements? I should say: either by seeing which laws are justified by the meaning-theory, or, at a deeper level, by determining which, of rival meaning-theories, is the correct one. But suppose someone says that it can be done by empirical investigation, by finding out whether our world is the sort of world in which the distributive law, or the law of excluded middle or of double negation, holds. How are we to do this? Since the laws are themselves schematic, it follows that, even to begin, we must be able to consider various statements which are instances of those laws, or are the premisses and conclusion of instances of the corresponding forms of inference; and we must know how to determine such statements as true or not true. Since these will necessarily be complex statements involving the relevant logical constants, we must appeal, at least tacitly, to the conditions for the truth of statements containing those constants. Now, if the only formulation of those conditions that we admit is one the correctness of which depends on first deciding the logical laws that are to hold, our investigation goes round in a circle.

Should we conclude, then, that a Tarskian truth-definition throws no light whatever on the concept of truth? By no means. Paradoxical as this may sound, it is to be regarded as providing the correct explanation of the use of 'it is true' as it occurs *within* the language—that is, within the object-language. The comment sounds paradoxical because Tarski insisted so strongly that the predicate 'is true' belongs only to the metalanguage and cannot be incorporated into the object-language without rendering it inconsistent. But we have to ask what is meant by talking about 'object-language' and 'metalanguage' in connection with a natural language. Natural languages contain many expressions, such as 'true', 'meaning', 'assertion', 'justification', 'definition', and so on, which relate to our use of language itself; in using them, we as it were take up a standpoint as from outside the language. Yet we draw no line; we observe no distinction, even in principle, between a primary part of the language and a secondary part in which we comment on our employment of the primary part. We do not, for example, reserve the use of such words for general abstract reflections on the use of language; on the contrary, they provide us with important instruments for use in everyday discourse. Precisely for this reason, as Tarski observed, we cannot prevent the semantic paradoxes from arising in our language as we have it: our linguistic practice is thus not perfectly coherent. We have, therefore, just as Frege believed for quite different reasons, to tidy up the language somewhat before we can begin to construct a systematic account of the way it functions: we seek an account of a slightly idealised version of the language. And one thing we need to do in this regard is to draw a line, where none previously existed, between the part of the language described and the part we use to describe it, between object-language and metalanguage.

At first it sounds ridiculous to say that a Tarskian truth-definition relates to the notion of truth employed within the object-language, because the definition is given in the metalanguage: precisely in order to avoid the paradoxes, the predicate 'is true' was taken to be a predicate of the metalanguage, not of the object-language. It nevertheless remains that the notion of truth for which it is obvious that each instance of the disquotational form of the (T) schema holds—and, to grasp which, we need know nothing more than that each instance of the (T) schema holds—is precisely the one that we employ in contexts in which we are not appealing to any ideas, however inchoate, about how our language functions: contrast with these such quasi-philosophical remarks as 'I think that a man's ethical principles are true for him'. The observation is in fact virtually a tautology. If the whole significance of the use of the word 'true' in such a statement as 'When you said a moment ago that Americans are even worse at learning foreign languages than English people, what you said was quite true' lies in the fact that the statement has the same force as 'You said a moment ago that Americans are even worse at learning foreign languages than English people, and Americans *are* even worse at learning foreign languages than English people', then it is not being used in such a way as to presuppose any general account of how language functions, nor, indeed, as to permit any such account in terms of such a use of 'true'. Certainly it does not presuppose such an account, since the explanation of 'true' formed a small part of an account of the language.

As for not permitting such an account, this depends upon the status accorded to the requirement that each instance of the (T) schema shall hold. If a specification of the conditions under which sentences of a given language are true is thought of as forming part of some meaning-theory for the language, then, whether that specification takes the form of a Tarski-style truth-theory or not, it has to be conceived of as being framed in some metalanguage. The meaning-theory must be capable of explaining the meanings of the sentences of the object-language. Hence, even if the object-language is in fact one we already know, and even if, because our interest lies in seeing what the meaning-theory looks like rather than in actually using it to achieve an understanding of the object-language, we in fact frame the meaning-theory in an extension of the object-language, we are still viewing the object-language *as if* it were one we did not understand. That is to say, the meaning-theory itself must make no appeal to our prior understanding of the object-language; it would not, for example, impair its adequacy as a meaning-theory if it were translated.

In such a case, therefore, the fact (if it be one) that all instances of the (T) schema, in its simple form, hold good is one of which we can take no official notice; its simple (or disquotational) form being that in which the sentence which replaces '**A**' is that named by the term which replaces '**S**'. As for the general form, in which that sentence may be only a translation of the one named by the term, we can take no official notice of its satisfaction, either; for, plainly, we should have to rely on our understanding of the object-language to recognise that the one sentence *was* a translation of the other. To speak more precisely, we can view the requirement that all instances of the (T) schema should hold as being formulated only at some third level, as a criterion for our stating the conditions for the truth of sentences of the object-language correctly. The intelligibility of the meaning-theory, and the fact that it serves the purposes of a meaning-theory, cannot depend upon our awareness that the requirement is satisfied. Rather, the significance of the word 'true', as employed in the meaning-theory, will depend jointly upon the specification of the conditions for sentences of the object-language to be true and those other principles of the meaning-theory that are expressed by means of the predicate 'true', namely, the connections established by the meaning-theory between the property of being true and the use that speakers make of the sentences. Conversely, therefore, an explanation of the use of 'true' by means of an outright stipulation that each instance of the (T) schema is to hold (perhaps, to avoid the paradoxes, for some restricted range of sentences) cannot be part of, or be extended to, any general account of how the language functions, precisely because it depends on and exploits the prior understanding of those sentences to which the predicate 'true' is to be applied. Even when the explanation is given, not by means of such an outright stipulation, but by means of a Tarski-style truth-definition, the same observation holds good, whether or not it is thought of as essential to the explanation that it be given in the same language as that to which those sentences belong, to which the predicate 'true' is being applied.

It is for these reasons that the observation made earlier is justified. The observation was that it is virtually a tautology to say that that notion of truth which can be grasped simply by recognising that each instance of the (T) schema holds good must be one that neither embodies nor subserves a conception of how our language functions. It amounts to this. If it is *not* thought of as essential that the truth-theory be stated in a language which contains the object-language, then the requirement about the (T) schema cannot play an essential role, since the notion of translation can be at best heuristic. In this case, we at least have a candidate for being an ingredient of a meaning-theory, although, for the reasons already given, an unsuccessful candidate. But if it *is* taken to be essential that the truth-theory be stated in a language the understanding of which presupposes an understanding of the object-language, then the predicate 'true', considered as so explained, cannot figure in any meaning-theory for that object-language, and, in fact, we have only an explanation designed to show how the object-language can be expanded to admit the employment *within* it of that predicate, restricted to sentences of the unexpanded language.

Knowledge of a Proposition and Knowledge of the Truth of a Sentence

The point may be put by saying that if the understanding of 'true', as applied to the sentence 'Sharks never sleep', consists in knowing that ' "Sharks never sleep" is true' is equivalent to 'Sharks never sleep', then an understanding of the sentence could not be taken to consist in a knowledge of the conditions under which it is true, where 'true' is so understood. A little care is needed in saying why not. We need, in general, to distinguish between knowing that a sentence is true and knowing the proposition expressed by the sentence. In using the latter phrase, I am not accepting any commitment to admitting propositions into our ontology: I mean merely to express the generalisation of the distinction between knowing that the sentence 'Kangaroos are marsupials' is true, on the one hand, and, on the other, knowing that kangaroos are marsupials, which I equate with knowing the proposition expressed by the sentence. To know the proposition expressed by a sentence, one need not understand that sentence: one may understand and accept some equivalent sentence in another language, or, to the extent that it is possible to grasp a thought without being able to express it, one may simply grasp the thought and judge it to be true. But if someone does know that a given sentence is true, then what has to be added to this knowledge, for him to arrive at a knowledge of the proposition which the sentence expresses, is simply a full understanding of that sentence. If someone who has never heard of Professor Quine or of semantics hears it authoritatively stated that Professor Quine is attending a conference on semantics, he would not claim, nor would anyone ascribe to him, the knowledge that Professor Quine is attending a conference on semantics; he knows only that the sentence 'Professor Quine is attending a conference on semantics' is true, or, as he might say, pinpointing the areas of his ignorance, that someone called 'Professor Quine' is attending a conference on something called 'semantics'. It should be noted that to ascribe to someone the knowledge that a sentence is true, in this sense, is *not* to attribute to him a grasp of the meaning of the word 'true', and certainly not that meaning which is explained by a Tarskian truth-definition; at the most, it involves his having some implicit grasp of the concept of truth, but not his having the means to express it.

In terms of this distinction, we may now ask whether an understanding of the predicate 'true', as applied to the sentence 'Sharks never sleep', is to be taken as the knowledge that the sentence ' "Sharks never sleep" is true if and only if sharks never sleep' is true, or of the proposition expressed by the latter sentence. If we think of the word 'true' as having been explained by an outright stipulation that every instance of the (T) schema is to hold, we might incline to the former alternative, in which case it amounts to knowing that the sentence 'The sentence "Sharks never sleep" is true' is true just in case the sentence 'Sharks never sleep' is true, where the two outermost occurrences of 'is true' do not invoke the use of 'true' explained by the truth-definition (but are, as it were, implicit in the grasp of the meaning of the connective 'if and only if'). Now, in this case, an understanding of the predicate 'true', as applied to 'Sharks never sleep', does not amount to the knowledge that 'Sharks never sleep' is true just in case sharks never sleep: what is needed, in order to advance to this knowledge, is precisely to acquire an understanding of the sentence 'Sharks never sleep'. Hence, on this way of taking it, it is correct that, given this explanation of the word 'true', someone will know that 'Sharks never sleep' is true just in case sharks never sleep if and only if he knows what 'Sharks never sleep' means. It is correct—but it is totally unexplanatory; that is what is so confusing. It is unexplanatory because we have characterised what it is to know the condition for 'Sharks never sleep' to be true only by appeal to the notion of knowing what that sentence means, and so we have not arrived at any characterisation of what knowing what it means consists in. If, on the other hand, we think of the word 'true' as having been explained by means of an actual truth-definition, for the understanding of which an understanding of all the words used in it was essential, then we shall say that an understanding of 'true', as applied to 'Sharks never sleep', consists in a knowledge of the proposition that the sentence 'Sharks never sleep' is true just in case sharks never sleep. But, in that case, a knowledge of the condition for 'Sharks never sleep' to be true is part of a grasp of the *definition* of the word 'true', and so cannot *also* constitute an understanding of the sentence; on the contrary, an understanding of the sentence was presupposed for a grasp of the definition. Notice that this reasoning purports to give no general argument against an explanation of meaning in terms of truth-conditions, but only one against such an explanation in the context of a particular account of the predicate 'true': one, namely, that relates to the use of the word *within* the language, and hence one to which it is essential that the explanation be formulated in the language itself, slightly expanded to include the word 'true'.

The presence in our language of various meaning-theoretic terms forces us, as we saw, to *impose* on it a distinction between object-language and metalanguage which is not there in reality. And we shall want to draw the line so as to put into the metalanguage only those terms, and those uses of such terms, which really do serve the purpose of expressing some imperfectly formed ideas we have about how our language functions—or, to put it differently, which could be understood only as having a place in a meaning-theory for the rest of the language. Now, if one of these terms, considered as subject to a certain type of characterisation, would not play any useful role in such a meaning-theory, it is either useless or belongs (in so far as it is so characterised) on the other side of the line, to what we ought to take as constituting the object-language. And that is how we ought to view the term 'true', considered as characterised either directly by the requirement that each instance of the (T) schema holds, or by a Tarskian truth-definition to which the fact that the metalanguage is an expansion of the object-language is taken as essential.

This view of 'true' as a predicate of the object-language is taken in Saul Kripke's article "Outline of a Theory of Truth" (*Journal of Philosophy,* vol. 72, 1975, pp. 690–716) and in the strikingly similar treatment in R. L. Martin and Peter Woodruff's article "On Representing 'true-in-*L*' in *L*" (*Philosophia,* vol. 5, 1975, pp. 213–217). In both articles the aim is to do justice to the fact that we apply the predicate 'true' to sentences which themselves contain that predicate without having recourse to a hierarchy of metalanguages. This is done by taking the language as containing the predicate 'true' and as admitting predicates that are not everywhere defined, of which the only one need be the predicate 'true'. To handle such an object-language, a semantic theory is framed in a metalanguage whose underlying logic is three-valued. It is then shown how, by considering in the metalanguage a chain of interpretations of the object-language, differing only with respect to the predicate 'true', we can arrive at an interpretation under which that predicate is true of the sentence **A** if and only if **A** is true under that interpretation, and false of **A** if and only if **A** is false under the interpretation. It is of importance, however, as Kripke emphasises, that the object-language so interpreted is still not a universal language, in the sense of one in which we can express everything that we want to say, for instance that a sentence of the object-language for which the truth-predicate of that language is undefined is not true. It is not that we cannot have a truth-predicate in the object-language, on pain of contradiction; but it remains that a significant distinction persists between the truth-predicate of the object-language and that of the metalanguage.

Classical Logic as the Logic of Natural Language

So far in this chapter I have quarrelled with the idea of taking a Tarski-style truth-theory as an ingredient of a meaning-theory for a natural language only on the ground that this, which specifies a particular programmatic interpretation, will not accomplish what we require of a meaning-theory, if the logic of natural language proves to be non-classical, and gives us no way of resolving disputed claims about what that logic is. Previously, however, I sought to establish the distinction between programmatic and semantic interpretations for the classical case also; and at the end of Chapter 2 I left unanswered an objection to that distinction. The objection was that, if we start with a purely programmatic interpretation, and assume that the classical laws of logic hold in the metalanguage, then we can *derive* the principles of two-valued semantics; and so, in this case, the distinction between a programmatic and a semantic interpretation shrinks only to one between what is left to be extracted and what is made explicit.

Vagueness

In order to evaluate this objection, let us suppose that we wish to give a semantic theory for a language which, like all natural languages, contains vague expressions, including vague predicates. Some people think that some of the laws of classical logic, in particular the law of excluded middle, must fail in such a language; but there is at least one plausible view according to which they would not. For every vague predicate, for instance 'red', we may consider the relation which a given predicate, say 'rouge', will have to it when 'rouge' is what I shall call an *acceptable sharpening* of 'red': 'rouge' is an acceptable sharpening of 'red' if (i) 'rouge' is a predicate with a quite determinate application, (ii) everything that is definitely red is rouge, (iii) nothing that is definitely not red is rouge, and (iv) everything that more nearly matches something that is definitely red than does some given thing that is rouge is itself rouge. (The last clause says that anything that is redder than something that is rouge is rouge.) The notion of an acceptable sharpening has here been explained by example, since the last clause would demand a considerable apparatus if we were to give a general definition. Moreover, what we really want to consider is the notion of an acceptable set or system of sharpenings, since we should not want simultaneously to admit sharpenings 'rouge' and 'rose' of 'red' and 'pink', respectively, which left things that we should normally say were on the borderline between red and pink as neither rouge nor rose. In terms of this notion, we now say that a sentence of the language is true if it would come out true under replacement of its vague predicates by their sharpenings in accordance with *any* acceptable system of sharpenings. It is evident that, when the notion of truth for the language is so understood, every logical law that holds for a language all of whose predicates are determinate also holds for this language; hence, if we favour a classical logic for a language devoid of vagueness, we shall accept it for a language containing vague expressions also.

Now, on this understanding of languages with vague expressions, the specification of a programmatic interpretation will look no different from one for a language without vagueness. The clauses for the logical constants will, as usual, be straightforward, and the underlying logic will be classical. Hence we can, by appeal to the laws of that logic, 'prove' in just the same way that the sentential operators obey the two-valued truth-tables; we can also 'prove' that two predicates are intersubstitutable provided that they are co-extensive. Of course, the notion of co-extensiveness, for vague predicates, is not simple: it is not sufficient that they should be definitely true of the same things, and definitely false of the same things; they must also be linked in such a way that no acceptable system of sharpenings could leave them with different extensions. But none of this will be apparent from the specification of the programmatic interpretation; it will merely inform our understanding of a sentence of the form ⌜For every x, $\mathbf{F}x$ if and only if $\mathbf{G}x$⌝.

Plainly, however, a semantics for such a language could not be a two-valued one. The only kind of objective condition of which we can say that every sentence determinately either does or does not possess it is some distribution of truth-values relative to the various acceptable systems of sharpenings. And the only one of these we can identify with truth, consonantly with the intuitive conception of truth as supplying the objective condition for the correctness of an assertion, is that it be true under all acceptable systems. Quite evidently, this is not a notion of truth which distributes over the logical operations, which is to say that it is not one for which straightforward clauses would be correct; it is not the case, for example, that ⌜Not $\mathbf{A}$⌝ is true in this sense whenever $\mathbf{A}$ is not true. Hence a semantic theory cannot be given for this language in terms only of a sentence's being true or not being true; what is needed, obviously, is a semantics employing a relativised notion of truth—truth under a given acceptable system of sharpenings—with the logical constants being explained by relatively straightforward clauses, or by truth-tables, in terms of relativised truth. In relation to a specific language, the hard work will come in laying down which systems of sharpenings are to count as acceptable.

Bivalence

What is important to us is that the derivation, from the specification of the programmatic interpretation, of the principle of bivalence and the other principles of two-valued semantics, is spurious. The principle of bivalence does not mean merely that, for every sentence $\mathbf{A}$, either $\mathbf{A}$ or ⌜Not $\mathbf{A}$⌝ is true under that sense of 'true' for which every instance of Tarski's (T) schema holds, for this amounts to no more than that every instance ⌜$\mathbf{A}$ or not $\mathbf{A}$⌝ of the law of excluded middle holds. On the contrary, the customary distinction between the principle of bivalence and the law of excluded middle is rightly drawn; the former does not reduce to the latter. The law of excluded middle, together with all other classical laws governing the standard logical constants, will hold in every language for which the semantic theory takes the form of a Boolean algebra; and it will also hold in some languages for which others of the classical laws fail (for instance, in the language of quantum mechanics as governed by quantum logic); but the principle of bivalence will hold only for a language for which the two-valued semantics is correct. More exactly, it will hold provided that the law of excluded middle holds and the notion of absolute truth commutes both with negation and with disjunction. If we have a possible-worlds semantics for a language with modal operators, this is far from being a two-valued semantics, but we can still say that every sentence of the language is either true or false, since we may identify absolute truth with truth in the actual world, and ⌜Not **A**⌝ is true in the actual world just in case **A** is not true in the actual world.

The Adverb 'Determinately'

The principle of bivalence is not fully expressed merely by saying that every statement is either true or false: it is the principle that every statement is *determinately* either true or false. What is the force of qualifying a disjunction by the adverb 'determinately'? Intuitively, to say that an object *a* is determinately either **F** or **G** is to say that there is a statement, which may be ⌜*a* is **F**⌝ or may be ⌜*a* is **G**⌝, that is more informative than the statement ⌜*a* is either **F** or **G**⌝, and is no less true than it. This is often expressed by saying that if, determinately, one of two possibilities holds, but not both, then there is an answer, not necessarily known to us, to the question which one. A logician's explanation is that if we can assert ⌜**A** or **B**⌝ in a sense according to which the connective 'or' will admit the qualification 'determinately', then the statement could have been derived by the rule of or-introduction from one of its two subsentences, no matter how it was in fact arrived at. Again, the idea may be expressed by appeal to the concept of knowledge: if, determinately, one of two possibilities holds, then, if someone neither knows that the first possibility holds nor knows that the second one does, there is something that he does not know. This may be put in terms of God's omniscience: God must know which of the two possibilities holds, that is, must either know that the first one does or know that the second one does.

None of these explanations is watertight. At least on the proposed manner of construing sentences involving vague predicates, we should be right to assert, of an object on the borderline between red and orange, 'It is either red or orange'. It would be natural to comment that the object was, nevertheless, not *determinately* one or the other; and equally natural to gloss this by saying that there is no answer to the question which of the two it is. But to say that the question which colour it is has no answer is to say that there is no one colour which it is; whereas, on our way of construing the language, it will be correct to assert, 'There is one of the two colours, red and orange, which it is', since this sentence, too, will be true under all acceptable systems of sharpenings. Likewise, to say that, when 'or' admits the qualifier 'determinately', ⌜**A** or **B**⌝ implies ⌜Either God knows that **A** or God knows that **B**⌝ is just to say that the operator 'God knows that' distributes over disjunction. Now, to attribute omniscience to God is just to hold that, whenever a statement **A** is true, so is ⌜God knows that **A**⌝. The thesis therefore reduces to the claim that 'it is true that' distributes over disjunction; and this is uninformative until the sense of 'true' has been specified. There is always one sense of 'true' which is bound to distribute over disjunction, namely that sense under which all instances of the (T) schema hold; until the relevant sense of 'true' has been distinguished from that sense, to say that truth distributes over disjunction is to say nothing.

From the vantage point of a semantic theory for the language in which whatever disjunctive sentence we are considering is framed, the distinction we are aiming at is easily formulated: the disjunction is determinate provided that not only is the disjunctive statement true absolutely but at least one of the two disjoined sentences is true absolutely. Thus '*a* is either red or orange' may be true absolutely, in that it is true under all admissible systems of sharpenings, and yet not determinately true, since neither '*a* is red' nor '*a* is orange' is true absolutely. In a similar way, 'The photon goes through slit 1 or through slit 2' may be true absolutely, in the sense that the possibility of verifying either is still open, but not determinately, since we are still capable of closing off the possibility of verifying either. However, the statement with which we are concerned, namely, 'Every statement of the object-language is determinately either true or false', must be taken as enunciated in the metalanguage. Hence, if we relied on an explanation of the adverb 'determinately' of this kind, we should have to appeal to a semantic theory, of higher level, for the metalanguage. This is not a pedantic difficulty. To rely upon a semantic explanation of 'determinately' presupposes that we have selected some semantic theory for the object-language as the correct one, whereas, if we had a criterion for whether true disjunctive statements of the object-language are true determinately that related directly to the actual employment of the object-language, we could use it as a test for whether or not a proposed semantic theory was correct, according as it yielded the same or a different result.

There are two such internal criteria that we can apply, which can be illustrated from the two examples we have used. A true intuitionistic disjunction is plainly determinately true: a proof of it must yield a method of proving one or other of the disjoined statements. Thus it is not a requirement, for the connective 'or' to be interpretable as always determinate, that the logic be classical. But a quantum-logical disjunction is equally clearly not, in general, determinate. A proof-theoretic ground for denying its determinacy is that in quantum logic the unrestricted rule of or-elimination fails to hold. Only a restricted form of the rule is valid, which allows us to infer a statement **C** from the premiss ⌜**A** or **B**⌝ provided that **C** can be shown to follow both from the hypothesis **A** alone and from the hypothesis **B** alone, without appeal to any collateral information. This is enough to validate the inference from ⌜Either **A** and **B** or **A** and **C**⌝ to ⌜**A** and either **B** or **C**⌝, since the latter obviously follows of itself from ⌜**A** and **B**⌝ and equally from ⌜**A** and **C**⌝. It does not allow the converse inference, however. Plainly ⌜Either **A** and **B** or **A** and **C**⌝ does not follow from **B** alone or from **C** alone but follows only from one or the other combined with **A** as collateral premiss: so the unrestricted rule of or-elimination is needed to effect the inference. This is why the distributive law fails in quantum logic. Now if it were determinately the case that either **B** was true or **C** was true—for example, that the photon went, determinately, either through slit 1 or through slit 2—an appeal to the unrestricted rule of or-elimination would manifestly be intuitively valid; hence the quantum-logical 'or' cannot in general be stiffened by the addition of the qualifier 'determinately'. We may therefore take it as a necessary condition for every true disjunction to be determinately true that the rule of or-elimination hold without restriction.

It cannot be a sufficient condition, however, as is shown by our example of a language with vague expressions, understood according to the foregoing proposal. On that proposal, all the laws of classical logic hold good for that language; and yet it cannot be claimed that every statement of the language is determinately either true or false, or that every true disjunctive statement of the language is true determinately. In this case, the decisive feature is that it is possible to add to the language the operator 'definitely', so understood that ⌜Definitely **A**⌝ implies **A**, but not vice versa, and that an assertion of **A** is unassailably correct, in the sense that it would be incorrect to refuse to accept it, if and only if ⌜Definitely **A**⌝ is true. In terms of the semantic theory, ⌜Definitely **A**⌝ will be true under each sharpening just in case **A** is true under all sharpenings; it thus resembles the operator 'necessarily' under the standard semantics for the modal logic S5. With such an addition to the language, the fact that an object is red or orange but not determinately one or the other may be expressed by saying that it is definitely either red or orange but neither definitely red nor definitely orange. It may thus be taken as a second necessary condition for every true disjunction to be considered determinately true that it be impossible to add to the language an operator possessing the stated properties.

The two necessary conditions are jointly sufficient. We cannot take the impossibility of adding an operator with the properties of 'definitely'—say, in general, an operator with the force 'it is true absolutely that'—as sufficient by itself; for there may be a variety of reasons why it should be impossible. When the logic is non-classical, the meaning-theory that supplies a rationale for the appropriate semantic theory may impose restrictions upon what is expressible in the language; thus, for example, it is impossible to say within the ordinary language of intuitionistic mathematics that a proposition has not yet been proved, or that it is provable but never will as a matter of fact be proved. It may be such restrictions that render it impossible to add a 'true absolutely' operator; and in that case we must fall back on the first criterion, concerning the validity of or-elimination. But, when the logic is classical, the second condition is sufficient as well as necessary. That a language has a classical logic is far from being a guarantee that the two-valued semantics is correct for it: any Boolean algebra may equally well supply the framework for the appropriate semantic theory. A Boolean algebra may always be represented as a field of subsets of some underlying set. It therefore lies ready to hand to frame the semantic theory in terms of truth relative to the elements of this underlying set; we may call these elements 'possible worlds'. This is not, so far, a modal logic, since we have as yet admitted no modal operators into the language: it is clear, however, that there can be no conceivable obstacle to the addition of a unary operator 'U' such that $\ulcorner U\,\mathbf{A}\urcorner$ is true at any world if and only if $\mathbf{A}$ is true at every world.

There are now two possibilities: (1) 'U' is a necessity-operator; (2) 'U' is a 'true absolutely' operator of the kind with which we are concerned. Which of these possibilities obtains depends on features of the use of the language that will be reflected in the semantic theory by whether or not all the worlds are treated as having the same status; and that in turn depends on how absolute truth is characterised in the theory. There are two salient alternatives. First, one of the worlds may be accorded a distinguished status, and absolute truth may be defined as truth in that world: in this case, the distinguished world is the actual world, and 'U' is a necessity-operator subject to the standard semantics for the modal system S5. Or, secondly, the worlds may be regarded as of equal rank, and absolute truth may be defined as truth in all worlds: in this case, 'U' is not, properly speaking, a modal operator but a 'true absolutely' operator. How absolute truth should be defined in the semantic theory depends upon the conventions prevailing in the use of the language. If the condition for a correct assertion of $\ulcorner$ U A$\urcorner$ is, in general, more stringent even than the condition for an unassailably correct assertion of **A**, 'U' is a necessity-operator; but if the condition for asserting $\ulcorner$ U A$\urcorner$ coincides with that for asserting **A**, or at least with that for an unassailably correct assertion of **A**, even though **A** does not imply $\ulcorner$ U A$\urcorner$, 'U' is merely a 'true absolutely' operator.

How can this happen? In application to the language containing vague expressions, the phrase 'correct assertion' is really too crude: we must distinguish between a case in which the assertion of a statement is *mandatory*, in the sense that anyone who has made the relevant observations and has been presented with the relevant inferential reasoning reveals a deficiency in his understanding of the language if he fails to accept the assertion, and one in which it is *permissible*, in the sense that someone who makes the assertion on the basis of certain observations and certain reasoning does not thereby show any defect in his mastery of the language, his observation, or his reasoning. A mandatory assertion will be one made under conditions that render it unassailably correct. By a 'permissible' assertion, in the present sense, is not meant one made on less than conclusive evidence, still less a guess. There is, of course, no question of barring utterances of this latter kind, which will occur whatever the appropriate semantics. When the sense of a sentence is vague, however, it may be used to make assertions which, even in the face of the best possible evidence, it is not wrong to make but which are not mandatory: it is such assertions that are here called 'permissible'. There will in general be a gap between the condition for an assertion to be permissible and that for it to be mandatory; in this case the 'U' operator assumes the sense of 'definitely', and then an assertion of $\ulcorner$ U A$\urcorner$ will be permissible precisely when the bare assertion of **A** is mandatory.

That is not the general case, however. A second example of a language admitting a 'true absolutely' operator would be the language of a community that did not believe that there is, in general, any present truth about whether or not some future event will take place. For the members of this community, there are many possible courses the future may take, no one of which has presently the status of the *actual* future course of events. A statement in the future tense must thus, in general, be considered as true relatively to certain possible courses of events, and false relatively to others: the ordinary logical constants operate pointwise, that is, ⌜**A** or **B**⌝ is true relatively to any given course of events if and only if either **A** or **B** is true relatively to it, and similarly in other cases. Here the force of asserting ⌜U **A**⌝ is no greater than that of asserting **A**, and the conditions for the two assertions to be correct will coincide. What prevents the two sentences from being equivalent is that the sentential operators are not explainable in terms of the conditions for the correct assertion of the sentences on which they act: the contents of ⌜If **A**, then **B**⌝ and of ⌜If U **A**, then **B**⌝, for example, will by no means be the same.

When the language has a classical logic, but the two-valued semantics is inappropriate, there can be nothing to block the introduction of a 'true absolutely' operator, whose presence will thereby show that not every true disjunction is determinate. It may be, for example, that in every possible future course of events either **A** will be true or **B** will be true, so that ⌜**A** or **B**⌝ is true absolutely but nevertheless not determinately. For a language with a classical logic, the impossibility of introducing such an operator will therefore serve as a sufficient condition for every true disjunction to be determinately true. It is also the condition for the two-valued semantics to be appropriate for the language, which is just what we wanted: it is precisely in that semantic theory that the principle of bivalence, properly understood as saying that every statement is determinately either true or false, holds good. Such a language is characterised by the fact that the logical operators can be explained in terms of an unqualified notion of truth, under which a statement will be true just in case it could be correctly asserted. Any attempt to introduce a 'true absolutely' operator 'U' will therefore fail, since ⌜U **A**⌝ will collapse into **A**, and the condition that **A** should not imply ⌜U **A**⌝ will be violated.

What can be derived, by appeal to the classical laws, from the specification of the programmatic interpretation, is thus not the principle of bivalence properly so called: it is only a surrogate, of the form 'Every statement is either true or false', where no assumption can be made that the disjunction admits the qualification 'determinately'. As we noted, the derivation depends on an appeal to the law of excluded middle as holding in the metalanguage. But we have seen that the mere fact that a language has a classical logic by no means guarantees that all true disjunctions formulated in the language are true determinately. To decide that, we should therefore have to enquire after the semantic theory governing the metalanguage. A programmatic interpretation is possible only in a metalanguage whose logic matches that of the object-language, and the contention we have been examining was that when the logic is classical, such an interpretation will yield the two-valued semantic theory. Now we see that to obtain the two-valued semantics by this means, we must appeal to the semantics of the meta-language, without which that of the object-language is by no means determined.

Semantic versus Algebraic Characterisations

An attempt might be made to stand this argument on its head. Given the programmatic interpretation—that is, essentially, a notion of truth which commutes with the logical operations—we can, by appeal to the classical laws, derive principles that are formally indistinguishable from those of the two-valued semantics. It might be concluded from this that these principles cannot, in themselves, have the kind of force we have been ascribing to them. This would be to misunderstand what a semantic theory is: such a theory relates not simply to any notion of truth which it is possible for us to introduce but only to that notion of truth which serves the purpose of a meaning-theory. That purpose is to give a systematic account of the practice of speaking the language, embodying many linguistic modes of which assertion is the most central. The concept of a semantic theory is not a mathematical one. The two-valued system will, of course, serve perfectly well to characterise, in an algebraic manner, the relation of entailment between sentences of the language that contains vague expressions. Nevertheless, it is not a semantic theory for that language, since we cannot make the right kind of connection between its two 'truth-values' and the employment of the sentences, and hence between an interpretation of a formula by replacing its schematic letters by arbitrary expressions of this language (of appropriate type) and an interpretation in this algebraic system. The same contrast obtains between the interpretation of the modal system S4 in terms of sets of real numbers under the usual topology and its interpretation in terms of possible worlds, or of intuitionistic logic in terms of open subsets of the real line and in terms of Beth trees. Mathematically speaking, the two kinds of interpretation are quite analogous. In fact, both are specialisations of the general topo-logical interpretation of S4 or of intuitionistic logic. But no one would think of calling the theory of interpretations in terms of the usual topology on the real line a *semantic* theory, since no one has any idea how to represent the meanings of the logical constants in terms of the operations on subsets of the real line which correspond, in either case, to those constants, and since, more generally, no one knows how to relate an interpretation in terms of this topology to a replacement of the schematic letters by actual expressions.

For something to be a semantic theory, it is essential that it be at least plausible that it can be extended to a complete meaning-theory for a language, so that it forms the base on which such a meaning-theory can be constructed. Unless this is taken as a distinguishing mark of a semantic theory, we have no way of drawing the distinction, which is not a mathematical one, between a semantic theory properly so called and a purely algebraic theory of valuations, whose ambition is only to characterise the appropriate relation of logical consequence in algebraic terms. Whether any given theory of valuations could serve as a base for a meaning-theory, and so deserves to be classified as a semantic theory, and therefore what interest that theory of valuations has for logic, is a question that lies outside the province of logic itself. It is a topic for the theory of meaning, to which logic thus becomes subservient. That is not yet to say that every meaning-theory must have some semantic theory as its base, since to say that is to assume that the notion of truth must play a crucial role in any meaning-theory, and so far we have found no argument for that.

chapter 4

Meaning, Knowledge, and Understanding

Meaning and Knowledge

We are now at last in a position to turn to a direct consideration of meaning-theories. There appears to be a connection between meaning and knowledge, expressible by saying that the meaning of an expression is the content of that knowledge possessed by the speakers which constitutes their understanding of it; it is what someone has to know about the expression if he is to be a competent speaker of the language, that is, in the common phraseology, to know the language. This connection seems intuitively very strong. When, for example, it is said that it is part of the meaning of the word 'valid', as applied to deductive arguments, that a valid argument whose premisses are true will have a true conclusion, it is natural to gloss this by saying that someone who does not know this fact will not be said to understand the word 'valid' in this use. If someone can in many cases distinguish valid arguments from invalid ones but does not realise that there is anything wrong with recognising an argument as valid and accepting its premisses as true while refusing to admit its conclusion as true, we shall say that he does not fully understand what 'valid' means. Or, again, asking whether it is part of the meaning of the word 'aunt' that an aunt is the sister of a parent may naturally be explained as asking whether a knowledge of this interconnection is required of someone for him to be said to know what 'aunt' means.

The Social Character of Language

The connection between meaning and knowledge was called into question by Putnam, on the ground of what he illuminatingly termed 'the division of linguistic labour'. In his well-known example, the word 'gold' may be correctly used by people of whom we should allow that they know its meaning, although they do not know the criteria for its application used by specialists such as chemists and jewellers but would accept the authority of these experts. A yet more telling example is the word 'temperature', which is certainly one in everyday usage but is also a technical term in physics. Its meaning, as it is employed in everyday speech, is certainly not exhausted by the lame explanations that are all that most speakers could offer, for they would themselves acknowledge that it requires someone with a knowledge of physical theory to say what temperature actually is, and hence what 'temperature' means.

These two examples, and many others that could be cited, illustrate a more general phenomenon. In speech, we constantly use words whose meanings we do not fully know, but we use them with confidence that what we are saying is true, and that we are therefore transmitting correct information. If someone does not know the rules of chess, he can have only a partial understanding of what the word 'chess' means; but this will not inhibit him from remarking that two of his friends play chess together one evening each week, any more than someone is inhibited from telling you that So-and-so is the British middleweight boxing champion by his ignorance of the relevant upper weight limit. As long as you know what sort of person is being referred to, you count as understanding the information that an inspector called, regardless of whether you can state the hierarchy of ranks in the police force; you may learn from me, who was told by the garage mechanic, that the gasket of my car was leaking, even though I have not the remotest idea what a gasket is. This last example differs from the others in that we should not say that I know what the word 'gasket' means, whereas Putnam's were so chosen that a non-expert speaker would be allowed to know the meaning of 'gold', for instance; but what is required for understanding a word, like what is required for knowing a language, is somewhat arbitrary. Nobody knows every Russian word, or every word of any language; but, unless you are a mathematician, your ignorance of the Russian for 'prime ideal' will not tell against your having a perfect knowledge of Russian, whereas your not knowing how to say 'February', 'Moscow', or 'Germany' would. You may be said to understand a word if you know about it what is known by most people who use it frequently; but, this apart, there is no difference between what happens when the average speaker uses the word 'volt' and when a mechanical ignoramus uses the word 'gasket'. In both cases, the speaker is exploiting the fact that the word has an established use in the common language, which he does not fully know. He has good ground for believing that what he says is true; but he holds himself responsible to the established use and would withdraw what he had said if it could be shown to be wrong by the standard of that use.

The existence of an established use of such words depends on there being those whose authority concerning their use is communally acknowledged. More generally, any speaker beyond the initial stages of mastering language must have some conception of what language he is speaking and hold himself responsible to that. It has become wearisomely familiar to read commendations of dictionaries for being descriptive rather than prescriptive: the implication is that it is an impertinence to tell anyone how to speak, like telling someone how to wear his hair. Whatever the intentions of the compiler, however, a dictionary cannot help being treated as authoritative, just as a book of rules of games acquires an authority to which its author may not have aspired. The reason is the same in both cases. Using language and playing a game are not like doing one's hair and taking a bath. One may do either of the last two things as one likes and still be doing it. But, if the game ceases to have rules, it ceases to be a game, and, if there cease to be right and wrong uses of a word, the word loses its meaning. The paradoxical character of language lies in the fact that while its practice must be subject to standards of correctness, there is no ultimate authority to impose those standards from without. The only ultimate determinant of what the standards of correctness are is the general practice of those recognised as primary speakers of the language. ('Primary speakers' means, roughly, those whose mother tongue it is, but the status may be lost by long disuse, and, more important, may be acquired by sustained practice.) Those who inveigh against a prescriptive attitude to the language sometimes stigmatise as superstitious the idea that a word may have a meaning 'in itself', as opposed to what a speaker means by it on a given occasion; but, when Alice told Humpty-Dumpty that 'glory' does not mean 'a nice knock-down argument', she was not being superstitious. Including as they do professors of English and even of linguistics, those who argue for these libertarian views must presumably *know* a great deal about language, but they have not *understood* the first thing about it; they have perceived only half of its paradoxical character, and are thus unaware of its paradoxicality.

The examples so far considered have all been of words of whose meanings some people—Putnam's experts—have a full knowledge. There are, however, words of whose meaning it would make no sense to ascribe to anyone a complete knowledge: place-names are the best example. The employment of a word of this kind rests on a complex of social practices. It depends, primarily, on our ability to get to the place it names and to know when we have arrived; and this is embedded in the practices of making and reading maps and the operation of our various systems of transport. Knowing where one is has to do with recognising landmarks, with being able to read roadsigns or names of railway stations, but also, where there are people living, with where they say one is. This involves a system of established correspondences between names in different languages, since the words 'Napoli', 'München', 'Deutschland', and 'Steiermark', for example, are not the names in English of Naples, Munich, Germany, and Styria. In addition to all this, a mastery of the use of names of famous places like Jerusalem, Mecca, Delhi, and Peking involves some minimal awareness of their historical and literary significance: someone who has not heard of the Roman Empire or of the Papacy cannot count as fully understanding the name 'Rome', even if he has been in Rome, can recognise places in it, and can pinpoint it on the map. But even if one learned by heart the encyclopaedia entry under 'Rome', one would not thereby know everything that goes to determine the use of the name in the language, because that use is interwoven with the functioning of a range of social practices and institutions such as travel agencies and railways. A knowledge of how they function cannot be replaced by anything that could be written down in a book.

Idiolects and Dialects

All this shows that any adequate description of how a language functions must take account of its social character and, indeed, not only of the conventions governing the speaking of any one language (in the ordinary sense in which English, Czech, Tamil, and Japanese are languages) but of those which determine standard modes of translation between languages. Many philosophers, including Frege, have spoken of language in such a way as to identify a language, in the strict sense, with that spoken by some one individual at some period in his life, in other words, an idiolect. On this picture, communication is possible because each adult possesses an idiolect, and sufficient overlap between idiolects constitutes a common dialect, or less far-reaching overlap a language. The picture misrepresents the nature both of a dialect and of an idiolect. In one sense of the word, a dialect is simply a language that has not achieved recognition by the establishment. Save for a little poetry and scholarly editions of ancient writings, it is never seen in print; no newspapers are printed in it, no novels published in it, and it is not used for public notices and hardly ever even for advertisements. Nor is it employed for formal spoken use: it is not sanctioned in parliament, the law courts, school classrooms, or university lecture halls; the liturgy is not celebrated in it, preachers do not preach in it, politicians do not orate in it. The citizens of Catalonia have successfully striven to prevent their language, in itself no nearer to Castilian than to French, from becoming a dialect in this sense; those of Brittany, or of Sicily and Venice, have not. In a different sense, a dialect is simply a way of speaking a language, as an accent is a way of pronouncing it. If a native of a foreign country addresses me in his language, it is only polite to pronounce and speak it as correctly as I am able. But if someone addresses me in a broad Yorkshire accent, he might think I was mocking him if I replied in an imitation of that accent. Likewise, if a Scotsman says something to me about wee bairns, he does not expect me to use the expression 'wee bairns' in reply: we are both speaking English, he in his way, I in mine. An English dialect does not stand to English as Italian stands to the Romance subfamily; rather, the English language exists at a higher level of abstraction than its dialects.

Davidson has proposed relativising the notion of an idiolect, not only to a speaker and a time but to a hearer as well: we are to take the basic linguistic unit to be how *A*, at a given period, speaks to *B*. It is obvious that we try to speak to others so as to be understood. But this is not well described by saying that we use words according to the senses we believe the hearer to attach to them; it is better to say that we try to use expressions that will be accessible to him. I shall not be deterred, by the thought that he may not know what a gasket is, from telling someone that the gasket in my car is leaking, any more than I am deterred by the fact that I myself do not know. The reason is that I know that he will know how to find out what a gasket is if he needs to. The occurrence of this word in our dialogue cannot be explained in terms of his idiolect or mine; it can only be explained by reference to the English language. A speaker may use periphrasis to avoid a word to which he knows his hearer attaches the wrong sense; he will very rarely make an unqualified use of it in that sense.

A language is not to be characterised as a set of overlapping idiolects. Rather, an idiolect is constituted by the partial and imperfect grasp that a speaker has of a language, which is related to the language as a player's grasp of the rules of a game is related to the game. It is largely determined by what the speaker rightly or wrongly takes the meanings of words in the language to be; the concept of such an idiolect therefore cannot be anterior to that of a common language. In some cases, such as a place-name, no speaker could be credited with a grasp of the whole use of the word, nor, therefore, with a belief about what its use is. The idiolect of someone familiar with the name will then be characterised both by his knowledge that it is a place-name belonging to the language and by the connection he personally makes between the name and the place it names, a connection he need not suppose to be any part of the use of the word as a constituent of the public language.

Idiolects, so understood, are philosophically important for two quite separate reasons. When an utterance is made, what the speaker *says* depends upon the meanings of his words in the common language; but, if he thereby expresses a belief, the content of that belief depends on his personal understanding of those words, and thus on his idiolect. (The same holds good when he expresses any other 'propositional attitude'.) In unhappy cases, therefore, his words, understood according to their meanings in the common language, may not be the best expression of his belief, or may even misrepresent it. Furthermore, his personal grasp of some words, particularly certain kinds of names, may embody personal associations or recognitional capacities that do not enter into the meaning of that or any other expression of the common language. In such a case, there will be no completely accurate verbal rendering of the content of his belief; it is just such a possibility that Kripke exploits in his article "A Puzzle about Belief".

Speech as a Rational Activity

Idiolects are of significance not only for epistemology but also for the theory of meaning. Whether or not it can be said of a theory of meaning that it *is* a theory of understanding, it must certainly give an account of a speaker's understanding of his language. This is because speech and writing are conscious activities on the part of rational agents, just as playing a game is such an activity. Suppose that a Martian observes human beings, without, however, realising that they are rational agents, to whom motive and intention can be ascribed. The Martian becomes intensely interested in the phenomenon of chess-playing and devises a theory on the basis of which he can, after examining both intending players with some of his remarkable instruments, predict precisely the course each particular game is going to take. Now can this Martian play chess? Does he even know what chess is? If he should play against some human player, he can make the moves that some particular other human player would make, and so pass himself off as capable of playing chess; but it would only be by accident that he played well, because he lacks the concept of playing chess well. He does not know that he should be trying to checkmate his opponent, because the notion of trying is applicable only to voluntary agents, and he thinks of human beings only as natural objects, not as agents. Furthermore, he does not even know the rules of the game. He has observed a great many regularities, to which, in playing, he will conform; but he cannot distinguish, among moves that are never made, between those that would be against the rules, those that, though legal, would be obviously stupid, and those so brilliant and unexpected that it has occurred to no one to make them. Rules, as opposed to regularities, presuppose purposive behaviour, and the Martian allows no place here for purposive behaviour.

It would be the same with language. The Martian might develop causal hypotheses about what, in human beings, prompts utterances and responses to the utterances of others, and so attain an accurate predictive theory of such utterances and responses in some one human language; but he would no more be able to speak that language or know what a language is than he could play chess or know what a game is. The idea of regarding language as a natural phenomenon finds expression in some of the writings of Wittgenstein.

> One can ... consider language as part of a psychological mechanism. The simplest case is if one uses a restricted concept of language in which language consists only of commands. One can then consider how a foreman directs the work of a group of people by shouting. One can imagine a man inventing language, imagine him discovering how to train other human beings to work in his place, training them through reward and punishment to perform certain tasks when he shouts. This discovery would be like the invention of a machine. Can one say that grammar describes language? If we consider language as part of the psychophysical mechanism which we use when we utter words—like pressing keys on a keyboard—to make a human machine work for us, then we can say that grammar describes that part of the machine. In that case a correct language would be one which would stimulate the desired activities. Clearly I can establish by experience that a human being (or animal) reacts to one sign as I want him to, and to another not ... I do not even need to fabricate a case, I have only to consider what is in fact the case; namely, that I can direct a man who has learned only German, only by using the German language. (For here I am looking at learning German as adjusting (conditioning) a mechanism to respond to a certain kind of influence; and it may be all one to us whether someone else has learned the language, or was perhaps from birth constituted to react to sentences in German like a normal person who has learned it.) (*Philosophical Grammar*, I, §135)

> We say: "The cock calls the hens by crowing"—but doesn't a comparison with our language lie at the bottom of this?—Isn't the aspect quite altered if we imagine the crowing to set the hens in motion by some kind of physical causation? But if it were shown how the words "Come to me" act on the person addressed, so that finally, given certain conditions, the muscles of his legs are innervated, and so on—should we feel that that sentence lost the character of a *sentence*? (*Philosophical Investigations*, I, §493)

A baby seeks its mother's nipple, and sucks upon it, by reflex action: that is to say, without calculation, based on knowledge, of the means to the end of satisfying its hunger. Much of what we do as adults, in the exercise of skills we have acquired by training, is likewise done by reflex action, though it is accessible to consciousness when this is needed, and can be consciously inhibited or controlled: when a motorist changes down from third to second gear, or a typist holds down the space bar for a certain period, neither has *selected* a means to an end. In moments of stress, particular verbal utterances can be like that. I may not know that I shouted, 'Look out!'; or I may know that I shouted a warning but have no idea in what words. To a certain degree, many linguistic utterances may be like that: someone who knows several languages well may, without noticing, lapse into German, say, when conversing with English speakers. We can, with difficulty, imagine how it would be if our employment of language were wholly unavailable to consciousness, as long as we still had a conception of the content of our utterances. That is, we could hear that someone else was speaking but should be unable to discriminate the sounds he was making from those of any other speaker, as when one hears through the wall someone speaking in the next room without being able to make out the words. When someone addressed us in a language in which we had been trained, this would convey to us a certain content: we should know that we were being told that the Conservative Party had won its eighth general election in succession, or being asked to lend the speaker a comb, or being advised not to go to London by car. But we should not know the language, as a piece of conscious knowledge; we should have no idea of the correlation between sounds and content. Likewise, when we ourselves wished to convey something to someone else, we should, as an intentional voluntary action, open our mouths and speak to him, but we should be no more capable of discriminating between the sounds we made then and those we made for other purposes on other occasions than we were for the speech of others.

Such a fantasy is barely intelligible; any adequate description of our use of language must make clear that it is not so for us. It would still hold good of speakers of this 'sotto voce' language that their saying something with a given content to a given hearer at a given time would be the intentional action of a rational agent. Since linguistic utterances have no one end, however general, to suppose that they were wholly inaccessible to consciousness, content as well as form, would be to imagine ourselves living three-quarters of our daily lives as automata. Someone approaches me and says something, of which I have no idea even of the meaning; I hear myself replying, but have no more idea of what I am saying than of what my interlocutor said. If speech, in such a world, is to be of any use, people must act on what they are told, when any action would be appropriate: perhaps on this occasion I go to another house, to which I had not intended to go and did not previously know the way, where I find a party beginning. Presumably the speaker told me of this party. Suppose, however, that I had, instead, been told about it the day before—should I then have known, during the interval, that there would be a party, without knowing how I knew, or should I simply go there at the appropriate time, without knowing where I was going? It is hardly worth filling out the details of this wilder fantasy, so far is it from the reality we experience.

The theory of meaning has, as its task, to explain what language is: that is, to describe, without making any presuppositions, what it is that we learn when we learn to speak. The fact that the use of language is a conscious rational activity—we might say *the* rational activity—of intelligent agents must be incorporated into any such description, because it is integral to the phenomenon of the use of human language. But it also affects the phenomenon itself. When we converse with others, we are continuously concerned to discern the *point* of what they say, that is, their reasons or motives for saying what they do, just as we are concerned to discern the point of their non-linguistic actions. The point of an utterance is to be distinguished from its meaning—not merely from the meaning which it has in virtue of what the words mean in the language, but from the meaning the speaker supposed it to have in the language and therefore intended to convey: we can ask after its point only when we know its meaning. Its meaning is specific to the language in which it is couched, or to the speaker's personal use or understanding of that language; the point is to be assessed in the same way that we assess someone's motives for a non-linguistic action. Very often, there is no problem in discerning the point of an utterance; at other times, we have to cast about to see what the speaker was driving at. Was he deliberately changing the subject, or did he see his remark as relevant to the previous conversation? If the former, why? If the latter, how? Was his last remark intended as an illustration of what had gone before? As an objection to it? As a ground for it? Or as a consequence of it? Did he mean it seriously, or was it a joke? Or was it meant ironically? Or was it, perhaps, a quotation or a parody? Was it intended to be understood literally or metaphorically? Was it meant soberly or as a piece of hyperbole? Did the speaker intend an allusion to such-and-such, or was that inadvertent? To what was he referring when he said 'that'? Which of the people named 'Joan' did he mean? When he said 'here', did he mean 'in this room', 'in this university', 'in this city', or 'in this country'? Why did he express himself in that roundabout way? These and a score of similar questions may present themselves, usually not explicitly formulated, as we strive to follow what someone is saying. All but the last few would arise for speakers of the 'sotto voce' language, because they can be put in the form, 'Why did he at that moment say something with that meaning?' All of them relate, in one way or another, to the intention with which the speaker said what he did, or the motive that prompted him to do so.

Now we can estimate someone's purpose, motive, or intention only against the background of what we presume him to know. Only by assuming him to understand or, occasionally, to misunderstand the words he uses can we give any substance to attributing to him one or another intention in using them: if someone has no idea what he is doing, he can have no purpose in doing it rather than something else. This becomes vivid when we are trying to understand the utterances of a foreigner with an imperfect grasp of the language: we assign quite different intentions to him from those we should assign to a native speaker who used the same words.

The theory of meaning need not undertake an account of the means by which we divine the intentions underlying an utterance, since these are in no way specific to the use of language, save in so far as they relate to expressly linguistic modes or figures such as parody, punning, sarcasm, and understatement. It must, however, acknowledge the role that estimation of intention plays in communication. To do this, it must make plain that a speaker's use of a language rests on his understanding of that language. It is therefore incumbent upon it to explain in what an individual's understanding of a language consists, an understanding embodied in his idiolect, or, if he speaks more than one language, one of his idiolects.

A meaning-theory should not, therefore, aspire to be a theory giving a *causal* account of linguistic utterances, in which human beings figure as natural objects, making and reacting to vocal sounds and marks on paper in accordance with certain natural laws. We have no need of such a theory. We can, in general, make some unfamiliar human activity—say, a social function or ceremony—intelligible without either circularity or anything resembling a causal theory (one which could, ideally, predict exactly what the participants would do). To do so, we describe the practice and the institutions that surround the practice, and then it becomes intelligible as an activity of rational agents. And that is all the understanding that we seek of language. What we implicitly grasp when we understand activities of this kind in which we do participate is precisely an account of this sort, and not any inchoate causal theory; indeed, if a causal theory were possible, it would not provide the sort of understanding that we seek.

Understanding and Knowledge

We have left two questions incompletely resolved. The mastery of a language (knowledge of that language) and the understanding of a word (knowing what it means) are closely akin to knowledge, which is why they are often expressed colloquially by means of the verb 'to know'. They have, like knowledge, to be acquired; they form, as knowledge does in other cases, the basis on which the intentions underlying our utterances rest. But are they instances of knowledge in the strict sense?

The alternative usually proposed is to regard an understanding of a word as a practical ability, and the mastery of a language as a vast complex of practical abilities: it is towards this view that Wittgenstein constantly drives in the *Philosophical Investigations*. It is indeed clear that someone's understanding of a word must *issue* in an ability to use it correctly. Someone might try to learn to waltz by studying one of those manuals with numbered foot positions. No matter how accurately he could reproduce the diagrams, however, he would not be said to know how to waltz unless he was able to use his knowledge to dance the waltz. Similarly, just knowing the Morse code, in the sense of being able to say what is the Morse symbol for each letter and numeral, does not, by itself, constitute an ability to send signals in Morse; you have to be able to apply your knowledge without hesitation. For all that, knowing the Morse code is an indispensable ingredient of being able to signal in Morse; you will never pick it up without committing the code to memory. To regard the understanding of a word or an expression purely as a practical ability is to render mysterious our capacity to know whether we understand. This capacity is not inerrant: we may have the illusion of understanding, say, a deceptively lucid lecture on a difficult topic and discover later that we cannot explain what we thought we understood. No one, moreover, is an authority on whether the sense he attaches to a word is really that which it has in the common language. It remains that we can usually say, without error, whether a word or sentence conveys a sense to us. Someone asks me, 'Do you understand the word "anaphora"?' If understanding were simply a practical ability, it would make sense for me to reply, 'I have no idea: try me out'. Unless I meant, 'I am not sure whether I understand it correctly', such a reply would be senseless. Or, suppose you are listening to a radio broadcast of a political speech in a language you know only imperfectly, in the company of a friend who knows it well, and at a certain point she asks you, 'Did you understand that remark?': you can answer straight off. This phenomenon, which nags Wittgenstein in the *Investigations,* so that he keeps coming back, not exactly to these but to related cases, is not easily explained if understanding is just a practical ability.

That it is not is shown by a joke of P. G. Wodehouse's. A character in one of his novels is asked, 'Can you speak Spanish?' and she replies, 'I don't know: I've never tried'. The joke does not turn merely on the fact that you have to have learned Spanish in order to be able to speak it. It is because we have to learn to swim that we speak of knowing how to swim. Someone who has never learned is thereby aware that he cannot swim; he could try to do so, all the same. It might be otherwise. Dogs do not have to be taught to swim but do so automatically when they first find themselves in water. It could have been that half the human race resembled dogs in this respect, while the other half had to be taught: then, to the question, 'Can you swim?' the answer, 'I don't know; I've never tried', would make good sense. But the same answer to the question, 'Can you speak Spanish?' would in no conceivable circumstances make sense. The reason is that, if you do not know Spanish, you cannot even try to speak it: you would not know what to do in order to try. Even if you cannot swim, you know what swimming is and can tell whether or not someone else is swimming; you can therefore try to swim. But if you do not know Spanish, you do not, properly speaking, know what it is to speak Spanish. You cannot tell whether someone else is speaking Spanish or not; you could be taken in, for example, by two pranksters uttering Spanish-sounding nonsense words with the demeanour of people engaged in conversation.

Explicit theoretical knowledge consists in the capacity to formulate the relevant propositions, to present them in a connected manner when there are connections between them, and to answer questions concerning them. Such knowledge presupposes mastery of some language within which to frame those propositions; hence knowledge of that language, or at least of one's mother tongue, cannot be of that kind. At the other extreme is simple practical knowledge of how to do something which has to be learned: it consists in the ability to do in practice what, even before one learned how to set about doing it, one knew what it was to do. Between these comes the knowledge of a language, which falls under neither of these heads: it is an acquired ability to engage in a practice of such a kind that one cannot know what engaging in it consists in until one has acquired the ability to do so. To classify mastery of a language as a practical ability is inept because when one already knows what it is to do something, the difficulty in learning to do it wholly concerns *how* to do it. You may, for example, be able to recognise the French vowel 'u' without knowing how to produce it; then someone tells you to try to say 'ee' while holding your lips in a position to say 'oo', and you have discovered how to say it. Learning to dance is an intermediate case: one has both to learn *what*, precisely, to do—what the steps are—and *how* to execute them. Most of what has to be learned in learning a language concerns what to do: learning how to do it—how to make unfamiliar vowel sounds, to pronounce unfamiliar consonants, or to impart an unfamiliar intonation to one's sentences—is a comparatively insignificant component, with which, of course, a meaning-theory is not concerned. Learning what to do is acquiring knowledge as substantial as any explicit theoretical knowledge. In other cases, such as the knowledge of the rules of a game, it frequently *is* explicit knowledge; but, when it relates to one's mother tongue, it cannot be.

What, then, is the mode of this knowledge that we have of our mother tongue and that underlies our ability to use it purposively? An infant at the earliest stage of language acquisition does not use it with a calculated purpose. He has been encouraged to say 'Doggie' when he sees a dog, and 'Pussie' when he sees a cat, and does so with no purpose save possibly to elicit the approval of adults. He therefore serves as an extension of his parents' means of observation; but they do not yet serve as an extension of his own. He does not understand the exclamation 'Doggie', said by his mother in the next room, as informing him that there is a dog there. He knows of his parents' use of the word only as an encouragement for him to say it; and therefore he cannot say it with an eye to its effect on others. He may well have been trained to say 'Water' when he is thirsty, and hence he says it with a purpose; but he cannot respond to anyone else's request for water, and so his purpose in asking for water is not a calculated one. A child at this stage has no linguistic knowledge but merely a training in certain linguistic practices. When he has reached a stage at which it is possible for him to lie, his utterances will have ceased to be mere responses to features of his environment or to experienced needs. They will have become purposive actions based upon a knowledge of their significance to others.

Implicit and Explicit Knowledge

There is no uniform answer to the question what the mode of our linguistic knowledge is, because it has no one mode. The concept of implicit knowledge is of little assistance here. The term should properly be reserved for knowledge which its possessor is incapable, unaided, of formulating verbally, but of which he can recognise a formulation when presented with one. Some of our linguistic knowledge, particularly of orthography and of syntax, is of this kind. There is then a possibility of eliciting assent to an explicit formulation, of bringing the speaker to recognise, not only that that which he is credited with knowing is true, but that it represents a principle that had been guiding his use of the language. For instance, someone who spells correctly may be unable to say when the final consonant of a verb is doubled before the termination '-ing', why, for example, we write 'fitting' but 'crediting', 'referring' but 'proffering', 'summing' but 'consuming'; but when told that the consonant is doubled only when the final syllable is stressed and the vowel is short, he is likely, after a little reflection, to acknowledge that that is the rule he follows.

The concept of explicit knowledge is elastic; that of implicit knowledge even more so. Someone has explicit knowledge of something if a statement of it can be elicited from him by suitable enquiry or prompting: we leave it vague how much prompting is allowable. A subject's inability to answer a question when woken in the middle of the night, in the midst of a crisis, when in an emotional state or preoccupied by some task, certainly does not count against his knowing the answer; even his acting inconsistently with that knowledge may be put down to a failure to bear it in mind. In the *Meno*, however, Plato undoubtedly went beyond all reasonable bounds in the degree of prompting he allowed; and there is no sharp line to be drawn. A piece of *implicit* knowledge may perhaps be attributed to someone who has only an implicit grasp of the concepts involved. If a speaker always uses the pairs 'I' / 'me', 'he' / 'him', 'she' / 'her' and 'who' / 'whom' correctly, but, never having been taught the rudiments of formal grammar, has never heard the words 'nominative' and 'accusative', can he be said to have an implicit grasp of the concepts they express? A statement of the rule he tacitly follows will involve an explicit formulation of those concepts and will necessarily be somewhat lengthy. Still, we may credit the speaker with an implicit knowledge of that rule, provided that, when he understands the statement of it, he acknowledges it as accurately describing his existing practice. The concept of implicit knowledge is not infinitely elastic, however: if we try to stretch it to cover our whole knowledge of our native tongue, it will snap. An explicit statement of the principles governing the use of the language will amount to a meaning-theory. It would be preposterous to suggest that all competent speakers would recognise such a theory as correct if it were presented to them. Most would not understand it; those who did would probably engage in disputes, far from easy to resolve, over whether it was correct.

Chomsky solves the difficulty by moving one step further down. For him, a speaker's competence consists in his knowing a complete syntactical and semantic theory, not implicitly in the sense explained but unconsciously; even presentation of an explicit statement of its content may well not serve to bring this knowledge to consciousness. Chomsky puts this forward not as a philosophical explanation but as a psychological hypothesis; and it is as such that it must be evaluated. He is prepared to relinquish the word 'knowledge', if objected to, in favour of 'cognition'. The important question about a body of knowledge possessed by a subject is, however, the form in which it is delivered, and of this Chomsky tells us little. A body of knowledge, however explicit, is obviously not continuously before our consciousness, being a store of items available, save when our memory betrays us, for use when needed. How the storage is effected is of no concern to philosophy: what matters to it is how each item is presented when summoned for use. When we ask in what kind of knowledge our understanding of our language consists, we are asking in what form it is delivered.

Some of it—principally knowledge of the meanings of specific words—is explicit knowledge. Beyond a certain stage, much of our acquisition of new vocabulary is effected by definitions or other verbal explanations, and our knowledge of the meanings of those words consists primarily in our ability so to explain them. Evidently, this cannot hold good for all the words of the language. Besides, although we usually understand a sentence when we understand all the words in it, we may fail to do so: the understanding of a sentence involves, but does not reduce to, the understanding of its constituent words.

Awareness

Philosophers often concentrate upon the concept of knowledge to the neglect of that of awareness: yet it is the latter that underlies motivation. What I know but have for the moment completely forgotten does not influence my present actions. What makes it possible to treat a speaker's utterance as having a point is that he was aware, when he made it, of what it meant. The fact that he could, if challenged, give a definition of some word he used has, *by itself*, no bearing on the intentional character of his use of it: what matters is that, when he used it, he was aware of its meaning. Plainly, to be aware of something is not, in general, to have it in the forefront of one's consciousness: but what is it? If I switch the light on, and someone says, 'Why did you do that?' I might reply, 'I was beginning to find it difficult to read'. I am probably reporting some actual mental event—perhaps the verbalised thought, 'It is getting hard to read', perhaps just an irritation at the reduced illumination. Now, supposing that I was in Europe, I should, to turn the light on, have pressed the switch down. Certainly, had anyone asked, 'Do you press the switch down or up to turn the light on?' I should have told him straight off; but equally certainly I in no way adverted to my knowledge of this fact when I turned the light on. Suppose that there had been two adjacent switches in opposite positions, and I turned one off. Someone asks, 'Why did you do that?' and I answer, 'Sorry, I meant to turn the other light on; having been so long in the United States, I forgot they go the other way here'. Probably, I could just as easily as before have answered the general question how the switches go, but I needed a higher level of awareness of the answer in order to perform the appropriate action than I should have done if I had been living in Europe for several months. But what does that consist in?

What happens when I resolve to bear in mind which way the switches go? I do not attempt to keep the matter continuously in mind but try to establish a new reflex whereby, whenever I go to switch a light on or off, the thought 'Up for off, down for on', or at least the thought 'There is something special about this', comes to mind before I act. So with anything I resolve to bear in mind, for instance that So-and-so's son was recently convicted on a drug charge. Knowing the meaning of a word, however, normally resembles knowing which way the switches work in cases where nothing has occurred to disturb this familiar knowledge. Or, better, it is like knowing the identity of a person well known to one. A word, like a person, strikes one as familiar or unfamiliar: the impression of familiarity generates a confidence that one could explain it, if asked, like the confidence that one could, if asked, say who someone is. The explanation might be only by example—'Strutting is walking in *this* fashion'; or only in context—'When he said I could come on any weekday, he meant that I could come on Monday *or* on Tuesday *or* on any one of the days up to Friday'; but it will suffice to transmit competence in the use of the word. The confidence the speaker feels is also confidence that his knowledge will be brought to bear on his actions, verbal or non-verbal. Not only can I tell you, if you ask, that Jones is a mediaeval historian, is the master of the college and has a vehement dislike of television, but my actions will reflect that knowledge: I shall not ask him whether he saw a recent broadcast or what string theory is, but may ask him about some historical point and shall introduce him as the master to my guest when I have one. My assurance that I understand a sentence comprises a similar familiarity with each of the words in it: to know what a word means is to know the word, in a sense akin to knowing a person. The understanding of a sentence comprises, in addition, the ability to construe it, that is, to apprehend the relations of the parts to one another. If someone says, 'It is not up to the man to whom the whole trouble is due to complain about the delay', I may be momentarily baffled, until I perceive that 'to complain' attaches to 'is not up to the man' and not to 'due': as we listen or read, we impose accustomed structures and groupings—grammatical constructions—upon the linear sequences of words.

Now how is it if I say that I understand a sentence? You are watching a film on television in the company of an Italian friend. The film is mostly in English, but there are some characters who speak in Italian. When some remark is made in Italian, your friend, knowing that your Italian is not very good, asks, 'Did you understand that?' and you say, 'Yes'. On what basis? First, that you had none of the perplexity characteristic of an inability to articulate a sentence into its component words, or, having articulated it, to construe it; secondly, that you knew—were familiar with—all the words; and, thirdly, that the utterance appeared to fit sufficiently well into the story, including the other characters' reactions to it. If the third feature had been absent, you might have replied, 'I don't think I can have done'. The immediate basis of your affirmative reply, though firm, may thus be very slender. It might have been more substantial: if, for instance, you had still been at the stage in which to interpret any Italian sentence you had mentally to translate it into English. All this is very different from a straightforward enquiry concerning a practical ability. Someone hands you one of those puzzles in boxes with transparent lids requiring you to manoeuvre a ball around an obstacle course and asks you, 'Can you do this?'; you have tried it often before and say, 'Sometimes, but not always'. Your answer is based on experience with that puzzle and relates to what will happen when you try. When you say that you understand the sentence, you are not talking about what will happen when you try.

For all that, your confidence that you understand an utterance, like your assurance that you know the identity of an individual you encounter or perceive, carries with it a conviction that you can do various relevant things—not merely that you could explain it if asked, but that you can react to it appropriately, comment on it, raise objections to it, act on it now or later, and so on—in short, that you know what to do with it. What differentiates this from a belief that you can solve the puzzle is that you know what to do with it *now*. That is obvious when—like 'Can you smell something burning?' or 'Do you know the time?'—it calls for an immediate response. But what constitutes knowing what to do with it when no immediate response is in place? Knowing what to do with an utterance is a particularly complex case of knowing what to make of something presented to the eye or ear. Very occasionally we are unable to interpret our visual impressions at all, in the sense of being unable to apprehend what part of three-dimensional space is occupied by the object seen. Less infrequently, we can do this but cannot tell the consistency of the object—whether it is liquid or solid, flexible or rigid. Less infrequently still, we can do this, too, but are baffled to identify the object. And more often yet we cannot identify a sound. For the most part, however, these two senses and the others contribute a continual flow of information which, except in moments of very conscious attention, is sifted and stored or discarded without any decisions on our part. An utterance in a language we understand provides multiple information: the information that a given individual made that assertion, asked that question, gave that advice, or the like, on that occasion; information about the speaker or others deducible from what he said; and, when the utterance is an assertion that we accept, the information it served to convey. Just as we continuously evaluate what we see and hear, noting it for future reference, drawing conclusions from it, reacting to it with pleasure, distaste, sympathy, and so on, so we evaluate each utterance as we hear it, forming expectations, awaiting with interest the responses of others, considering whether the speaker is reliable or unreliable, drawing consequences from his assertions, comparing them with our own beliefs, and the like. Understanding is more the exercise than the possession of a practical capacity. Its exercise will in some cases have no enduring effect; in others, it will result in the storage of some or all of the information acquired, perhaps producing a more overt response to the utterance at a later date.

Words and Sentences

It is the current exercise of this capacity, even when merely mute, that enables us to say without uncertainty whether we understand, though without knowing when we misunderstand any more than we know when we misperceive. So described, however, the activity appears consequent upon our understanding rather than constitutive of it. We can perceive the consequences of a statement, or its incompatibility with a belief we hold, because we know what it means: and the discussion so far seems to have failed to hit on what that knowledge consists in. Just this is the central problem of the theory of meaning. Since Frege, it has become evident to all who study the subject that a grasp of the meaning of a word is a grasp of how, in general, it contributes to the meanings of sentences in which it occurs. This was not obvious before Frege; nor is it obvious to ordinary speakers. It needs reflection to notice that the explanations we give others of the meanings of words usually exploit grammatical clues to indicate the part of speech to which the words belong, and thereby the role they will have in sentences. Thus verbs are usually explained by using an infinitive or a gerund; 'To scowl is to make a face like this' indicates that 'scowl' is an intransitive verb (and moreover that its subject must be a person or creature with a face). Moreover, the relationship between word and sentence is subtle. The *concept* of word-meaning is dependent, though unobviously so, upon that of sentence-meaning. But our capacity to understand sentences resides in our ability to arrive at the meaning of the particular sentence from our understanding of its familiar component words and the modes of phrase- and sentence-formation involved.

Given the conceptual dependence of word-meaning on sentence-meaning, then, the question is: what does knowing what a sentence means consist in? Why should this be a philosophical problem? We all know what countless sentences mean and can say, of any sentence, whether or not we know what it means, so how can it be a problem for us what it is to know the meaning of a sentence? When, as children, we learn to use language, we learn to do a variety of different things involving it. We learn, on the one side, to recognise certain situations as entitling us to make this or that assertion, and to judge the correctness, or likelihood, of assertions made by others. At the same time, we learn the far more complex skill of using language to build up our picture of the world. This picture, which we carry around with us and continually modify, all our lives, is a connected body of stored information (including some misinformation). It is stored, in the memory of an adult, to a large extent in verbal form, though also in images (of faces, scenes, voices, tunes, and so on) and diagrammatically (particularly when the information is topographical). Adopting the practice of registering information in this way goes hand in hand with using the utterances of others as a means of acquiring information, so vastly increasing the information available to us by our own observation. But, while we are taught how to recognise the application of certain words and forms of expression, and some of this teaching is quite formal—think, for example, of how a child is first taught to use colour words, or to count, or to tell the time—we are in no sense taught how to treat the statements of others as contributing to our picture of the world: we fall into this practice automatically. We are confident that we can convey to other language-users—to others who have mastered the general practice of using language—the meanings of individual words we employ. We are confident that we know what to do with sentences which we are aware of understanding—that we know how, in favourable circumstances, we may judge of their truth or falsity, but also what it is to accept them as true, that is, how doing so would modify our picture of the world. Because we do know these things, our understanding does constitute genuine knowledge; but because our acquisition of the general practice of using language is so inexplicit, we do not know exactly what that knowledge consists in. It is the task of the theory of meaning to make it explicit.

This means that its central task is to give the correct general representation of our grasp of the content of a sentence. To grasp the content of an assertoric sentence is, primarily, to know the immediate consequences to us of accepting as true an assertion it makes, although the long-term consequences may be quite unforeseeable—that is, to know what difference will be made to our picture of the world if we accept it.

Now how is that to be explained? Can it be displayed as derivable from a knowledge of what is needed to establish such an assertion as true? If so, we shall have, in broad terms, a verificationist meaning-theory. Or is a knowledge of content, rather, as the pragmatists thought, a grasp of the consequences for action of accepting any such assertion as true, something from which, in turn, a knowledge of what will establish its truth is derived? Or is it, as the tradition of Frege, the *Tractatus,* and Davidson would have it, a grasp of what would make such an assertion true, independently of whether we have any means of determining that it does or does not obtain? This would yield a truth-conditional meaning-theory; to vindicate a theory of this kind, it would have to be shown how both features of use—what acting on the truth of the statement involves, and what is required to establish it as true—can be derived from a knowledge of the condition that must hold for it to be true. Obviously, a decision between these three representations of a speaker's understanding of a sentence, and other conceivable ones, is far beyond the scope of a speaker purely in virtue of his having that understanding. In the first place, he knows a great many things about his language, but, having learned them piecemeal, he has never had occasion to apprehend their systematic connection; and, in the second, much of his knowledge lies deeper than his capacity to represent it. His principal means of representation is by means of language, aided by ocular and auditory demonstration. The most fundamental components of his knowledge of the language were attained neither by verbal explanation nor by the acquisition of any single demonstrable skill.

The question, what the mode of a speaker's knowledge of his language is, has no uniform answer. Some of it consists of explicit knowledge; some of a purely practical ability to follow tacit rules of inflection, phrase-formation, and so on, which the speaker is unable to formulate; and some—the deepest and most interesting components—of a complex of acquired practices that together constitute a grasp of content. Philosophers sometimes argue whether the primary function of language is as an instrument of communication or as a vehicle of thought; but its essence lies in the fact that, acquired by interaction with others, it cannot serve for further successful communication unless it has been made a vehicle for thought. Mastering the role in communication of some form of sentence requires a grasp of what Wittgenstein called its 'use'. There are two aspects of the use of any assertoric sentence, which provide the answers to the questions, 'When should I use it?' and 'What can I do with it?' To know when I should use the sentence is to know what evidence establishes it as true and from what premises it may be inferred. To know what to do with it is to know what bearing its truth may have on my actions; and this involves knowing what consequences flow from it, together with other statements accepted as true, and how such consequences may affect the outcome of my actions. All this we learn in the course of acquiring language, but in a haphazard, unsystematic way: it constitutes our grasp of the contents of the sentences of the language. Our grasp of their contents could not exist, however, as a mastery of a purely external practice. By the very nature of language, we could not learn its use as a means of interacting with others without simultaneously learning to use it as a vehicle for our own thoughts. It is precisely because this interior use of language as a medium of our thinking, and of our representation of reality, is from an early stage integral to our whole conscious life that we travesty the facts if we call it a 'practical ability', even though it is never severed from, and remains responsible to, the use of language in conversing with others.

The Content of Knowledge and Its Manifestation

Although our competence with our language is thus rightly to be classified as knowledge, a meaning-theory aims at providing, not a faithful representation of a speaker's linguistic knowledge, but a systematisation of it. This explains the hesitancy concerning the status of a meaning-theory which we find in writers like Davidson. In his earlier essays, he was disposed to attribute to actual speakers an implicit knowledge of a correct meaning-theory for their language. In later writings, he forswore this attribution, claiming only that the meaning-theory constituted a body of knowledge whose possession by a subject would enable him to speak the language. To this the natural response is to ask why we should adopt so roundabout a route to describing a practical competence: why not simply describe what it is that a competent speaker has the capacity to do? The right answer is that knowledge of a language is not merely a species of practical competence but is also genuine knowledge, and that the meaning-theory is intended as an organised and fully explicit representation of the content of that knowledge. The gap between such a systematic representation and the inexplicit and unorganised character of an actual speaker's knowledge nevertheless has the consequence that we can never give a complete characterisation of a piece of the speaker's knowledge simply by stating the *content* of that knowledge, that is, by saying what it is that someone knows who has that knowledge. At least, this must be so if the knowledge in question is stated in terms that do not directly relate to linguistic practice, as in a truth-conditional meaning-theory. We have then also to explain how each component of the speaker's knowledge guides his utterances and his verbal and non-verbal responses to those of others, in other words, what counts as a manifestation of his linguistic knowledge. This may be vividly expressed as the requirement that we say in what that knowledge consists.

The necessity for this is also apparent from the need to distinguish between knowing that a sentence is true and knowing the proposition expressed by the sentence. Often it is unproblematic to make out that distinction, since we may explain a knowledge of the proposition expressed by a sentence as requiring an understanding of that sentence, or some equivalent one. This happens when we are giving a philosophical explanation of some concept in terms of what an agent knows (the propositions that he knows, not the sentences he knows to be true), and we are assuming that the agent may be taken as equipped with the mastery of some language. But, when that of which we are trying to give an account is itself the mastery of a language, we cannot by that means explain what it is to know some proposition of the meaning-theory without gross circularity. Plainly, in using the meaning-theory to represent the speaker's knowledge, what we want to ascribe to him is a knowledge of the propositions expressed by the sentences of the theory, and not the knowledge that those sentences are true. Hence a statement of *what* a speaker knows is, in this context, not enough. To explain the force of ascribing such knowledge to him, we must say how his possession of that knowledge is manifested, which is to say in what it consists.

Quine was therefore right to say, 'When I define the understanding of a sentence as knowledge of its truth conditions I am certainly not offering a definition to rest with; my term "knowledge" is as poor a resting-point as the term "understanding" itself' ("Mind and Verbal Dispositions", in *Mind and Language*, ed. S. Guttenplan, Oxford, 1975, p. 88). We should not seek to *eliminate* the term 'knowledge'; but we should also not be content with saying *what* is known, without saying what it is to have that knowledge, that is, how it is manifested by one who has it.

If linguistic competence could be straightforwardly classified as a practical ability, we could say, as I once did say, that in framing a meaning-theory we are giving a theoretical representation of a practical ability—the ability to speak the language. We are representing this complex ability as consisting in the knowledge of a theory, that is, of an articulated structure of propositions. On this account, we are analysing a complex of practical abilities by feigning to attribute to one who has these abilities a knowledge of the theory. The analysis will fail, however, if it does not at the same time explain the method of representation, by saying how the knowledge of each proposition of the theory is manifested. By this means, we shall arrive at an articulation of the complex practical ability which constitutes mastery of the language into a network of more particular, though interrelated, practical abilities. Although in fact linguistic competence is not a pure practical ability but is properly described as knowledge, the point still stands. It is precisely the failure of certain conceptions of a meaning-theory to take account of the need to say in what the knowledge ascribed to speakers consists, and how it is manifested, that causes descriptions of a meaning-theory based on them to give the impression, on which it may seem hard to put one's finger, of failing to elucidate what they claimed to elucidate. We shall never succeed in saying where such conceptions fail until we reject their tacit presupposition: that all that is required is a statement of what it is that a speaker knows.

The Idiolect and the Common Language

We are now better equipped to answer the second question previously touched on: is the fundamental unit of the theory of meaning a common language, like English or Malay, or an idiolect? We saw that a speaker's use of a common language is not explicable as his use of his idiolect: he both holds himself responsible to the common meanings of his words and exploits the existence of those common meanings. We saw also that his idiolect is to a large extent comprised by his imperfect grasp of his language, informed by his beliefs, sometimes mistaken, about what the common meanings are. These observations do not settle the question, however. It is probably unavoidable that in sketching the shape of a meaning-theory we should at the first stage idealise, prescinding from complicating factors such as linguistic change or imperfect competence. Should we start from a meaning-theory presented as a theory of the language of an individual speaker at a given time? Or should we address from the outset the functioning of a language in the common possession of a whole society or group of societies?

If someone had a perfect knowledge of a language, would not his idiolect coincide with that language? Granted, he could not know that his knowledge was perfect, and so, in conversation with others, he would still hold himself responsible to the common meanings of his words; moreover, as we saw, there are words of the common language whose use essentially rests on complex social cooperation, of which no one can be said to have a complete knowledge of the meaning. These are minor reservations, however. If we take as our fundamental unit a language as known by a single individual, are we committing any greater crime than idealising to the case of a perfectly competent speaker?

To draw this conclusion is to make a mistake complementary to that of those who would relegate the use of language as a vehicle of thought to a derivative status. We could not use language solely as a medium of discourse and not also as a vehicle of thought, because learning to use it as a medium of discourse involves coming to grasp it as a means of representing reality. Conversely, our capacity to store and retrieve information in linguistic form, to act upon the information so retrieved, and to operate with language in the course of inner reflections all depend equally upon our ability to engage in linguistic interchange. A grasp of the content of a statement derives from an understanding both of its consequences and of what it follows from, where, in general, a chain of consequences will terminate in action and a chain of grounds in observation. An individual may draw consequences; he cannot, by himself, determine what they should be. More exactly, he cannot do this quite generally. He may set up objective criteria which he can apply instead of relying on unchecked judgement, but the chain of criteria must come to an end. Likewise, neither the common judgement nor even the established practice is in all cases decisive, for there may be objective criteria before which they stand for assessment. But the chain of criteria and principles must come to an end here, too, although philosophers must beware of declaring it at an end prematurely. When the chain terminates, the individual stands to be judged only by his peers, the general accord of the society from which he originally learned to handle words and symbols. If we isolate him in thought from this society, there ceases to be any right or wrong in his use of his personal language; and consequently all meaning evaporates from it. Even as an idealisation, we may regard language solely as a medium of thought and of soliloquy as little as we may regard it solely as a medium of discourse.

chapter 5

Ingredients of Meaning

Modest Meaning-Theories

We saw that if a truth-theory, in Tarski's style, were to be used as part of a meaning-theory, we could take no official notice, that is, no notice *in* the meaning-theory, of the fact that it yielded instances of the (T) schema. One way to put this would be as follows: on the one hand, it would be preposterous to maintain that, say, a meaning-theory for Greek could be stated only in Greek; and, on the other, to give the more general explanation of the (T) schema, we have to appeal to the notion of translation or of sameness of sense between languages, and such an appeal is illicit in constructing a meaning-theory. Could we replace the requirement that each instance of the (T) schema be derivable by the requirement that each stipulation governing a primitive expression of the object-language be straightforward? The difficulty here is that, unless the metalanguage is an expansion of the object-language, or else we appeal to the notion of translation, we have no way of saying, for non-logical expressions, what a 'straightforward' stipulation is. In the case of a logical constant, we characterised a straightforward stipulation in part by the requirement that the meta-linguistic logical constant used in the stipulation should obey the same logical laws as the logical constant of the object-language to which the stipulation relates; but we have no parallel conception of the 'laws' obeyed by a non-logical primitive. Some may still feel that a meaning-theory embodying a Tarski-style truth-theory framed in a meta-language which is an expansion of the object-language, though not mandatory, has the advantage of encouraging a suitable attitude to what a meaning-theory can and cannot be expected to accomplish. The right attitude to this, in their view, is a modest one. We said previously of semantic theories that, in so far as they serve the purposes of logic, it is no part of their business to *explain* the meanings of the logical constants, but that a meaning-theory, by contrast, must be capable of explaining the meanings of the sentences of the object-language. This latter claim expresses an attitude which the proponents of modest meaning-theories reject as inflated. On their conception, a meaning-theory cannot hope to give an account of the concepts expressible by the primitive vocabulary of the object-language: it can seek only to explain, to someone who already has those concepts, what it is that a speaker must know if he is to know the meanings of words and expressions of the language, and hence to attach those concepts to the words which, in that language, express them.

This formulation may make it appear that no meaning-theory can aspire to be more than modest. We can, by means of a verbal explanation, convey to someone a concept that he did not previously have. A meaning-theory might well incorporate, as specifications of the meanings of various words in the object-language, many explanations that would serve this purpose. But to understand such an explanation, one must understand the words in which it is framed: one must, therefore, already have *some* concepts. How could a meaning-theory possibly give, for all the words of the language, explanations that would convey the concepts they express to someone who, previously, possessed none of them?

Such a demand would obviously be exorbitant: the demand which proponents of a modest meaning-theory resist should be stated in a more conciliatory form. A modest meaning-theory assumes not merely that those to whom it is addressed have the concepts expressible in the object-language but that they require no explanation of what it is to grasp those concepts. A more robust conception of what is to be expected of a meaning-theory is that it should, in all cases, make explicit in what a grasp of those concepts consists—the grasp which a speaker of the language must have of the concepts expressed by the words belonging to it.

In a lecture called "What is a Theory of Meaning?" (*Mind and Language*, ed. S. Guttenplan, Oxford, 1975), I criticised Davidson's account of a meaning-theory for a natural language, mistakenly as it now appears to me, as being a modest theory in this sense. The reason why, as he presents his idea, a meaning-theory appears to be a modest theory is that he speaks of it as being constituted by a truth-theory after the mode of Tarski, and the truth-theory as founded upon 'evidence' relating to which statements the speakers hold true. A statement is here an actual or hypothetical utterance of a sentence by a particular speaker at a particular time. In Davidson's formulation, 'holds S true' is not to be construed as 'holds that S is true', that is, as appealing to an already understood notion of a statement's being true. Rather, it is meant to express a relation between a speaker and a possible utterance, by him or another, which we can grasp before we attain the concept of a statement's being true. The reason why a meaning-theory of Davidson's kind is not after all a modest one is that, contrary to the way he presents it, the so-called evidence is not an external support on which we rest our confidence in it but, rather, is integral to it; it is part of the theory itself. A helpful analogy is Wittgenstein's celebrated account of a proper name such as 'Moses'. According to Wittgenstein, the referent of the name 'Moses' is that one man, if any, of whom a large number of the sentences involving the name, and commonly held by us to be true, are in fact true; sentences such as 'Moses was brought up in a royal palace', 'Moses led his people out of slavery in Egypt', and so on. For the name 'Moses' to have a bearer, no one of these sentences has to be true of anyone; but there has to be some one person of whom a large number of them are true.

Now suppose that, against the background of such an account of proper names, it were said that to know the use of the name 'Moses' was to know that the name 'Moses' refers to the man Moses. To make this out, we must distinguish between knowing that the sentence 'The name "Moses" refers to Moses' is true, and knowing the proposition expressed by that sentence, that is, knowing that the name 'Moses' refers to Moses. Anyone who knows that 'Moses' is a proper name, and that it has a reference, and who also knows the use of the expression 'refers to', knows that the sentence 'The name "Moses" refers to Moses' is true; but, for someone to be said to know that the name 'Moses' refers to Moses, we must demand more than this, if it is to be plausible that, in knowing this fact, he thereby knows the use of the name. After all, we can hardly deny that someone who knows that the name 'Moses' refers to Moses knows the reference of the name. But, if we follow Wittgenstein's account of proper names, when we come to say what more someone must know, beyond the truth of the sentence 'The name "Moses" refers to Moses', in order to know the proposition expressed by that sentence, we cannot allow that it consists just in knowing that the name refers to that man of whom a large number of the sentences involving it, and commonly held to be true, hold good, whatever those sentences may be. For him to know that, it would be enough that he knew that 'Moses' was a personal name, and have come to grasp the correctness (as we are supposing) of Wittgenstein's general account of proper names; he would not have to know anything peculiar to the name 'Moses'. Rather, he must know what the sentences are that we commonly hold to be true and that contain the name 'Moses': it is these which, on Wittgenstein's account, give to the name its particular use.

Just the same holds good for the language taken as a whole, on Davidson's original account of what the mastery of a language consists in. On this account, such a mastery is constituted by a knowledge of the axioms of the truth-theory; and, in formulating those axioms, we may just as well frame them within a metalanguage of which the object-language is a proper part as in one that is disjoint from it. A formulation of the former kind has, indeed, the merit of bringing out clearly the fact that the knowledge that constitutes a mastery of the language cannot consist merely in a knowledge that the sentences embodying the axioms are true; it has to be taken as a knowledge of the propositions expressed by those sentences. This entitles us to ask what is required of someone if he is to be said to have a knowledge of those propositions. As soon as we ask this question, it becomes plain that, just as in the simpler case of Wittgenstein's account of proper names, he must, in order to know those propositions, also know a large part of the so-called 'evidence' on which the truth-theory is said to be based: he must know *which* statements are generally held true by speakers of the language. So far as I know, Davidson has never put the matter in this way himself; but if we adopt it as the most plausible interpretation of his theory, it will cease to be accurate to describe him as contenting himself with saying *what* a speaker must know, without explaining in what that knowledge consists.

Davidson's theory, thus understood, is therefore not a modest theory, although some of his followers may perhaps have taken it for one. To obtain a genuinely modest meaning-theory, we should have to propose something like a truth-theory without any background constraints, masquerading as evidence, on the form it should take, save for the requirement—empty in the absence of further constraints—that it be a correct theory. Such a theory would tell us *which* proposition it is that someone must know, concerning any given word, if he is to have a mastery of the language. It would not, however, tell us in what a knowledge of those propositions consists, nor, therefore, how it is manifested; and, as we have seen, an explanation of the latter kind is required, if we are to maintain the necessary distinction between knowing that a sentence is true and knowing the proposition expressed by that sentence.

For someone to advance from the knowledge that some sentence containing the word 'sheep' is true to a knowledge of the proposition expressed by that sentence, he must acquire an understanding of the word 'sheep' (and of the other words in the sentence); and, for him to have a knowledge of the proposition expressed by the sentence, whether or not he knows that that particular sentence is true, he must grasp the concept of a sheep. Hence, if we explain his knowledge of the meaning of the word 'sheep' as consisting in the knowledge of the proposition expressed by some axiom which uses, as well as mentions, the word 'sheep', we are attributing to him a grasp of the concept of a sheep. His grasp of this concept may be being thought of in either of two ways. Either it is thought of as prior to his understanding of the English word 'sheep', or it is thought of as attained precisely by gaining an understanding of that word. In the former case, the claim of the meaning-theory to be in any way explanatory rests on the possibility of giving an explanation of what it is to grasp a concept which is independent of taking some word to express that concept; for if we could explain what it is to grasp the concept expressed by the word 'sheep' only by stating what it is to take *some* word (not necessarily that one) as expressing that concept, we should not need any explanation of what it is for someone who already grasps that concept to associate it with the particular English word 'sheep'.

Viewed in this way, a modest meaning-theory would obviously be almost wholly destitute of explanatory power, since we characterised such a theory as one which took as already known, and did not seek to explain, what it is to grasp the concepts expressed by the primitive words of the object-language. Would it not be possible to divest such a theory of its modesty, and supplement it by explanations of the possession of those concepts independently of the knowledge of any language? The ground for scepticism about the feasibility of this proposal is not the difficulty of explaining what the possession of a concept by a being devoid of language would consist in. Undoubtedly, some concepts, such as numerical ones, are available only to those equipped to manipulate words or symbolic devices; for simpler concepts, the question is debatable. The difficulty of the proposal turns, rather, on how, once we had an account of what it was to grasp a given concept, we might set about explaining the nature of the association between that concept and some particular word. As Frege insisted, concepts, or what he called 'senses'—the senses of words considered independently of their being expressed by words—are not contents of the mind, as mental images are. We therefore cannot explain what it is for a subject to understand a certain sense as attaching to a word by means of a simple associationist model, according to which the hearing of a word brings that sense into his consciousness: a concept or a sense cannot come into the mind like a tune or a face remembered from long ago. It is dubious whether there is any way to explain what it is to take a word as expressing a certain sense save by describing the use made of the word which constitutes its having that sense. This, however, will be an explanation which, while not denying a prior grasp of that sense or concept, does not presuppose it, either, and which therefore simply fails to exploit the assumption of an antecedent grasp of the concept.

The reason why analytical philosophy, in all its varied manifestations, has accorded a central place in philosophy to the theory of meaning lies in the belief that thought is best explained by giving a direct account of the means whereby we express thoughts; a 'direct account' is to be taken as meaning one which does not presuppose it as already understood what it is to have the thoughts that are expressed. An account of language that presupposes what it is to grasp the senses, if not of whole sentences, at least of individual words, therefore destroys the greater part of the interest which, as philosophers, we have learned to take in language. That, of course, does not prove that it is wrong; on the contrary, if it could be shown to be feasible, the underlying assumption of all analytical philosophy would have been refuted. But this result would follow only from a theory which demonstrated the possibility of explaining the association between words and their senses in a manner that exploited, and depended essentially upon, the assumption of a prior grasp of those senses—a theory that was therefore very far from being modest. A modest theory attempts no such explanation: it merely issues a promissory note that one will be forthcoming.

The alternative is that in ascribing to a speaker a knowledge of a proposition expressed by a sentence involving the use, in the metalanguage, of the word 'sheep', we are attributing to him merely that grasp of the concept of a sheep which he attains by coming to understand the word 'sheep' in his language—that is, in what we are taking to be the object-language—in other words, by gaining a knowledge of that very proposition. It is, of course, incontestable that anyone who knows whatever it is necessary to know to understand the word 'sheep' must grasp the concept that that word expresses. The theory will therefore be unobjectionable if it goes on to explain in what a knowledge of the proposition expressed by the axiom consists, as, on the proposed way of construing it, Davidson's theory does, though of course it may give some totally different explanation. If it does this, *that* explanation will be the heart of the meaning-theory. But, if it is a modest theory, it renounces any such further explanation; and a modest theory, so understood, is in an even worse condition than on the way of understanding it we just reviewed. Understood in the former way, there was at least the possibility of supplementing it by a non-linguistic explanation of a grasp of the relevant concepts; but, on the present way of viewing the matter, we are being told that an understanding of the word 'sheep' consists in a knowledge of the proposition expressed by a certain sentence, that a knowledge of this proposition requires a grasp of the concept of a sheep, and that a grasp of that concept by a speaker of the language in question will consist in his understanding of the word 'sheep'. Since no more paradigmatic case of a circular explanation could be devised, we may conclude that the conception of a modest meaning-theory is a phantasm.

Truth as the Central Notion of a Meaning-Theory

For the time being, we may continue to assume that the notion of truth plays a crucial role in a meaning-theory, which is to say that it is the central notion of such a theory in the weaker of the two senses of this phrase we previously distinguished; the grounds for making such an assumption will be examined in the next chapter. It will be recalled that truth is said to be the central notion of a meaning-theory, in the weaker sense, if the meaning-theory displays how a sentence is determined as true in accordance with its composition, and hence incorporates a semantic theory, and if, further, an important part of the meaning of a sentence relates to the way it is determined as true, if it is true. It is of a meaning-theory of this type that a semantic theory must form a base, and it is with such theories in mind that the somewhat nebulous expression is sometimes used that to know the meaning of a sentence is to grasp the condition for it to be true. In the strong sense, truth is the central notion of a meaning-theory only if that meaning-theory has a two-valued semantics as a base, that is, if the semantic value of a sentence is identified with its being true or not being true. In a somewhat more generous sense, but still much stronger than the weak sense just stated, we may take as having truth as their central notion those meaning-theories whose base is a many-valued semantics, in which the values are divided into designated and undesignated ones, the content of a sentence being taken as given by the condition for it to have a designated value. As long as every statement is thought of as having, determinately and permanently, some particular one of those values, such a meaning-theory differs from one based on a two-valued semantics only in a comparatively superficial way, namely, in taking the way in which it is determined whether or not a complex sentence has a designated value to be more complicated than in the two-valued semantics. The formulation 'To understand a sentence is to know the condition for it to be true' is sometimes construed as an endorsement of a meaning-theory for which truth is a central notion in this stronger, or even in the strongest, sense; this is a good reason for being chary of that ambiguous expression.

Sense, Force, and Tone

Now, if it is assumed that truth must, in the weak sense, be the central notion of a meaning-theory, an important ingredient in the meaning of any expression will be that part of its meaning which is relevant to the determination of a sentence in which it occurs as true or otherwise. Adopting Frege's terminology, we may call this ingredient of meaning the *sense* of the expression; the following discussion of it aims to accord as closely as possible with Frege's account, without assuming, as Frege did, that the correct semantic theory is the two-valued one. What other ingredients in meaning may there be? Frege distinguished two, force and tone. Force, or, more properly, the indication of force, is the significance possessed by a linguistic element which serves to indicate which type of linguistic act is being performed: whether the speaker is making an assertion, expressing a wish, making a request, giving advice, asking a question, or something else of the kind. The theory of force is a most important ingredient in a meaning-theory because it is the part which connects the rest with the actual employment of sentences in discourse and which, we may say, goes to tell us what truth is. Of course, in everyday speech, we apply the terms 'true' and 'false' only to assertions or to sentences whose syntactic form would allow them, if used on their own, to be uttered assertorically. But it was an important insight of Frege's that certain non-assertoric utterances, for instance those which serve to ask sentential questions (questions requiring the answer 'Yes' or 'No'), have the same specific content as the corresponding assertoric ones and may therefore be regarded as differing from them only in the force they carry (for instance, interrogative rather than assertoric force). If the specific content of the assertoric sentence is regarded as given by the condition for it to be true, then that of the non-assertoric sentence may likewise be so regarded, by an extension of the word 'true' beyond its everyday application; it is just that, in such a case, the speaker is not asserting that the sentence (more properly, the thought expressed by it) is true but, for instance, asking whether it is true.

Frege himself did not make a thoroughgoing distinction between sense and force. He regarded assertoric sentences and sentences used to ask questions requiring the answer 'Yes' or 'No' as both expressing thoughts: in the one case we assert that the thought is true, in the other we ask whether it is true. In Frege's terminology, a 'thought' does not involve any judgement that it is true but is, rather, the *content* of such a judgement and, equally, of a doubt or a question; the characteristic of a thought is that it may be judged to be, absolutely, true or false. However, without exploring the topic any further, he classified optative sentences as expressing wishes and imperative sentences as expressing commands, where wishes and commands stand on the same level as thoughts. This is plainly a mistake: a wish may have exactly the same content as an assertion or a question, as the following unlikely but perfectly intelligible fragment of dialogue illustrates:

Nancy: Jesse Jackson is President of the United States.

Oscar: *Is* Jesse Jackson President of the United States?

Patsy: Would that he were!

A thought, in Frege's terminology, is the content of an assertion or a sentential question, and also of a subsentence forming part of a complex sentence used assertorically or interrogatively. Since an optative or imperative utterance may have the same content as an assertoric one, it, too, must have a thought as content. The notions of a command or declared wish must therefore be correlative with that of an assertion or question, rather than with that of a thought in the technical Fregean sense. The resulting extension of the sense/force distinction was perhaps first made by R. M. Hare, independently of Frege, and with a clumsy terminology of 'phrastics' and 'neustics'; it was subsequently explored by Stenius in his book on the *Tractatus*.

The imperative mood serves a variety of functions: not only to issue a command but, somewhat rarely, to make a request ('Pass the butter, please', 'Give me the price of a cup of coffee'), to make an offer ('Let me take your suitcase'), to give instructions ('Simmer gently for twenty minutes') or to offer advice ('Don't tell the dean what you intend to do'). It is natural to say that the parts of an imperative sentence contribute to the meaning of the whole by going to determine what constitutes compliance—obeying the command, acceding to the request or offer, following the instructions or advice. It is as essential to see the imperative force as attaching to the sentence as a whole, and not to any of its subsentences, as it is to see assertoric force in the same way. Someone who asserts a conditional statement is not asserting the antecedent: it is senseless to think of assertoric force—or force of any other kind—as attaching to the antecedent clause. Nor is it a good description to say that he asserted the consequent conditionally, as if he had handed his hearers a sealed envelope marked 'Open only in the event that . . .': someone who believes the speaker, and knows the consequent to be false, may infer the falsity of the antecedent. Likewise, if we failed to grasp that the force attaches to the sentence only as a whole, we might be puzzled why the antecedent of a conditional does not tolerate the imperative mood (or the interrogative word order), whereas a clause in a disjunctive sentence tolerates both. Our puzzlement is resolved when we realise that the inflection of the verb, or the word order, in the main clause (or in each of the two coordinate clauses) signals the attachment of imperative or interrogative force to the sentence as a whole, rather than to any clause or clauses within it. But, if we do not observe that the content of a command, request, instruction, or piece of advice can coincide with that of an assertion or sentential question, we shall be perplexed to explain our compelling intuition that most words have the *same* sense in assertoric and in imperative contexts: the words 'simmer' and 'twenty' do not change their senses from those they bore in the cookery book when the cook reports, 'I simmered it for twenty minutes'. Waismann, indeed, somewhat unfairly made it a reproach to Frege's analysis of statements of number that it explained 'There are four plates on the table', but failed to explain 'Put four plates on the table'. Plainly, the words 'four' and 'plate' do not merely have *analogous* senses in these two sentences. They have *identical* senses: we therefore need a *uniform* account of what these senses are. Such an account is attainable only if we separate the content of an utterance from the force attaching to it, regarding words like 'simmer', 'four', 'plate', and so on, as contributing to determining the content independently of the force.

It is plain that some words or linguistic elements such as verb inflections serve solely to indicate the force attached to an utterance; and these demand explanation by any meaning-theory for the language to which they belong. It is equally evident that language has insufficiently few forms to differentiate the various types of linguistic act it may be used to effect. To what extent this is true depends upon how fine are the distinctions we allow between the types of act. If we distinguish between all the different acts listed above as capable of being effected by the use of the imperative, the disparity between the linguistic forms available and the kinds of force attachable to an utterance becomes very great; and, at that, the list was not comprehensive. If I shout, 'Get back!' to someone about to step in front of a lorry, I should hardly be said to be offering advice; and if I yell, 'Stop that infernal noise!' my exclamation falls somewhere between a command and a request, and may perhaps belong to the intermediate category of demands. A question at issue between philosophers of language—Davidson and myself, for example—has been how far the possibility of using language in these various ways depends on conventions, both linguistic and social, that have to be learned, and how far merely on underlying intentions that have only to be discerned. There is undoubtedly some line to be drawn here. I may wonder why someone asked a certain question; his motive is clearly separable from the linguistic act he performed—it is necessary to know that he asked a particular question before you can know what the motive being sought was a motive *for*. Indeed, explanations of interrogative force frequently fail by making it an expression of an inner state, of uncertainty about the fact in question or of a desire to resolve it—an account which makes examiners and barristers into frauds; the significance of a question lies solely in its conventionally calling for a reply. The clear distinction that exists in this instance between the linguistic act performed and the motive for performing it—invoked in the injunction, 'Never mind why I am asking, just answer the question'—depends upon the existence of the linguistic form; yet the distinction can be blurred in such a case as 'Do you have a match?' On rare occasions this form of words might serve solely to ask a question; normally, however, just answering the question would either be a piece of irritating facetiousness or display a misunderstanding. The misunderstanding might merely be a misreading of the speaker's intention by a hearer who knew perfectly well that that form of words was normally used to convey a request; what is difficult—perhaps in principle impossible—to say is whether ignorance of this fact would constitute a defect in his knowledge of the *language*. The equivalent, for the imperative, of 'Just answer the question' is 'Never mind why: just do as I tell you'. To understand a question—to grasp the significance of the utterance in the language—one must be familiar with the practice of asking and answering questions; if you do not know what an answer is, you also do not know what a question is. You do not need to know why the speaker asked the question to know *what* he said—to grasp the significance of his utterance in the language: hence the validity of the distinction between the linguistic act and the intention behind it. To understand an utterance in the imperative mood, then, one has to understand that the speaker is telling his hearer to do something. One must therefore be familiar with the practice of telling someone to do something. Is this a true parallel? Could we add, 'To understand what was said, you do not have to know why the speaker said it'?

What is it to know the practice of asking and answering questions? One must know, first, what constitutes an answer to any given question. Secondly, one should know that the answer may be given in an abbreviated form, and in particular that to say 'Yes' or 'No' in response to a sentential question is tantamount to making an assertion whose content depends on that of the question. And, thirdly, one must know that a question calls for an answer. If an adult were asked what it means to say that a question calls for an answer, he might embark on a summary of the social conventions governing the answering and evasion of questions; but a child will be acknowledged as understanding the interrogative form if he knows merely that others will usually answer a question he asks, and that he is supposed to answer one addressed to him. Likewise, any adequate analysis of the concept of an order or command would have to explain the concept of socially recognised authority, whereby an individual is accorded the right to give orders of a certain scope to another; for instance, we recognise everyone but a small child as having a right to say who may enter or remain in his room. But the concept of telling someone to do something is much broader than that of ordering him to do it. A child understands the use of the imperative mood as soon as he knows that he is supposed to do what he is told, and that telling people to do things is sometimes a way of getting them to do it. When he says, 'Go away', to his mother, he is being rude and disrespectful, but he is not violating linguistic propriety.

At this point we enter a very blurred area. The child has much to learn, but does his learning cover only social conventions, or is he at the same time deepening his understanding of the use of the imperative? The child quickly invents, or perhaps learns by imitation, two blocking responses to being told to do something: 'Shan't' and 'Why?' Things would be very different with us if it were the common practice to acquiesce in a refusal, and the child of course soon learns that this is not the common practice of his parents and other adults. Is he thereby learning more of the meaning of imperatives? Well, would imperatives mean something different in a society in which it was the usual practice to acquiesce in a refusal? If they would, then of course the child is learning more of their meaning in our language—but would they? Similarly, when the child drives one of his parents to say, 'Because I tell you!' he learns that an order, to be effective, does not always have to be backed by a stated reason. A society in which it did would again differ greatly from ours; but an analogously difficult question arises about whether the imperative would then have a different meaning.

These questions may be left in abeyance, and perhaps lack any definitive answer. Even when we set aside the varied uses of the imperative, there remains an imperfect match between sentential form and linguistic act, most evident in the dual use of the interrogative for questions and requests; but confusion is generated by exaggerating the mismatch. If, at quarter to four, the chairman says to the guest lecturer, 'Several people have to leave at four', he is obviously indicating that he should bring his lecture to a close; but it needlessly blurs the distinction between what is said and the reason for saying it if this is proffered as an instance of an assertoric form being used to make a request. The chairman did *not* ask the lecturer to finish; he merely gave him what he ought to have recognised as a compelling reason for finishing, and if the lecturer failed to recognise it as such, it was not his linguistic competence that was at fault. By contrast, in colloquial speech the sentence 'Can you speak French?' is genuinely ambiguous between a question and a request; a misunderstanding could occur. If Mr. Smith is telling M. André an anecdote about his recent visit to France, M. André might use the sentence to enquire about a relevant background detail, while Mr. Smith, replying, 'Mais, certainement', and continuing his story in French, took him to be asking him to speak in that language. When an utterance is ambiguous, what the speaker said is determined by how he intended to be understood; Smith's mis-apprehension concerns *what* André said, not his reason for saying it. We have to recognise this as a genuine ambiguity in the language, because there is no neutral way of stating the content of the utterance, save by a paraphrase that matches the ambiguity: the question and the request call for difference responses.

When the force attached to an utterance is signalled by its linguistic form (word order or inflection of the verb) and is unambiguous in the context, no appeal to the speaker's intention is relevant to the linguis-tic act he performed. In these cases, the force cannot be attributed to an intention behind the utterance, because that would deprive the lin-guistic form of its evident conventional significance. When there is an undeniable ambiguity, produced by there being two distinct conven-tional uses of the linguistic form, what determines the force attached to the utterance is how the speaker intends it to be understood: this intention *selects* between two existing linguistic practices but *creates* neither of them.

It is Davidson's contention, however, that force is characteristically created by the speaker's perceived intention rather than by any con-vention that has to be learned in learning the language. On this ac-count, force ceases to be part of what is said and is assimilated to the point of saying it. A language, on this view, has no need of any device for indicating interrogative force, for example. In a language without such a device, what a speaker says is determined wholly by the Fregean thought he expresses; the hearer must discern whether the point of his expressing it was to convey that the thought was true or to prompt the hearer to pronounce on whether the thought was true, or, perhaps, something else again. It is probably true that a child not in-troduced to the practice of asking questions would be driven by need to invent it for himself and could probably succeed in conveying what response he was seeking; and it is probably also true that there could be a language without explicit interrogative forms, or at least without a form signalling a sentential question—Italian approximates to being such a language. But a language of this kind would not be one in which 'to say that . . .' meant 'to express the Fregean thought that . . .'. If the practice of asking questions were widespread, it would be gener-ally recognised and count as a distinct and admissible use of sentences, even though not signalled by any explicit verbal device; this would be a mere ambiguity, comparable to that, in English, between questions and requests. In this case, the utterance of a sentence to ask a question would be one of the ways of using the language that a child would learn at an early stage; there would be no sense in which each speaker had to invent it for himself. If the asking of questions were very rare, however, someone who used a sentence for this purpose would have to acknowledge that he had in fact made the corresponding assertion, while explaining that he had not meant it to be taken seriously, just as happens, among us, to those who speak ironically.

We should beware of distinguishing too many varieties of force. Austin's criterion for there being any given kind of what he called 'illocutionary force' was whether one could say that someone had performed a certain action by uttering certain words. By this criterion, giving a warning is a species of illocutionary force. But you do not have to have the concept of a warning in order to understand a warning, in the way in which you have to have the concept of a question to understand a question. If you understand the sentence 'The steps are very slippery', and you know that someone uttering it is making a serious assertion, you do not have further to grasp that he is giving you a warning: you already completely understand what he is saying. Illocutionary force distinguishable by Austin's criterion is not, in general, an ingredient in meaning. To be that, two conditions must be satisfied. First, it must be impossible to understand an utterance to which the force in question is attached without grasping that it has that force; and, secondly, it must be impossible to perceive it as having that force simply by grasping its content and being aware that it has some other, or more general, type of force.

This formulation leaves the issue between Davidson and myself unresolved, however, because we frequently include, as part of understanding, an apprehension of what the speaker was driving at—of his purpose in saying what he did. If I fail to perceive that someone is speaking ironically, I have certainly misunderstood him, but have I merely missed his point in saying what he did, or have I actually mistaken what he was saying? The case is difficult because irony, like hyperbole, is a parasitic form. The employment of a special inflection of the verb to indicate the ironic character of an utterance would be almost as self-defeating as an inflection reserved for lying. An ironic utterance gains its effect by mimicking a straightforward assertion. It is not, however, to be characterised as a straightforward assertion made with a particular purpose in view; the hearer is meant to perceive that the speaker does not intend to be taken as making that assertion at all. Irony thus stands at an intermediate level, that of a figure of speech, between force and overall intention. Asked in court, 'Did you say that . . .?' (where 'say' has the sense of 'assert'), a witness may reply, 'I did not; I only asked whether . . .'. But, when the relevant utterance was ironic, he cannot truly declare that he did not make the assertion; he will have to say, 'I did, but I was speaking (or: I meant it) ironically'. In a language that employed an explicit assertion sign, an ironic utterance, unlike a question, would have to have the assertion sign as a prefix; that is why figures of speech must be seen as lying at a deeper level than force properly so called. They do not lie at the base level, however: given that someone spoke ironically, there is still room to ask *why* he made that ironic remark. In fact, there is a level deeper yet, that at which utterances *in propria persona* are distinguished from those made by an actor on the stage. We may ask why the character spoke as he did; the character makes assertions, asks questions, speaks ironically, and so on, but the actor, while on the stage, does none of these things.

The topic is complex. All that matters in the present context is that any systematic meaning-theory must separate sense from force—the specific content of an utterance from the type of linguistic act it is used to effect—if it is to handle its task of explaining the meanings of that majority of words and expressions that may occur without change of meaning in assertions, questions, commands, and other types of utterance.

The other ingredient of meaning distinguished by Frege from sense may conveniently be labelled 'tone'. It is not really a single type of ingredient but comprises disparate components associated only by belonging neither to force nor to sense. They do not go to determine the kind of linguistic act effected, and hence are not force-indicators; but they also cannot affect the truth or falsity of what is said, and so are not part of the sense expressed, on Frege's technical understanding of the term 'sense'. A favourite example, both of Frege and of subsequent philosophers, is the difference in meaning between 'and' and 'but', when the latter is used as a conjunction. Frege states this difference incorrectly, declaring that to say $\ulcorner$**A** but **B**$\urcorner$ is to make a statement that is true just in case $\ulcorner$**A** and **B**$\urcorner$ is true, while also hinting that the truth of **B** is unexpected, given that of **A**. If this were right, it would be difficult to explain why we should want to distinguish, in such a case, between hinting something and asserting it outright. It is not right, however: a sentence like 'She is a brilliant performer, but she never appears for a fee smaller than £200' cannot be explained in Frege's way. 'But' is apposite when a contrast of *any* kind is involved; it is its lack of any precise content that keeps it from contributing to the sense of the sentence.

The difference between 'and' and 'but' does not concern the mental images or feelings the speaker wishes to arouse in the hearer, which is how Frege often characterises tone; nor has it to do with the speaker's adoption of any general stance or attitude. It serves merely to indicate, with great vagueness, something that he would be prepared to add but takes for granted that his hearer will realise. More characteristic are the differences between 'dead' and 'deceased', 'woman' and 'lady', '*vous*' and '*tu*' in French, 'rabbit' and 'bunny', 'womb' and 'uterus', 'enemy' and 'foe', 'meal' and 'repast', 'politician' and 'statesman'. The choice between such twins serves to convey, and sometimes also to evoke, an attitude to the subject or, more particularly, to the hearers. It serves to define the proposed *style* of discourse, which, in turn, determines the kind of thing that may appropriately be said. We may speak to one another solemnly or light-heartedly, dispassionately or intimately, frankly or with reserve, formally or colloquially, poetically or prosaically; and all these modes represent particular forms of transaction between us. These complex social aspects of linguistic interchange are signalled by our choice of words; and, in so far as it is capable of serving to give such a signal, that capacity is part of the meaning of a word. When a dictionary notes, after its definition of a word, 'archaic', 'vulgar', or the like, it is, quite properly, indicating its tone. But this feature, important as it is in our dealings with one another, and complex as it is to describe in detail, is evidently peripheral to the problem of explaining what it is for something to be a language. We can hint only at what we could express; we can adopt one or another style of saying things only because we are able to say them at all.

Sense and Reference

To characterise the meaning, or any aspect of the meaning, of an expression is to talk about what the speakers know about that expression; that is, about the knowledge possessed by the community of speakers of the language, or, at least, that knowledge which it possesses by virtue of being the community *of speakers*. Hence to characterise the *sense* of an expression is to give a complete account of something that the speakers know about that expression; not in general, however, of everything that the speakers know about it, since the sense of the expression may not be the only ingredient in its meaning. It appears to follow immediately that the sense of an expression cannot be identified with its semantic value, since to understand the expression is not, in general, to know its semantic value. At least this seems clear whenever the semantic theory belongs to that large class for which the semantic value of a sentence determines whether or not it is true; otherwise it would follow from the sense of a sentence that it was true or that it was not. Moreover, a similar objection would hold against identifying the sense of a sentence with its being compounded in a certain way out of primitive expressions having certain semantic values. So construed, it would not follow that anyone who understood the sentence would thereby know whether or not it was true, but it would follow that he would know enough to be able to infer that it was or was not true, and this is equally unacceptable. Thus, to know the semantic value of an expression is to know *more* than is needed to know its sense. To know the sense of an expression is, by definition, to know everything relevant to determining its semantic value that needs to be known about it by anyone who knows the language. Sense therefore determines semantic value; that is to say, the semantic value of an expression follows from its sense together with relevant features of external reality. The phrase 'external reality' is not here a metaphysical one: it simply signifies any relevant facts that are not facts known to speakers by virtue of their knowledge of the language. But, if whether or not a sentence is true is to follow from the semantic values of its components, then, in ascribing a semantic value to an expression, the contribution of external reality has already been taken into account. Hence, relative to a semantic theory of this kind, sense is not to be identified with semantic value: to know the sense falls short of knowing the semantic value.

These observations are in line with the most celebrated of the arguments used by Frege for distinguishing sense from reference. Some of his arguments turn merely on his using the term '*Bedeutung*' for the thing referred to, rather than for the expression's referring to it. Thus he says that the various thoughts that can be expressed by sentences containing the name 'Etna' must have a common constituent, but that this common constituent, which comprises the sense of the name 'Etna', is not the mountain itself, which cannot be part of my thought. This argument, for what it is worth, does not show that the sense of the name 'Etna' amounts to more than its referring to that mountain. It therefore does not show that to know the sense of the name is to be distinguished from knowing its reference. The interesting arguments are those that aim to show precisely this.

The sense of an expression determines its reference, inasmuch as its reference follows from its sense, taken together with relevant facts about extra-linguistic reality; but the reference is not part of the meaning—it is not part of whatever is known by anyone who understands the expression. For Frege, the reference of a proper name or other singular term is its bearer, the object which we use the name or term to talk about. Hence to know the reference of a name is to know, of a certain object, that the name refers to it. Frege's most celebrated argument for the sense/reference distinction starts from the question how identity-statements can be informative. A statement is informative if, by coming to know that it is true, we thereby come to know something more; more, that is, than the bare fact that that statement is true. Plainly, we shall learn something more than that bare fact only if we understand the words by which the statement is expressed. The informational content of a statement may therefore be taken as what someone who understands those words, but has no other relevant knowledge, may come to know by learning that the statement is true. Frege's question therefore was in what the understanding of a name must consist if an identity-statement containing it was to be capable of being informative.

In introducing the notion of semantic value, we made no appeal to the notions of knowledge or understanding. But meaning, of which sense is the salient ingredient, is entirely correlative to understanding: to ask after the meaning of an expression is to ask what has to be grasped in order to understand it. Frege's argument was that, if to understand a name were to know its reference, then, where ⌜**a** = **b**⌝ is a true statement of identity, anyone who understood the two names **a** and **b**, and who knew what the relation of identity was, would already know that the identity-statement was true: for he would know, of some object, both that **a** stood for it and that **b** stood for it. Hence, to understand the name, to grasp its sense, we need not, in general, know its reference; we need only know something which, taken together with something that we may not know, and that is therefore not part of its meaning, determines its reference. Let us call this famous argument the 'identity argument'.

The identity argument could be extended to any atomic statement. To know the reference of a predicate $F(x)$ is to know, of each object, whether or not the predicate is true of it. Hence anyone who knows the reference of a name **a** and the reference of the predicate $F(x)$ already knows whether or not the sentence ⌜$F(a)$⌝ is true, since he knows, of some object, that **a** refers to it, and he also knows, of that object (as of others), whether or not $F(x)$ is true of it. Moreover, even if we should do well to resist the extension of the argument to more complex sentences, it is plain that anyone who knows the references of the parts of such a sentence will know enough to be able to infer its truth or falsity, even if he does not necessarily already know whether or not it is true; and this is quite enough to show that sense cannot be identified with having a certain reference.

Semantic theories involving many truth-values, and those based on relativised truth-values, are all such that the semantic values of the components of a sentence are sufficient to determine the sentence as true (absolutely) or otherwise. No notion of sense relating to a semantic theory of either of these two kinds can therefore be identified with the corresponding notion of semantic value. It is different with those semantic theories in which absolute truth is defined by existential quantification. The semantic value of a mathematical sentence, on Heyting's account, is an effective classification of mathematical constructions into those which do and those which do not prove the sentence. Anyone who knows the semantic value of a sentence is accordingly able to recognise a proof of it when he is presented with one: but it does not follow that he knows whether or not the sentence is true, that is, whether or not there *exists* a construction that proves it.

It is true that, even in such a case, there will be a small gap between sense and semantic value, since the semantic value of a term is an object; two terms refer to the same object if the identity-statement connecting them is true, and hence two terms may have the same semantic value without having the same sense. But since, in an intuitionistic language, identity is required to be an effectively decidable relation, the gap between sense and semantic value will be very narrow: sense will be related to semantic value as a programme to its execution. Frege's identity argument will still hold good, but not its generalisation to atomic sentences of other forms. There is, in fact, a profound difference between the conception of an object in classical and intuitionistic semantics. For the classical mathematician, mathematics treats of objects considered independently of the way they are given to us, that is, of how we conceive of them or identify them. For the intuitionist, we cannot so consider them; we cannot, as it were, conceive of them independently of the way we conceive of them. Identity, in the strict sense, is for him a decidable relation in that we may in certain cases be able to decide, from two ways in which an object is given, that the same object is given in each of those ways. We shall always know whether or not we can decide this: if we can, strict identity holds, if not, it does not. For instance, a natural number may be given by a numeral or by a numerical term involving addition and multiplication; we can effectively decide whether or not the term denotes the same number as the numeral. This requires us to distinguish between strict identity and extensional equality; from two ways of being given a species or a function, we cannot in general decide whether the species or functions so given are extensionally equal. An object, considered as the semantic value of a singular term, is then an equivalence class of senses, under the relation of strict identity, not of extensional equality. There is therefore no general assumption to be made that all mathematical predicates will be extensional, namely that such a predicate will apply to anything extensionally equal to anything to which it applies: many interesting predicates will be extensional, but no principle requires that all should be. There is accordingly no room for Frege's notion of indirect reference, or for any special treatment of singular terms in intensional contexts: intensional contexts, not extensional ones, are the norm.

By contrast, in Frege's celebrated example, the sense of 'the Morning Star' and 'the Evening Star' cannot be related to their joint reference as a programme to its execution. That is because he made the substantial assumption that the 'is' of his example was the sign of identity in the sense of being that relational expression an atomic sentence formed from which holds just in case both terms have the same semantic value. This assumption is substantial in the presence of his further tacit assumption that the semantic value of both terms will be a heavenly body; and this assumption goes far beyond the merely formal requirement that the semantic value of a singular term be an object.

Knowledge-That and Knowledge-What

Is Frege's identity argument valid? That turns on our understanding of the phrase ⌜knowing, of an object **b**, that the name *a* refers to it⌝. Both the original argument, and its extension to all atomic statements, turned on the assumption, which we may call 'the conjunction assumption', that ⌜*X* knows, of **b**, that it is **F**⌝ and ⌜*X* knows, of **b**, that it is **G**⌝ together entail ⌜*X* knows, of **b**, that it is both **F** and **G**⌝. Thus, if you know, of Venus, that 'the Morning Star' refers to it, and you also know, of Venus, that 'the Evening Star' refers to it, then you must know, of Venus, that both 'the Morning Star' and 'the Evening Star' refer to it. Likewise, if you know, of the Earth, that the term 'the Earth' refers to it, and you also know, of the Earth, whether or not the predicate '*x* spins' is true of it, then you must know, of the Earth, both that 'the Earth' refers to it and that it does (or that it does not) spin. Is the conjunction assumption reasonable?

Frege made implicit use of an argument to show the need for distinguishing sense from reference which explores the notion of knowing the reference, and is thus complementary to the identity argument; we might call it the 'cognitive' argument. Where the identity argument can be expressed by saying that to know the reference of a word is to know more than is involved in knowing its sense, the cognitive argument may be stated, conversely, by saying that more is involved in knowing the sense than just knowing the reference: more exactly, that there cannot be such a thing as a *bare* knowledge of the reference of an expression. We took a knowledge of the reference of a name *a* to consist in knowing, of some object, that *a* refers to it; and, by analogy, we took a knowledge of the reference of a predicate $F(x)$ to consist in knowing, of each object, whether or not $F(x)$ is true of it. A *bare* knowledge of the reference of the name *a* will consist, therefore, in knowing, of some object, that *a* refers to it, where this is a *complete* characterisation of this particular piece of knowledge; and similarly for a predicate. Thus the thesis tacitly maintained by Frege is that an ascription to someone of a knowledge of the reference of an expression, so understood, could never be a complete characterisation of that piece of knowledge on his part.

What justifies this explanation of what it is to know the reference of an expression? For simplicity, we may, for this discussion, confine ourselves to the case of a proper name or other singular term. Then, evidently, 'X knows the reference of *a*' is to be understood as meaning, not 'X knows the object to which *a* refers', where 'knows' means 'is acquainted with', but 'X knows what the reference of *a* is', understood as meaning 'X knows to which object *a* refers'. Here we have a particular instance of a very common locution, which I shall call 'an ascription of knowledge-what'; ascriptions of knowledge-who, knowledge-which, knowledge-when, knowledge-where, and so on, are special kinds of ascription of knowledge-what. The general form of an ascription of knowledge-what is ⌜X knows what is F⌝, where F is a predicate. An ascription of knowledge-what stands in contrast with an ascription of knowledge-that, which has the general form ⌜X knows that P⌝, where P is a sentence. Following the terminology already introduced, we may also call a statement of this latter form 'a propositional knowledge-ascription' or, specifically, either 'an ascription of a knowledge of the proposition expressed by the sentence P' or simply ⌜an ascription of a knowledge of the proposition that P⌝.

Propositional and Predicative Knowledge-Ascriptions

How are we to explain ascriptions of knowledge-what? A moment's reflection makes it irresistible to construe such an ascription as involving an existential quantification. The statement ⌜X knows what is F⌝ invites the question ⌜What does X know to be F?⌝; for instance, if you tell me, 'The police know who murdered Sandford', it is always in place for me to ask, 'Whom do they know to have murdered Sandford?' You may not know the answer, of course; but there must be a true answer, if your original assertion was correct. Such a statement as, 'The police know Tremayne to have murdered Sandford' we may, for the sake of clarity, render as, 'The police know, of Tremayne, that he murdered Sandford'; and we may call a statement of this form 'a predicative knowledge-ascription'. It is important to observe that what have so far been distinguished are not two distinct types of *knowledge* but merely two linguistic modes by which knowledge may be ascribed to someone. It has been left completely open whether there are types of knowledge that can properly be ascribed only in the one mode or in the other.

The general form of a predicative knowledge-ascription is ⌜X knows, of **b**, that it is **F**⌝. It differs from the corresponding propositional knowledge-ascription, ⌜X knows that **b** is **F**⌝, by the fact that in the former but not in the latter, the singular term **b** stands in a transparent context: ⌜**b** = **c**⌝ and ⌜X knows, of **b**, that it is **F**⌝ together entail ⌜X knows, of **c**, that it is **F**⌝, whereas, notoriously, ⌜**b** = **c**⌝ and ⌜X knows that **b** is **F**⌝ do not entail ⌜X knows that **c** is **F**⌝. The suggestion then is that an ascription of knowledge-what, ⌜X knows what is **F**⌝, is equivalent to an existential quantification of a predicative knowledge-ascription, that is, to ⌜For some y, X knows, of y, that it is **F**⌝. For example, the police know who murdered Sandford just in case there is someone of whom they know that he murdered Sandford. Thus, as was previously claimed, 'X knows the reference of a', meaning 'X knows what a refers to', comes out as equivalent to 'For some object y, X knows, of y, that a refers to it'.

It is easy to give a plausible account of how ascriptions of knowledge-what are related to predicative knowledge-ascriptions; the difficult problem is to say how the latter are related to propositional knowledge-ascriptions. It might be proposed that any ascription of a knowledge of the proposition expressed by a singular sentence, ⌜X knows that **c** is **F**⌝, entails the corresponding predicative knowledge-ascription, ⌜X knows, of **c**, that it is **F**⌝, and hence that ⌜**b** = **c**⌝ and ⌜X knows that **c** is **F**⌝ entail ⌜X knows, of **b**, that it is **F**⌝. But this cannot be combined with our analysis of ascriptions of knowledge-what in terms of predicative knowledge-ascriptions. For it would be universally admitted that 'The police know that Sandford's blackmail victim murdered him' does not entail 'The police know who murdered Sandford'; hence, given our analysis of ascriptions of knowledge-what, it cannot entail 'The police know, of Sandford's blackmail victim, that he murdered Sandford', nor, taken together with 'Sandford's blackmail victim was Tremayne', can it entail 'The police know, of Tremayne, that he murdered Sandford'.

The intuitive reason why 'The police know that Sandford's blackmail victim murdered him' does not entail 'The police know who murdered Sandford' is that the police may not know who Sandford's blackmail victim is. But, if this is the obstacle to the entailment, then it seems not merely that some propositional knowledge-ascriptions will *not* entail the corresponding predicative knowledge-ascriptions, and therefore the corresponding ascriptions of knowledge-what, but that others *will*: for instance, that 'The police know that Tremayne murdered Sandford' will entail 'The police know, of Tremayne, that he murdered Sandford', and hence 'The police know who murdered Sandford'. The reason is that the corresponding obstacle cannot occur in this case. We cannot argue that the police may know that Tremayne murdered Sandford, but may not know who Tremayne is, and therefore not know who murdered Sandford. We cannot argue thus, because it is a necessary condition for knowing that Tremayne murdered Sandford (or anything else about Tremayne) that one should know who Tremayne is. Here we need to invoke the distinction drawn previously, between knowing the proposition expressed by a sentence and knowing that the sentence is true. If the police do not know who Tremayne is, they cannot know that Tremayne murdered Sandford but can know, at best, that Sandford's murderer is called 'Tremayne'. Thus it is a precondition of knowing that Tremayne murdered Sandford that one should know who Tremayne is; there is therefore no obstacle to concluding, from the fact that the police know that Tremayne murdered Sandford, that they know who murdered him.

This example shows only that there may be an entailment from a propositional knowledge-ascription to an ascription of knowledge-what. It does not determine the direction of analysis, because we have not established that, for every true ascription of knowledge-what, there is a true propositional knowledge-ascription that entails it. In particular, we have not established this for such a statement as 'The police know who Tremayne is'. In fact, sentences of this particular form provide examples to which our analysis of ascriptions of knowledge-what in terms of predicative knowledge-ascriptions does not very naturally fit. It appears correct, but not very illuminating, to equate knowing who Tremayne is with knowing, of someone, that he is Tremayne; and, if we actually wish to analyse predicative knowledge-ascriptions in terms of propositional ones, even less illuminating to explain knowing, of Tremayne, that he is Tremayne as knowing that Tremayne is Tremayne—though still not incorrect to *equate* the two, if we keep in mind the distinction between knowing that a sentence is true and knowing the proposition it expresses.

It seems natural and, indeed, correct to say that the sense in which it is a precondition of knowing that Tremayne murdered Sandford that one should know who Tremayne is coincides with that in which it is a precondition of knowing that Tremayne was Sandford's blackmail victim that one should know what blackmail is. It is equally natural to gloss this by saying that what must be known is, respectively, the use of the term 'blackmail' and the use of the name 'Tremayne'. It is, however, only because 'Tremayne' is a *standard* personal name that there is no *other* sense of 'knowing who Tremayne is' relevant to the step from a propositional knowledge-ascription to an ascription of knowledge-what. If the police do not yet know who Sandford's blackmail victim is but, for convenience of private communication, have adopted the name 'Beardsley' for that blackmail victim, whoever he may be, and later determine that Sandford was murdered by his blackmail victim, then they know that Beardsley murdered Sandford, and they know the use of the proper name 'Beardsley'; but they do not yet know who murdered Sandford, because they do not, in the relevant sense, know who Beardsley is.

Frege's 'cognitive' argument for the distinction between sense and reference (which was presented by him only allusively and in metaphor) can be reconstructed as resting on two premisses. Premiss (1) is that all theoretical knowledge—knowledge of what is the case, rather than of how to do something—is, ultimately, propositional knowledge; otherwise expressed, for every true predicative knowledge-ascription, there is some true propositional knowledge-ascription which entails it or, as we may say, on which it *rests*. Premiss (2) is that every predicative knowledge-ascription entailed by an ascription of the knowledge of some true proposition is always also entailed by an ascription of the knowledge of some true but non-equivalent proposition; here the ascriptions themselves need not be true. (For this purpose, we may adopt Frege's not wholly satisfactory criterion: two propositions are equivalent just in case it is impossible to know either without knowing the other.) It follows that there can be no such thing as *bare* predicative knowledge, sometimes called 'knowledge *de re*'; that is, no predicative knowledge-ascription can be a complete characterisation of that piece of knowledge on the part of the subject. Hence, in particular, there can be no such thing as a *bare* knowledge of the reference of an expression, in the sense already explained. To say of someone that he knows the reference of a term is to say that there is some object such that he knows, of that object, that the term refers to it. According to premiss (1), this predicative knowledge-ascription, if true, must rest on some true propositional knowledge-ascription; it must be true in virtue of some piece of propositional knowledge that the subject has. According to premiss (2), the proposition which he knows, and which renders the predicative knowledge-ascription true, is not determined by that ascription; there will be some other true proposition such that, if he knew it, his knowledge of it would also entail that same predicative knowledge-ascription. Hence, even if the knowledge which someone has when he grasps the sense of the term is taken as entailing that he knows its reference, that knowledge is not completely characterised by his knowing the reference of the term.

These two premisses do not amount to an analysis of predicative knowledge-ascriptions; they tell us only that such an ascription is entailed by an ascription of a knowledge of various distinct propositions. We have seen that $\ulcorner X$ knows, of **b**, that it is $\mathbf{F}\urcorner$ is entailed by, and can perhaps be analysed as, the conjunction of $\ulcorner X$ knows that **b** is $\mathbf{F}\urcorner$ and $\ulcorner X$ knows what **b** is$\urcorner$. (This latter sentence is to be understood as the general case of $\ulcorner X$ knows who **b** is$\urcorner$; it means that X knows which object **b** denotes, not merely what kind of thing it denotes.) The proper analysis of this 'knows what' statement is extremely obscure. Probably it has no uniform analysis: what is demanded for a knowledge of what a thing is or who a person is may vary from context to context.

The ground for the two premisses of the 'cognitive' argument may be taken to be something like this. Anything which serves to manifest possession of a piece of knowledge will serve to manifest knowledge of some proposition; in particular, this will hold good of whatever serves to manifest possession of that knowledge the subject's possession of which renders a predicative knowledge-ascription true. For instance, the police may manifest their knowledge of the identity of Sandford's murderer, that is, their knowing, of some man, that he murdered Sandford, by arresting someone and charging him with the murder. But, in order to be able to arrest anyone, you have to be able to identify him: hence the action of the police will also serve to manifest their knowledge of the proposition that the man identifiable in such-and-such a way murdered Sandford. Furthermore, there will always be some non-equivalent proposition a manifestation of a knowledge of which will equally serve to justify the very same predicative knowledge-ascription. Thus, there would always be other possible ways of identifying the man whom the police arrested. Of some of these, the police may have known that they provided means of identifying the man they knew to have committed the murder, of others, not; but that is irrelevant. What matters is that if they had used any of them, they would have manifested knowledge of a different proposition but, at the same time, would have justified our saying that they knew, of that same man, that he committed the murder.

Premiss (1) is highly plausible: even in default of an analysis of predicative knowledge-ascriptions, it is difficult to think how they could possibly be explained save in terms of propositional ones. Premiss (2) is much more doubtful. Indeed, if we accept Frege's identity argument, it will be wrong to suppose that knowing the sense of a term involves knowing its reference at all; in this case the propositional knowledge that constitutes knowledge of its sense will not necessarily ground the predicative knowledge-ascription which attributes a knowledge of its reference.

However, since the two arguments are complementary, we may, by taking them in tandem, recognise the need to distinguish sense from reference without having to decide whether any of their premisses is true, or, in particular, what should count as knowing the reference of a term or of a predicate. Premiss (1) of the 'cognitive' argument was that, for every true predicative knowledge-ascription, there is some true propositional knowledge-ascription on which it rests. If this premiss fails, a true predicative knowledge-ascription need not rest upon the knowledge of any proposition; there can be knowledge *de re* (bare predicative knowledge). In this case, the conjunction assumption, which was the premiss of the identity argument, is certainly plausible. For, if you know, of Venus, that 'the Morning Star' refers to it, and you also know, of Venus, that 'the Evening Star' refers to it, and if neither piece of knowledge consists in your knowing a complete proposition, then you have bare knowledge of the reference of 'the Morning Star' and of 'the Evening Star'; and it is then difficult to see how it can fail to follow that you know, of Venus, that both 'the Morning Star' and 'the Evening Star' refer to it. Suppose, next, that premiss (2) of the 'cognitive' argument fails, even if premiss (1) holds. Premiss (2) says that there will be more than one proposition a knowledge of which will imply the truth of a given predicative knowledge-ascription. Assume that this is false, so that every true predicative knowledge-ascription rests upon the knowledge of some unique proposition.

The conjunction assumption then again becomes plausible; at least, it becomes plausible provided that the form of the singular term in the sentence expressing that unique proposition depends only on the object to which the predicative knowledge-ascription relates, and not on the particular predicate involved. That is to say, if there is a unique proposition that you must know if it is to be true of you that you know, of Venus, that 'the Morning Star' refers to it, it must, presumably, be the proposition that 'the Morning Star' refers to Venus. If you can also be credited, on the same grounds, with knowing the proposition that 'the Evening Star' refers to Venus, then you surely know that both 'the Morning Star' and 'the Evening Star' refer to Venus. The conjunction assumption is *not* plausible, however, if both premisses of the 'cognitive' argument hold. In this case, the identity argument fails. A speaker might be said to know both the reference of 'the Morning Star' and that of 'the Evening Star' without his knowing, of any object, that both terms referred to it; if so, the identity-statement would supply information not even latent in his understanding of the language.

It is now that the 'cognitive' argument will come into play. Its conclusion was that to ascribe to someone a knowledge of the reference of a term could never be a complete characterisation of his knowledge. The complete characterisation of the relevant piece of knowledge will cite a proposition on a knowledge of which his knowledge of the reference rests: his knowledge of this proposition will constitute his grasp of the sense of the term.

In Frege's writings, the grounds for the two arguments appear, not in parallel, but in series; and there is a reason for this. Taken by itself, even if its premisses are accepted, the cognitive argument shows only that each speaker must attach a sense to any given term, a sense which requires a richer characterisation than that he knows its reference. It has no tendency to show that different speakers must all attach the same sense to the term, that, therefore, the sense of a term is a feature of the *language;* the argument would be met by their all attaching different senses to it, provided only that these determined the same reference. The first argument provides a ground for setting aside this possibility and regarding sense as common to all speakers, since it concerns the use of language for *communication,* which depends upon the informational content of a sentence being constant from speaker to speaker. If language is to serve as a medium of communication, it is not sufficient that a sentence should in fact be true under the interpretation placed on it by one speaker just in case it is true under that placed on it by another; it is also necessary that both speakers should be aware of the fact.

It is for this reason that some importance attaches to the observation that Frege's first argument could be extended to all atomic sentences. If we do not observe this, we shall be in danger of thinking that the argument for distinguishing sense from reference depends upon rejecting Russell's theory of descriptions. That theory offers an alternative account of a posteriori identity-statements without invoking the sense/reference distinction: to apply it to an identity-statement connecting two syntactically proper names, it is not necessary to adopt the 'description theory of names' in any stronger sense than that which is involved in Quine's elimination of proper names in favour of uniquely applicable predicates. Nevertheless, the necessity for the distinction between sense and reference in no way depends upon the need to explain how identity-statements can be informative, despite the fact that, as Frege perceived, the case of identity-statements forms the best possible heuristic basis for introducing the distinction.

All the same, the extension of Frege's identity argument to atomic sentences in general rests on a stronger assumption than does the original application of it to identity-statements. As we have seen, to say that in general the semantic value of a singular term is an object does not in any way restrict the kind of semantic theory that we adopt, unless some particular ontology, some doctrine about the kinds of objects which the world contains, is presupposed. Hence Frege's original argument concerning identity-statements does not depend upon the adoption of classical, two-valued, semantics, though admittedly its application to particular cases involves a large assumption about what is to count as an object and hence about the form of the semantic theory. But the extension of the argument to other atomic sentences depends upon assuming that the semantic value of a predicate is its extension, that is, its being determinately true or false of each object in the domain; and this holds good only within a two-valued semantics. However, just as the assumption underlying the extended argument is stronger, so the conclusion is more powerful. Frege's original argument about identity-statements would be met by supposing the sense of a term to be related to its reference as a programme to its execution—by supposing that the sense provides an effective procedure, by means of physical and mental operations, whereby the reference could be determined. For, without appeal to the assumption that every meaningful sentence *has* a determinate truth-value, we cannot claim that the semantic value of each sentence is its truth-value. Hence, although we may say that it is possible to understand a sentence without knowing its semantic value, we do not have a ground for arguing that one may understand it without even being able effectively to discover its semantic value. Thus, granted that the semantic value of a singular term is the object to which it refers, we cannot assume, without appeal to the principle of bivalence or, at least, to some suitable principle of multivalence, that there can be admissible singular terms whose reference cannot be effectively determined, nor, therefore, any identity-statements whose truth-value cannot be effectively decided. By contrast, the extension of the argument to all atomic sentences does presuppose bivalence: it therefore leaves open the possibility that the language may contain primitive predicates whose application cannot be decided effectively, and which we can accordingly understand without being able to determine their semantic value, since the semantic value of a predicate is being assumed to be its extension. Some distinction between sense and semantic value must be admitted whatever semantic theory we adopt. It is only in certain semantic theories, however, above all in two- and many-valued semantics, that we require a notion of sense as determining the semantic value of an expression, but not in general in an effective manner.

Reference, Sense, and Modesty

The advocates of a modest meaning-theory will strenuously deny that they ascribe to a speaker a knowledge only of the reference, not of the sense, of a word. They do not represent a speaker's grasp of the use of the name 'Boston' as consisting in his knowing, of Boston, that the name refers to it; rather, they take it as consisting in his knowing that the name 'Boston' refers to Boston—a piece of propositional knowledge. Whether or not, in cases of this particular kind, knowing the sense entails knowing the reference, they do not have to decide; their business is with expounding what knowledge of sense consists in. In this way, they can explain how two names can have the same reference but different senses. Anyone who knows the language knows that 'the Morning Star' refers to the Morning Star and that 'the Evening Star' refers to the Evening Star; but, since he need not, in virtue of his knowing the language, know that the Morning Star is the Evening Star, he need not know that 'the Morning Star' and 'the Evening Star' refer to the same thing. If, in cases of this kind, a knowledge of sense does entail a knowledge of the reference, then anyone who knows the language must know, of the planet Venus, that 'the Morning Star' refers to it, and must know, of that planet, that 'the Evening Star' refers to it. If so, however, the conjunction assumption must fail; it will therefore be illegitimate to infer that anyone who knows these two things will also know, of the planet Venus, that both 'the Morning Star' and 'the Evening Star' refer to it.

A good case can be made that a modest meaning-theory accords with Frege's ideas. His practice, in Part I of *Grundgesetze der Arithmetik*, in which he systematically expounded the syntax and semantics of his formal theory, is consistent with the view that it is in principle impossible to *say* what the sense of a symbolic expression is, but that this can only be *shown* by the particular manner in which we say what its reference is. There is certainly nothing in any of Frege's arguments for distinguishing sense from reference to conflict with the thesis that knowing the sense of the name 'Boston' consists in knowing that the name 'Boston' refers to Boston. If this thesis is to be maintained, however, it is strictly necessary to draw the distinction between knowing that a sentence is true and knowing the proposition expressed by that sentence. Anyone who knows that 'Boston' is a name having reference knows that the sentence 'The name "Boston" refers to Boston' is true. Hence, if the thesis is to be defended against the criticism that it confuses knowing the sense of a name with knowing that the name has a reference, knowing that 'Boston' refers to Boston must be distinguished from knowing that the sentence '"Boston" refers to Boston' is true. To make out this distinction, it is essential to recognise that, in order to know that the name 'Boston' refers to Boston, or to know anything else about Boston, it is necessary to know what Boston is; and this, plainly, involves knowing both that Boston is a city, and which city Boston is. Until we are told what constitutes knowing which city Boston is, we shall not have an analysis of what it is to know the sense of the name 'Boston'. As 'Boston' is the standard name of the city, we can equate knowing what Boston is with knowing the use of the name 'Boston'. Since this may in turn be equated with knowing the sense of the name, the claim that to know the sense of the name 'Boston' is to know that the name refers to Boston, while quite possibly correct, takes us not one step towards explaining what it is to know the sense of that name: for, in order to interpret the claim, we have already to know not merely the sense of the name 'Boston' but what it is to know its sense. This is simply one application of the general principle that the need to distinguish knowing that a sentence is true from knowing the proposition expressed by it imposes on a meaning-theory the necessity to say not only *what* the speakers know in knowing the meanings of the words of the language, but in what that knowledge consists.

Frege's Principles Concerning Sense

As is well known, Frege contented himself with laying down certain principles about sense and never attempted a specific account of the sense of any particular expression. Most of his writing is consistent with the view that no such account is possible, save by equating the sense of one expression with that of another. It does not *demand* that view, however; and there seems no sufficient reason to maintain it. The project of giving, within some one language, a non-circular system of explanations of the meanings of all words of the language *is*, of course, unrealisable; but that is not what is required. There is no intrinsic absurdity in the project of explaining, for every word, what a grasp of its meaning amounts to and how that grasp is manifested. Equally, there is no intrinsic absurdity in the project of describing, for every word, how it is used, in such a way as to exhibit what constitutes its meaning what it does. The projects are the same: for it is by the way a speaker uses a word that he manifests his grasp of its meaning. It is in just this project, described in the one way or the other, that the task of constructing a meaning-theory consists. There is no ground for declaring that task impossible, rather than merely difficult.

The principles Frege stated tell us a great deal about what form a specific theory of sense would take. The first of these principles that we have already noted is:

(i) To give the sense of an expression is to specify something that the speakers of the language grasp concerning it and to give a complete characterisation of what their grasp of it consists in.

If we interpret a speaker's grasp of the sense of the expression as a piece of knowledge that he has, we can render this:

(ia) To give the sense of an expression is to give a complete characterisation of a piece of knowledge that the speakers have concerning it.

A further principle that we have noted is:

(ii) Given how the world is, sense determines reference.

If we equate Frege's notion of reference, as applied to expressions of different logical types, with our notion of semantic value, this becomes:

(iia) Given how the world is, sense determines semantic value.

The complementary principle is:

(iii) Given principle (i), nothing belongs to sense save what is required to determine reference (semantic value).

Yet another principle, equally fundamental, is:

(iv) The sense of a complex expression is compounded out of the senses of its constituents.

This fourth principle involves not merely that we in fact derive the sense of the complex expression from knowing the senses of the components and understanding how they are put together, but that we can apprehend that sense only as expressible by a complex expression with just that structure, that is, compounded in the same way out of constituents having those senses. We therefore could not attach that same sense to another expression, perhaps one of a different syntactic complexity, without understanding it as capable of being expressed by one of the same structure as the original expression.

A principle of rather a different character from these is:

(v) An expression has sense only in the context of a sentence.

Frege originally stated this principle in his *Grundlagen der Arithmetik,* in terms of an undifferentiated notion of meaning, before he had arrived at the distinction between sense and reference; but his thesis, in *Grundgesetze,* that the sense of a constituent of a sentence consists in its contribution to the thought expressed by the sentence as a whole, is completely consonant with it. The content of the principle is that it is integral to the sense of any expression that it can be combined in certain ways with other expressions to form a sentence whose semantic value (in Frege's semantics, its being true or not being true) is determined by its sense, which, in accordance with principle (iv), will be given by the senses of the components and the way they are put together. By principle (iv), it is necessary, in order to grasp the sense expressed by a complex expression, that we understand it as having a complexity corresponding to that of the expression. By principle (v), it is also sufficient, since a complex expression (when complete) is one that is formed at some stage in the construction of a whole sentence, or else (when incomplete) is one extractable from a sentence by omission of some of its constituents. Principle (iv) therefore makes it necessary that we should have a conception of the kind of semantic value that can be possessed by a complex expression, as well as by a simple or primitive expression; otherwise we have no way of grasping how the senses of the components of a complex expression cohere to form the sense of the whole. But, by principle (v), the sense of any expression must be given as determining a semantic value that combines with those of other expressions, which, together with it, would make up a sentence, to yield a semantic value for the whole.

This is not yet quite accurately expressed, since we defined the semantic value of an expression, at the outset, as that feature of it which goes to determine the truth or otherwise of a sentence in which it occurs. When 'semantic value' is so understood, what principle (v) expresses is that semantic value was the right notion to invoke in explaining the notion of sense; semantic value is precisely what we must take sense as determining. That is, the sense of any expression must be taken as given in terms of the way in which the semantic value of a compound—ultimately, of a sentence—that is formed by combining that expression with others is determined. Since the sense of an expression must always determine *its* semantic value, that means that the semantic value of an incomplete expression, say, a predicate, must always be taken to consist in a mapping—in the case of a predicate, from objects to statement-values. In a classical semantics, the statement-values—the semantic values of sentences—are, of course, simply truth-values.

Semantic Theories as Bases for Meaning-Theories

It should now have become more apparent what is meant by saying that a meaning-theory has a semantic theory as its base, and why it must have a semantic theory as its base (given that truth is, in the weak sense, the central notion of the meaning-theory). To say that the sense of an expression must be something grasped by the speakers, or that it is the content of some knowledge possessed by them, and, further, that it must determine the semantic value of the expression, does not yet tell us what that sense is, even when we know the semantic value. Nevertheless, given that we have selected a particular semantic theory, it places strong constraints upon what an acceptable account of sense must be like. If, however, we do not have a semantic theory, we do not have the least idea what will constitute an account of the senses of expressions, that is, how to explain that part of the speakers' understanding of expressions that bears on how sentences are determined as true or otherwise. A merely programmatic interpretation of a language gives us no clue as to what is required of an explanation of sense; what we need, in order to know what is required, is a semantic interpretation. Even when we are concerned to specify one particular semantic interpretation, what makes it a *semantic* interpretation is the fact that it is specified against the background of a semantic theory which says what, in general, such an interpretation consists in. That is why, although, in giving a meaning-theory, we need only to lay down one specific interpretation of language, the meaning-theory must incorporate a general account of what constitutes an interpretation, that is, a statement of what, in general, the semantic value of an expression of each category is to be, and how these jointly determine the semantic value of a sentence.

In a certain sense, a programmatic interpretation is all we need in the classical two-valued semantics, since we can, by appeal to the classical laws of logic, derive what the semantic values of expressions are. Nevertheless, even in this case, if we are to be able to construct that part of the meaning-theory which constitutes the theory of sense, we shall need to make an overt appeal to the semantic theory, that is, to the principles which state what kind of semantic value an expression of each type must have. It is easy to think that, because in the theory of meaning we are concerned with only one interpretation of a language, our task is much more straightforward, and conclude that we may neglect some of the complications that arise in logic because, in it, we are concerned with the range of all possible interpretations. It is this illusion that leads to the conception of a modest meaning-theory, and more particularly of a meaning-theory as specifying a programmatic interpretation. This tendency is strongly reinforced by an exclusive concentration upon languages with a classical logic. It is nevertheless a mistake, engendered by a failure to see what is required of a theory of sense, and the only possible path to constructing such a theory. The answer to the question raised earlier, whether it makes an essential difference that in the theory of meaning we are concerned with only one interpretation for each language, is 'No'. It is now also evident why, if we assume that truth is the central notion for a meaning-theory, it follows that the meaning-theory must incorporate an account of how a sentence is determined as true or otherwise in accordance with its composition, and not just any statement of the condition for the truth of a sentence in terms of the truth of its subsentences. The reason is that without such an account we cannot construct a theory of sense for the words of the language.

It is thus wrong to suppose that Frege's contribution to elucidating the notion of sense was confined to providing arguments that there must be such a thing as sense, taken as distinct from reference. By supplying an explicit theory of reference, that is, a semantic theory, he enunciated a *programme* for a theory of sense; in the light of his general principles concerning the relation of sense to reference, he determined the *form* that the sense of a word of given type must assume, if that semantic theory is correct.

chapter 6

Truth and Meaning-Theories

Is the Sense of a Predicate a Function?

The principle that sense determines semantic value, or, in Frege's terminology, that sense determines reference, is one not always clearly held in mind, even by those with a deep insight into Frege's theory of meaning. This comes out if we consider what might at first seem a highly esoteric point in Fregean exegesis. Geach has criticised me for denying that the sense of an incomplete expression, such as a predicate, is a function. Consider a unary predicate, say 'x stammers'. Frege says that the reference of such a predicate is a concept, that is to say, a function which carries every object into one of the two truth-values, *true* and *false*. Given a two-valued semantics, this is unobjectionable, provided that the truth-values are not taken themselves to be objects. Now what is the sense of such a predicate? It cannot also be a concept, say, a function mapping senses of names of objects onto truth-values, for otherwise anyone who knew the sense of the predicate 'x stammers' and the sense of the name 'Colonel North' would thereby know the truth-value of the sentence 'Colonel North stammers', which is absurd. But may it not be a function from senses to senses, specifically, a function taking the sense of any name to the sense of the sentence formed by inserting that name in the argument-place of the predicate? That is, may not the sense of the predicate 'x stammers' be that function which maps the sense of the name 'Colonel North' onto the thought that Colonel North stammers, the sense of the name 'Henry Kissinger' onto the thought that Henry Kissinger stammers, and so on? There must, after all, be such a function; and do we not achieve economy by the identification of the sense of the predicate with that function? Geach adduces positive advantages for this identification. By making it, we acknowledge an incompleteness in the *senses* of incomplete expressions (expressions containing one or more argument-places) parallel to the incompleteness of their referents, and, in so doing, do justice to the passages in which Frege says expressly that the sense of an incomplete expression is itself incomplete. If the sense of an incomplete expression is not any kind of function, then, in Frege's ontology, it must be an object. How, in that case, can we explain how the three objects, the sense of 'John', the sense of 'hit', and the sense of 'Mary', cohere into a whole, the thought that John hit Mary, and into the right whole at that, rather than into the thought that Mary hit John?

Geach acknowledges that Frege repeatedly said that the sense of a complex expression, including a sentence, is composed of the senses of its constituent words. He asks, however, whether Frege is to be imitated or only charitably expounded (as Aquinas says concerning the Fathers), and goes on to allude to the blunder which Frege at one time made, and later retracted, in saying that the referent of an expression is composed of the referents of its constituents (a mistake which could hardly be made if one distinguished verbally between the reference and the referent). Here is a late passage from Frege (*Nachgelassene Schriften*, p. 275) in which he retracts his blunder about reference and strongly reaffirms what Geach believes to be his parallel blunder about sense:

> A distinction is to be made between the sense and the reference of a sign (word, expression). When an astronomer says something about the Moon, the Moon itself is not part of the thought he expresses. The Moon itself is the reference of the expression 'the Moon'. This expression must, therefore, have, besides its reference a sense, which can be a constituent of thought. The sentence can be regarded as a representation of the thought, in such a manner that to the part-whole relation between the parts of the thought and the thought there corresponds, by and large, the same relation between the parts of the sentence and the sentence. It is otherwise in the realm of reference. One cannot say that Sweden is a part of the capital of Sweden.

Geach concludes that we should regard the sense of a predicate as a function mapping senses of names onto thoughts (senses of sentences), though he admits that Frege never actually said this. On the contrary, the thesis is inconsistent with Frege's whole conception of sense. Geach recognises that it *is* inconsistent with Frege's principle that the sense of a complex expression, including a sentence, is composed of the senses of the component parts of that expression. If the sense of 'x shines' is a function which maps the sense of the phrase 'the sun' onto the thought that the sun shines, then that thought no more contains the sense of 'the sun' as a part than Stockholm contains Sweden as a part. Geach's proposal involves inattention to what we want the notion of sense for. Suppose that the sense of the predicate 'x stammers' is given to us as a function which carries us from, for example, the sense of the name 'Mrs. Thatcher' to the thought expressed by the sentence 'Mrs. Thatcher stammers'. On Frege's conception of the sense of a sentence, the content of the thought expressed by the sentence depends on the condition for the sentence to be true. What, then, is that condition? What *does* determine the sentence as true or as false? On this picture of the sense of the predicate, we are left unable to say; or, if we can say, then it must be the satisfaction of some condition, given by the predicate, by the *sense* of the name 'Mrs. Thatcher'. The reference of the name will not then come into the determination of the truth or falsity of the sentence. At best, it is relevant only to how we grasp the sense of the name.

Obviously, this is wrong: the determination of the truth-value of the sentence goes via the referent of the name. The sense of the name determines an object as its referent; and the sense of the predicate determines a mapping from objects to truth-values—in Frege's terminology, a concept. The sentence is true or false according as the object does or does not fall under that concept, that is, according as it is mapped by it onto the value *true* or onto the value *false*. The mapping of objects onto truth-values is not the *sense*, but the referent of the predicate; the sense is, rather, some particular way, which we can grasp, of determining such a mapping. But the sense of the predicate is to be thought of not as being given directly in terms of a mapping from the *senses* of names onto anything (such as thoughts) but, rather, in terms of a mapping of *objects* onto truth-values. If the thesis that there can be no such thing as a *bare* knowledge of reference is right for this case, too, as it certainly appears to be, then we could not simply be given such a mapping: that is, it could not be a complete characterisation of any piece of knowledge that we might possess that we knew, of each object, onto which truth-value it was mapped. And if the thesis that a knowledge of the sense does not entail a knowledge of the reference is also correct, as it must surely be in the context of a two-valued semantics, then, by knowing the sense of the predicate, we do not necessarily know, or even have any effective means of discovering, what the mapping is. But, for all that, if to grasp the sense of the predicate is to grasp something that determines its reference, and if it is to lead us to apprehend the condition for a sentence formed by means of that predicate to be true, then it must be given to us as a grasp of the condition that must be satisfied, by any object, for it to be mapped onto the value *true* or for it to be mapped onto the value *false*.

There are two possible interpretations, weak and strong, of the thesis that sense determines reference. On the weak interpretation, it is just that two expressions with the same sense could not have different references; on the strong interpretation, to know the sense of an expression is just to know the condition for it to have a given reference. It is clear enough from what Frege expressly says that we need the strong interpretation so far as the sense of a sentence—a thought—is concerned: to grasp a thought is to know the condition for it to be true. It is reasonably plain, also, that we need it for proper names as well: to know the sense of the name is to know the condition that must hold, of any given object, for it to be the referent of that name. Not only does this accord with Frege's saying that the sense of a word is the way in which the referent is given to us, but it provides the only means by which we can attain any conception of what the sense of a proper name consists in; if we reject the suggestion, we are left without any idea of what the sense of a name is supposed to be. But if we adopt the strong interpretation of the thesis that sense determines reference—roughly speaking, that the sense of a word is given to us *as* a means of determining its reference—both for sentences as a whole and for proper names, we are virtually forced to adopt it for predicates also; and this means that the sense of the predicate is not given to us as a function from the senses of names to the senses of sentences, though it readily induces such a function, but as a means of determining a function from objects to truth-values.

If Geach's interpretation were right, there would indeed be no more reason to say, with Frege, that the sense of the predicate was a constituent of the sense of the sentence in which it occurs than to say that the function which is the referent of the expression 'the capital of *x*' is a constituent of Stockholm; the function maps Sweden onto Stockholm but is no more a part of Stockholm than Sweden is; and so it is with the function that maps the sense of the name 'Mrs. Thatcher' onto the sense of the sentence 'Mrs. Thatcher stammers'. Hence Frege's reiterated insistence that the senses of the parts are parts of the sense of the whole is strong evidence that he did not intend that the sense of the predicate should be construed as identical with this function. Frege's conception of the sense of a complex expression cannot in fact be understood at all if one rejects altogether the doctrine which Geach thinks should only be charitably expounded. To say that the sense of the whole is compounded out of the senses of the parts is to say, first, that we understand the complex expression as having the sense it does by understanding its parts and the way they are put together, and, secondly, that we could not grasp that sense without conceiving of it as having just that complexity. The second of these two constituent theses is a very strong one. It is, in my view, correct; but it needs a very deep argument to support it, or, indeed, to refute it. The first of the two theses, by contrast, is all but banal and is affirmed, in one form or another, by almost everyone who thinks that a meaning-theory is possible at all: how else are we going to explain how we come to associate those senses which we do with complex expressions of our language (including, as frequently remarked, new ones that we have never heard before)?

Frege's theory, correctly interpreted, does allow the senses of incomplete expressions to have a kind of incompleteness: they have the sort of incompleteness appropriate to the senses of expressions, not that attributable to the referents of incomplete expressions. The sense of a binary relational expression, say that of 'x hit y' (which, having a tense inflection, is not a *primitive* relational expression), is given to us as a means of determining a mapping from ordered pairs of objects to truth-values. Hence, by inserting names into the two argument-places, we obtain a sentence with which we associate a condition for it to be true and a condition for it to be false; if we switch the two names around, we obtain a sentence with which we associate a different such condition. There is thus no problem in explaining how the senses of the parts of a sentence cohere to form the expression of a thought. The sense of a predicate is incomplete in so far as what it determines is a concept; grasping its sense involves grasping how, by inserting a name in its argument-place, we determine a truth-value as the value, for the corresponding argument, of the function which comprises the concept. There is no need to attribute to the sense of the predicate any further incompleteness by saying that it is itself a function.

The Determination of Reference by Sense

We cannot adopt the strong interpretation of the thesis that sense determines reference for some types of expression but not for others: it is all or none. To reject the strong interpretation altogether is to make the notion of reference wholly otiose in the theory of meaning. Reference—or, more generally, semantic value—is not an ingredient in meaning; but it, like the notion of truth, is a notion belonging to the theory of meaning. This is so precisely because the sense of an expression—which *is* a part, and often the whole, of its meaning—is given to us as a means of determining its reference (or its semantic value), that is to say, because sense determines reference in the way that the strong interpretation requires. If we reject the strong interpretation, then reference may still be a notion that can be satisfactorily explained; but it would have no particular interest, at least for the theory of meaning, since it would play no role in the meaning-theory. A meaning-theory aims to describe how the language functions; the most familiar model for such a theory is a representation of what a speaker of the language knows in virtue of being a speaker. If the strong interpretation fails, then not only would speakers not know the references of their words, but their understanding of the language would in no way involve their having any conception of an expression's having a reference, and an account could be given of what that understanding consisted in which likewise did not invoke the notion of reference. When it comes to sentences, that would mean that an understanding of a sentence need involve no conception of what it is for a sentence to be true, and an account could be given of what such an understanding consists in which would not appeal to the notion of truth or to any notion in terms of which truth could be explained. This is intuitively preposterous, for reasons yet to be explored; for the time being, we are merely assuming the contrary.

Once we allow that an understanding of a sentence involves a grasp of the condition for it to be true, then, provided that we agree that the understanding of a sentence is derived from an understanding of its parts and the way they are put together, it will be extremely hard for us to resist thinking that the understanding of the constituents of the sentence likewise involves a grasp of what determines their semantic values, since it is their semantic values which, by definition, determine the sentence as true or otherwise. Consider, for example, Frege's doctrine that proper names, and indeed all expressions, have, in intensional contexts, an indirect reference, namely, to their senses rather than to their ordinary referents. Given that Frege held that the referent of 'Napoleon' is a man, of 'Mont Blanc' a mountain, and so on, and given that he allowed that the appearance of proper names in intensional contexts was not illusory, this doctrine was mandatory for him: for a sentence containing a proper name is true or false according as the predicate is true or false of the referent of the name, and hence, if the truth-value changes when one name is replaced by another, the reference must change. But suppose that we think that the sense is not given as a means of determining the reference, and that the sense of a predicate is given as a function defined on the senses of proper names. Then the reference of a name has nothing to do with our understanding of sentences in which the name occurs, and there will therefore be no difference between our understanding of an extensional and of an intensional occurrence: the fact that the same name will have a different reference in the two types of occurrence will simply be irrelevant to our understanding of the sentences. The sense of the (complex) predicate that is yielded by extracting the name from an occurrence of either kind will, in each case, be a function defined on the sense of the name. If we take it as a function from senses of names to truth-values, then in both cases our means of recognising the sentence as true or as false will relate solely to the sense of the name, and the reference of the name will not come into it. We shall understand the sentence in which the name occurs in an extensional context and recognise it as true or as false in just the same way as we do with the sentence in which it occurs in an intensional context. The distinction between intensional and extensional contexts will not disappear, indeed: an extensional context will still be one where we can replace the name by any other with the same ordinary reference without change of truth-value. But we shall not in any way need to be aware that a context is extensional in order to understand it—indeed, we may not have the notion of the ordinary reference of a name.

If, instead, we take the sense of the predicate, as Geach does, as being given as a (presumably effective) function from senses of names to thoughts, then, again, we shall understand sentences of the two kinds in exactly the same way. As for how we then recognise them as true or as false, nothing has been said about that. Either it involves going back to determine the reference of the name, or it does not. If it does not, then, once more, an account of how we recognise the sentences as true or as false has no need to invoke the notion of reference, and there will be no discernible difference in how we do this, whether the name occurs in an extensional or in an intensional context. If, to determine the truth-value of the sentence, we do need to determine the reference of the name, then this must be done by appeal to the sense of the name, and we must allow, after all, that the sense of the name yields a means of recognising an object as its referent; but now the referent will depend not only on the sense but also on the context. Having determined the referent, we need, in order to determine the truth-value of the sentence, to determine whether or not the predicate is true of the referent of the name: so now we must also regard the sense of the predicate as yielding a means of determining whether or not it is true of objects of the appropriate kind, and nothing is left of our rejection of the strong interpretation of the thesis that sense determines reference.

If the strong interpretation of that thesis is correct, then the determination of the truth-value of the sentence goes via the determination of the referent of the name. The sense of the predicate must therefore relate solely to a function defined over *objects,* objects of the sort for which the name stands, not over senses. Once we have determined the object for which the name stands, the sense of the name has been fully exploited. The sentence will then be true if that object satisfies the condition determined by the sense of the predicate for the truth of the whole, and we need no longer consult the sense of the name in order to tell whether or not this condition is satisfied. That is why Frege saw such a radical difference in our mode of understanding sentences involving intensional contexts and those that do not.

The Semantic Base of a Meaning-Theory

The point under discussion originally arose in the exegesis of Frege. It has therefore been treated in terms of Frege's notion of reference, which carries with it the whole background of a two-valued semantics, rather than in terms of the more general notion of semantic value, which does not presuppose any particular semantic theory. It should nevertheless be clear that the argument is perfectly general, although, in those semantic theories which admit only a narrow gap between sense and semantic value, it is of much less importance. If it is correct that the meaning of a sentence is to be explained by reference to the notion of truth—to our grasp of what it is for the sentence to be true— then a large ingredient in the meaning of expressions which form constituents of sentences has to be taken as given to us as a means of determining the semantic values of those expressions. Not only is this point of view forced on us, but we have no grip at all on the notion of meaning if we do not acknowledge it. The selection of the appropriate semantic theory to serve as a base is therefore the first step in the construction of a meaning-theory, and, if it is wrong, the whole of the rest of the meaning-theory will be wrong. It is also the most momentous step: it is this choice which has repercussions both on which logical laws we should hold to be valid and on which metaphysical views we ought to favour. When the choice of a semantic base has been correctly made, we still face vast problems in constructing a meaning-theory—quite apart from that of first finding an adequate syntactic analysis of the language: we have to construct a theory of sense, a theory of force, and a theory of tone. But in the remainder of this book I shall largely ignore these, challenging and important as they are; I shall largely be concerned with the justification of the assumption so far made, that truth is, in the weak sense, the central notion of any meaning-theory, and, more particularly, with the question by what principles we should be guided in selecting a semantic theory, and the repercussions of that choice. In discussing this, we shall have to attend to the question which semantic theories make a theory of sense possible, but we shall not otherwise be concerned to ask what such a theory will be like.

We are not quite finished with the notion of sense, however. Yet another principle concerning sense which we may attribute to Frege is:

(vi) A stipulation of what the reference (semantic value) of an expression is to be confers on it a particular sense.

This can seem confusing at first; one has the inclination to say, 'I thought that sense determined reference, but that reference did not determine sense', and feel that the whole distinction has vanished. Since reference does not determine sense, a correct statement of the reference of some expression that already has a definite sense, in virtue of having an existing use in some actual language, may very well not display the sense that that expression has. But just because in stating the reference of the expression some one out of many possible, non-equivalent, means of stating it must be chosen, the specification of its reference will correspond to *a* sense which determines that reference. When we are concerned, not with an already existing expression, but with laying down, say, in a formalised language, what the interpretation of a newly introduced symbol is to be, the particular specification of the reference may be taken as conferring simultaneously a definite corresponding sense. That is not to say that the specification of the reference *states* what the sense is to be: all that it *states* is what the reference is to be; it is the particular manner that has been adopted for stating that reference that determines a definite sense. We may here adapt, in expounding a doctrine of Frege's, the famous distinction between *saying* and *showing* that Wittgenstein used in the *Tractatus:* the specification of the reference *says* what the reference is to be, and, by saying it in a particular manner, *shows* what the sense is to be.

That is *not* to say that in a meaning-theory nothing will be required save a specification of the semantic values of the words of the language, on the ground that, by formulating the statement of their semantic values in a particular manner, we thereby show what sense they have. To say that would be incorrect, since a meaning-theory is required to do more than merely show (to someone who understands the metalanguage in which it is formulated) what the senses of the words of the object-language are. There is a temptation to say that the meaning-theory is required not merely to *show* what senses the words have but also to *state* their senses. This would, however, be mystifying, since strictly speaking one cannot state the sense of an expression, save by saying that it is the same as that of some other expression already understood. What one can state, and what the meaning-theory is required to state, is what it is to attach a given sense to a word, what constitutes taking the word as having that sense. The meaning-theory must, ultimately, explain this by describing how a speaker manifests his attachment of a particular sense to the word, namely, by displaying his ability to use it correctly in some canonical range of contexts. We cannot, therefore, claim that a specification of the reference, or semantic value, of a word is in itself a possible contribution to the theory of sense. We can claim only that, whenever such a specification is stipulative—that is, to be understood as laying down what the reference is to be—then, given that we understand the terms in which the specification was framed, it also confers on the word a particular sense. There can be no justice in a complaint of the form, 'You have told us what the symbols of your language are to stand for, but you have not told us what they *mean*'.

This has consequences both for what a theory of sense is and for what a semantic theory is. Any meaning-theory for a natural language must take due account of the levels that exist within it: the understanding of certain parts of the language depends on the prior understanding of other parts. A speaker's understanding of some expressions of the language is verbalisable knowledge. In some cases, his knowledge may be required to be fully explicit. More frequently, such a requirement would be too strong; but the knowledge which he must have to understand the expression in question would still be verbalisable in the following sense. In order to come to understand the expression, a speaker must first understand the words that would be used in stating, in that language, what must be known if one is to understand the expression; moreover, a speaker who does understand it must be willing to acknowledge that statement as correct. The simplest case is that in which a word admits an explicit definition in the language, and it is plausible that any speaker who understands the word must have an explicit, or nearly explicit, knowledge of this definition, as, for example, the word 'aunt' admits the definition 'sister of a parent'. In all such cases, the meaning-theory discharges its task by simply stating what a speaker has to know in order to understand the word, without there being any special problem about saying in what that knowledge consists; what it consists in is shown by the account given of the speaker's understanding of that part of the language which would be needed to state the knowledge in question. When a purely verbal explanation of meaning is possible, we may legitimately speak of stating the sense of the word; and we may then say that all the meaning-theory has to do is to state that sense.

For a word to be of this kind, there must be some part of the language which a speaker must understand before he can understand that word. It follows that not all words and expressions can be of this kind, and hence that not all knowledge that constitutes grasping the sense of a word can be verbalisable knowledge. It is to words and expressions that are not of this kind that the various theses previously enunciated relate: it is their senses that the meaning-theory cannot attempt to state; the theory can attempt to state only what it is to know them. It is in giving an account of this knowledge that it must say not merely what is known but in what the knowledge consists. From this it is clear that what lies at the base of the meaning-theory is not a specification of a particular semantic interpretation, of the actual semantic values of expressions, but a semantic theory. We might otherwise be tempted to think of the semantic interpretation—what corresponds, in Frege, to a specification of the references of the words—as giving what the speakers must know, and the theory of sense as a kind of elaboration on this, stating in what that knowledge consisted. But this would be a misconception. In so far as a knowledge of the semantic value of an expression goes beyond what is required for an understanding of it, as on Frege's identity argument for the distinction between sense and reference, its semantic value is not an ingredient in its meaning, and the specification of it no part of a meaning-theory. In so far as the meaning-theory must assign specific interpretations to the words of the language, that will be accomplished entirely by the theory of sense. What lies at the base of the meaning-theory is, therefore, a general semantic theory, one that states what *kind* of semantic value an expression of each type is required to have: that is what forms an indispensable foundation for the theory of sense. This is why it is so utterly mistaken to suppose that the fact that a meaning-theorist is concerned only with a single interpretation relieves him of any of the labour involved in devising a semantic theory for the purposes of logic.

Skeletal Theories

A further consequence of principle (vi) is that we must view certain theories which, hitherto, we have been regarding as semantic theories as only the skeletons of such theories. Suppose that we have a particular formula of first-order classical logic, containing only a single, binary, predicate-letter, and we wish to demonstrate that it is satisfiable over the domain of the natural numbers. We therefore specify within standard two-valued semantics a particular interpretation, by laying down, in this or that manner, which ordered pairs of natural numbers are to satisfy the predicate-letter under our interpretation, and we demonstrate that, so interpreted, the formula comes out true. What goes for a stipulation of the fixed interpretation of a newly introduced symbol goes equally for the specification of a possible interpretation for a schematic letter. It would be absurd for someone to remark, 'You have shown that there is a possible extension of a binary predicate for which the corresponding sentence would be true, but we have still to discover an actual number-theoretic predicate which has the extension'. By stating the required extension, we have already specified a particular such predicate and have displayed the sense which one such predicate might bear. (At least, we have done so provided that two-valued semantics is a tenable semantic theory for arithmetical statements, that it forms the basis of an acceptable meaning-theory for the language of arithmetic. It would, of course, be a different matter if the objector were concerned with whether such a predicate could be expressed within some restricted language.)

But now consider the Beth trees. In a first flush of excitement after the discovery of a means of generalising the notion of a Beth tree so as to permit an intuitionistic proof of the completeness, with respect to the generalised Beth trees, of intuitionistic first-order predicate logic, a member of the Nijmegen school (which jointly made this discovery) gave an argument to show that the Beth trees provided *the* correct semantics for an intuitionistic language, and went on to claim that, by their use, it was possible to show that there is an interpretation, over the natural numbers, of the unary predicate-letter 'F' which will bring out true the formula '¬ ∀ x (Fx ∨ ¬ Fx)'. The interpretation he gives is the following. On the full binary tree, we take the atomic formula Fn to be verified at a node just in case, to reach that node from the vertex, we have to take at least $n + 1$ steps to the right, not necessarily in succession. That is, if we represent each node by a finite sequence of 0's and 1's, F1, for instance, will be verified at the node <1, 1>, and also at the nodes <0, 1, 1>, <1, 0, 1>, and at all other nodes represented by a sequence of which at least two terms are 1. It is then evident that at no node of level n is the formula 'Fn ∨ ¬ Fn' true, and hence that at no node is the formula '∀x (Fx ∨ ¬ Fx)' true; the formula '¬∀x (Fx ∨ ¬ Fx)' is, therefore, true at the vertex.

Now, if the Beth trees indeed constituted a complete formulation of a semantic theory, this example would certainly settle the matter. And yet the author of the example went on, in the very next sentence, to concede that he did not know of any actual number-theoretic predicate for which the formula holds. This is very strange. It would be absurd, in the classical case, to give an interpretation of a predicate-letter under which a formula came out true, and then to say that one did not know of actual predicate for which the formula held. Yet, in this case, the concession seems correct: the description of the interpretation on the Beth tree does not allow us to cite any specific number-theoretic predicate $A(x)$ such that $\ulcorner ¬ ∀x(A(x) ∨ ¬ A(x)) \urcorner$ is intuitionistically true. And that must mean that the Beth trees do not, after all, provide a fully fledged semantic theory. For otherwise a specification of the semantic value of a predicate, within the theory of Beth trees, *would* determine a definite sense for that predicate, in accordance with our general principle that a specific statement of the semantic value an expression is to have shows what the sense of that expression is to be. We are concerned here not with whether the Beth trees provide a semantic theory acceptable to intuitionists, who take the meanings of the logical constants to be those given by Heyting's intuitive explanation of them, but solely with whether they provide a semantic theory at all.

The particular Beth tree specified above represents our situation, in respect of verifying sentences of the form 'Fn', when we are able to assert certain complex sentences involving the predicate 'Fx'. As usual, the nodes below the vertex represent the possibilities now open that we may later verify atomic sentences involving that predicate. The complex sentences we are being assumed to be in a position to assert are:

(i) $\forall x \, (Fx \rightarrow \forall y \, (y < x \rightarrow Fy))$,
(ii) $\forall x \, \neg \neg Fx$

and

(iii) $\neg \forall x \, Fx$.

By (i), we can never verify 'Fn' unless we have previously verified 'Fm' for each $m < n$; by (ii), we can never verify '$\neg$Fn' for any n; and by (iii), taken together with (i), we can never verify 'Fn' for more than finitely many n. Given the requirement that we should be able to assert (i), (ii), and (iii), the Beth tree represents the most general possible situation; but given that there is a predicate which satisfies these conditions, there is no reason whatever why it should be unique. To represent ourselves as knowing all three propositions, and as knowing no stronger proposition expressible by means only of the predicate 'F' and of '<', no doubt restricts the sense that the predicate can bear but certainly does not determine its sense. Furthermore, no reason is apparent why we should feel assured that there is *any* predicate that satisfies these conditions. The Beth trees provide an admirable means of summarising the possibilities of verifying statements constructed with a given, limited, vocabulary, once we have understood that vocabulary and seen what those possibilities are; but no guarantee has been given that any Beth tree we like to construct will represent a genuinely possible situation. We can, indeed, show how we may know conditions (i) and (ii) to be satisfied, by construing 'F' as itself having a suitable internal complexity. If, for some predicate 'G', we take 'Fx' to be '$\forall y \, (y \leq x \rightarrow Gy)$', then it is evident that condition (i) must hold, namely, that we cannot verify 'Fn' until we have verified 'Fm' for each $m < n$. If, further, we take 'Gy', for some predicate 'Hy', to be equivalent to 'H$y \lor \neg$Hy', then we shall never be able to assert '$\neg$Gn' for any n, and therefore cannot ever assert '$\neg$Fn' either, so that condition

(ii) is satisfied. The condition that we shall never be able to assert '$\forall x\, Fx$' now comes out as the condition that we can never assert

$$\forall x\, \forall y\, (y \leq x \to Hy \lor \neg Hy),$$

which is equivalent to requiring the truth of '$\neg \forall x\, (Hx \lor \neg Hx)$'; and we do not have at hand a way of specifying further the internal structure of 'Hx' so as to guarantee that this condition is satisfied. Indeed, since the whole object was to demonstrate the existence of a number-theoretic predicate 'Fx' for which

$$\neg \forall x\, (Fx \lor \neg Fx)$$

is true, it is apparent that the procedure has merely gone round in a circle and accomplished nothing.

Such considerations do not show the theory of Beth trees to be no more than a purely algebraic theory of interpretations. Rather, they show the theory to be a skeleton or abstract form of a semantic theory. What is needed, in order to put flesh on the skeleton and so transform it into a genuine semantic theory, is to provide a means of *identifying* the various possible states of information represented by the nodes of a tree otherwise than by reference to their position on the tree and the atomic sentences taken as verified at those nodes. This means that we should be able to specify, for each atomic sentence, in what a verification of it will consist. Such a specification will then enable us to recognise which combinations of atomic sentences may be verified together, and, given that any particular such combination has been verified, which further combinations are still possible; this array of possibilities can then be represented by a Beth tree. The Beth tree itself, however, gives only the abstract structure of the situation; what will determine specific senses for the predicates and sentences will be the statement of what, concretely, is to count as a verification of each atomic sentence.

The situation here is the same as with a possible-worlds semantics for a language involving modalities. The most devoted proponent of such a semantics does not suppose that, by merely describing some abstract structure of possible worlds, and laying down the extensions of the predicate-letters of some formula over the domains of those possible worlds, we have thereby associated definite senses with those predicate-letters. The abstract structure is not enough: we have to say, specifically, *which* possible worlds we are speaking of, that is, to provide some means of identifying them other than their position in the abstract structure and the interpretation, relative to them, of the predicate-letters. The point is worth dwelling on, because there is a sharp difference here between two-valued semantics and possible-worlds semantics. Suppose we are giving an interpretation of the predicate-letters of some formula of classical logic, and we take as the domain the set of all animals presently existing on Earth, laying down that 'Fx' is to be true of a member of the domain if and only if it is a dog. Then the manner of specifying the extension of the predicate-letter under this interpretation, in this case a very simple one, displays a sense which would determine that extension, namely, the sense which the predicate 'x is a dog' bears in the metalanguage (English). Now suppose that we want to give a counter-example to some formula of modal predicate logic, and we assume that besides the actual world w there are two worlds w_1 and w_2, each possible relatively to w and to each other, but with w possible relatively to neither. The domain of w is again to be the set of all existing terrestrial animals, and the domains of w_1 and w_2 are to be the same (or isomorphic). Suppose, first, that we specify the interpretation of a predicate-letter 'F' by taking it to be true, in w, of all animals with brown eyes, in w_1 of everything of which it is true in w except of Rover, and in w_2 of everything of which it is true in w and, in addition, of Felix. Then we may be tempted to think that this specification determines a possible sense for 'Fx', namely, the sense of 'x has brown eyes', and, in part, an identification of the possible worlds w_1 and w_2: w_1 is a world in which every animal save Rover has eyes of the same colour as they in fact are, but in which Rover's eyes are not brown, while w_2 is a world in which every animal save Felix has eyes of the colour they in fact are, and Felix's eyes are brown. But now let us change the example, and have 'F' true in w just of those animals that are dogs, while again in w_1 it is true of all those things save Rover of which it is true in w, and in w_2 it is true of Felix, together with all those things of which it is true in w. Now is the sense of 'x is a dog' a possible sense for 'Fx', and is w_1 a world in which Rover is not a dog and w_2 a world in which Felix is one? Here we run up against the notion of essential properties. *Can* we meaningfully say, 'Suppose Rover were a cat'? Or 'a yacht' or 'an island in the Caribbean'? It is plain that some limitation on the range of intelligible supposition is required, whether imposed by nominal or by real essence. To accept such limitations is to restrict the range of admissible descriptions of possible worlds, not to rule out such interpretations of a predicate-letter over those worlds as that which was specified above; for there is no reason to deny that there may be some sense for a unary predicate such that, as things are, that predicate is true of all dogs, and only of them, but such that it might not have been true of some dog, or, alternatively, might have been true of some cat. Rather, what follows from the imposition of such limitations is that we cannot take the means that is employed to specify the extension of a predicate in the actual world as showing the sense of that predicate. For just this reason, we also cannot take the specification of an interpretation of a vocabulary, over a number of arbitrarily labelled possible worlds, as itself providing a means of identifying those possible worlds.

The natural idea that, since the sense of an expression is not determined just by what things it actually applies to, we may take it as determined by what things it *would* apply to in any possible state of affairs is open to various objections. In the first place, it will work only if we construe 'possible' as meaning 'possible so far as that knowledge goes which constitutes our knowledge of the language', that is, 'not excluded by our knowledge of the language'. If we employ any other notion of possibility, for instance 'not demonstrably false by purely a priori reasoning', and, particularly, if we postulate that possibility is not an epistemic notion at all, then we shall arrive by this means at some concept of intension that does not answer to the purpose for which we need the notion of sense. Moreover, the idea that the divergence in meaning between, say, 'person' and 'human being' is shown by the fact that there are at least possible circumstances in which the extension of the former would be wider than that of the latter was never intended to imply that we could display that divergence in meaning by simply stipulating a possible state of affairs as being one in which there were persons who were not human, since, obviously, in order to know what state of affairs has been specified one would have already to know the meanings of the expressions. Rather, the idea was that the meanings would emerge from a statement of the extensions of the terms in various independently describable possible circumstances. Thus a semantic interpretation of a vocabulary, in terms of possible worlds, cannot purport to determine corresponding senses for the expressions in that vocabulary, so long as the possible worlds are only arbitrarily labelled, and we know only the abstract structure of the relation of relative possibility between them. To obtain something sufficient to characterise their sense, we should have to add some means of identifying the different possible worlds otherwise than by using that vocabulary.

Here the same question arises as in the case of the Beth trees; do we have a guarantee that there exists a set of possible worlds corresponding to any abstract structure we care to describe and a range of predicates having, over these possible worlds, whatever extension we choose to specify? For example, can we form the three-element set of possible worlds that was instanced earlier? Are there two possible worlds, each possible relative to each other, but relative to which the actual world is not possible? To answer this, we should have to know not only how a possible world can be identified or described but also what, precisely, the relation of relative possibility is. Possible-worlds semantics, like the theory of Beth trees, provides only the skeleton of a semantic theory, not a genuine, full-fledged one. This fact is unimportant for the purposes of logic, for proofs of soundness or of completeness, since for such purposes only the abstract structure matters (though a completeness proof may be affected by which abstract structures represent genuine possibilities and are therefore admissible). But, although the mathematical character of such a theory remains the same, its interest (and the interest of proofs of soundness or of completeness relative to it) depend heavily upon whether it is a genuine semantic theory or not, that is, on whether a meaning-theory can be constructed on it as foundation. Given my thesis that every meaning-theory must have a semantic theory as its base, a base on which will rest the theory of sense, with the theory of force as an essential buttress and the theory of tone as an ornamental surround, it is incumbent on me to make clear how much, within the meaning-theory, is to belong to the base, that is, to the semantic part of the theory as the word 'semantic' is here being used.

The Concept of Truth and Its Habitat

So far we have *assumed* that truth is, in the weak sense, a central notion for any meaning-theory, an assumption which many writers on this subject are content to leave as intuitively obvious. We have, however, seen enough to be clear that truth is not a single, univocal notion, explicated once for all time by Tarski, but a cluster of different notions, adhering together by being governed by various closely related principles. We have therefore to ask from where we get the notion, or the cluster of notions, and what we want it for.

A stock argument was formerly used by philosophers against the correspondence theory, the coherence theory, and any other theory attempting to characterise in some general manner what it is for something to be true. This argument was to the effect that no such general characterisation is possible, because to determine the condition that has to be satisfied for a particular sentence to be true is to fix its meaning, or is at least an indispensable ingredient in the determination of its meaning. It is clear, however, that there is no a priori ground to accept the premiss of this argument, which amounts, in our terms, to saying that truth is the central notion of a meaning-theory in the *strong* sense, that the meaning of a sentence is directly given, at least in part, by the way its truth-condition is determined. If, for instance, the correct meaning-theory for a language were one whose base was a games-theoretic semantics of the kind advocated by Hintikka, for which the semantic values of the sentences are not given in terms of any variant whatever of the notion of truth (save that a notion of truth is assumed for atomic sentences), it is evident that we should be able to give what the argument purports to show impossible, namely, a quite general characterisation of the condition for an arbitrary sentence to be true: it is true if a player uttering it has a winning strategy. The semantic theory does not merely permit but *requires* such a characterisation.

There was, nevertheless, something right about the criticism of philosophical theories of truth such as the correspondence theory embodied in the stock argument against them; only the claim made was too strong. The criticism of such theories ought to have been, not that they attempted to give a general characterisation of truth, but that they did so without the background of an account of meaning, of the outlines of a meaning-theory, which alone could provide the terms in which it would be possible to state the general condition for a sentence to be true. Indeed, the traditional theories of truth advertised themselves as explaining the predicate 'is true' as applied, not to *sentences*, but to *propositions*. What proposition a sentence expresses obviously depends upon its meaning; and so these theories assumed that we could grasp the meaning of sentences of our language and also, presumably, give a philosophical analysis of the concept of meaning in advance of knowing how the concept of truth applied to those sentences. Their proponents failed to realise that the concepts of meaning and of truth can only be explained together.

From this it is apparent that the concept of truth belongs to the theory of meaning; to explain the concept of truth, we have to give an account of that in which the meaning of a sentence consists. But there are two distinct ways in which this might be so. That envisaged by the stock criticism of philosophical theories of truth was that truth is related to a proposition as winning is to a game. There can be no description of any particular game, not itself invoking the concept of winning, from which one can derive, by appeal to some general characterisation of what winning an arbitrary game consists in, what constitutes winning that particular game. What makes this clear is that there are distinct games which differ *only* in what constitutes winning. If this is a correct analogy, then any account of meaning must *invoke* the concept of truth: meaning must, in part at least, be *given* by determining the conditions for a sentence to be true. But we have no proof that the analogy is correct, because we are not in a position to say that there are non-equivalent sentences whose meanings differ *only* in what constitutes the condition for them to be true. A natural suggestion would be a pair consisting of a sentence and its negation; the operation of negation compares with the result of reversing the conditions for winning and losing a game. But this is not the only way to vary conditions for winning and losing a game. One can keep constant the rules of play—those which specify the initial position and how it is arrived at and those which specify what counts as a legal play or move—while imposing what criteria one likes for determining who, if anyone, has won; the rules governing winning and losing form a separate compartment of the rules of the game. Nothing similar occurs with sentences; one cannot conceive of a specification of the meaning of a sentence which provides *everything but* the conditions for its truth or falsity. A defender of the stock argument might protest that this shows only that the connection between the meaning of a sentence and the criterion for its truth is even more intimate than that between a game and the criterion for winning it; but he still needs to make this out and cannot rely upon an analogy that has proved to be faulty.

The alternative possibility is that the concept of truth is related to that of meaning as that of a winning strategy is to that of a game; here only an *analogy* is intended, not an *application* such as that made by Hintikka. What constitutes a winning strategy depends upon, and only upon, the rules of the game. In describing a game, however, we do not need to invoke the notion of a strategy at all: we can characterise the notion of a winning strategy in terms of the general concepts, such as those of a 'play' or 'move', of an 'opponent' and of 'winning' the game, that are used in describing it. If *this* is a correct analogy, then a meaning-theory will not need itself to invoke the concept of truth; but a characterisation of that concept will have to appeal to the concepts that are employed in the meaning-theory.

The condition for a sentence to be true surely depends solely upon the meaning of that sentence. At least, this seems clear provided that it is possible to disentangle meaning from the background information which bears upon our propensity to judge the sentence as true or not true, and can likewise so disentangle the notion of the condition for the truth of the statement. If we cannot, then the notions of meaning and of truth-conditions will be contaminated in like degree, so that they will remain correlative to one another. Other things than truth-conditions depend upon meaning, however. For instance, it depends upon the meaning of a sentence what constitutes evidence for it, or, again, what a speaker commits himself to in accepting it as true. For every feature of a sentence or expression which depends upon its meaning, a successful meaning-theory must display this dependence; and, just as for truth, there are for each such feature only two possible ways in which this can be done. Either the meaning-theory will represent the meaning as being given, in whole or part, by the way in which that feature is determined for the particular expression; or else the meaning will be given in some different way, but there will be some general characterisation of that feature in terms of whichever other feature has been chosen as that by means of which the meaning is given. In the second case, this characterisation will constitute a uniform manner of deriving the former feature from the latter. Now, with some relatively trivial exceptions, it is highly repugnant to us to suppose that different features of expressions, both intuitively dependent upon their meaning, are not systematically connected—for instance, that even after it has been determined under what conditions a sentence is true there remains some room in which we are free to decide what we shall choose to count as evidence for its truth. It is for this reason that it has been so popular among philosophers to suppose that there is just *one* type of feature of a sentence which supplies the central notion of the theory of meaning. Such conceptions are often summarised in slogans, such as 'To know the meaning of a sentence is to know the condition for it to be true', 'The meaning of a sentence is the method of its verification', and the like. On such a conception, the meaning-theory will consist of two parts: one which describes how particular words contribute to determining this central feature of any sentence in which they occur and how this feature is determined for any sentence in accordance with its composition; and the other which displays the uniform connection between this central feature and every other feature which is dependent upon meaning.

It is clear that we need to distinguish between a feature of an expression which is *dependent upon* its meaning and one that is actually *part of* that meaning. This distinction underlies our intuitive inclination to take meaning as something that we *confer* on an expression, to treat saying that some feature of it is part of its meaning as involving that it might have lacked, or could be deprived of, that feature. In so far as this is taken literally as a historical account of how, in general, meanings are acquired or modified, it is obviously open to telling criticism, and no doubt some varieties of conventionalism depend upon supposing that it can be taken almost literally: but it has its origin in a perception of the distinction between being merely dependent on and actually being part of the meaning of an expression. If some feature of an expression is merely dependent on its meaning, then it did not have to be conferred and cannot be altered; that is, it cannot be altered without altering something else to which it is responsible, and from which it derived. If, however, it is actually part of the meaning, then, in the sense in which it is we who make our words mean what they mean, we could alter it without there being anything else which we should, as it were, have to alter first.

An Inconclusive Test Case

There is, however, a disanalogy between truth-conditions and other features of sentences. Consider the case of a child who knows what the natural numbers are, and who knows how to add them and find their squares, but has never seen a mathematical proof (as opposed to computation). The child hears someone assert, 'Every number is the sum of four squares'. He has not the remotest idea on what basis such an assertion might be made; perhaps he supposes that it has been tested for a large number of natural numbers and never found to fail; more likely, it will just not occur to him to wonder how adults know things like that. Does the child understand the statement that he has heard? This may seem a good test case for deciding between the conception of meaning as given by truth-conditions and that which takes meaning as given by knowing what counts as a ground for assertion. If, on the one hand, you favour the former conception, you will be inclined to say that the child certainly understands the statement, since he knows what it is for it to be true: after all, he can believe the statement, accept it as true, and apply it; he might even win bets as a result of applying it to particular numbers. He does not, indeed, yet know how we come to recognise such a statement as true, but that does not impair his grasp of what it *is* for it to be true, nor, therefore, his grasp of its meaning. If, on the other hand, you favour a conception according to which an understanding of a mathematical statement involves a knowledge, not of an actual proof of it but of the kind of thing necessary for a proof of it, then you will be disposed to say that the child has, as yet, only a partial understanding of the statement and will fully understand it only when he has learned more mathematics.

The opposition between the two views has not yet been rightly stated. If you take the second view, you will *not* say that, while the child indeed knows the condition for the statement to be true, that knowledge does not constitute understanding it. Rather, you will say that it is only an illusion on our part that the child knows what it is for the statement to be true; you will say that we have no legitimate notion of truth for mathematical statements other than that of our being able to prove them, and that therefore the child has yet to learn what the truth of such a statement consists in. But the proponent of the first view does not say that, by knowing the condition for the truth of the statement, the child already knows implicitly what counts as a proof of it: he readily admits that the child does *not* have any idea as yet what a proof of such a statement is like. The opposition between the two views does not concern whether truth is, in the *weak* sense, the central notion of a correct meaning-theory—both are agreed that it is. It is a disagreement about whether truth is the central notion in the *strong* sense, whether it is the notion in terms of which the semantic value of a sentence is to be given. Both sides are agreed that one knows the meaning of a statement just in case one knows what it is for it to be true. They differ over whether truth is an irreducible notion, or one to be explained in terms of something else.

The relation between the central and the secondary notions is different on the two accounts. If what is in the strong sense the central notion of the meaning-theory is that of proof or, more generally, of evidence for the truth of a statement, then truth is to be explained in terms of it: namely, as consisting in our having evidence for the statement, or in there being evidence of a kind such that, if we knew of it, we should acknowledge it as such, or something of that sort. If the meaning of a statement is given in terms of what is to count as evidence for it, there is no question of our having an imperfect or incorrect notion of truth for the statement (except in so far as we become philosophically confused): the only legitimate notion of truth we can have for it must be explained in terms of the existence of evidence.

Conversely, if truth is the central notion in the strong sense, if meaning is given directly in terms of the condition for the statement to be true, then the way in which we are able to recognise the statement as true must be explained in terms of our grasp of its meaning; what we take as showing the statement to be true must be derived from our understanding of it, because it is dependent on that meaning, and not an independently assignable part of the meaning. (If it were the latter, the child would *not* fully understand the statement.) In particular, the forms of deductive reasoning that we employ must be open to justification in the light of the meanings of the statements involved, meanings which were not given in terms of how they figure in deductive arguments; the child's understanding of the mathematical statement preceded his knowledge of how it could be proved, and, when he sees a proof, his recognition of its validity will be derived from his understanding of the statements that appear in it. This time, however, there is room for our apprehension of the means of coming to recognise the statement as true to be imperfect, or even incorrect. Guided by a grasp of the meanings of mathematical statements that does not depend on, and can in principle precede, any knowledge of the practice of giving mathematical proofs, we may become aware that new forms of reasoning, which it had not previously occurred to us to use, are truth-preserving; such a change will not induce any shift in the meanings of our statements, but will be made in the light of our grasp of the meanings they have always had. Indeed, in that light we might also come to see that principles of reasoning we had been accustomed to use do not, after all, transmit truth from premises to conclusion. Thus, on such a view, forms of reasoning, or other means of coming to recognise a statement as true, that we employ in practice are not determinative of the meanings we attach to our statements but are subject to criticism as well as justification in the light of those meanings. Actual practice is only an uncertain guide to meaning: what meaning determines, on this view, is not how we do reason, or what we do count as evidence, but only how we should reason, and what we should count as evidence.

A Tentative Conclusion

It thus appears that, from any standpoint, knowing what a sentence means will be taken as entailing knowing what it is for it to be true: the objections to regarding truth as the central notion of a meaning-theory all relate to taking it as the central notion in the strong (not in the weak) sense. That does not, indeed, prove that truth is the central notion of a meaning-theory, even in the weak sense: one might want to jettison the concept of truth altogether or, rather, restrict it to its employment *within* the language and explain meaning in some quite different way which did not make use of the concept of truth at all. Such a project seems to be what Wittgenstein had in mind in the *Philosophical Investigations,* but whether this amounted to a denial that any systematic meaning-theory for a natural language was possible, or only to a proposal to build a totally new kind of meaning-theory, we are hard put to it to say. Most kinds of meaning-theory that we envisage would work equally well if we were a kind of intelligent trees, able to observe the world and to communicate with one another but otherwise powerless to affect the course of events; and this was precisely what Wittgenstein objected to about them, believing as he did that language can be explained only as interwoven with all our other activities. If most accounts of meaning are right, we might say, that, if a lion could talk, we should understand him perfectly well. The language-games that Wittgenstein offers as illustrative of his conception of language suggest that he did think a systematic account of how language functions to be possible, since, in describing them, he does give a completely systematic account of the functioning of a miniature language. Nevertheless, it is difficult to see how we are meant to extend this model to the languages we actually have, since what distinguished the language-games is that, in them, language is used only as an adjunct to some one specific activity, whereas, however dependent the significance of our utterances may be on their bearing on our non-linguistic activities, the striking thing about our language is that its employment is not, for the most part, connected with any one such activity. What has here been urged has not amounted to a proof that truth is an essential notion for a meaning-theory, and, therefore, that a meaning-theory must have a semantic theory as its base; but we have not been given even a sketch of what a meaning-theory would be like that was of a quite different character.

chapter 7

The Origin and Role of the Concept of Truth

The Root Notion of Truth

What do we need the concept of truth for, and where do we get it from? Without doubt, the source of the concept lies in our general conception of the linguistic practice of assertion. It is fundamental to this practice that an assertion may be judged as correct or incorrect: it may be accepted as correct, or rejected as incorrect, by a hearer; the speaker may subsequently be compelled to withdraw it as incorrect, or the hearer to acknowledge it as correct. This is, of course, to appeal to an intuitive conception of the correctness or incorrectness of assertions, without offering any analysis of it. That analysis will be given by the part of the meaning-theory which makes up the theory of force, which will describe the various linguistic practices of making assertions, requests, and so forth. The description of the practice of assertion will, among other things, delineate the situation in which a speaker is compelled to withdraw an assertion as incorrect, and that in which a hearer is compelled to acknowledge it as correct. The description must aim, as far as possible, to be uniform over the senses of different assertoric sentences. The explanations of those senses, as given in the theory of sense, will issue in an account of what a speaker's grasp of the condition for each sentence to be true consists in. It is, therefore, here that the connection will be established between the notion of truth and the practice of making assertions.

Our present task is not to formulate such a description of assertion but to enquire what features of our linguistic practice make it plausible that the way the sense of a sentence is given to us may be characterised in terms of the notion of its being true. Given that the application of the concept of truth to particular sentences is to be specified by the theory of sense, we have to ask how that concept will figure within the theory of force. It is plain that any account of the practice of assertion will supply us with a general notion of the correctness and incorrectness of assertions. The root notion of truth is then that a sentence is true just in case, if uttered assertorically, it would have served to make a correct assertion. From this we derive what was earlier called the 'underlying principle' of the Tarski (T) schema, namely, that the specific content of any assertion is given by what is taken as rendering it correct, that is, what renders true the sentence used to make the assertion. From this we may go on to extend the notion of truth to non-assertoric utterances, in a manner not customary in everyday speech. This extension will enable us to explain in a similar way what gives them their specific content—what determines what command has been given, what question asked, and the like.

Thus the content of an assertion is taken as determined by the condition for it to be correct, and this in turn is identified with the condition for the sentence to be true: just as we know what bet has been made when we know when the bettor wins and when he loses, so we know what has been asserted when we know in what case the assertion is correct. This is not to say that each assertion amounts to asserting that the sentence uttered is true. We need to maintain a distinction betweeen asserting that a conference on semantics is taking place in Brescia and asserting that the sentence, 'A conference on semantics is taking place in Brescia', is true, parallel to that between knowing the proposition and knowing that the sentence is true. It is sometimes alleged that what makes a given notion a notion *of truth* is that it satisfies all instances of the (T) schema. This is wrong: what is required is that it accord with the principle that the truth-conditions of an utterance determine its content. If a constructivist proposes that the only intelligible notion of truth we can have for mathematical statements is that under which they are true just in case we presently possess a proof of them, he is offering a characterisation of truth for which the (T) schema fails, since truth, so understood, does not commute with negation. What nevertheless makes it not improper for him to claim it as a notion of truth is that he can still say that a mathematical assertion is correct just in case the asserted statement is true. The same holds good for one who takes a neutralist position about the future and holds that the only notion of truth we can have for future-tense statements is that under which a statement is true if it accords with present tendencies.

How the Concept of Truth Diverges from that of Correctness

For all that, what gives the concept of truth its most characteristic features are precisely those considerations which lead us to distinguish a sentence's being true from the general notion of the justifiability of an assertion made by means of it. These considerations are very various in character. They can be classified under two main heads: (i) those that relate to the need for distinguishing between the truth of a statement and the existence of grounds for making it; and (ii) those that relate to the distinction between what is (literally) said and the point of saying it.

If we already have a notion of truth, and if this notion is such that there is no guarantee that for any true statement there must exist a ground for asserting it, and no guarantee that there will be a point in doing so, these distinctions force themselves upon us. That is to say, *given* a concept of truth, it is unproblematic how we come to distinguish between a statement's being true and there being grounds for asserting it. The question before us is the opposite. The concepts of the truth of a statement, the ground of an assertion, and the point of making one indeed belong to our ordinary linguistic repertoire; they are nevertheless second-level concepts, used to comment on our employment of our language. We can therefore perfectly well imagine people equipped with a language containing our whole first-level vocabulary, but without explicit means of expressing these second-level ones. Those who had such a language would grasp the significance of any utterance in that language: they would know what, by making any such utterance, a speaker intended to convey. Now we, deploying our second-level concepts, should say that part of what a speaker communicates to a hearer by means of an assertoric utterance is that he believes himself to have grounds for what he asserts; and we should add that a further part of what he communicates is that he takes it to be worth saying in that context, in other words, that the context is such that it can serve one of the possible purposes of making it. From *our* standpoint, therefore, what is conveyed by an assertoric utterance—beyond the bare fact that the speaker made that assertion at that time—is multiple: that the statement is true; that the speaker thought he had grounds for it; and that he thought there was a point in saying it. The speakers of the first-level language are innocent of such distinctions: they merely apprehend all that anyone making an assertion in that language wishes to convey. The question before us is why, when we reflect upon our use of language, and come to operate with second-level notions, we feel forced to distinguish these ingredients in what is communicated. Why do we not include them all in the content of an assertoric utterance? We differentiate between diverse ways in which such an utterance may be at fault: it may be false, even though well-grounded; or groundless, even if true; or pointless, even if true and well-grounded. What impels us to draw these distinctions?

The point of raising this question is not to call the distinctions into doubt but to understand how they arise. The root notion of truth is that of the correctness of an assertion. At this basic level, however, the notion of correctness is undifferentiated: we invoked the distinction between a correct and an incorrect assertion as the minimum required for a grasp of the significance of an assertoric utterance. To make an assertion for which one has no grounds is, save in quite particular circumstances, to violate linguistic convention, and therefore to say something incorrect, in the basic sense of 'incorrect'. Likewise, to say one thing when there is no point in saying it rather than something more usual in those circumstances can be misleading if it prompts the hearers to suppose a point that does not exist; it, too, is therefore incorrect in the general sense. We accordingly need to ask what features of our linguistic practice make it necessary to distinguish these different ways in which an assertoric utterance may be incorrect. By so doing, we shall bring to light fundamental components of our concept of truth. As long as we remain content with simply reiterating, without justification, that a grasp of the meaning of a sentence consists in a knowledge of its truth-conditions, and, especially, if we suppose that we have taken a significant step by *replacing* the notion of meaning by that of truth-conditions, so that the question of justification cannot even be raised, we shall fail to ask ourselves why we need a notion of truth that allows us to draw these distinctions instead of resting content to understand truth in such a way that everything that is conveyed by an assertion becomes part of the condition for the truth of the sentence.

The distinction between the truth of a statement and the existence of grounds for it is principally forced upon us by the behaviour of the sentence as it occurs as a constituent of complex sentences. This is very clear for sentences in the future tense. If I assert, 'I shall be in New York next week', my hearer's understanding of my statement is very much conditioned by his knowledge of the kind of ground I may have for it: indeed, there is a strong temptation to say that the utterance may bear two possible senses, according as it is meant as an expression of my intention or as a prediction. But if the existence of such grounds were taken to be included in the condition for its truth, then we could not explain the content of or truth-condition for such sentences as 'I shall be in either New York or Chicago next week' and 'If I am in New York next week, I shall meet my friends' in terms of the truth-conditions of their constituents. 'If I am in New York next week, . . .' does not mean either 'If I now intend to be in New York next week, . . .' or 'If it now looks as though I shall be in New York next week, . . .'—even though the conditional utterance as a whole may have the force of 'I intend to meet my friends if I am in New

York next week' or of 'It looks as though I shall meet my friends if I am in New York next week'. (By contrast, where intuitionistic truth is equated with provability, the truth of a disjunction is to be explained as the truth of one or other disjunct; and the condition stated by the antecedent of a conditional is that there be a proof of the sentence in that clause: in neither case is there a gap between assertoric content and ingredient sense.)

For statements about the future, we have a choice. If we want to explain disjunctions directly in terms of the truth of the disjuncts, or to take the condition expressed by the antecedent of a conditional to be the condition for it to be true, then we are compelled to distinguish between the truth of a sentence and the existence of grounds for it; such a distinction thus becomes mandatory if truth is to be, in the strong sense, the central notion of our meaning-theory. If we adopt this option, then, on pain of having to admit two independent ingredients of the assertoric content of a sentence, some account must be forthcoming of how we determine, from the meaning of a sentence as given by its truth-conditions, what we count as evidence for it.

We have an alternative, however: to explain the logical operations in terms of some semantic theory in which the semantic value of a sentence is not simply truth or the lack of it. In this way we may be able to avoid making a distinction between the truth of a statement and the existence of grounds for asserting it. The simplest means of doing this is to appeal to a relativised notion of truth. Thus, for statements about the future, we may consider all possible future histories of the world that are, in some suitable sense, consistent with the present evidence; we may then take the meaning of each sentence in the future tense to be given in terms of its truth or falsity relative to each such possible future history. We can proceed to explain the sentential operators by the two-valued truth-tables relativised to each possible future history, and truth *simpliciter*—absolute truth—as truth in all possible future histories. Absolute truth would then attach only to sentences for which there was present evidence, and no need would arise to distinguish between truth, in the absolute sense, and the existence of evidence.

This semantic device does not remove that need altogether, however; it merely renders the distinction less stark. The term 'evidence' is ambiguous in this context: it might be taken to mean either 'evidence (whether known to us or not)' or 'evidence in our possession'. The notion of a possible future world history, consistent with the present evidence, can be construed according to either interpretation of 'evidence'. When it is construed in accordance with the first interpretation, we must admit a distinction between truth and actual grounds for assertion, as opposed to what would be a ground if we knew of it.

Even when it is the second interpretation of 'evidence' that governs our conception of a possible future world history, it will be necessary to admit a distinction between the truth of a statement and the individual speaker's being justified in making it; without it, we shall relapse into a version of solipsism. Moreover, if absolute truth is to be a persisting quality, the term 'consistent' must be so interpreted that a future in which a given event does not take place is nevertheless consistent with present evidence that it will, whenever that evidence falls short of being conclusive—for instance, when it consists of an intention (whether the speaker's or another's) that may be frustrated or abandoned. This need not be understood in the sense in which no evidence for a future event can be conclusive, in view of its bare logical compatibility with that event's non-occurrence; we may regard the evidence as conclusive whenever it renders the empirical probability of the event only negligibly lower than 1. The upshot of all this is that no semantic theory can obviate the necessity for drawing some distinction between the truth of a statement in the future tense and the existence of present evidence for it; but, contrary to what one might at first think, the need for an account of the sentential operators, as applied to such statements, cannot of itself force upon us a realist conception of their truth and falsity according to which each of them is determinately either true or false.

The choice between the two alternatives is not a matter of indifference: it relates to genuine metaphysical divergences, in this case divergences about the reality of the future. We have here to recognise that, within the everyday use of natural language, appeals are made to the concept of truth which cannot be accounted for as invoking only that notion of truth which belongs to the object-language; they can by no means be explained by appeal to the 'disquotational' principle that 'The sun will rise tomorrow' (said today) is true just in case the sun will rise tomorrow. Rather, they must be seen as embodying an inchoate conception of the relation of truth and meaning, a vague outline of a meaning-theory. A great part of what we take as belonging to the intuitive notion of truth derives from the perceived need for distinguishing truth from the existence of evidence. That this perception concerns the behaviour of sentences as constituents of more complex sentences is something we are not normally aware of; still less are we aware that it is motivated by a disposition to prefer a notion of truth that distributes over disjunction and the conditional to one that does not.

It is the behaviour of sentences when they figure as antecedents of conditionals that most powerfully influences what we take to be the 'intuitive' conception of truth. What most vividly testifies to this is our uncertainty about how to apply the notion of truth to conditionals themselves, that is, to the indicative conditionals of natural language. Philosophers argue about the circumstances in which such conditionals are to be called 'true'. In the light of the thesis that to grasp the meaning of a sentence is to know its truth-condition, this seems surprising; for the philosophers surely know how to use the indicative conditional form in their language, and therefore can be presumed to know what indicative conditionals mean. Their disputes are not about how those conditionals are to be used but solely about when they should be called 'true'. An enthusiast for the disquotational principle might suppose that we could settle the matter by appeal to the (T) schema. This tells us two things: (a) that if the statement 'If an election is held, the Socialists will win' is true, then, if an election is held, the Socialists will win; and (b) that if the Socialists will win if an election is held, then the statement 'If an election is held, the Socialists will win' is true. Principle (a) is intuitively clear; and from it we might expect, by contraposition, to learn in what circumstances the conditional statement will not be true. Unfortunately, we do not know how to perform the contraposition. Performed mechanically, the operation yields the conclusion that if it is not the case that the Socialists will win if an election is held, then the conditional statement is not true: but we do not know how to interpret this, because it is not our normal practice to apply negation to an entire conditional statement, and we can therefore attach no precise sense to the clause beginning 'it is not the case that . . .'.

Discouraged by this failure, we turn to principle (b) to discover when our conditional statement *will* be true; but we suffer a second disappointment, for we do not know how to apply it. We can readily accept that, whenever we are justified in affirming that, if an election is held, the Socialists will win, we shall be equally justified in affirming that the conditional statement is true. But we wanted to know when that statement *is* in fact true, and that we are no closer to discovering. Why is that? Because we have hardly any use, in natural language, for conditional sentences of the form ⌜If, if **A**, then **B**, then **C**⌝, in which the antecedent is itself a conditional, and hence we cannot grasp the content of the principle.

This requires a more precise formulation; for, as the qualification 'hardly' indicates, the form ⌜If, if **A**, then **B**, then **C**⌝ (or ⌜If **B** if **A**, then **C**⌝) is not actually syntactically ill-formed or devoid of all use. For instance, a fragment of dialogue might conceivably, and certainly intelligibly, assume the following form:

X: If A, then D.

Y: I don't know about that, but at any rate, if A, then B.

X: Well, if, if A, then B, then, if A, then D; for, if B, then D, because . . .

Or another fragment might run:

X: Not A.

Y: I wouldn't go as far as that: but, if A, then B.

X: Well, if, if A, then B, then not A, as I said, because I happen to know that not B.

What these slightly forced examples illustrate is that a conditional assertion of the form ⌜If, if **A**, then **B**, then **C**⌝ will be admitted as correct if the speaker can produce a purely logical argument by which the consequent **C** can be deduced from the hypothesis ⌜If **A**, then **B**⌝, together with other premisses acknowledged on independent grounds as true; and it will be regarded as intelligible if the speaker can produce such an argument, even if its premisses are rejected.

This is, of course, to characterise this form of sentence in terms of whether an utterance of it is *justified* rather than whether it is *true*. It is justified if the speaker can produce a justification of a certain form; compare the fact that a speaker's use of 'but' in place of 'and' is justified if he can cite some relevant point of contrast. It would be possible, but it would be idle, to call an utterance of the form ⌜If, if **A**, then **B**, then **C**⌝ 'true' if a justification of the required kind existed, even if the speaker could not produce it. It would be idle for three reasons. The first and most important is that we have no need to determine truth-conditions for sentences of this form, since they cannot in turn figure as subsentences in yet more complex ones. Secondly, we have no use for a notion of falsity as applied to such sentences. And, thirdly, sentences of this form have no peripheral uses. An ordinary assertion is improper if the speaker has no ground for supposing it to be correct; but there are special contexts in which this requirement is waived. An assertoric sentence may be used, quite properly, to make a groundless assertion if it is the expression of a hunch, the response to an invitation to guess, a profession of faith, a prophetic utterance, or the laying of a bet. These are peripheral uses and must be signalled as such: they could not be typical cases. The existence of the first four of these modes encourages, although it does not always require, a separation of the condition for the truth of the assertion from the existence of grounds for it; the possibility of betting strictly requires them to be cleanly separated. But the existence of a justification for propounding a conditional of the form ⌜If, if **A**, then **B**, then **C**⌝ cannot be an article of faith for one who knows no such justification, and it is not suitable material for a hunch, guess, or bet; so we need no notion of truth for such sentences, as opposed to that of the justification for advancing them.

Conditionals of this special form differ from indicative conditionals in general in the very restricted type of justification required for them. We can certainly say that every well-grounded conditional assertion can be arrived at by means of an argument terminating in an application of if-introduction. For instance, if you have grounds for asserting that, if an election is held, the Socialists will win, you will be able to defend your assertion by an argument beginning, 'Suppose an election is held', and concluding, 'So the Socialists will win'. The argument will, as before, invoke additional premisses you regard as true; it will not, however, be a purely logical deduction. It might, for example, after the initial statement of the hypothesis, proceed, 'In that case, the Conservatives will focus attention on inflation'; but this assertion is neither a premiss nor a logical consequence of the hypothesis. Rather, it expresses a belief that it would be correct to say, 'If an election is held, the Conservatives will focus attention on inflation'. The argument could, indeed, be formally converted into a purely logical one by making this last conditional into an explicit premiss. Even if this manoeuvre is allowed, we can still distinguish a justification of an ordinary indicative conditional from one of a conditional of the special form ⌜If, if **A**, then **B**, then **C**⌝ by imposing a further constraint on an admissible justification of the latter: namely, that none of its premisses may themselves be conditionals with the antecedent ⌜if **A**, then **B**⌝.

Unlike the subspecies of conditionals whose antecedents are themselves conditionals, indicative conditionals in general do admit peripheral uses: one can have a hunch that, if an election is held, the Socialists will win; one can have faith that, if one's friend is offered a bribe, he will refuse it; one can prophesy that, if the citizens do not repent, Nineveh will be destroyed. This is so because the content of the hunch, act of faith, or prophecy is readily taken to be the material conditional: they will be falsified only if the antecedent is realised, but the consequent then proves false. As against this, one cannot bet on the truth of a conditional: a conditional bet is quite another matter. It is, above all, our lack of any general use for conditionals whose antecedents are conditionals that dispenses us from any need for an intuitive notion of the truth of a conditional. Our understanding of the use of the indicative conditional form—an understanding possessed in advance by philosophers who dispute how 'true' should be applied to sentences of that form—depends not on any grasp of the condition for their truth, in the strict sense, but only on the more primitive conception of what entitles a speaker to assert a conditional. The intelligibility of sentences in other positions within more complex ones—including that of consequent of a conditional—is often explicable without appeal to more than this primitive conception: their use as antecedents of conditionals demands a conception of their being true, as opposed to our being justified in asserting them.

Truth and the Point of an Assertion

The second natural distinction which tends to confer on the notion of truth its characteristic lineaments is that between what a speaker actually says and the point of his saying it, what he conveys by saying it in that context. If, in a plague-stricken city, someone says to me, 'Either you are going to contract cholera or you aren't', he is probably wishing to exhort me to an attitude of untroubled fatalism, saying, in effect, 'Stop worrying: you can't do anything about it'; but the natural comment is that that is only what he *conveys*, not what he literally *says*. But why, if his utterance has the force of an exhortation, should we insist on treating it as an assertion at all, particularly one with such a ludicrously thin content? Not just because the sentence could conceivably be used in some other way: it would make no difference if we recognised no other use. Nor because it would be difficult to extract the actual force of the remark from its internal structure: we are, in many cases, compelled to acknowledge the existence of idiom. Rather, it is because, as soon as we attempt to systematise our accepted modes of reasoning, we are bound to acknowledge principles by means of which we should be able to justify the assertion of any such instance of the law of excluded middle (on the assumption that we reason classically). There would be no such thing as recognising arguments as valid if there were no general principles that guided us in doing so; and we obtain a smoother description of our linguistic practice if we do not posit special exceptions to those principles, blocking us from justifying what is too obvious to need justification. We obtain a smoother description, too, if we appeal to idiom only as a last resort. We achieve a more economical explanation when, without making any such appeal, we can account for the force of an utterance by treating it, not as part of the meaning of the sentence, but as due to the hearer's seeking the point, in a given context, of an utterance whose meaning as a sentence-type he already understands. All this we already acknowledge, in a rough and ready way, in our everyday comments on things that are said, particularly in the distinction between what a sentence means and what a speaker means, and in our customary application of the predicate 'true'. To give a systematic account of the principles to which we appeal in drawing this distinction is a complex task, which Grice's theory of implicature is a largely successful attempt to accomplish; but perhaps no complete systematisation is possible.

Truth and Deductive Inference

Of the two kinds of distinction which, for these reasons, we find it natural to make, that between the truth of a statement and the existence of grounds for it has the deeper significance. This comes out, above all, when we look with a philosophical eye at the practice of deductive reasoning. A form of argument is deductively sound only if, given that it would be correct to assert its premisses, it would also be correct to assert its conclusion; that is to say, if it is truth-preserving, where the correctness of an assertion is equated with the truth of the sentence asserted. But the argument-form is of value to us only if, from premisses that we have recognised as true, it does not always lead to a conclusion that we have thereby already recognised as true.

Here a distinction must be drawn. A mode of reasoning is of value if it can be used to advance our knowledge; but we must here distinguish the collective from the distributive 'our'. Any valid form of inference with more than one essential premiss can serve to advance the knowledge of an individual; for he might have learned of the truth of the premisses from different sources, say by the testimony of distinct informants. Indeed, this applies whenever the premisses have been accepted on grounds that fall short of being conclusive. Thus the usefulness of *modus tollendo ponens* would not be impaired in cases of this kind, even if it were conceded that, in recognising ⌜A or B⌝ and ⌜Not A⌝ as both true, one has thereby already recognised the truth of **B**. Again, if it were part of the meaning of a certain form of statement that its truth could be recognised by appeal to a particular rule of inference, then the fact, if it were one, that we could not recognise the premisses as true without thereby already recognising the conclusion as true could not render that rule of inference otiose, since, by hypothesis, the enunciation of the rule would be an essential part of an explanation of the meaning of the conclusion. A possible example would be a statement of the form ⌜A and B⌝. It could plausibly be maintained that it is part of the meaning of the conjunction that its truth can be established by establishing the truth of **A** and of **B** separately. Here it is essential to invoke the distinction between what is *part* of the meaning and what is only *dependent on* the meaning: it would not be enough to say that the validity of the inference was a consequence of the meanings of the premisses and conclusion, for that is true of every inference.

Thus the usefulness of deductive reasoning to an individual cannot be called into question. Nevertheless, if to recognise the truth of the premisses were always thereby to recognise that of the conclusion, then deductive reasoning could never increase our collective knowledge; and this it obviously does. If it did not, then everyone would recognise all the logical consequences of all the truths he recognised. Anyone who had recognised the axioms of a mathematical theory as true would thereby have recognised the truth of all the theorems; there would then be no discoveries for mathematicians to make. This was Mill's dilemma. Deductive reasoning is like the growth of a child: a son cannot surpass his mother in height in the course of a day, but he can in 365 days. Deductive reasoning can lead us where we never expected to get; but we can account for its doing so only if we acknowledge that a single step takes us a definite distance; and although a spatial distance may be imperceptible, it does not make sense to speak of an imperceptible epistemic distance.

What has all this to do with truth? Surely it has to do with the recognition of truth, not with truth itself. Well, that is just the point: we cannot explain the utility of deductive reasoning if the notion of truth is straightforwardly explicable in terms of that by means of which we can recognise a statement as true. If a deductive argument is justified, and if we can see that it is justified, that must be because we can perceive that it preserves some property of statements that renders an assertion of them correct. If the argument advances our knowledge, however minimally, this property cannot consist in our ability, in some given favourable situation, to recognise a statement as true, independently of the argument itself. The existence of deductive reasoning thus compels us to admit some gap between truth and that which enables us to recognise truth: how the two are related will depend upon the form of the meaning-theory that we adopt.

Recognition of truth is an active process, perhaps involving physical operations such as measurement, or intellectual ones such as counting, and at any rate requiring the discernment of a pattern: it is not a mere automatic response to exposure to sense impressions. A single deductive step involves a small alteration in the operations performed or in the pattern discerned. A whole deductive argument, or, more exactly, a constructive one, provides an effective procedure for rearranging the operations accompanying any given observations which yielded a pattern amounting to recognition of the truth of the initial premisses, so as to yield one constituting recognition of the truth of the conclusion. Consider, for example, Euler's proof that anyone who, in the course of one journey, crossed every bridge at Königsberg crossed at least one of them at least twice. The proof shows us an effective means, given observations establishing that someone had crossed every bridge, to make observations establishing that he crossed some bridge twice; and it does this by providing an overall pattern which will be displayed whenever the two kinds of observation are carried on simultaneously.

The proof does not bring us into the position of recognising directly the truth of the conclusion: it shows how we could arrive at that position, if we began by being in a position to recognise directly the truth of the premisses. By doing this, it provides us with an *indirect* means of seeing that the conclusion is true. To put it in this way assumes that we already have a notion of what it is for the conclusion to be true, even though its truth has not been directly recognised, and that, by adopting the practice of deductive reasoning, we acquire a new means of coming to know its truth. Not merely this, however: the practice of deductive reasoning is itself one of the sources of our notion of truth, and one of great importance at that. More accurately expressed, therefore, the effect of the proof is that, if we started with no other means of establishing our statements as true save the most direct one, it would *extend* our means of coming to recognise those statements as true. To this extent, therefore, Wittgenstein was right in saying that a proof introduces a new criterion; if an individual proof does not do so, then at least the practice of arguing in accordance with certain principles does.

In intuitionistic mathematics, this fact is reflected by the necessity for the distinction between a canonical proof and the sort of proof which normally appears in a mathematical textbook or article, which may be called a 'demonstration'. A canonical proof is a proof of the specially restricted kind in terms of which the meanings of mathematical statements, and of the logical constants in particular, are given— the kind of proof referred to in Heyting's explanations in terms of constructions. For these explanations to avoid circularity, there must be an upper bound on the complexity of a canonical proof of any given statement, depending on the complexity of that statement; but the complexity of a demonstration—any argument that serves to establish the truth of a theorem without question—can exceed any assigned bound. The restrictions on the form of a canonical proof flow from the explanations of the logical operators. For instance, a canonical proof of an arithmetical statement of the form ⌜For some x, $A(x)$⌝ is required to take the form of a proof of some specific statement ⌜$A(n)$⌝; but, in the course of a demonstration, we can assert ⌜For some x, $A(x)$⌝ on the strength merely of an effective procedure for finding such an n, without our having to carry out that procedure. In general, a demonstration consists in anything we can recognise to be an effective procedure for finding a canonical proof. Thus, if we started only with the practice of giving canonical proofs, the introduction of ordinary demonstrative proof would extend our methods of establishing mathematical statements as true, and in practice greatly extend the range of theorems that we actually proved.

It does not, of course, happen this way. Neither in mathematics nor in any other sphere do we begin with a limited range of ways of establishing our statements as true, and then, by introducing more general forms of deductive reasoning, extend them. In actual fact, we begin to learn the practice of deductive reasoning at quite an early stage in our acquisition of language: the word 'so' is one frequently heard on the tongue of a small child. Yet the distinction between direct and indirect means of establishing a statement as true is in no way peculiar to intuitionistic mathematics. The direct means—which may possibly itself involve some deductive argument, and, except in the simplest cases, will certainly involve some intellectual operations (of which counting may be taken as the prototype)—is that which, step by step, reflects the structure of the sentence; it is that in terms of which it is natural to say that the meaning is given—at least, whenever we seek to explain meaning by reference to verification. Thus, when you want in this way to explain sentences of the form 'There are more apples than oranges in the basket', you do not think of a case in which you say, 'We paid so much for the oranges, and so much for the apples, and each of those amounts admits only the following factorisations, as the products of two primes, and so we must have bought so many apples and so many oranges, and then we gave five oranges to So-and-so, and put just under half the apples in the carrier bag, so . . .'. That is a perfectly good means of verifying the statement, but you would not cite it, or even think of it, if you were aiming to explain what the statement means; for it is a method of verifying the statement of which it may rightly be said that it can be recognised as such only when the meaning of the statement is already known. Rather, you would fasten on the canonical procedure, saying, 'If you paired off the apples with the oranges one by one, there would be some apples left over'. That illustrates what is meant by speaking of the *direct* way of establishing the truth of a statement. The practice of deductive reasoning extends the meanings of our statements beyond those which they would bear if we appealed only to the direct means of establishing them. But, since we do not first learn one practice, and then enrich it by adding the other, we do not apprehend deductive reasoning as extending the meanings of our statements but as faithful to those meanings. This is why we are not wholly comfortable with a conception of meaning as given solely by reference to the direct verification of our statements, but find it more natural to think in terms of meaning as given by what makes a statement true, where the truth of a statement is *not* to be identified with the occurrence of a direct verification.

In the case of constructive mathematics, the effect is not a strong one. It is possible to argue thus: an assertion should amount to a claim that the statement asserted is true; you are prepared to assert a statement of which you have only a demonstration; therefore your notion of truth for a statement must be the existence of a demonstration, not of a canonical proof (where by 'existence' is meant actual existence, not existence in the realm of possibility or of abstract objects). But a constructive mathematician might reply that this connection between assertion and truth has been imported from elsewhere, and that, for him, assertion embodies no more than a claim to have an effective method of finding a canonical proof, not that such a proof is at hand. In any case, the notion of a demonstration is itself to be explained in terms of that of a canonical proof, so that the original explanations of meaning in terms of canonical proofs remain in force. The constructivist can therefore consistently continue, if he wishes, to regard what makes a mathematical statement true as being the actual existence of a canonical proof. On his way of speaking, a mathematical assertion amounts not to a claim that the statement asserted is true but only to possession of a means, effective in principle, of making it true.

In the case of empirical statements, however, the matter stands quite differently. The crucial difference lies in the fact that what corresponds, within mathematics, to the making of observations, namely the effecting of a construction, can be repeated at any time; but an observation cannot. If a proof shows me how to convert one construction into another, then, if I have once carried out the first construction, I can always carry out the second, whenever I like. But suppose that I have made observations which directly establish a certain statement as true, and I have a deductive argument, from it as premiss, which convinces me of the truth of its conclusion by showing how to make observations that would establish it: it does not follow that I can make those observations, since the phenomenon to be observed may have come to an end, or be no longer accessible to observation. All the same, the argument convinces me that, if I could have made the observations, and had done so, they would have established its conclusion. Why should we treat this as a reason to accept that statement? Here the chain of justifications comes to an end: we simply do. Not only our language, but our entire conception of the world, would be transformed if we did not; we should find ourselves with a radically impoverished grasp on the reality that exists around us. So we may say, more exactly, that it is the fact that I speak the language, and thus engage in the practice of reasoning in this way, that commits me to treating such a deductive argument, too, as a ground for accepting the statement, although indirect. This is how it can come about that there are grounds for asserting a statement, and hence for according it the status of being true, when it not only has not been directly established, but can no longer be.

When the distinction between a statement's being true and the existence of grounds for asserting it was first introduced into our discussion, it may have appeared that this was simply a line we all find it convenient to draw between different kinds of condition which we know to be required for an assertion to be correct. But not everyone need see it in this way. One who holds a neutralist view about the future will not so regard the distinction we are accustomed to draw between the truth of a statement in the future tense and the existence of present evidence for it, the statement being determinately true or false according as the event in question is or is not going to take place. In *that* case, the proper course for the neutralist was to reject that notion of truth, and with it, that way of drawing the distinction. But in the present context, it is not so easy to replace our ordinary notion of truth.

The thesis I have been arguing is that the mere existence of deductive reasoning, no matter how constructive the principles of inference to which it appeals, has an effect upon the notion of truth, provided only that that reasoning is of a kind which lead us to new knowledge. Suppose that a sceptic rejects the resulting notion of truth. Unlike the neutralist, who has an alternative means of treating statements about the future, the sceptic does not appear to have any other means of accounting for the facts of linguistic practice, that is to say, in this case, of representing such modes of reasoning as justified. I spoke earlier of truth as a property which is transmitted from premisses to conclusion of a valid deductive argument, and which entitles us to assert a statement that possesses it. We have not, however, discovered any means of describing how we *find* such a property: hence nothing has yet been said to rebut the sceptical contention that we simply make it up. Having the practice of accepting arguments which provide a means of transforming observations that establish the premisses into ones which establish the conclusion, we *ascribe* to the conclusion of such an argument a property of truth; and all we know about this property is that it is possessed by any statement which has been directly established by observation, and that it is transmitted by valid arguments; but what it consists in, we have no means of saying. Or so, at least, the sceptic will say.

We are, of course, dominated by a picture. The picture is that, in making observations, we are observing what is *there* independently of whether we observe it or can observe it. Moreover, if this external reality becomes inaccessible to us, so that we can no longer observe it, still, when it appears that, if we *could* make further observations, they would turn out in such-and-such a way, we take it that this can only be because of the constitution of that reality in itself; namely, because it is as the statement we should have established by means of those observations (had we made them) says it is. Now, someone may say, is that not just what the word 'observation' *means*? To speak of observation at all is to assume that the observation gives us information about a reality which exists independently of our observations and is unaffected by them—a reality which would have existed, and would have been as our observation shows it to be, even if we had not made those observations. Exactly so. In the course of the discussion, I deliberately moved from speaking about directly recognising a statement as true to speaking of making observations that establish it as true—two phrases that were intended to apply to precisely the same processes—in order to mark the adoption of this picture. The picture is, indeed, the one we have of what an observation is: we speak of 'observations' only when we have that picture.

But *can* we not characterise the required notion of truth? True statements must comprise, though they are not necessarily confined to, all those which would have been established as true had the relevant observations been made; 'observation' is, as before, not to be taken as mere passive exposure to sense experience but to include physical and mental operations and the discernment of structure (of patterns). In particular, we are able to say that a statement is true, in this sense, whenever we can show how observations that were made *could have* been transformed into ones that would have established it. Is that not sufficient explanation?

The appearance of a counterfactual is characteristic of many justifications of some form or degree of realism. Counterfactuals do not have to do with possible worlds: they have to do with the *actual* world. You may, if you wish, suppose that what renders a counterfactual true is how things stand in certain possible worlds. Still, if that is so, we can know them to be true only if we can find something in the actual world which will tell us what possible worlds there are and are not, and how things are in them. Moreover, a counterfactual can bear on how things are in the actual world only if, whether we know it or not, there is some feature of the actual world that determines the relevant structure of the possible worlds. Counterfactuals therefore interest us only in so far as there is some aspect of actuality that is sufficient to determine them as true.

Let us call two counterfactuals 'opposites' if they have the same antecedent and contradictory consequents. Then the conviction that one of a given pair of opposite counterfactuals must be true—that, for certain particular statements **A** and **B**, either the statement ⌜If it had been the case that **A**, then it would have been the case that **B**⌝ or its opposite, ⌜If it had been the case that **A**, then it would have been the case that not **B**⌝, must hold—is frequently exceedingly compelling. This conviction is a characteristic expression of a realist view, of a belief that there is an underlying objective reality that must determine one or other opposite counterfactual as true: an expression of realism that we meet with over and again in discussions of one or another realist claim. Of course, it is not a *logical* law that one or another of the two opposite counterfactuals must be true. Since, for example, whether or not Allen would have told Bailey of his inheritance if he had met him might have depended on *where* they met, neither the unqualified statement that he would have told him had they met, nor its opposite, can rank as true. But if we take the antecedent as being 'If both groups had been counted', and the consequent as 'Their numbers would have been found to be equal', the conviction that one or other counterfactual must hold good, despite our inability to determine which, is irresistible.

Unfortunately, this conviction has little explanatory power: we have no way of saying what makes a counterfactual of the relevant kind true save by reference to the supposed aspect of reality. For example, whichever of the pair of counterfactuals concerning the result of counting the two groups is true, it will be true in virtue of the numbers of members of the groups. (If someone wants to say that what *makes* the counterfactual true is the way things are in possible worlds, then we shall have to say here, 'We have no way of saying how things in the actual world determine such a counterfactual as true save by reference to the supposed aspect of reality'.) We therefore shall achieve nothing if we try to characterise the aspect of reality in question in terms of the truth of the relevant counterfactuals.

It is not, of course, a possible option that we should abandon altogether the practice of deductive reasoning: scepticism of that kind is too extreme for serious consideration. It does hold good—or so I shall maintain—that particular forms of accepted deductive practice may be up for revision in the light of philosophical criticism; but that the entire practice of deductive argument is exposed to such criticism only someone on the verge of solipsism could maintain. The moral of our whole discussion is that there are certain respects in which the notion of truth has built into it from the outset a certain bias toward realism: a bias which by no means forces us to return a realist answer to any of the various metaphysical questions listed in the Introduction, but does give us an initial tilt in that direction. This is partly why, to people like Dr. Johnson and others, realism can seem the merest common sense. It also sets a bound on how far it is possible to go in rejecting realism without doing violence to the concept of truth itself, without flouting the purposes for which we needed the concept in the first place.

It should also have become clear that, even at this preliminary stage, the same sort of impasse that appears to arise in live disputes over this or that form of realism arises here as well. The impasse arises because, at a certain point, the only characterisation we can achieve for the notion of truth we wish to justify is in terms of the holding of certain counterfactuals; and because such an appeal has no probative force, since to assume that counterfactuals of the relevant kind determinately either hold or fail is just to assume that we already have the desired notion of truth for non-counterfactual statements, where a counterfactual 'fails' only when the opposite counterfactual holds. It is wrong to think that, in live disputes over realism, such an impasse is insurmountable: if it were, those disputes would be for ever irresoluble. But the impasse that arises over those basic features of the concept of truth which it must have if there is to be such a practice as deductive reasoning at all really seems to be insurmountable: here we have reached the outermost limits of philosophical space.

chapter 8

The Justification of Deduction

Logical Laws

Is it possible to justify a logical law, or putative logical law? Is it possible to show it to be devoid of justification? In order to answer these questions, we have first to ask what is meant, in this connection, by a 'logical law'. The narrowest notion of a logical law is that illustrated by the law of excluded middle: such a law stipulates the truth (and hence the logical truth) of every statement of a given form. But the interest of a logical truth lies wholly in the fact that it can be appealed to in the course of deductive reasoning; that is to say, in the presence of one rule of inference, it will license another. Given *modus tollendo tollens,* for example, the law of excluded middle will license the rule of double negation; given the rule of or-elimination, it will license the simple constructive dilemma, which authorises us to assert a statement **B** whenever it can be shown to follow both from a statement **A** and from its negation. If we had a means of isolating logical truths from non-logical ones, so that, while we acknowledged them as true, it was forbidden to assert them in the course of a piece of deductive reasoning, they would be quite idle and of no interest: what matter are the principles we employ for deriving non-logical truths from other non-logical truths. Hence we must understand the term 'logical law' in the more general sense in which we speak of 'de Morgan's laws' or of 'the distributive law', namely, as applying to a principle of inference; more exactly, to a principle of inference that turns only on the structure of the premises and conclusion and on the presence in them of purely logical expressions.

In asking the questions with which we began, we are concerned with principles or rules of inference as they are actually observed in the course of informal, or at least unformalised, reasoning, in everyday life, in the law courts, in political argumentation, in scientific literature, in mathematical proofs and elsewhere. Nevertheless, before we tackle those questions, it will be best to be as precise as possible about what we take a rule of inference to be. The easiest and most accurate way to do this is to consider how, in general, such a rule is to be formally represented; for formalisation is the only means we have of attaining precision either about what a rule of inference is in general or about the content of a specific rule. We are interested in the *rule*, as applied in inferential practice, not in the formalisation as such; our question is whether the rule, as it is or might be so applied, can be shown to be justified or to be invalid, not whether a given formalised rule succeeds in capturing the rule as it is in practice applied. We have therefore to consider only such methods of formalisation as correspond in an obvious and unproblematic way to the unformalised principles of inference we use in ordinary contexts, even though the formalised versions do not precisely match our informal modes of expression.

What notion of a rule of inference is used by logicians depends upon the formalisation of logic they are considering. The simplest notion is that according to which a rule of inference is a principle licensing the assertion of a statement expressed by a sentence of a certain form, given the prior assertion of a finite number of other statements, expressed by sentences of related forms: the statement whose assertion is licensed is the *conclusion* of the inference, those whose prior assertion warranted the assertion of the conclusion, in the light of the rule, are its *premisses*.

This, however, contains too narrow a conception of the form an inference may take. It does not, for instance, allow for inferences by *reductio ad absurdum,* or by any other principle that permits us first to introduce a supposition 'for the sake of argument', and then to discharge it, that is, to make an assertion outright, no longer dependent upon the supposition. To admit rules of inference of this kind, we must explain them after the manner of a natural deduction formalisation of logic. The technically simpler, though intuitively less transparent, way of doing this is to take the premisses and conclusion of an inference to be not individual sentences but *sequents.* The notion of a sequent has already been explained, but it may be helpful to repeat the explanation here. A sequent is a pair whose first term, called the *antecedent,* is a finite (possibly empty) set of sentences and whose second term, called the *succedent,* is a sentence. Intuitively, the succedent expresses the statement being asserted at that point in the deductive argument, while the sentences belonging to the antecedent express the hypotheses on which it is being presented as depending; 'hypotheses' here covers both suppositions to be discharged in the later course of the argument and premisses of the argument as a whole which have been asserted outright as starting points for the argument. If we regard an inference as a step from some finite number of sequents as premises to a new sequent as conclusion, we can allow that the antecedent of the conclusion need not be the union of the antecedents of the premisses, and hence admit rules of inference that allow the discharge of hypotheses.

It is essential to bear in mind that a sequent, unlike a sentence, is not up for assessment as contingently true: it is either logically valid, or it is invalid and will therefore never appear in any correct deduction. A sequent is simply a device for carrying along the premisses on the strength of which the succedent is asserted at a particular stage of the deduction, or the hypotheses under which it is asserted, with the sentence asserted. Sequents can thus be used to represent a deduction from contingent premisses to a contingent conclusion; and we may call the succedent of the last sequent in a deduction so represented the *final conclusion* of the whole deduction, and the sentences comprising its antecedent the *initial premisses* of the deduction. But the whole point of allowing inferences that discharge hypotheses is that, in such a case, we cannot describe the inference as a transition from the assertion of certain statements as premisses to the assertion of some other statement as conclusion: the conclusion is asserted on the strength of its being possible to derive certain statements from certain hypotheses. At least one of the premisses of the inference is therefore not a statement but a deduction, most easily representable by a sequent; for convenience, we therefore represent every line as a sequent, whether a hypothesis is discharged or not. When we take the premisses and conclusion of an individual inference to be sequents, the transition, if the inference is sound, will be from *valid* premisses to one that is also valid, not from true statements to a true statement.

A natural deduction formalisation of logic does not allow of any operation upon antecedents of sequents except those of forming the union of two or more and of deleting one member. This corresponds to requiring that every hypothesis, whether a supposition to be discharged or a premiss of the deduction as a whole, must be introduced independently of any prior logical operation. If we represent the deduction in tree form, we can say that each hypothesis must be introduced *before* any other operation (on the same branch of the tree). A sequent calculus allows of a more general notion of a rule of inference and, in addition, of a more general notion of a sequent. A rule of inference may now involve the introduction into the antecedent of the conclusion of a sentence that did not appear in the antecedent of any of the premisses, perhaps simultaneously with the deletion of one or more sentences that do so appear; these are the rules of introduction on the left. Intuitively, they allow us to infer the succedent, as depen-

dent on certain hypotheses, on the strength of its having been shown
to follow from certain other hypotheses. Since we should aim at the
greatest reasonable generality, we should take our notion of a rule of
inference as covering rules of this kind also.

The second generalisation made in the classical sequent calculus,
that of the notion of a sequent, admits sequents whose succedent is a
finite, possibly empty, *set* of sentences rather than a single sentence. A
sequent with an empty succedent expresses that the sentences comprised by the antecedent are contradictory: the same effect can be
obtained by employing a particular constant absurd sentence. We may
therefore allow the notion of a sequent to be extended to cover those
with empty succedents, since, although it is greatly at variance with
our practice in natural language, it is readily intelligible and easily
replaceable by something more in conformity with ordinary practice.
Sequents with two or more sentences in the succedent, by contrast,
have no straightforwardly intelligible meaning, explicable without recourse to any logical constant. Asserting **A** and asserting **B** is tantamount to asserting ⌈**A** and **B**⌉; so, although the sentences in the
antecedent of a sequent are in a sense conjunctively connected, we can
understand the significance of a sequent with more than one sentence
in the antecedent without having to know the meaning of 'and'. But,
in a succedent comprising more than one sentence, the sentences are
connected disjunctively; and it is not possible to grasp the sense of
such a connection otherwise than by learning the meaning of the constant 'or'. A sequent of the form **A** : **B, C** cannot be explained by saying, 'If you have asserted **A**, you may with equal right assert either **B**
or **C**', for that would imply that you can assert either one at your
choice; and the formulation, 'If you have asserted **A**, then either you
may assert **B** or you may assert **C**', does not entitle you to make *any*
further assertion until you learn *which* of them you may assert. A general explanation of this form of sequent becomes possible only when
we can say, 'Having asserted **A**, you are thereby entitled to assert ⌈**B** or
C⌉'. An explanation of this kind, assuming the understanding of a
particular logical constant, is useless for our purposes, for a reason
that will shortly become evident; so we shall allow only those rules of
inference licensing a conclusion to a sequent with at most one sentence
in the succedent, as is usually done in the standard sequent calculus
for intuitionistic logic.

A logical law in the narrowest sense, discussed above, illustrated by
the law of excluded middle—namely, one stipulating the truth of
every sentence of a given form—can be subsumed under our present
definition if we represent it as an inference with an arbitrary sequent
as premiss and a sequent with a null antecedent as conclusion, for

example a sequent of the form : $A \lor \neg A$; or alternatively we could take it as an inference without premisses. An actual inference has as premisses and conclusion sequents composed of sentences; a rule of inference is general and licenses particular inferences characterised by their form. A rule of inference is therefore expressed by means of an inference-schema, in which syntactical variables represent sentences (which in one sequent may stand on their own, and, in another, form a subsentence of a more complex one), sets of sentences, or parts of sentences; we may speak of the premisses and conclusion of such an inference-schema as 'schematic sequents'. For such a rule to be a *logical* one, the only actual expressions occurring in the schema must be logical constants; for the present, we need not pause to draw any explicit distinction between logical constants and non-logical ones.

Justification and Criticism of Logical Laws

Equipped with this clarification, we may reiterate our original questions: is it possible to justify a logical law, or putative logical law, and is it possible to show one to be devoid of justification? Obvious affirmative answers to both questions spring to mind. In ordinary life, we seldom formulate general principles of inference: we seek to justify, or to criticise, particular inferences. We vindicate an inference by breaking it down into shorter steps, that is, by constructing a whole deductive argument, using simpler principles of inference, whose initial premisses are the premisses of the inference under challenge and whose final conclusion is the conclusion of that inference. This has been expressed for the simplest type of inference, in which the premisses and conclusion may be taken as actual statements. When such an inference is formulated by means of sequents, it is one in which no hypothesis is discharged and none is modified, but the antecedent of the conclusion is the union of the antecedents of the premisses. In the general case, under our official notion of an inference as one whose premisses and conclusion are sequents, what is needed for a justification is the tail end of a deduction which, when added to deductions of the premisses, will yield a deduction of the conclusion. The analogous procedure, applied to an inference-schema representing a formalised rule of inference, demonstrates that it is derivable from the rules of inference figuring in the formalised deduction-schema, in other words what is usually known as a *derived rule* in any formalisation of logic in which those rules hold good. This is obviously a proof-theoretic, rather than a model-theoretic or semantic, justification: we may call it a 'proof-theoretic justification of the first grade'. It shows unarguably that, if we accept certain rules of inference, then we must also accept the one under challenge.

In an everyday context, there is a well-known procedure, to which we frequently resort, for subjecting an inference to criticism. Let us for simplicity again assume that the inference in question is of the simplest kind, namely, with statements rather than sequents as premisses and conclusion. We cannot conclusively show a particular such inference to be invalid save by demonstrating that the premisses are true and the conclusion is not. The opponent therefore makes a guess at the principle of inference to which the proponent is appealing and constructs what we may call a 'recognisably strong counter-example' to this rule of inference, namely, a putative inference exemplifying the rule in question whose premisses are recognisably true and whose conclusion is recognisably false. In ordinary life, the production of such a counter-example is usually preceded by the words 'You might as well say . . .'. Such a counter-example is to be called 'strong' because the conclusion is actually false. Given the principle of bivalence, that every statement is determinately either true or false, every counter-example must be strong. But, when bivalence is not accepted, we cannot regard it as sufficient, for the validity of a rule of inference, that no application can arise in which the premisses are true but the conclusion false, because that would not guarantee that, whenever the premisses were true, the conclusion would also be true. A recognisably weak counter-example will be one in which the premisses are recognisably true but the conclusion recognisably not true, but not recognisably false. In intuitionistic sentential logic, for example, a rule of inference that is classically, but not intuitionistically, valid can never have a strong counter-example. We have then to use subtler methods in order to exhibit a counter-example in which the conclusion can be recognised not to be true in some suitable sense, such as that we are not entitled to assert it, but cannot be claimed as false in the sense that we are entitled to assert its negation.

In an everyday context, the proponent will attempt to defend himself from the criticism by seeking to show a significant difference between the inference he made and that whose invalidity the opponent demonstrated; he will say, 'But that is not a fair analogy', and go on to make out that the principle of inference to which he was appealing was not that which his opponent refuted. We, however, are concerned with the justification and criticism of *principles* of inference, not of specific inferences; and the production of a recognisably strong counter-example is an unassailable refutation of a purported principle of inference. Such a refutation is not proof-theoretic in character but, in a loose sense, semantic; it relies on the requirement, for the validity of an inference-schema, that there be no interpretation of it under which the premisses come out true and the conclusion false. The interpretation it employs is simply an interpretation by replacing the schematic letters by actual expressions, so that no semantic apparatus is involved and no semantic theory underlies the procedure. In the general case, in which the premisses and conclusion are sequents, the requirement would be that there be no interpretation under which the premisses come out valid and the conclusion strongly invalid, where a sequent is 'strongly invalid' when the sentences in its antecedent are all true and its succedent is false.

Proof-theoretic procedures for refuting purported rules of inference are never employed in everyday practice but occupy a modest place in the repertoire of logicians. Łukasiewicz introduced a refutation-procedure adequate for demonstrating, in a quasi-deductive manner, the invalidity of any invalid formula of classical sentential logic, and hence of any classically invalid quantifier-free schematic sequent; but the procedure was parasitic upon the proof-procedure whereby the validity of formulas was demonstrated and hence rested upon quite heavy assumptions. Łukasiewicz attempted to extend his refutation-procedure to intuitionistic sentential logic, but Kreisel and Putnam showed his method to be incomplete; Dana Scott devised a complete method, but one far from perspicuous. In any case, such refutation-procedures have never been devised for predicate logic and, if they were, could not be complete, since the joint existence of complete effective proof- and refutation-procedures would contradict the undecidability of first-order logic. Moreover, there is something highly unnatural about a purely *deductive* refutation of a (purported) logical law. We may therefore ignore this approach henceforward.

Disputes over Fundamental Laws

The existence of proof-theoretic justifications of the first grade and of refutations by means of recognisably strong counter-examples, and our frequent appeals to these procedures in everyday practice, are quite obvious. One who raises the question, as a philosophical problem, whether a logical law can be justified or refuted is therefore likely to be impatient at being referred to them in reply. He will naturally point out that such procedures have limited scope, and can be invoked only in essentially unproblematic cases. A proof-theoretic justification of the first grade is only a *relative* justification: it assumes the validity of the rules of inference appealed to in the justificatory deduction. We therefore cannot, by such means, justify *fundamental* laws of logic, that is to say, of an entire logical system such as classical or intuitionistic logic. The notion of a fundamental law is, of course, not absolute; in systematising our logical practice, we have a choice which laws we shall stipulate as valid outright, and which we shall leave to be recognised as derivable from them. In any systematisation, some must be stipulated outright, however: relative to such a systematisation, these cannot be justified by showing them to be derivable from other laws treated as being more basic. Our enquirer wants to know whether any means exists for justifying the laws considered as having been stipulated, not derived.

The production of recognisably strong counter-examples is an equally limited procedure. We have seen that, unless the principle of bivalence is accepted, there may be invalid rules of inference to which no strong counter-example exists. Even for an adherent of classical logic, however, there is no guarantee that a *recognisably* strong counter-example to any invalid rule is to be found. Essentially problematic disputes over logical laws—disputes that are not easily settled by one or the other of the two procedures we have been considering—are of two kinds. There are those which relate to elementary laws—laws within the scope of first-order, including sentential, logic: such are the disputes between adherents of classical logic and intuitionists or proponents of quantum logic. Other disputes relate to laws belonging to higher-order logic, and typically arise, in the first instance, within mathematics. The dispute that arose over the Axiom of Choice, when it was first isolated as a distinct principle of reasoning, not reducible to or derivable from other principles, was a characteristic example. Most of those who rejected the Axiom of Choice as an illegitimate device inadmissible in mathematical proofs harboured no doubts about classical logic. They must therefore have believed in the existence of strong counter-examples to the Axiom, instances in which its hypotheses were satisfied but no choice function existed. They did not expect to be able to refute the Axiom by producing such a strong counter-example, however; they did not believe that there were any *recognisably* strong counter-examples to it. They did not suppose that they could, in any particular case, *demonstrate* the non-existence of a choice function; they simply believed the assumption of its existence in every case to be unwarranted.

Those who engage in disputes of either of these kinds do not behave as though there were nothing to be said, as when one person expresses a liking for celery and another declares that it revolts him. Neither rests content with saying that the logical law in question strikes him as valid or as invalid; rather, they treat it as capable of justification and of criticism. One side defends the status of the Axiom of Choice, or of the law of excluded middle, as a law of logic, and the other gives arguments for calling that claim into question. Their arguments characteristically turn on the meanings that the relevant logical constants ought to be taken as having—for instance, the meaning of existential quantification over sets or functions. In other cases, as in disputes between constructivist and classical mathematicians, their arguments strike deeper still; the issue now is not the meanings to be assigned to specific logical constants, but the terms in which the meanings of any logical constants, or even of mathematical statements in general, ought to be framed.

It is unsurprising that arguments for or against the validity of a purported fundamental law of logic should take this form: for logical laws are certainly correlative to the meanings of the logical constants. It is often said that two people cannot disagree over the validity of some principle of inference unless they attach different meanings to the logical constants involved. This is far from obvious. If there is such a thing as a justification of a logical law, it will presumably take a characterisation of the meanings of the relevant logical constants as its starting point. It is not evident that it would not be possible to understand those logical constants in just that way without perceiving that the law is valid when they are so understood. Indeed, it is manifestly possible for someone to fail to recognise the validity of a law capable of a proof-theoretic justification of the first grade by appeal to simpler laws which he does recognise as valid; the same presumably holds good for justifications of other kinds, if these exist. What *is* true is that, if two people really agree about the meanings of the logical constants, they cannot *with equal right* take different views of the validity of a logical law; in the light of those meanings, one must be right, and the other wrong. The contraposition of course holds equally: if both are equally entitled to take the attitudes to the law that they do, then they must attach different meanings to the constants, whether or not they realise that they do.

To enquire how disputes over the validity of some principle of reasoning may be resolved, if at all, thus affords a particularly vivid way of enquiring how the meanings of the logical constants should be regarded as being given to us. This latter enquiry is one in which we must in any case engage. The logical constants form a small but vital part of the vocabulary of a language, since it is by means of them that sentences of arbitrary complexity can be generated from the basis of simple ones. An important feature of a meaning-theory is therefore the means it employs for representing the meanings of the logical constants. That is why it would have undermined the purpose of our enquiry to employ a notion of a sequent allowing more than one sentence in the succedent, since the significance of such a sequent can be explained only by appeal to the connective 'or': we needed, as our general notion of a logical law, one that did not presuppose the meaning of any logical constant.

The fact that any disagreement over the validity of a logical law in which neither side is straightforwardly mistaken according to his own lights always reflects a divergence in the meanings each attaches to some or all the logical constants does not imply that it can be dismissed as a mere verbal disagreement. Disagreements about the meaning to be attached to a word or expression are of two kinds: those which, however linguistically important, are conceptually trivial; and those which are conceptually deep. Such a disagreement is conceptually trivial when it could be resolved (save for considerations of linguistic propriety) by introducing two new words which both sides could agree to understand alike, one to bear the meaning attached by one disputant to the disputed word, the other to bear that attached to it by the other. Disagreements about the meanings of the logical constants are seldom conceptually trivial: typically, one or both of the parties to the dispute denies that the other has hold of any coherent meaning at all. An intuitionist, for example, does not merely want to hijack the classical mathematician's particle 'not' for his own peculiar purposes, and he would not be content with a proposal to use some other word to mean what the classical mathematician means by it: he denies that one can treat any word as meaning what the classical mathematician thinks he means by it. That is why disputes over fundamental logical laws go so deep. They turn on different conceptions of what it is possible to mean, and hence, ultimately, on different conceptions of what meaning is.

The Philosopher's Concern with Justification

It is not only when a logical law comes under challenge that we are interested in the possibility of justifying it. Deductive inference is an integral component of a linguistic practice, more prominent in some contexts than in others, but never out of order. It is not an isolable subpractice, like fictional narrative, which leaves virtually unaffected anything subsequently said or written, save that which has it as its subject matter, like literary history and criticism. The point about a deductive argument is that it is connected at start and finish with the ordinary assertoric use of language. It is required to start from statements whose assertion is warranted, and it serves as a warrant for asserting the conclusion. The rest of our practice governing the assertoric use of language may naturally be supposed to endow the statements which figure as premises and conclusion of a deductive argument with definite meanings. Those meanings must surely suffice to determine both what warrants the assertion of any of those statements and what consequences result from taking any one of them to be true. What, then, justifies the procedure of deductive argument?

This is a philosopher's question. In everyday life, we do not wait upon a justification, or ask for one. It is not rational to entertain any serious doubt about the matter; both thought and discourse would break down if we attempted to eschew all deductive inference until a justification of the practice was forthcoming, which it would never be, because any such justification must involve some deductive argument. But the philosopher is not content merely to conform with established linguistic practice; he wants, in Wittgenstein's phrase, to command a clear view of its operation. Without doubting that deductive inference is justifiable, he wants to know what its justification is. What relation do our inferential practices bear to our other criteria for when an assertion is warranted? Is it true that our linguistic practices other than deductive argument fully determine the meanings of the assertoric sentences of the language? If so, by what right do we *also* treat an assertion as warranted when it is arrived at by deductive inference? How is it that doing so does not distort its meaning, but, instead, can be viewed as a way of being faithful to it? Or is it, rather, that our inferential practice essentially modifies the meanings that all our assertoric sentences would otherwise possess? If so, *how* does it modify them? In what respect does it do so, and how do we come to grasp that it does?

When we restrict our attention to purely *logical* deduction, the meanings with which we are concerned are those of the logical constants; but still, not exclusively of them, since any sentence can figure as the conclusion of a purely logical deductive argument, and the question remains to be answered whether the possibility of so arriving at it does not essentially modify its meaning. We have, apparently, two alternatives before us.

(1) The meanings of our assertoric sentences generally, and of the logical constants in particular, are given us in such a way that the forms of deductive inference we admit as valid can be exhibited as faithful to, and licensed by, those meanings and involve no modification of them. In this case, these principles of inference will indeed be capable of justification, possibly together with other principles we have failed, but are entitled, to acknowledge.

(2) Our principles of inference admit no justification, because they are not faithful to the meanings of our statements as antecedently given, but instead serve to determine the meanings of our logical constants and, in part, of sentences not containing them.

If we are to command a clear view of the workings of our language, we have to decide between these two alternatives and then to flesh out the one we have chosen.

A philosophical enquiry into the justification of deductive inference resembles a philosophical investigation of the concept of meaning. In both cases the interest of the enquiry is general. In both cases, however, it can be answered only by illustrative examples. There can be, at best, a vacuous general answer to the question, 'What is it for a linguistic expression to have a meaning?': we can answer it only by showing how we might set about specifying the meanings of representative expressions of different types. For this to be a way of answering the general question, the answers cannot collectively presuppose it known what it is for any other expressions to have the meanings that they do; that is why we need to sketch the form that may be taken by an entire meaning-theory for a language. Similarly for deductive inference. We can give, at best, a purely vacuous answer to the question what justifies the practice of drawing such inferences. To give any substance to our answer, we have to show how specific rules of inference could either be justified or shown to need no justification; and we have to do so in such a way as to indicate how an entire logic could be justified.

The Ability of Deductive Inference to Extend Our Knowledge

An enquiry of this kind into the justification of deduction is subject to a severe constraint. Once the justification of deductive inference is perceived as philosophically problematic at all, the temptation to which most philosophers succumb is to offer too strong a justification: to say, for instance, that when we recognise the premisses of a valid inference as true, we have thereby already recognised the truth of the conclusion. If that were correct, all that deductive inference could accomplish would be to render explicit knowledge that we already possessed: mathematics would be merely a matter of getting things down on paper, since, as soon as we had acknowledged the truth of the axioms of a mathematical theory, we should thereby know all the theorems. Obviously, this is nonsense: deductive reasoning has here been justified at the expense of its power to extend our knowledge and hence of any genuine utility.

Frege is virtually the only philosopher who both recognised the power of deductive reasoning to yield knowledge that we did not previously possess and tried to explain what gave it this power. His explanation was too specific, but surely of the right general form. Frege's semantic theory differed from Tarski's in that he took as the basis from which complex sentences are formed, not open atomic sentences as Tarski did, but simply (closed) atomic sentences. This obviated the need for a notion of satisfaction by an infinite sequence of objects (or by an unrestrictedly long finite sequence) but required an operation of forming a complex one-place predicate from a sentence as a preliminary to attaching a quantifier to the predicate to form a new sentence (with a correlative notion of the satisfaction of such a predicate by a *single* object); parallel notions of one-place higher-order predicates were needed to explain the formation of sentences with higher-order quantifiers. However readily it came to hand in application to a symbolism involving variables bound by quantifiers, Tarski's device of using open sentences—expressions like sentences except that they contain indefinitely many free variables—was unashamedly a technical device, not corresponding to any natural operation of thought. Frege, in contrast, regarded the operation of extracting the predicate from a complex sentence by omitting one or more occurrences of some one term as a linguistic reflection of an intellectual operation of the highest importance, constituting one of the most fruitful methods of concept-formation. The extraction of the predicate from the sentence depends upon recognising that the sentence displays a pattern in common with certain other sentences; a grasp of the sense of that predicate constitutes a grasp of a pattern in common between the thought expressed by the sentence and other thoughts. In apprehending the common pattern, we attain a new concept; but what makes this concept *new* is that it was not a constituent of the original thought. That is to say, we did not need to perceive the original sentence as displaying that pattern in order to grasp the thought it expressed: the pattern was there to be perceived, but it was not essential, in order to understand the sentence, that we should perceive it. For instance, the sentence 'A Harvard professor was appointed president of Harvard' has one pattern in common with 'A Harvard professor was appointed president of Princeton', another in common with 'A Stanford professor was apointed president of Harvard' and yet a third in common with 'A Columbia professor was appointed president of Columbia'. These three similarities correspond to three distinct predicates that can be extracted from the first of these four sentences; but, in order to grasp the thought expressed by it, we do not need to notice or have in mind any of the three patterns or similarities. When we notice the pattern common to the first sentence and the fourth, we have attained a new concept, that of an internally appointed university president, which, if we cared to do so, we could embody in a definition.

Whether crystallised in a definition or not, such an operation is an essential step in the formation of a quantified statement. In order to recognise the validity of an inference involving a quantified statement, it may well be necessary to be able to see some unquantified sentence as containing the predicate in question; not, indeed, as having been constructed by first forming the predicate and then inserting a term in its argument-place, but as exhibiting the pattern that constitutes the predicate. Thus, to grasp that 'Every university that appoints as president a professor of that university solves its financial problems' and 'Harvard has appointed a Harvard professor president' together entail 'Harvard will solve its financial problems', it is necessary to perceive the minor premiss as containing the predicate 'x (university) has appointed a professor of x university president' (which, using one of the devices of natural language for explicitly marking the reiteration of a term, we should express as '. . . has appointed one of its own professors president').

A generalisation of this process leads to the extraction of relational expressions—two- or more-placed predicates—and to the formation of new concepts of relations. As long as we employ only unary quantifiers, and unary second-level operators such as the abstraction operator, the generalised operation of extraction is not needed in order to explain the actual construction of complex sentences. It is needed, however, for the recognition of inferences as valid, for instance one involving quantification over relations. Strictly speaking, it is unnecessary for the recognition of inferences not involving higher-level quantification, because we can always formulate the rules of inference so that it is never required to view any relational expression as occurring in different sentences. In practice, we do not confine our reasoning to that effected by the primitive rules in, say, a formalisation of logic by natural deduction, but invoke principles of inference derivable from them; and these will include rules formulable only by means of schematic letters for relational expressions.

No one was better aware than Frege that deductive inference can be formalised: he in effect invented the first formal system for reducing the presentation (not, of course, the discovery) of mathematical proofs to a completely effective procedure, and, as Gödel remarked, was in this respect many years in advance of Russell and Whitehead; he did not, of course, know about the limitations on formalisation which Gödel's incompleteness theorem made apparent. Yet we can surely also attribute to him an awareness that an understanding of a proof demands more than an ability to recognise that it is correct. To verify that every line of a formal proof follows from earlier lines by one of a list of transformation rules is to be convinced, within the limits of human error, that it is correct; but it takes one very little way towards understanding the proof. The proof has an architecture that must be comprehended as a whole; but the first necessity for gaining such comprehension is to be intuitively convinced, for each step, that it genuinely follows from the earlier lines from which it was derived. On Frege's account, this will in general require a creative act. It is not enough merely to grasp the thought expressed by each line of the proof; in addition, one must perceive patterns common to those thoughts and others, patterns which are not given with the thoughts as a condition for grasping them but which require a further insight to apprehend. That is why, on Frege's account, even to follow a proof is an intellectually active process, in general requiring the formation of new concepts as it proceeds. It is, of course, a platitude to say the same about devising proofs; but some explanations by philosophers why deductive reasoning is justified would leave it mysterious how devising a proof can be any less mechanical than, on their picture of it, merely following one. Frege's picture makes it quite unsurprising that devising proofs requires creative imagination, not a mere application of algorithms that can be applied without thought.

Frege's account of the extraction of concepts from thoughts, effected by the extraction of predicates from sentences; his thesis that this is a process of concept-formation, since the concept extracted was not a *constituent* of the thought, nor the predicate extracted one formed in the process of constructing the sentence; and his insistence on the importance of these ideas—all these may, and should, be acknowledged to be sound. Nevertheless, in seeking to explain the fruitfulness of deductive reasoning by appeal to them alone, he laid upon them a weight greater than they can bear. He deserves our thanks, however, for seriously addressing the problem, which scarcely any other philosopher has attempted to do; and his explanation is surely along the right general lines. The fundamental idea is that inference involves the discernment of pattern. The pattern is not, in general, *imposed:* it is *there* to be discerned. But it is not normally presented together with that in which it is discerned; we can be fully aware of that without apprehending the pattern. Now *all* thought may be said to involve the discernment of pattern; even to recognise the truth of the rawest of observation statements requires us to attend to particular features or notice particular similarities in the welter of detail before us. One of the ways in which deductive inference frequently operates is to reveal a higher-order pattern—a pattern that relates different patterns to one another. Consider, for example, the proof that an even number is perfect if and only if it is of the form $2^{k-1} \cdot (2^k - 1)$, where $2^k - 1$ is prime. The procedures of checking that a number is of the given form and that it is even and perfect are quite different; the proof shows how they might be carried out simultaneously, step by step, in such a way that their results must agree. An exactly similar remark could be made about the Königsberg bridge theorem. It has no air of paradox to describe a mathematical proof as effecting such a feat: what misleads us, when we reflect on deductive inference in general, is the amazing fact that an operation of this kind can be accomplished by a sequence of such tiny transitions.

Kant made the mistake of supposing that what is arrived at by analysis cannot be new; and so he relegated analytic truths to the rank of trivialities. To insist that whatever involves new perceptions is synthetic, because creative, is not helpful: for if it is not supposed to comprise any form of deductive inference, Kant's mistake is repeated; and, if it is, the distinction Kant intended to draw between what can and what cannot be achieved by deductive means alone is blurred. Although he acknowledged, and even stressed, the creative component of deductive reasoning, Frege did not repudiate Kant's term 'analytic' for what could be attained by it alone. On the contrary, he described the process of extracting a concept from a thought as one of analysis *(Zerlegung)*: we have to distinguish the creative act of discerning what is not immediately apparent, but was there to be discerned, from the construction or imposition of what was not there before; and the former is more properly described as analysis than as synthesis.

chapter 9

Circularity, Consistency, and Harmony

Must Any Justification of a Logical Law Be Circular?

The generally received opinion among philosophers is that no effective justification of a logical law is possible, since any attempted justification must involve argument, and such argument will always appeal to the law we are seeking to justify: any justification will therefore be circular, and hence useless.

The fable of the sour grapes ought to have been told about a philosopher rather than a fox. Philosophers can never be content with demonstrating that some demand we naturally make cannot be satisfied. They feel compelled to go on to argue that it was an empty, nonsensical demand in the first place. So those who deny that logical laws are capable of any but a useless circular justification normally also deny that they need any justification; logical laws are not things of a kind that are up for justification, even if a justification were possible. Their arguments on this score are less persuasive than their arguments against the possibility of justification. It is therefore best to concentrate on the charge of unavoidable circularity.

A good exposition by Dag Prawitz of this accusation is to be found in his article "On the Idea of a General Proof Theory" (*Synthese*, vol. 27, 1974, pp. 63–77). This formulation is unusual in two ways. First, Prawitz writes as a logician, and logicians are usually inclined to take soundness and completeness proofs at their face value, as justifying formalisations of logic in terms of the semantic theory which gives the intended meanings of the logical constants; the accusation is usually made by philosophers with no great respect for mathematical logic. Secondly, Prawitz does not direct his accusation at *all* attempted justifications of logical laws but only at those formulated in *semantic* or *model-theoretic* terms; it is of course these that proponents of the circularity have normally had in mind, not conceiving that there could be a *proof-theoretic* justification of a fundamental law. Prawitz uses as an example the inference from $\neg\, \forall x\, \mathbf{P}(x)$ to $\exists x\, \neg\, \mathbf{P}(x)$, and argues thus:

Whether e.g. a sentence $\exists x \neg P(x)$ follows logically from a sentence $\neg \forall x\, P(x)$ depends according to this [model-theoretic] definition on whether $\exists x \neg P(x)$ is true in each model $(\mathbf{D}, \mathbf{S})$ in which $\neg \forall x\, P(x)$ is true. And this again is the same as to ask whether there is an element e in $\mathbf{D}$ that does not belong to $\mathbf{S}$ whenever it is not the case that every e in $\mathbf{D}$ belongs to $\mathbf{S}$, i.e. we are essentially back to the question whether $\exists x \neg A(x)$ follows from $\neg \forall x\, A(x)$.

It is natural to object that the example does not admit of unrestricted generalisation. When, for example, we wish to persuade a beginner that the formula $\exists x\, \forall y\, (P(y) \to P(x))$ is (classically) valid, we do not say to him, 'Well, you see, in every model $(\mathbf{D}, \mathbf{S})$ there will be an element e in $\mathbf{D}$ such that, for every element d in $\mathbf{D}$, if d is in $\mathbf{S}$, then e is in $\mathbf{S}$', since this is very far from being intuitively true. We should, rather, argue as follows: 'In any model $(\mathbf{D}, \mathbf{S})$, either $\exists x\, P(x)$ is true or it is not. If it is true, choose some element e in $\mathbf{S}$: since $P(x)$ is true of it, so is $\forall y\, (P(y) \to P(x))$, and so $\exists x\, \forall y\, (P(y) \to P(x))$ is true. If $\exists x\, P(x)$ is not true, choose e as any element in $\mathbf{D}$: since $P(y)$ is false of every element d in $\mathbf{D}$, $P(y) \to P(x)$ will be true of any such d when e is assigned to x, and so $\forall y\, (P(y) \to P(x))$ will be true of e; so again the formula $\exists x\, \forall y\, (P(y) \to P(x))$ will be true in the model'.

Prawitz's claim is thus evidently too strong: not every semantic justification of a logical law must appeal to that very law in the course of the reasoning. It may be urged on Prawitz's behalf, however, that he did not need to make so strong a claim. The proponent of inevitable circularity may say that his thesis is meant to apply only to *fundamental* logical laws. When, as in the foregoing example, we construct, in the semantic metalanguage, a non-circular argument for the validity of some formula or rule of inference, then, he argues, we are merely imitating in the metalanguage some formal derivation that could be given in the logical system. His contention is, therefore, that the best we can do, by appeal to a semantic theory, is to show that certain logical laws hold if certain others are assumed to hold; and, whenever we can do this, we can also show that law to be derivable from those others without any appeal to semantic notions. In such a case, we are not treating the law as fundamental, and the resort to the semantic theory has accomplished nothing for us.

It is far from obvious that this contention is universally cogent. If the Axiom of Choice may be regarded as a law of logic, it is a fundamental law in the sense of one not derivable from others more fundamental. Yet it is not apparent that no convincing argument—as opposed to a mathematical proof—can be constructed for its validity which does not itself appeal to that Axiom or some equivalent of it. Nevertheless, the contention looks extremely plausible for elementary laws—laws of sentential or first-order logic—such as *modus ponens* or the distributive law. On first examination, then, the proponent of the circularity thesis has a highly plausible case.

We need therefore to enquire whether circularity of this kind deprives of all value any justification that displays it. It is not immediately obvious that it does; for the circularity complained of is not the ordinary gross circularity that consists of including the conclusion to be reached among the initial premises of the argument. We have some argument that purports to arrive at the conclusion that such-and-such a logical law is valid; and the charge is not that this argument must include among its premises the statement that that logical law is valid, but only that at least one of the inferential steps in the argument must be taken in accordance with that law. We may call this a 'pragmatic' circularity. Our first question must be whether a pragmatic circularity vitiates an argument as incontestably as does a gross circularity.

The answer depends in part on the purpose for which the justification is being given, and in part on the character of the argument. If the justification is intended as suasive, then the pragmatic circularity will defeat its principal objective. That is to say, if the justification is addressed to someone who genuinely doubts whether the law is valid, and is intended to persuade him that it is, it will fail of its purpose, since he will not accept the argument. If, on the other hand, it is intended to satisfy the philosopher's perplexity about our entitlement to reason in accordance with such a law, it may well do so. The philosopher does not seriously doubt the validity of the law and is therefore prepared to accept an argument constructed in accordance with it. He does not need to be persuaded of the truth of the conclusion; what he is seeking is an *explanation* of its being true. An explanation frequently takes the form of a deductive argument, in which the conclusion is the fact to be explained. There is therefore no uncertainty about the conclusion, which we already know; and often the best reason for believing the premises is that they offer an explanation for the conclusion's being true. A gross circularity is as damaging to an explanatory argument as to a suasive one; but a pragmatic circularity need do it no harm at all.

We should ask ourselves *why* a gross circularity should be so damaging. The reason is that if one sets oneself to derive a conclusion from a set of premises that contains that conclusion, one cannot fail; and succeeding at a task at which one cannot fail neither proves anything nor explains anything. The mere occurrence of a pragmatic circularity does not guarantee success: it depends upon the theoretical framework to which the argument appeals. When this framework consists of

a programmatic interpretation—with so-called disquotational specifications of the meanings of the logical constants—then success *is*
guaranteed: whatever laws are treated as valid in the metalanguage
will be demonstrably valid in the object-language. For just that reason,
a justification in terms of a programmatic interpretation will lack
either suasive or explanatory power. Tarski, indeed, did not make
the mistake of supposing otherwise, that is, of thinking that a truth-
definition of his kind could serve simultaneously as a means of specifying the meanings of the logical constants or of any other expressions
of the object-language. On the contrary, he specifically proposed
that the meanings of the classical sentential operators be regarded as
being fixed by the logical laws stipulated as governing them. But a
similar situation does not obtain for all conceivable justifications of
logical laws. If, for example, we adopt the semantics given by the
Beth trees for the sentential operators, no licence to employ classical
reasoning in the metalanguage will enable us to exhibit, as valid, laws
holding classically but not intuitionistically. Against a background
such as this, there is no guarantee that a law treated as holding in
the metalanguage will be able to be shown to be valid in the object-
language; and hence, when, in any given case, we *are* able to show
some law to be valid in the object-language, we have certainly proved
something, even if the demonstration was pragmatically circular, because we have succeeded in a task whose success was not guaranteed
in advance.

Thus, from the standpoint of a philosopher seeking an explanation
of the possibility of deductive inference in general, or perplexed about
some particular principle of inference we habitually employ, there is
nothing problematic about a justification given in terms of some
semantic theory which he finds satisfactory, that is, which he views as
cohering with the type of meaning-theory for the language as a whole
which he is disposed to favour. Such a justification is very likely to be
pragmatically circular; but he has no reason to dismiss it on that
ground. A justification given in terms of a semantic theory will not, by
itself, solve his problem, which is not purely semantic but also epistemological. He wants to know how we can both recognise the law as
valid and use it to attain knowledge we did not possess before; but he
may use a semantic justification of the law as a base for his answer to
the epistemological problem.

In the presence of a genuine dispute over the validity of a logical
law, by contrast, pragmatic circularity has to be avoided. Here the interest of the participants to this dispute is likely to be more narrowly
semantic. Since a justification of a logical law will take the form of a
deductive argument, there can be no justification that appeals to no

other laws whatever; but that does not matter, since there is no sceptic who denies the validity of *all* principles of deductive reasoning, and, if there were, there would obviously be no reasoning with him. Hence the ideal, in a dispute between adherents of different logics, would be the use, by each, of a semantic theory that allowed a justification of the laws disputed by the other that appealed only to laws that the other accepted, and hence was not pragmatically circular. A semantic theory can also be used for demonstrating a purported logical law to be invalid, and in such a dispute this has an equal importance in establishing communication between the disputants and explaining to each the other's point of view. No question of pragmatic circularity arises in this case; but, once again, the demonstration ought, if possible, to appeal only to laws accepted as valid by the other. This ideal may often be only imperfectly attainable. Yet even an approach to it may suffice to give to each some understanding of how the matter is seen by the other, and of the meanings he attaches to the logical constants, both of which were previously quite opaque to him. Neither is likely to persuade the other, because each will reject the other's semantic theory, but they will no longer be baffled by each other's disagreement. Moreover, they will have reduced that disagreement to something they have sufficient common ground to argue about, namely, the appropriate semantic theory to adopt: and this will ultimately turn upon what type of meaning-theory is the proper one in terms of which to describe the workings of our language.

Do Logical Laws Need Any Justification?

It is of little use to argue for the possibility of justifying logical laws without circularity, or at least without vicious circularity, if any justification of them is otiose; such justifications are otiose if there is no criticism that can be directed against those laws. Philosophers have supplemented their attempted demonstration that a justification of a logical law is *impossible* with a further argument to show that it is in any case *unneeded*. For, they maintain, it is by our choice of the logical laws governing them that we determine the meanings of the logical constants. We have the right to make them mean what we like; and therefore we have the right to adopt what logical laws we choose. The question of any justification of these laws accordingly does not arise: logical laws are *self-justifying*, that is to say, justified simply by being the laws we *treat* as valid.

This is very unlike saying that the rules of a board game need no justification, being justified simply by being the rules that we have chosen to observe when playing that game. The pieces used in the game have no significance outside the game: they are not used for anything but playing it. The logical constants, however, are used in sentences that are not figuring, on a given occasion of utterance, in any deductive inference—sentences that may be used in any of the manifold ways in which sentences, whether or not they contain any logical constants, may be used: as expressions of intention, as inductively supported generalisations, as hypotheses, as stipulations, rules, or laws, and in all other conceivable ways in which assertoric statements can be employed, including fictional narrative. Moreover, logical constants figure equally in non-assertoric sentences. The meanings of the logical constants cannot, therefore, *consist* in their role in deductive inferences: they must have meanings of a more general kind whereby they contribute to the meanings of sentences containing them just as other words do. It may still be that the meanings of the logical constants are *determined* by the logical laws that govern their use in deductive arguments; but this cannot be assumed—it needs to be *shown*. To show it, we have first to explain in what their meanings, in general, consist, in such a way as to make clear how they go to fix the content of sentences in which they occur just as the other words in those sentences do. Having thus formulated an adequate general conception of what the logical constants mean, we have then to show that these meanings stand in one-to-one correspondence with the logical laws that govern them: if the meanings were different, the logical laws would also be different. But this is not enough. A biunique correspondence might obtain, although the logical laws might be derivable from the meanings of the logical constants only with some ingenuity, while the converse derivation could not be humanly, and perhaps not even in principle effectively, carried out. That would be just such a situation in which a justification of the logical laws was urgently required: for it to be otiose, it has to be maintained that we can fix the meanings of the logical constants *by* selecting whatever logical laws we choose to recognise, that is, that their meanings can be *read off* from the laws.

Just this is what we do not know how to do. If someone simply announces that *he* understands, or proposes to understand, one or more logical constants in such a way that certain logical laws that we count as valid no longer hold, we can only ask, 'And what way is that?' Anyone familiar with quantum logic will know that in it the rule of or-elimination holds only in a restricted form: **C** can be inferred from ⌜**A** ∨ **B**⌝ only if it follows from each of **A** and **B** *without* any collateral premisses or hypotheses. Thus an inference of the form

$$\frac{\mathbf{D}:\mathbf{A}\vee\mathbf{B} \qquad \mathbf{A}:\mathbf{C} \qquad \mathbf{B}:\mathbf{C}}{\mathbf{D}:\mathbf{C}}$$

is valid in quantum logic, but not one of the form

$$\frac{\mathbf{D : A \vee B} \qquad \mathbf{A, E : C} \qquad \mathbf{B, F : C}}{\mathbf{D, E, F : C}}$$

which, of course, is valid under the full or-elimination rule. Now suppose that someone announces that he so understands the connective 'or' that only the restricted, not the full, or-elimination rule holds good for it. Can someone, who may never have heard of quantum logic, recognise, or work out, how this individual does understand it? He attaches a weaker meaning to ⌜**A** or **B**⌝ than we do, since, for him, it does not have all the implications that it has for us. What meaning *does* he attach to it, then? If he tells you, 'Either deforestation is halted within the next ten years, or human life will be extinct before the end of the next century', and you are disposed to think he knows what he is talking about, how alarmed should you be? Just *what* is he asserting? How can we, or he, be sure that there *is* a meaning that can be attached to the word 'or' in accordance with which the restricted, but not the full, elimination rule is valid? Is there a guarantee that there are appropriate meanings for the logical constants to fit *any* set of logical laws that we choose to select, but no laws not derivable from that set?

What holds good for someone who announces that he rejects a logical law that we are accustomed to treat as valid holds good equally for someone who announces that he proposes to regard as valid a logical law that we should be disposed to reject. If we use the notation ⌜**A** □→ **B**⌝ for the counterfactual conditional ⌜If it had been the case that **A**, then it would have been the case that **B**⌝, a little reflection shows that the rule of inference

$$\frac{\mathbf{A} \,\square\!\!\rightarrow \mathbf{B} \vee \mathbf{C}}{(\mathbf{A} \,\square\!\!\rightarrow \mathbf{B}) \vee (\mathbf{A} \,\square\!\!\rightarrow \mathbf{C})}$$

is not intuitively valid. Suppose, nevertheless, that someone announced that *he* used counterfactual conditionals in such a way that the law did hold for him. Evidently, he would be able to arrive at conclusions, in particular, counterfactual conclusions, that we could not: but how would this affect the *content* of the counterfactual assertions that he made? He would, of necessity, mean something different by a statement of the form ⌜If it had been the case that **A**, then it would have been the case that **B**⌝ from what we should mean by it: but *what* exactly would he mean? How could we set about answering that question?

These perplexities go to the heart of the concept of understanding. Suppose that there were an International Academy of Logic, with the authority to issue edicts, from time to time, laying down which logical laws were, until further notice, to be treated as valid or invalid; and assume that its decrees were universally respected. If it were to pronounce that henceforward only the restricted or-elimination rule was to be recognised, or that the above rule allowing counterfactual implication to distribute across disjunction was henceforth to be counted as valid, we could obey these decrees; but we should lose the sense that we any longer understood what we were saying. The *rules* of the language-game would be clear enough; but its *point* would now escape us. It is not enough, in order to understand utterances in a given language, to be master of a practice. The practice imposed at any stage by the Academy would be clear enough, but we should quickly lose the sense of understanding. This would not affect our understanding only of those sentences containing the relevant logical constant, the word 'or' or the counterfactual 'if'. The rule of or-elimination enables us to infer a non-disjunctive conclusion from a disjunctive premiss; a weakening of that rule is therefore likely to deprive us of grounds for asserting statements not containing the connective 'or' that we should previously have been in a position to assert. We have no way of circumscribing the range of sentences whose use would be affected by such a change in our practice, and hence, presumably, their content: the meanings of all the sentences in the language would, or at least might, undergo a shift in consequence of the change in what we were willing to recognise as valid reasoning. The same would hold good for the adoption of an essentially new rule, such as that envisaged for counterfactual conditionals. On the face of it, the new rule allows us only to conclude from a counterfactual premiss to a statement also involving the counterfactual 'if'. But our use of counterfactual conditionals is not a part of our linguistic practice fenced off from the rest: we seek to determine which counterfactual conditionals it is right to assert in order to decide which statements of other types are to be accepted, for instance, assessments of probability, on which will depend a variety of judgements that we make, and attributions of moral or legal responsibility. Hence, again, a change in the principles governing our reasoning about counterfactual matters may have consequences for our use of a range of non-counterfactual statements.

It might be objected that all this is to confuse understanding with the mere *feeling* of understanding. To be sure, we sometimes have a feeling or impression of understanding, and likewise a feeling or impression of not understanding, but such feelings matter little. Genuine understanding of a statement or form of statement consists, according to the objector, in knowing how to use it; and, after the Academy of Logic had issued its decree, we should know as much about how disjunctive statements, or counterfactual conditionals, were henceforward to be used as there was to be known. The criticism is misplaced: the missing component of understanding is not to be stigmatised as a 'mere' feeling. Someone is taught a new game, sits down to play, and remarks, 'I don't really know what I am doing': he has grasped the rules but can perceive nothing of the strategy. For all that, he plays very well; and this proves to be not just beginner's luck, because he continues to do so on later occasions, while still protesting that he does not know what he is doing. Should we dismiss this as merely an irrelevant feeling, since he has shown himself a master of the *practice*? It depends upon the point of the game—what the enjoyment is derived from. The enjoyment of horse racing comes from winning and the excitement of seeing one's horse draw ahead; so someone who is very good at picking winners loses very little if he has no idea how he does it. But the enjoyment of games of strategy consists principally in devising one's strategy and seeing whether it works; so one who does not know why he plays as he does loses most of that enjoyment, like someone playing according to the instructions of another. What he lacks is not the *feeling* of understanding, but the *knowledge* that is an essential component of understanding. It is that knowledge that we should lack if we were compelled to reason in accordance with principles that appeared to us invalid or gratuitously restricted: we could rightly confess that we no longer knew what we were saying. Fully to know what one says is to command a completely clear view of the working of the language. Whether that is possible without explicitly apprehending the shape of a meaning-theory for the language is unclear; but, to achieve the level of understanding that we ordinarily have of our own utterances, some inchoate conception of what gives them significance and determines their content is needed. The conception of this possessed by ordinary speakers is so inchoate that we hardly know we have it until we are brought, in fact or in imagination, into a situation in which we lack it, like that produced by an unmotivated change in the logical laws to be observed; in such a situation, we should no longer know what our words meant, however adept we were at using them in accordance with the rules imposed on us.

The thesis that any arbitrary set of logical laws is self-justifying may well be called 'logical formalism'. The analogy with mathematical formalism is quite close. Quine's *New Foundations* system of set theory is one of the very few formal systems to have been constructed on strict formalist principles: that is, with no idea in mind of what a model for the theory would be like, but, in its place, a hunch that a purely syntactical restriction on admissible instances of the comprehension axiom would hold the set-theoretic paradoxes at bay. The result was not a mathematical theory but an *object* of mathematical theorising, most of it directed towards trying to find a model of the formal theory. It would occur to very few to regard proving theorems in *New Foundations* as establishing facts about a well-defined mathematical structure or class of structures, those, namely, that satisfy the axioms of *New Foundations*. Without some intuitive conception of the character of such a structure, one cannot talk *about* it, because one literally would not know what one was talking about: one can only wonder whether any such thing exists.

Are Logical Laws Subject to Criticism?

Arthur Prior, in a famous short article, long ago pointed out an objection to unrestricted licence to adopt what logical laws one chooses: they might render the entire language inconsistent. His example was a binary connective * having its introduction rules in common with 'or' and its elimination rules in common with 'and'. Inconsistency is immediate: from **A** we could derive $\ulcorner$**A** * **B**$\urcorner$, for any statement **B**, and, from $\ulcorner$**A** * **B**$\urcorner$, we could then derive **B**; from any statement one could derive any other. Wittgenstein, one of the strongest advocates of logical formalism, was the only one not to balk even at such an outcome. The appearance of a contradiction was not, he thought, to be regarded with superstitious dread; rather, we should simply go round it. Obviously, once a contradiction has been discovered, no one is going to go *through* it: to exploit it to show that the train leaves at 11:52 or that the next Pope will be a woman. The problem is, of course, to know *how* to go round the contradiction. In Prior's example, for instance, we could not be safe from the contradiction simply by avoiding an application of *-elimination immediately after an application of *-introduction; contradictions will lurk as long as we continue to use the connective * as subject to those two pairs of rules. Moreover, as is well known, once a given set of assumptions or of rules is known to lead to contradiction, we can no longer have any confidence in the truth of conclusions reached from those assumptions or in accordance with those rules; for, if we had a warrant for supposing such conclusions true, there could be no contradiction.

What can have prompted Wittgenstein to deny such obvious truths? Paradoxically, his overpowering drive for absolute consistency of thought, which deflected him from ever being content to allow one or two exceptions to any thesis that he maintained. He utterly rejected the idea, prominent in Frege's writings and eagerly adopted by Tarski, that natural languages have defects that impair their functioning as languages; he opposed the supposition that any conceivable language ever *could* have such defects. Hence his logical formalism: any set of logical laws comprises the fundamental laws of some conceivable language, and thus no such set can be subject to legitimate criticism. Now it is evidently possible that the principles embodied in the practice of using a given language can generate contradictions; Wittgenstein was therefore driven to maintain that inconsistency was no defect.

There can be no a priori ground, however, for denying that a natural language can be defective in the sense of operating imperfectly and thereby failing fully to realise the ends it is intended to serve. The ends of language are *internal:* there is no form of description of what a language is required to do—to communicate thoughts, for example—that would represent it as something in principle achievable without the use of language. But this is not to say that a language does not have ends, which one who has language can apprehend, and which it may attain more successfully or less successfully. The possibility of failure arises primarily because of the multiplicity of principles governing our linguistic practice. For the language to function as intended, these principles must be in harmony with one another; but the mere fact that certain principles are observed in no way guarantees that the necessary harmony will obtain. Inconsistency is the grossest type of malfunction to which a language, considered as governed by a complex of accepted practices in using it, may be subject. That it is no superstition to fear the occurrence, in natural languages as in formal theories, of this worst of calamities is evidenced by the existence of paradoxes properly so called. A paradox is either a strong counterexample to a whole deductive argument, rather than to a single rule, the puzzle being to find the step at which the error occurred; or it is an instance of a rule of inference such that our confidence in the validity of the rule is exactly counter-balanced by our confidence that the premisses of this instance are true and the conclusion false. In either case, we have a conflict between our inferential practice and those other features of linguistic practice that dictate our acceptance of the premisses and our rejection of the conclusion. Until the paradox is resolved, we cannot fully trust the practices we learned in learning the language. It may be that, when the resolution is found, we can continue for most of the time to observe those practices, knowing now just where the danger lies and how it may be avoided; that does not alter the fact that the paradox highlighted an imperfection in the functioning of the language.

We can do much better than to speak vaguely of the multiplicity of principles embodied in our linguistic practice: we can distinguish two general categories of such principles. The first category consists of those that have to do with the circumstances that warrant an assertion, the basis on which we may recognise a statement as having been established. There is multiplicity within this category, according as we are concerned with when an assertion is *conclusively* established, or with what merely warrants its being made, though defeasibly: but principles of both these kinds fall within the same broad category. Plainly, such principles form an important part of what we have to learn when we acquire language: we need to know when we are *entitled* to make any given assertion, and when we are *required* to acknowledge it as true. We may permit ourselves to speak of them as principles of *verification*, provided that we do not make the mistake of the logical positivists in regarding a possible verification of a given statement as attaching to it independently of the rest of the language, and hence as constituted by a sequence of raw sense experiences; just this mistake was one of the two dogmas of empiricism repudiated by Quine. In general, what we actually treat as establishing a statement as true involves both observation and inference. Reports of observation occupy one end of a scale, being arrived at without any inferential process, while mathematical theorems, not dependent on observation, occupy the other; most of the statements we make occupy some intermediate position. A realistic characterisation of what, from our understanding of a statement, we recognise as required to verify it, will need, in almost all cases, to be formulated relatively to our acceptance of other statements which may enter into an inference to the given statement as conclusion. This is demanded by the interconnectedness of language, expressed by Wittgenstein in the slogan, 'To understand a sentence is to understand a language'.

This aspect of linguistic use was proposed by the positivists as determinative of meaning. Their theory of meaning—more accurately, their proposal for the construction of a meaning-theory—was that *verification* should be taken as the central notion: we should regard the content of a statement as determined by what is required for its verification. Clearly, however, our use of the language cannot be exhaustively described in terms of our application of principles of verification. If that were all, we should be skilled at making assertions but incapable of responding to the assertions of others. The pragmatists should be understood as making the converse proposal that the content of a statement should be regarded as determined by its *consequences* for one who accepts it as true: my understanding of the statement consists in my grasp of the difference it would make to me if I were to believe it. A related notion belonging to the same broad category is that of what a speaker commits himself to by making a given assertion. These notions both fall under the general head of the *difference made* by an utterance. The significance of an utterance—assertoric or otherwise—can be seen as consisting in the (potential) difference the utterance makes to what subsequently happens: in what way are things now different, in virtue of its having been made, from how they would have been if it had not been made? In acquiring language, we learn a variety of principles determining the consequences of possible utterances; these compose the second of our two categories of principles which govern our linguistic practice.

It is easier to acknowledge this general distinction between two aspects of the use of sentences than to apply it to specific expressions. The difficulty of application is that which always bedevils the analysis of complex systems: how to partition the circumstances in which an effect is produced into significantly distinguishable components, and how to apportion to those multiple components their respective contributions to the resultant effect. The problem is sufficiently acute for the verificationist, but more acute yet for the pragmatist. What someone counts as establishing the truth of a given statement depends upon what other propositions he knows or believes to be true. What counts for him as acting on the truth of a given statement, however, notoriously also depends on what he wants, that is, on his goals and desires. We should nevertheless beware of speaking too hastily of 'holistic' systems in this connection, since to describe a system as holistic, if it means more than just that it involves a multiplicity of interacting factors, is to deny that any partition of it into distinguishable factors can ever be descriptively adequate; and this is to surrender before the opening shots have been fired.

We should also beware of placing much reliance on our intuitive inclinations about what is required for the understanding of an individual word or expression. What someone must know, and of what he may be ignorant, if he is to be credited with knowing what a given expression means, common parlance does not decide on any systematic principle. It varies from expression to expression and depends heavily both on what happens to be known by ordinarily well-informed speakers of the language and on the contexts in which an average speaker is most likely to have to use the expression. The theorist of meaning is certainly concerned to say what it is for an individual word, of any of the many kinds of words there are, to have a meaning. Since a word can have a meaning only as a word belonging to some language, the theorist can say what it is for it to have a meaning only by saying what it is for a system of which it forms part to function as a language; and his account of this will have the greatest interest when he takes the language to be an existing natural language, or at least a simplified or idealised version of one. But even when the word is one drawn from an actual language, and he wishes to describe it as meaning just what it does in that language, the theorist has no responsibility to identify its meaning with what we should ordinarily say had to be known by anyone to whom we should be willing to ascribe a full understanding of the word. What is demanded of a meaning-theory is that it give an acceptable explanation of what a mastery of a whole language consists in. It can do this only if it associates with each word, and with each general construction by means of which sentences are formed from words, something that must be known about that word or that construction: the sum total of this knowledge will then constitute a knowledge of the whole language. It is not required, however, that possession of the knowledge associated by the meaning-theory with each word or construction should be sufficient for us, in everyday contexts in which we are not constructing any systematic meaning-theory, to say that someone who has that knowledge understands that word or construction. On the contrary, it is sufficient that the meaning-theory be such that, for every given expression of the language, anyone who knows the whole theory will know everything that someone is required to know if he is to be said to understand that expression.

This observation affords a rebuttal of a crude type of criticism that may be aimed either at a verificationist or at a pragmatist meaning-theory, the one taking the canonical verification of a statement, the other the consequences of accepting a statement, as its central notion. Someone would not be said to understand the phrase 'valid argument', for instance, if he knew *only* how to establish (in a large range of cases) that an argument was valid but had no idea that, by accepting an argument as valid, he has committed himself to accepting the conclusion if he accepts the premises. The analogue holds good for a great many expressions: we should not say of someone who could recognise when a statement involving such an expression had been conclusively established but did not know the point of making that statement, or what could be inferred from it, that he understood the expression. But this fact has no tendency to show it impossible to construct a meaning-theory whose central notion is that of what would establish the truth of a statement, and which therefore represents the sense of any word as the way in which it contributes to determining, for any sentence in which it occurs, how a statement made by uttering that sentence may be established as true. The positivist slogan, 'The meaning of a sentence is the method of its verification', was not meant, or ought not to have been meant, as an analysis of what we ordinarily *call* 'knowing the meaning of a sentence'. It constituted, rather, a proposal for what should be taken to be the central notion of a meaning-theory. Exactly the same holds good for the pragmatist conception of meaning. It is fruitless to criticise this on the ground that someone would not ordinarily be credited with understanding the phrase 'valid argument' if he knew only that the conclusion of a valid argument is guaranteed to be true if the premisses are, but had no idea which arguments are valid and which are not, and that the analogue holds good for a great many expressions of the language. 'The meaning of a judgment is the sum of its consequences' is, likewise, not to be interpreted as an analysis of our hazy everyday notion of the meanings of the expressions composing a sentence, but as a proposal for the correct form that a meaning-theory ought to take.

The difficulty in applying the twin notions of verification and of consequences is therefore not so much one of *discerning* the relevant feature amidst a welter of irrelevant detail as of making the right *selection* of that feature which, within the framework of an entire meaning-theory, may be taken as representing the meaning of the given word or expression. Whatever has been chosen to be the central notion of the meaning-theory—verification in a positivist theory, consequences in a pragmatist one—will, within that theory, constitute the core meaning of any sentence of the language; and the feature selected as composing the meaning of the given expression will then constitute the contribution of that expression to the core meaning of any sentence containing it. There is no algorithm to determine what this feature is, nor even any criterion for deciding between alternative proposals. What the theorist aims at is simply to make the right choices, in all cases, that will collectively yield a tractable theory, and yet one that will deliver an adequate account of all that is involved in a mastery of the language as a whole.

Our immediate concern is not with the question which, if either, of these aspects of our use of sentences should be taken as the central notion of the meaning-theory, but with the mere fact that linguistic practice *has* these two aspects. The fundamental problem at issue is whether a language, which is to say an entire linguistic practice, can be flawed or defective. This question bifurcates. First, is there anything that would count as a defect? If so, then, secondly, could it pass undetected? Once we have allowed that the principles by which assertions are warranted can be inconsistent, and that such inconsistency undermines the reliability we expect such principles to possess, we have agreed that defects are theoretically possible. When we go on, as we must, to acknowledge that an inconsistency may be hidden, we have recognised that the mere fact that it is established affords no ground for assuming a linguistic practice free from defect. With that, we perceive that our linguistic practice is no more sacrosanct, no more certain to achieve the ends at which it is aimed, no more immune to criticism or proposals for revision, than our social, political, or economic practice.

Inconsistency, however, though the worst, is not the only possible defect of a linguistic practice. The two complementary features of any such practice ought to be in harmony with each other: and there is no automatic mechanism to ensure that they will be. The notion of harmony is difficult to make precise but intuitively compelling: it is obviously not possible for the two features of the use of any expression to be determined quite independently. Given what is conventionally accepted as serving to establish the truth of a given statement, the consequences of accepting it as true cannot be fixed arbitrarily; conversely, given what accepting a statement as true is taken to involve, it cannot be arbitrarily determined what is to count as establishing it as true. The supposition that the two features could be determined independently was the error of the theory, now long discarded, of descriptive and emotive meaning. The 'descriptive' meaning represented the criterion for applying the term, and the miscalled 'emotive' meaning what one commited oneself to by applying it; the theory assumed that the glue holding them together was nothing more than impermanent convention. On the contrary, the requirement that each be in full harmony with the other is far more stringent than that there be some degree of natural congruence between them. The failure to observe this was the fallacy in the notorious 'paradigm case' argument. The case cited in an application of this argument was a paradigm for the conventional application of the term. It was then assumed that there could be nothing problematic in drawing the standard consequences from its being applied to this case, whereas it had been precisely these which had been challenged by the philosophical contention supposedly refuted by the argument. There is even less reason to presume that perfect harmony prevails within our linguistic practice than to presume consistency, and even greater difficulty in discerning whether the practice is harmonious than whether it is consistent.

Harmony and the Logical Constants

The logical constants are much easier to think about, in relation to our two aspects of linguistic use, and hence in the framework of either a verificationist or a pragmatist meaning-theory, than any other words of our language. For, although we have no right to assume it a priori, we may at least hope that, in their case, the matter can be treated entirely in terms of logical laws. If we are wishing to formulate the meaning of, say, a binary sentential connective (), our task will be to explain the meaning of a sentence in which that connective is the principal operator, assuming that the meanings of the two sub-sentences are given. If we are working in the context of a verificationist meaning-theory, we have to find a means of specifying what, in general, is to constitute a canonical means of verifying a statement made by uttering a sentence of the form ⌜A ( ) B⌝, given how A and B are to be verified. The hope is that this can be done by appeal to the introduction rule or rules for the connective ( ) in a natural deduction formalisation of logic. For instance, it is highly plausible to say that a canonical verification of a statement of the form ⌜A and B⌝ will proceed by verifying both A and B, and then applying the standard introduction rule for 'and'. It is almost equally plausible to say that a canonical verification of an existential statement ⌜For some x, A(x)⌝ will consist in the verification of some instance ⌜A(t)⌝, followed by an application of the existential quantifier-introduction rule, that is to say, the rule often known as existential generalisation. It is by no means obvious that these tactics will always be successful; for instance, the claim that the canonical verification of a statement such as 'If you leave the kettle on the ring too long, all the water will boil away' will proceed by constructing a deduction of the consequent from the antecedent lacks immediate plausibility. Nevertheless, we have for the logical constants a hope that a verificationist account of their meanings can be given in terms of a familiar type of logical law, allowing us, in their case, a gratifyingly sharp notion of what those meanings consist in.

Just the same holds good for pragmatist meaning-theories. In this case, we shall have to explain the canonical means of drawing the consequences of a statement of the form ⌜A ( ) B⌝, given that we know the consequences of A and of B. The hope here will be that this can be done by appeal to the *elimination* rule or rules for the connective in a natural deduction system. Thus, again, it is highly plausible that the canonical means for arriving at the consequences of a conjunctive statement ⌜A and B⌝ will consist in applying either or both of the standard elimination rules for 'and', and then drawing consequences from A or from B or both. It is almost equally plausible to say that the canonical derivation of the consequences of a universally quantified statement ⌜For every x, A(x)⌝ will consist in one or more applications of the universal quantifier-elimination rule, namely, the rule often known as universal instantiation, to obtain one or more instances of the form ⌜A(t)⌝, from which further consequences can then be drawn. In this case, the conditional gives rise to no doubts: it is reasonable to think that *modus ponens*—the standard elimination rule for 'if'—constitutes the canonical means of deriving consequences from a statement of the form ⌜If A, then B⌝.

It is precisely a fear of disharmony that blocks any easy acceptance of a change in the rules of inference we recognise; for, if there is harmony already, a change will disturb it, or, at the least, risks doing so. A weakening of the introduction rules, while leaving the elimination rules unchanged, or a strengthening of the elimination rules, while leaving the introduction rules unchanged, must upset a harmony that prevailed previously: we can now draw conclusions not warranted by our methods of arriving at the premisses. The adoption of a new rule, such as that allowing distribution of the counterfactual 'if' across disjunction, which is neither an introduction rule nor an elimination rule in the usual sense, will produce an unpredictable readjustment, which might move from one equilibrium to another but might simply destroy existing harmony. A strengthening of the introduction rules, while leaving the elimination rules unchanged, or a weakening of the elimination rules, while leaving the introduction rules unchanged (as with the restriction of or-elimination), will not produce so deleterious an effect. Still, if harmony prevailed before, it will mean that we are now either demanding, in justification for asserting a logically complex statement, unnecessarily much for any consequences we admit as following from it, or, conversely, failing to draw all the consequences our methods of coming to recognise such a statement as true would warrant.

Someone who has not opted for any particular theory of meaning, whether verificationist or pragmatist, but wants to characterise our understanding of the logical constants in terms of our mastery of the use of sentences containing them, is likely to invoke the introduction rule for the existential quantifier and the elimination rule for the universal one. Wittgenstein, for instance, does precisely this in scattered places in his writings. But this can hardly be meant as more than illustrative. No one can be said to understand either quantifier unless he at least knows *both* the introduction and elimination rules for it: only a systematic theory, which will provide for the derivation of all other features of use from that which has been selected as the central notion of the theory, can afford to pick out one or the other type of rule as *the* distinguished determinant of meaning.

Conservative Extensions

The best hope for a more precise characterisation of the notion of harmony lies in an adaptation of the logicians' concept of a conservative extension. Given a formal theory, we may strengthen it by expanding the formal language, adding new primitive predicates, terms, or functors, and introducing new axioms or rules of inference to govern expressions formed by means of the new vocabulary. In the new theory, we can prove much that we could not even express in the old one; but it is a 'conservative extension' of the original theory if we can prove in it no statement expressed in the original restricted vocabulary that we could not already prove in the original theory.

Consider, now, not a formal theory but a natural language; and suppose it contains an expression **E** such that the conventional consequences of applying **E** are in disharmony with the conventional warrant for doing so. By means of **E**, we may be able to say things we should have no way of saying if the language did not contain that expression; but the disharmony means that we are accustomed to draw conclusions from statements made by means of **E** that what we treat as justifying the assertion of those statements does not entitle us to draw. Now those conclusions, if expressed verbally at all, cannot consist of statements containing **E**; for the drawing of *such* conclusions must count as part of our conventions governing the justification of assertions involving **E**. If there is disharmony, it must manifest itself in consequences not themselves involving the expression **E** but taken by us to follow from the acceptance of a statement **S** containing **E**. Acceptance of **S** might issue directly in actions not warranted by the grounds, rated adequate under our linguistic conventions, on which the statement **S** had been made; or our having accepted **S** as true might be taken to justify some further assertion not involving **E**, likewise not warranted by the grounds for making **S**. The grounds, here, must equally be capable of being formulated without the use of **E**; if this is not true of the *immediate* grounds, we must trace them back to those of which it does hold. Now to say that the action or the assertion was not warranted by our grounds for making the statement **S** is to say that we should not have treated it as so warranted but for our introduction of that statement; and that is precisely to say that our language, as we have it, is not a conservative extension of what remains of the language if we delete from it the expression **E**. We should not regard the grounds for asserting **S** as on their own having the consequences that that assertion has; if, lacking **E**, we could not formulate **S**, we should have no way of arriving at those consequences. The conventions we have adopted as governing **E**, however, allow us first to assert **S** on those grounds and then to draw those consequences: so, when **E** is added to the 'fragment' consisting of the rest of the language, we obtain a non-conservative extension of that fragment.

A conservative extension in the logicians' sense is conservative with respect to formal provability. In adapting the concept to natural language, we must take conservatism or non-conservatism as relative to whatever means exist in the language for justifying an assertion or an action consequent upon the acceptance of an assertion. The concept thus adapted offers us at least a provisional method of saying more precisely what we understand by 'harmony': namely, that there is harmony between the two aspects of the use of any given expression if the language as a whole is, in this adapted sense, a conservative extension of what remains of the language when that expression is subtracted from it. As before, this characterisation can most readily be applied to the logical constants. Any one given logical constant, considered as governed by some set of logical laws, will satisfy the criterion for harmony provided that it is never possible, by appeal to those laws, to derive from premisses not containing that constant a conclusion not containing it and not attainable from those premisses by other laws that we accept.

The requirement that this criterion for harmony be satisfied conforms to our fundamental conception of what deductive inference accomplishes. An argument or proof convinces us because we construe it as showing that, given that the premisses hold good according to our ordinary criteria, the conclusion must also hold *according to the criteria we already have for its holding*. We counted the apples and the pears separately and found that there were eight apples and five pears. Though they have now been eaten, an argument, which we do not ordinarily bother to make explicit, convinces us that, if we had counted all the fruit together, we should have found that there were thirteen of them: thirteen, that is, according to the criterion we had, namely counting, before we were ever introduced to the procedure of addition. Some philosophers, such as Wittgenstein, have maintained otherwise, holding that addition, when introduced, constituted a *new* criterion for assigning cardinalities to finite sets. To call it a 'new' criterion is to say something banal unless it is meant that we might have counted eight apples, five pears, and fourteen fruit altogether, and *have made no mistake*—no mistake, that is, that we could have been brought to recognise as such before we were introduced to addition. This is highly counter-intuitive, because it is precisely this possibility which we take the proof as ruling out; if we could be persuaded that it is a genuine possibility, we should reject the proof as fallacious and rate the procedure of addition as of only restricted application. Exactly the same holds good for somewhat more sophisticated examples; we regard the proof as showing us, of someone observed to cross every bridge at Königsberg, that he crossed at least one bridge twice, *by the criteria we already possessed for crossing a bridge twice*. Doubtless it is perplexing that we should be capable of discovering so much about what we should observe, were we able to make certain observations, or what we should have observed, if we had chosen to make certain others; but this is far less perplexing than to be told that we discover nothing of the kind, but merely adopt certain conventions in accordance with which we *say* that we make such discoveries.

If that is what deductive inference achieves, the requirement of harmony springs from its very nature. When an expression, including a logical constant, is introduced into the language, the rules for its use should determine its meaning, but its introduction should not be allowed to affect the meanings of sentences already in the language. If, by its means, it becomes possible for the first time to derive certain such sentences from other such sentences, then either their meanings *have* changed, or those meanings were not, after all, fully determined by the use made of them. In either case, it will not be true that such a derivation demonstrates that the conclusion holds good according to previously acknowledged criteria. The introduction of the new constant has created new criteria for the truth of statements not containing it.

The conservative extension criterion is not, however, to be applied to more than a single logical constant at a time. If we so apply it, we allow for the prior existence, in the practice of using the language, of deductive inference, since there are a number of logical constants. Unless, perhaps, 'and' is an exception, the addition of just one logical constant to a language devoid of them, or, more generally, the insertion of deductive inference into a linguistic practice previously innocent of it, cannot yield a conservative extension. We already saw that, if deductive inference is ever to be said to be able to increase our knowledge, then it must sometimes enable us to recognise as true a statement that we should not, without its use, have been able so to recognise, even though the meaning of that statement has not been given by providing for it to be arrived at by those means. The existence of deductive reasoning, as an accepted practice, causes us to adopt a more generous conception of truth for our statements than, without such a practice, our use of our language would have compelled us to do. For, in the absence both of the logical constants and of any mode of deductive inference, there is no obstacle to a meagre restriction of truth to those statements for which actual observations have been made that warrant their assertion. In the presence of deductive inference, we must at least admit a notion of truth explained in counterfactual terms as attaching to what we *should have* observed to be so had we had, or taken, the opportunity to do so. Whether, having taken this first step, necessitated by the existence of deductive inference, to differentiate the condition for the truth of a statement and the means available to us for recognising it as true, we are compelled to take yet further steps is a large question essential to the resolution of the metaphysical questions which form the eventual summit of the expedition which I am aiming to conduct no further than the foothills.

chapter 10

Holism

Compositionality

The verificationist and pragmatist meaning-theories, as we have been discussing them, exhibit a character often called 'compositional'; this is equally true of truth-conditional meaning-theories, as usually conceived. The term is somewhat opaque, since *any* meaning-theory must represent the meaning of a sentence as depending on its composition. The meaning of a sentence will normally differ from that of another sentence, and all that there is to differentiate the two sentences from each other is their composition—the words of which they are composed and the order in which these are put together. What, then, is the principle of compositionality to which certain meaning-theories conform but others can violate?

We can lay hold on this as follows. In order to know what a sentence of a language means, a speaker must certainly know *which* sentence it is; and that means that he must know of which words it is composed and in what order. He must obviously also know something more: the question is whether what he has, in addition, to know is constant from one sentence to another or varies from sentence to sentence. On one picture, the holistic picture, it is constant from sentence to sentence. Given that he knows *which* sentence is in question, what someone has, in addition, to know in order to understand is the entire language to which it belongs. Thus, if the two sentences **A** and **B** belong to the same language, what someone has to know, in order to know what **A** means, is (i) the words of which **A** is composed and the order in which they occur, and (ii) the language; and what he has to know, in order to know what **B** means, is (i) the words of which **B** is composed and the order in which they occur, and (ii) the language; the second component of his understanding of **A** is the same as the second component of his understanding of **B**.

A first, commonsense reaction is that this is absurd: what someone has to know in order to understand **A** is the meanings of the words in

A, and the modes of phrase- and sentence-construction involved in the formation of **A** from them, whereas what he has to know in order to understand **B** is the meanings of the words in **B**, and the modes of phrase- and sentence-construction involved in forming *it*. Common sense is here in agreement with compositional meaning-theories. A simple analogy shows, however, that the holistic picture is not as evidently absurd as it appears at first sight: the analogy with the game of dominoes. (There are many games that can be played with dominoes, as there are with playing cards; but we may pretend that there is only the one.) Different dominoes of course have different significance in the game: the double 3 is by no means interchangeable with the 5-2. In order to know the significance of a given domino, one must know which domino it is, that is, how many dots appear on each half of its face. But what one has to know, in addition, is the same for every domino, namely, the rules of the game in their entirety. In a substitution code, by contrast, like that of the dancing men in the Sherlock Holmes story, a word can be deciphered letter by letter: to do so, you do not have to know the entire code, but need know only the symbols that occur in the given word. The issue is whether sentences of a language are like dominoes or code words.

The principle of compositionality is most easily illustrated by the logical constants. On a compositional meaning-theory, to know the meaning of 'or', for example, is to be able to derive, from the meanings of any sentences **A** and **B**, the meaning of ⌜**A** or **B**⌝, where the meaning of a sentence consists in what counts as verifying it, or in the consequences of accepting it as true, or in the condition for it to be true. To understand ⌜**A** or **B**⌝, therefore, you must (i) observe the composition of the sentence, (ii) know what 'or' means, and (iii) know what **A** and **B** mean, whereas the third component of an understanding of ⌜**C** or **D**⌝ will be different, namely knowing what **C** and **D** mean.

Wittgenstein said that to understand a sentence is to understand a language. This is clearly true. There could be no such thing as understanding a single isolated sentence, however simple, without being able to understand any other. This is made more explicit in Gareth Evans's 'generality constraint'. One could not understand the sentence 'That cow is lying down' unless one could also understand other sentences such as 'This cow is standing up', 'That horse is lying down', and so on. Wittgenstein's observation was not an endorsement of holism, however: he did not mean that one cannot understand a German sentence without knowing the whole German language. To understand a sentence of a given language, one must know some fragment of that language, in which, of course, much would be incapable of being expressed, but which could in principle constitute an entire language.

Thus, to understand a logically complex sentence, one certainly need not understand any sentences of higher logical complexity; an explanation of a logical constant given by induction on the complexity of the sentences on which it operates is therefore perfectly in order. The logical constants form a uniquely simple case, however, since they do not satisfy the generality constraint: to understand ⌜A or B⌝, one need not understand ⌜A and B⌝ or ⌜If A, then B⌝. The principle of compositionality allows that a range of coordinate expressions—usually pairs or small sets of contrary predicates—may be capable of being understood only *together*. Colour-words of maximum generality, such as 'red', 'green', 'blue', and 'brown', constitute a plausible example; so do the pair 'male' and 'female', and the trio 'father of', 'mother of', and 'child of'. It also allows that, to understand sentences of a certain type, it may be necessary already to understand sentences of a different type, not differing in *logical* complexity. For example, to understand any sentence ascribing a certain character trait to an individual, it is necessary first to understand ascriptions of the corresponding characteristic to actions; to understand what it means to say that someone is vindictive, one must first know what it is to perform a vindictive act. We may speak of the relation that obtains between one expression and another when an understanding of the former requires an understanding of the latter as that of 'dependence'. What the principle of compositionality essentially requires is that the relation of dependence between expressions and sentence-forms be asymmetric. More exactly, to allow for the existence of sets of co-dependent expressions, the relation should be taken as holding between ranges of expressions rather than between single ones. This concession blunts the theoretical sharpness of application of the notion of compositionality: what is to stop the holist from simply declaring that all the words of the language form a single range? In practice, the concept remains clear enough; the only admissible ranges will be of words and expressions which can always replace one another without destroying the meaningfulness of the sentence. Compositionality demands that the relation of dependence imposes upon the sentences of the language a hierarchical structure deviating only slightly from being a partial ordering. The deviation allows for there being ranges of expressions a grasp of whose meanings can only be acquired simultaneously; as between these ranges, however, an understanding of the expressions in a given range can depend only upon the understanding of expressions occupying a lower position in the hierarchy.

We commonly take it for granted, in everyday converse, that a failure to understand a sentence must spring from a failure to grasp some constituent or feature of it. This is not always true: the failure may reside in inability to apprehend the structure of the sentence as a whole. But, when it is genuinely the sentence that the hearer fails to understand, rather than the point of the utterance or the possible ground of the assertion, his failure can usually be traced to his ignorance of some word or expression as used in a context of the kind in question. In such a case, his failure to understand the sentence casts no doubt upon his understanding of the other words in it: quite obviously, we cannot demand, for the understanding of a given word, that the subject should be capable of understanding every sentence containing it.

At the same time, the priority of sentence-meaning over word-meaning requires the understanding of a word to consist in the ability to understand *certain* sentences, or, more exactly, at least some of the sentences of a certain range, in which it occurs. This is readily accommodated within a compositional meaning-theory. The compositional principle demands that, for any given expression, we should distinguish between two kinds of sentence containing it. An understanding of the expression will consist in the ability to understand representative sentences of the first kind and does not, therefore, *precede* the understanding of sentences of that kind. By contrast, an antecedent understanding of the expression will combine with an understanding of the other constituent expressions to *yield* an understanding of a sentence of the second kind, which demands an understanding of the expression but is not demanded by it. The logical constants again provide a readily intelligible model for this. The understanding of a logical constant *consists* in the ability to understand any sentence of which it is the principal operator: the understanding of a sentence in which it occurs otherwise than as the principal operator *depends on,* but does not go to constitute, an understanding of the constant. It was his clear perception of this distinction that enabled Frege to construct a semantic theory for his formal language in which an explicit explanation of each logical constant is given only for contexts in which it is the principal operator. Such explanations rest on the explanations of the subsentences; hence, when the semantic account of a sentence in which a given logical constant is a subordinate operator is spelled out in full, it will explain the role of that constant in the given sentence by adverting to the explanation of a simpler sentence in which it is the principal operator.

The same holds good for all the words and expressions of the language, save that there is no comparably simple way to determine the range of sentences an understanding of which comprises the understanding of a given word. Thus, to understand the word 'fragile', for example, it is necessary to understand its use for some simple predications like 'That plate is fragile'; an understanding of such a sentence as 'I'm afraid that I forgot that it was fragile' *builds on* and *requires* an antecedent understanding of the word 'fragile' but is not a condition of understanding it. Holistic meaning-theories are in principle incapable of drawing this distinction. For them, it is a condition of understanding any sentence of the language that one be capable of understanding any other sentence of the language. The principle of compositionality is not the mere truism, which even a holist must acknowledge, that the meaning of a sentence is determined by its composition. Its bite comes from the thesis that the understanding of a word consists in the ability to understand characteristic members of a particular range of sentences containing that word. If we now apply the truism to that thesis, we arrive at the substantial doctrine that an understanding of any sentence containing the word must exploit the prior understanding of sentences in that range, in a manner depending on the context in which the word occurs. A compositional meaning-theory will represent the words occurring in any sentence **S**, and the modes of sentence composition in accordance with which those words have been connected, as together determining which are the sentences of lower complexity on whose understanding that of **S** depends; and it will describe how the meaning of **S** is derived from those of the less complex sentences. A holistic meaning-theory is powerless to endow the truism with such substance. It can say only that a knowledge of the entire language will, in particular, enable us to grasp the use of a sentence as depending on its composition, just as a knowledge of the game of dominoes enables us to know how each particular domino can be used.

An Example of Holism

Holism is capable of being applied, not to an entire natural language, but just to some large specialised fragment of it. As is well known, Duhem applied it to the languages of the various natural sciences, taken separately. Since all natural sciences lean on mathematics, a Duhemian holist will think of mathematical theories as interchangeable parts of scientific theories. A mathematical theory has no significance on its own, according to him, but gains significance from being incorporated into empirical theories, which then stand or fall as a whole; what is distinctive about the mathematical theory, and makes us view it in isolation from the rest of the scientific theory, is that it remains available for similar incorporation into other scientific theories. This view becomes in practice indistinguishable from that variety of formalism which holds that mathematical statements are intrinsically meaningless though of interest to us because they lend themselves to the imposition, from without, of various empirical interpretations. A holistic philosophy of mathematics—not, so far as I know, actually advanced by anyone—might conceivably be entertained by a mathematician relatively unconcerned with applications. He would, like the intuitionists, identify mathematical truth with provability; but he would take the relevant type of proof to be that accepted in practice by classical mathematicians. Such a view stands in opposition to platonism, which appeals to a two-valued semantics for the language of mathematics but cannot rule out the possibility of absolutely undecidable statements—ones neither provable nor refutable by any intuitively valid argument. If there are any such statements, there will be no sense, on the holistic view, in which they are either true or false, whereas, for the platonist, they must be determinately one or the other.

This pure mathematical holism also risks collapsing into formalism, this time of the radical type according to which mathematical sentences are not genuinely meaningful statements at all, but merely moves in a game of theorem-proving. It is common to all forms of holism that a meaning-theory which requires statements to be true that are not determined as such by observation goes beyond what is required to explain linguistic practice; and, if we take computations and proofs as corresponding, in mathematics, to observations in empirical discourse, mathematical holism conforms to this principle. It does not, however, embody the specifically Duhemian claim that there are statements whose affirmation or denial would be equally warranted. On the contrary, it holds that, if a statement is neither provable nor refutable, we shall never be warranted in asserting either it or its negation.

What makes it nevertheless a version of *holism,* and what differentiates it from intuitionism, is that, while the two agree that to understand a statement is to know how to recognise a proof of it, holism admits no way of explaining, in terms of the structure of a given statement, how a proof of it is to be recognised as such. Intuitionism respects the principle of compositionality inasmuch as it requires that, for each logical constant, there be a uniform explanation of what is to count as a proof of a statement in which that constant is the principal operator, in terms of proofs of its subsentences or (when the constant is a quantifier) of its instances. If all classical proofs are to be admitted as valid, no such requirement can be satisfied. If we could impose a hierarchical ordering on proofs in classical mathematics such that, if a given statement was provable at all, it had a proof of less than a bounded complexity, and hence a proof within some circumscribed fragment of mathematical theory, we could regard an understanding of that statement as depending solely on an understanding of that fragment. Except for effectively decidable statements, however, there is no way to do this. There is no bar in principle to the complexity of mathematical theory that might be appealed to in giving an intuitively acceptable proof of any one mathematical statement. Hence, on the holistic view, one cannot fully understand any mathematical statement until one knows the whole of mathematics; much as Wittgenstein believed, any significant advance in mathematics will modify the meanings of all mathematical statements.

Something similar may be said, indeed, about intuitionism. The standard stipulation of what is to count as a proof of a conditional statement is that it must be an operation of which we can recognise that, applied to any proof of the antecedent, it will yield a proof of the consequent. Since no restriction is placed on the operation, other than that it be effective, or on our means of recognising its effect, a highly sophisticated proof might in principle be needed for a relatively elementary conditional. There is thus no bound upon how much mathematics one might need to know to recognise a proof of such a conditional statement. The intuitionist account of the meaning of the statement nevertheless stands in contrast with that given by the holist. For the holist, our understanding of the statement, in so far as we understand it fully, simply *resides* in the knowledge we possess of the whole of mathematics. For the intuitionist, it does not. His explanation presumes that we may be credited with a general idea of an effective operation, an idea we can grasp without having the means to recognise each effective operation as such. Our understanding of the conditional statement rests upon our grasp of that idea, together with our knowledge of what will constitute a proof of each of the two subsentences. It therefore reflects only our understanding of the constituents of that particular statement, rather than a piece of background knowledge which, as a whole, informs our understanding of every mathematical statement. That is why intuitionism is in a position to criticise certain forms of classical reasoning, whereas, for the holist, it can neither be criticised nor justified, but is simply in place as an accepted practice.

Holism and Logical Laws

From this example it is apparent that holism, taken as applying either to the language as a whole or to some large sector of it, sanctions the claim that we have a right to adopt whatever logical laws we choose. One may combine holism with a verificationist answer to the question, 'In what does the meaning of a sentence consist?': namely, that it consists in what is required to establish the truth of a statement made by a particular utterance of that sentence. This answer, when given against the background of a holistic conception of language, means that the meaning of a given sentence is constituted by the *totality* of means by which such a statement could be shown to be true, including deductive arguments, however roundabout. A change in the logical laws whose acceptance is part of the practice of using the language, or sector of the language, therefore has the potential to change the meanings of all the sentences that can be formulated in it; but, since we have the right to make our words mean whatever we choose that they shall mean, there can be no objection in principle to such a change. Our logical laws are not, on a holistic view, *responsible* to the meanings of the logical constants, as determined by anything else; nor are they required to keep invariant the meanings of sentences not containing the relevant logical constants, considered as already determined by some other part of our linguistic practice. The meanings of all the expressions of the language are, on this view, determined by our linguistic practice *as a whole*. If we change any part of the practice, we may change the meanings of indefinitely many—in the limiting case, of all—the expressions in the language. That is our right to do if we wish, and no objection to our exercising it can be in order.

Alternatively, a holist may, without inconsistency, treat the meaning of a sentence as consisting in the consequences of a statement it is used to make; but, again, he means the *totality* of consequences that can be drawn from such a statement, including those arrived at by deductive reasoning, however indirect. The result is the same: *all* the logical laws we recognise as holding are potentially relevant to the meaning of every sentence in the language. If we change those laws, we may change the meaning of every such sentence; but, since we cannot regard the meaning of any sentence as having been fixed independently of those laws, we have the right to make any such change that we wish. There is, however, no particular point for the holist in fastening on one of the two aspects of use as determinative of meaning. To know the totality of possible means of establishing a given statement as true is not the same as to know the totality of possible consequences that follow from accepting it as true; but it is evident that one could not in practice know either without knowing the entire language. The holist may therefore as well say quite generally that to know the meaning of a sentence is to know its use under all its aspects. To understand a sentence is to understand a language; and since, for the holist, the sentence cannot be counted on to retain the meaning which it has in the language to which it belongs when we consider it as part of some proper fragment of that language, to know the meaning of a sentence requires a complete knowledge of the whole language.

In a compositional meaning-theory, matters stand quite differently. The meaning of a sentence must be explicable in a way that presupposes the meanings only of a restricted range of other sentences—sentences with a lower degree of complexity, in a generalised sense of 'complexity'. It follows that, in a verificationist theory, the content of a statement cannot be taken as fixed by the totality of means by which its truth could be established, since these will include deductive arguments involving sentences of an unbounded degree of complexity. It is this that requires us to distinguish between *direct* and *indirect* verifications of a statement, or, in mathematics, between canonical proofs and demonstrations of a more general kind. A direct verification of a statement is one which proceeds in accordance with the composition of the sentence by means of which it is expressed; on a compositional meaning-theory of verificationist type, our understanding of the statement will consist in a capacity to recognise such direct verifications of it. It is not necessarily the simplest possible verification of the statement that qualifies as direct. A direct verification of 'There are thirty desks in the classroom' would consist in counting the desks, even if they were arranged in five rows of six each; a direct verification of '119 is either prime or composite' would consist in factorising it, rather than in invoking the decidability of factorisation. When a direct verification involves deductive reasoning, this reasoning must always proceed from less complex premisses to a more complex conclusion: by no means *every* valid deductive argument can therefore figure in such a verification. The converse applies to pragmatist meaning-theories: we have to distinguish between consequences that follow directly and those that follow only indirectly. The consequences that go to determine the content of a statement, in so far as they take the form of other statements inferred from it, can only be those expressible by sentences of lower complexity. When the consequences are arrived at by deductive argument, the argument must lead to a conclusion of lower complexity than the statement figuring as the principal premiss.

From either a verificationist or a pragmatist standpoint, therefore, many deductive arguments will not be constitutive of the meanings of either their conclusions or their premisses, but will contribute to *indirect* means of establishing the former or of drawing consequences from the latter. As such, they stand in need of justification. The validity of such arguments must flow from the meanings of the logical constants, or of non-logical expressions occurring essentially in them. It has to be shown that the argument is valid in virtue of the meanings of those expressions, as independently given: in a verificationist meaning-theory, as given by what is required for a direct verification of statements involving them, in a pragmatist one, by what their direct consequences are. In a verificationist theory, a step in such an argument is to be justified by showing that, if we were in a position to verify the premises directly, we should be able to verify the conclusion directly; in a pragmatist theory, that any consequence drawn directly from the conclusion could already be drawn from the premises. A truth-conditional meaning-theory that respects the principle of compositionality must yield a specification of the condition for the truth of each statement, presupposing only the conditions for the truth of statements of lower complexity. Hence, on such a theory, *every* form of inference will be up for justification by showing that the conclusion will be determined as true whenever that holds good of the premises.

Thus a compositional meaning-theory, whatever its form, must require a justification at least for some logical laws: those laws will be held responsible to the meanings of the logical constants, as antecedently given, rather than being stipulated to hold as part of the process of fixing their meanings. A holistic conception of language therefore does not merely *allow* an arbitrary stipulation of the logical laws to be regarded as holding: such a conception is *demanded* by the claim that they may be arbitrarily stipulated.

Global Holism

Global holism takes the entire language as its scope. It is of course consistent with a generally holistic outlook to concede, as Quine did in his article "On Empirically Equivalent Systems of the World" (*Erkenntnis*, vol. 9, 1975, pp. 313–328), that there are some sentences—namely, those used to make observation statements—which can be largely understood without a knowledge of the more theoretical parts of the language, on the ground that, while capable of being rejected on the ground of conflict with theory, they are nevertheless separately susceptible to tests of observation which, when positive, create a strong presumption in their favour. It is also consistent with such an outlook to concede, as Quine does in the same article, that in practice the unit responsible to observation is usually considerably smaller than the whole of science, namely, one of those articulated bodies of scientific doctrine that we ordinarily refer to as 'theories'. This is merely to allow that an accurate holistic meaning-theory would frequently approximate locally to a compositional one, much as Einstein's theory of gravity approximates to Newton's. Our concern is whether the central *principle* of holism should or should not be sustained.

It is tempting to describe holism as the doctrine that a sentence does not have an individual content; but this is unsatisfactory. On any meaning-theory, a sentence, like every other component of discourse, must have a semantic value and a sense that determines that semantic value. Holism is better characterised as the doctrine that the application of the predicate 'true' to a sentence cannot be explained in terms of its composition; more exactly, that no meaning-theory according to which each sentence is determined as true or otherwise in a manner corresponding to its internal composition can do justice to every feature of our use of the language. What ground can there be for this doctrine?

One possible ground is the celebrated thesis that was propounded by Duhem for distinguishable scientific theories, and generalised by Quine to science as a whole and, more broadly yet, to our entire language. This thesis is that, although observation may conflict with an assignment of truth-values to a whole range of sentences, it never conflicts with an assignment of a particular truth-value to any one sentence, taken in isolation. This formulation is deceptively simple. Naturally, no observation can conflict with a truth-value assignment to sentences, considered merely as (uninterpreted) sequences of phonemes. What is intended is that any meaning-theory which has the effect of rendering any individual sentence true or false, given a particular set of observations, must both embody principles not needed to account for the existing practice of the speakers and rule out certain behaviour on their part which would be in accord with that practice.

The first component of this thesis does not give a *ground* for holism but is merely a particularly strong assertion of it. We can perfectly well imagine a meaning-theory according to which no finite set of observations entails the truth of any sentence, although it may nevertheless be determinately true. Perhaps, on such a theory, what renders a sentence true is an infinite set of observations, which at no time can we have made; perhaps it is a set of actual observations together with the (determinate) outcome of certain hypothetical observations (each in principle possible for us, but together impossible to combine with the actual ones); perhaps it is some sector of reality of which all possible observations give us only an incomplete knowledge. It admittedly requires demonstration that there is any feature of our use of the language which can be accounted for only by a meaning-theory which operates with such a notion of truth; at the same time, it equally requires demonstration that there is not.

The second component of the Duhem-Quine thesis, if correct, *does* give a ground for holism: it claims that linguistic practice is such that, for any sentence, one and the same set of observations will, in the presence of certain assignments to other sentences, warrant our assigning to that sentence the value *true* and, in the presence of different assignments to the other sentences, warrant our assigning to it the value *false*. Admittedly, even if such a claim were justified, this fact would not be strictly inconsistent with a meaning-theory according to which any truth-value assignment to some one sentence is, determinately, correct or erroneous, although no observations that we can make can ever definitively decide the matter; but it would create a presumption against such a meaning-theory.

Holism is not to be *identified* with the Duhem-Quine thesis, which, in virtue of its second component, is merely one possible ground for holism; the example of pure mathematical holism shows that there are other possible grounds. The principal objection to the Duhem-Quine thesis, as applied globally, is simply the difficulty of believing it. We may distinguish between a narrow and a broad sense of the term 'theory'. A theory in the broad sense is any deductively organised body of explanatory hypotheses (even this definition excludes group theory, and the like). A theory in the narrow sense is one containing at least one theoretical term. We may take a theoretical term to be one whose significance, as it occurs in statements of the theory, depends solely on its role within the theory, and not at all on its use, if any, in extra-theoretical statements, and one which, furthermore, does not, according to that theory, stand for anything that is even in principle directly observable. As a thesis about scientific theories, in the narrow sense, the Duhem-Quine thesis is credible enough. There is not enough continuity, however, between the sector of language used in a scientific theory and other sectors of language to justify extension of the Duhemian principle to the use of the language as a whole.

Against this it may be said, first, that everyday language is subject to constant invasion by scientific terms, such as 'electricity' and 'temperature'. It would be wrong to say that, when someone without any scientific education says of a household thermometer that it measures temperature, what he means by 'temperature' is something quite crude like 'how hot a thing feels'; rather, we have yet one more example of the linguistic division of labour. He knows some simple effects of temperature, like freezing, melting, cooking, scalding, and so on, but would readily admit that he does not know what temperature is, although there are those who do. Secondly, it may be said that certain everyday concepts shade into scientific ones: that of distance, for example. To have the everyday concept of distance, one must know a good deal besides basic principles about how it is measured, much of which belongs to the earliest things we learn: one must know about the comparative rigidity of a large number of material objects, the fact that our limbs, though jointed, are not compressible, the fact that we and other animals move, when we do, at a roughly constant velocity, so that a measure of distance is also a measure of time taken to travel, and so forth; and we must know some basic geometrical facts as well. 'Distance', as a term of physical theory, can be allowed to be a theoretical one if its use in physics is not actually *responsible* to the everyday use, but it is surely *continuous* with it.

Moreover, these reflections illustrate the degree to which the everyday concept of distance is embedded in a primitive theory; and even the thinking of the least scientifically informed is permeated by certain fragments of scientific doctrine known or half-known to all. Consider, for example, the view of Aquinas, which sounds so silly to us, that, when a small amount of water is mixed with wine, it is transformed into wine. This sounds silly not merely because we know, as Aquinas did not, that wine is already a mixture, but because we take the molecular structure of matter for granted. Once the phenomenon of mixing liquids is viewed against the background of the belief, that he had, that they are completely homogeneous substances, his remark no longer appears silly; but it also becomes apparent how utterly alien that conception, which once must have appeared the merest common sense, has become to us. (Fill up a half-empty glass of water with water from a jug, and now pour away again half the glassful: given the conception of water as entirely homogeneous, it would not so much as make sense to raise the question whether the water now in the glass is the same as that which was there before.) Or, again, consider almost anybody's reaction now to the question whether, when a lump of ice slithers down the side of Everest, and there is no creature near enough to hear it, there was or was not a sound. Virtually no one would now find this conceptually puzzling: practically everyone would say, 'Well, there would have been the *sound waves*'.

Yet the strong links between scientific theory and everyday discourse and thought do not afford sufficient ground for extending the Duhemian thesis to the language as a whole. Naturally, to the extent that scientific terms get into everyday language, speakers will tend to hold their use of such terms responsible to current scientific theory, even if they do not know it; but, just for that reason, such uses will be dependent upon the parent theories and the changes they undergo, so that, when revision is necessary, it will still be only the body of scientific doctrine, and not any propositions of everyday discourse, whose modification has to be decided. We may compare the use made, in the language of the seventeenth century, of the notion of the 'humours', and how it evaporated once the theory was abandoned, leaving no greater legacy than a handful of adjectives like 'phlegmatic'. It is undoubtedly important that some scientific concepts, like that of distance, are extensions, and are seen as extensions, of everyday ones: it is probably unintelligible to suppose that we might have a physics all of whose primitive concepts were devoid of any relation to those we employ in ordinary speech. Here, however, we ought to treat with extreme caution the treacherous word 'theory'. The use of such expressions as '225 yards away' is indeed connected with a considerable complex of practices and applications, which are made possible by regularities that we take for granted and that, with an effort, we can imagine to fail. The sense in which the concept of distance is embodied in a theory is that to have the concept is to make a number of general assumptions and to engage in a network of interrelated practices; but these assumptions lack the hypothetical character that may be attributed to even the best established scientific theory. The question of their breaking down does not arise: since Duhem's thesis is about what happens when a revision is called for, it simply does not apply to this case. To say that the question of their breaking down does not arise is not to offer any transcendental deduction of certain general features of the world as we experience it: it means only that the possibility is not provided for in the language. If certain familiar regularities failed, we should lose our concept of distance or of time or both; for instance, we should lose our concept of duration if the comparability of repeatable processes were to fail. We should not apply the well-known Duhemian procedure for finding a suitable revision of our theory; there is just no saying what we should say.

The Duhemian thesis cannot be convincingly applied to observation statements, either. The thesis says that we have not given to a theoretical sentence a meaning which makes it capable of being determinately true independently of what other sentences (not logically related to it) are true. If, therefore, some revision is called for in our theory, the thesis implies that we cannot sensibly enquire whether that sentence or some other is more *likely* to *be* false: we can ask only which it is more *convenient* to *treat as being* false. For observation statements, it is not merely that there exists a presumption in their favour (which might merely mean that we found it especially inconvenient to reject those we had accepted as true); it is that their defeasibility is not plausibly explained in this way. The commonsense explanation is that we weigh the probability that an observational error has occurred, of the kind we can sometimes directly establish, against the probability that our theory is wrong, where the supposition that one rather than the other is wrong is one that has substance, and may therefore properly be treated as having a high or low degree of likelihood. The reasons that may be given against taking such a view of competing individual theoretical statements do not tell against it when the choice lies between an observation statement and a theory.

Much more important than such reactions to an extension of Duhem's thesis beyond scientific theories in the narrow sense is the near impossibility of envisaging a meaning-theory for a language for which a thoroughgoing holism holds good. It is an insidious illusion to suppose that, on a holistic account, we can get on without any meaning-theory at all, that in some mysterious manner a set of sentences, taken without any particular interpretation, by itself determines which observations permit us to take the sentences in that set as all being true. This illusion has sometimes been voiced by claiming that holism renders the notion of meaning superfluous. Certainly a holistic meaning-theory will be one in which the notion of a statement's being true plays no role, and does not figure in its account of the practice of assertion. Either we shall think of truth as being wholly explained by means of a Tarski-type truth-definition; or else, when the linguistic practice is known, we shall identify the truth of a statement with our willingness to assert it: in neither case will the notion belong to the meaning-theory.

Now any meaning-theory is subject to the requirement that there be some linguistic unit which satisfies two conditions: (1) it is the smallest unit the correctness of an utterance of which is independent of what else is said; and (2) the sense of a complex expression constituting such a unit is systematically derivable from the senses of its components. This requirement places a particularly heavy burden on a holistic theory. Most of our discussion hitherto has proceeded on the assumption that such a unit is the sentence, since it is by the utterance of sentences that communication is effected. It is true that, in practice, what is conveyed by a sentence will often depend on what other sentences were previously uttered by the speaker or his hearers. This dependence is in part trivial, for example when it is due to anaphora: by eliminating the anaphora, we produce stylistic inelegance but restore condition (1) above. Of much greater importance is the fact that what is conveyed by a speech—that is, any connected sequence of utterances, whether as a lecture, political speech, or the like, or just an uninterrupted contribution to a dialogue—is not merely the sum of what is conveyed by the component sentences, so that it would make no difference if these were rearranged. That is because the statements made and questions asked during the course of the speech are meant to stand in various relations to one another, which the hearers are intended to apprehend: a given statement may serve as a ground for what is coming or for what went before, as a consequence or an illustration of it, as an objection to be answered, or in many other relations to it. This, however, does not invalidate the choice of the sentence as the fundamental unit: a speech stands in a quite different relation to its component sentences from that in which a sentence stands to its component words. We do not *both* grasp what the individual words say *and* apprehend the relations the speaker intends us to take them as bearing to one another: the words do not, by themselves, serve to *say* anything at all but instead combine in sentences which say something. Although the speech is more than an unordered set of sentences, the sentences, on our ordinary way of regarding them, do satisfy condition (1): we can ask, of each statement, not merely whether it followed from or illustrated what had gone before, but also whether, in itself, it is *true*.

On a holistic meaning-theory, however, the relevant unit cannot be the sentence, because, according to the theory, what is conveyed by the utterance of a sentence is not determinable from that sentence alone: either because, as from the Duhem-Quine standpoint, it has to be understood against a background knowledge (or presumption) on the hearer's part of what other sentences the speaker holds true; or simply because, as in pure mathematical holism, it is impossible to explain what renders the sentence true in terms merely of its internal structure. The central notion of a holistic meaning-theory must therefore be some property of a *set* of statements, considered as forming the totality of those which at any given time a speaker might wish to hold as true. A natural choice for this property would be that of being consonant with certain observations and not with others.

When a restricted Duhemian thesis is applied to a circumscribed scientific theory, this amounts, from a meaning-theoretic standpoint, to saying that the theory functions as a single unit. If we know the rules in accordance with which observation statements are deduced from other observation statements by appeal to the theory, this is not perplexing, so long as those observation statements are thought of as given content independently of the theory. If we took the role of a scientific theory to be purely predictive, we could then identify the meaning of the theory with its empirical or observational content, as given by the sets of observation statements with which it conflicts. Clearly the role of a scientific theory is also to *explain*, so this would be inadequate. But what require explanation are the phenomena we can observe: it lies ready to hand to add, as part of the meaning of such a theory, its explanatory power, as given by those sets of observation statements which it would serve to explain. Just as holism applied to mathematical statements tends in practice to reduce to some kind of formalism, so this restricted holism becomes in practice difficult to distinguish from instrumentalism: it becomes hard to suppose that there is any significant difference between theories which have the same observational content and explanatory power, still more that there is a difference of a kind that might make one theory correct and the other incorrect. There is then a temptation to generalise the holistic principle to the rest of language, to say that all sentences work as do theoretical ones; there will then be no hard facts expressed by non-theoretical statements to contrast with the soft ones expressed by statements of the theory, so that instrumentalism appears to lose its sting. But, as soon as the holistic principle is applied globally, to the language as a whole, we lose our grasp of how a systematic account might be given of the way in which the language functions. This global holism can be definitively refuted only by the production of a convincing non-holistic meaning-theory. Holism, however, does not have any better claim to escape the burden of proof: it will not have been shown to be even a tenable thesis until some sketch has been given of what a holistic meaning-theory would be like. There is ground for the deepest scepticism over whether such a theory is possible.

Another Form of Global Holism

According to global holism of the Duhem-Quine variety, to understand what someone says, you have in principle to know every sentence he holds to be true. This, of course, is not enough: you have also implicitly to know a holistic meaning-theory for the language, that is, to know which observations are compatible with any given set of assignments of truth-values to its sentences. Given that, for any observations incompatible with the current assignments of truth-values, there will be numerous distinct revised assignments compatible with them, it is apparent that such a theory must be extremely complicated. Two speakers, who start by assigning truth to exactly the same sentences, and who make the same series of observations, but at every stage choose to revise their truth-value assignments in different ways, will end up with very different sets of sentences they hold true, even though these are, in the light of the meaning-theory, equivalent sets. The theory must be very complex if it is to accommodate situations of this kind; but it equally appears unlikely that the two speakers will ever discover that there is no disagreement of substance between them. This form of holism leaves it a mystery how we manage to communicate with one another as successfully as we do.

Another version of global holism is also possible. It was remarked above that the purely mathematical holism used as an initial example was not based on any variation of the Duhemian thesis; and a global holism can be envisaged which is the analogue, for an entire language, of that purely mathematical holism. According to this variety of holism, you do not have to know everything a man holds to be true in order to understand what he says; but you do have to know the entire language in order to understand what any one sentence means.

A possible way in which this may arise is from the idea that the meaning of an expression is given by whatever someone would have to know in order to be said to understand it. When we try to apply this principle to some actual expression or range of expressions, we see that knowing how to determine as true a statement involving the expression would not be enough, on its own, for someone to be said to understand it: he would also have to know what such a statement was used *for*. If, for instance, we are considering the example, cited earlier, of statements about the spatial distance between objects, he would need to know that they are used to determine how long it will take to get from one place to another, or whether it will be possible to place some third object between the given two. In making these applications, we invoke a large number of empirical assumptions, about the relative dimensions and velocities of familiar objects, and of less clearly empirical assumptions, about elementary geometrical relations. Thus the understanding of some one form of expression seems to lead off, in two opposite directions (justification and application), to a knowledge of a great deal else in the language. Furthermore, each of the expressions on an understanding of which an understanding of the given expression depends will in their turn lead off in both directions to a yet larger fragment of the language. Thus we feel driven to think that an understanding of any expression of the language must involve a knowledge of the *whole* of it.

The mistake here is to suppose that a systematic meaning-theory must incorporate, as part of the meaning of any expression, everything that we should intuitively regard as necessary for a complete understanding of it. The aim of a meaning-theory is to explain in what a mastery of the language as a whole consists. It can do this systematically only if it parcels out the components of a knowledge of the language among its constituent expressions and among general principles permitting the derivation, from the central feature of the meaning of an expression, of other features of its use. As we have already seen, however, what is *not* demanded of the partitioning is that it correspond to our naive, unsystematic allocations of abilities required for the understanding of individual expressions.

Global holism of this variety does not, like that inspired by the Duhem-Quine thesis, propose a larger fundamental unit than the sentence: to say that the unit was the entire language would simply be to say that there is no unit. Nor does it, like global Duhemian holism, hold out a prospect of a meaning-theory of unmanageable complexity. Rather, it in effect denies that a systematic meaning-theory is possible at all. It condemns any attempt to construct one to an inescapable circularity; and that means that there can be no such theory.

This charge may provoke protest. All that the holist claims is that one can know the meaning of any expression only by knowing its role in the language, and that one can know this only by knowing the whole language: and is not this knowledge finite and therefore specifiable? There are only finitely many logical laws that we recognise outright, only finitely many principles of justification, only finitely many bases for eliciting consequences. The holist does not claim that they cannot be made explicit, but maintains only that they interact with one another, so that none in isolation determines the meaning of any expression or sentence. Consider purely mathematical holism, which serves as an analogue for the global variety. According to mathematical holism, one cannot fully understand any mathematical proposition unless one knows the whole corpus of existing classical mathematics, including accepted modes of mathematical reasoning; as this corpus is expanded, so the meanings of all our mathematical statements shift, noticeably in some cases, imperceptibly in others. But the corpus of existing classical mathematics is a finite body of knowledge, which it is possible to acquire and to set out. Why should the holist be accused of making it ineffable?

The problem looms large in the career of L. E. J. Brouwer. Brouwer regarded classical mathematics as meaningless. More exactly, he held that classical mathematicians reason as if their propositions had meanings of a kind quite different from any that could be ascribed to them. Above all, they treated infinite processes as if they could be completed, whereas it is of the essence of the infinite that it cannot be completed. Yet Brouwer made himself famous with his great series of discoveries in classical topology. His principal motive for doing so was to obtain the chair of mathematics at Amsterdam, from which he could preach the necessity for replacing classical by intuitionistic mathematics; but, by proving these classical theorems, he demonstrated that he had a profound grasp of classical mathematics. He could play the game of classical mathematics as skilfully as any classical mathematician, and more skilfully than most. He knew what would count, for classical mathematicians, as a valid proof, and what would not. How, then, *could* he maintain that classical mathematics is meaningless?

This question contains the nub of the issue between compositionality and holism. One might almost say between philosophy and intellectual incuriosity; or, since some philosophers preach that the answer to all riddles is that there is no answer, between philosophers who seek foundations and those who deny that anything needs a foundation. Frege wrote *The Foundations of Arithmetic* not because he thought, as

Brouwer did, that mathematicians proceeded in an incorrect manner, but because he thought that they could give no clear account, since they lacked any clear perception, of what it was that they were doing. Philip Kitcher contrasts his work unfavourably with that of those who sorted out the foundations of analysis by presenting well-defined concepts of limit, continuity, and differentiation. His idea is that the latter work was rendered necessary by the antinomies that arose *within* analysis and that therefore hampered progress while they remained unresolved. By contrast, there was no crisis within number theory: the work of number theorists could proceed untroubled by uncertainties about what the natural numbers are, how number theory could be axiomatised, and what the source of our belief in its axioms is. Even Frege's work on the foundations of analysis, in the second volume of *Grundgesetze*, was from this standpoint superfluous. The problems that led to the antinomies had already been resolved, and further curiosity about the fundamental concepts was therefore mere self-indulgence, of no importance to *real* mathematics. It is vain, in reply to this, to point to the substantial mathematical gains made in the process of investigating the foundations: the invention of mathematical logic in the modern sense, or Frege's contributions to the theory of groups with orderings. Such discoveries were not the central point of the enquiry into foundations; to justify that enquiry by appeal to them is to admit it to be, save for by-products, unjustified. Since, however, it has no purpose beyond itself, there is no justification that can be offered to the sceptic, any more than art can be justified to the philistine. For someone to whom it was of no concern if we had no clear idea of what we were doing—who was content with an assurance that what we are agreed on was true, even though we did not know what it meant, what made it true, or on what basis we believed it—all enquiry into these matters is vanity. The philosopher seeks not to know more but to understand what he already knows. He continues to seek unless he is seduced by the scepticism that denies that understanding is possible. Kitcher's position is more extreme: he does not deny that understanding is to be had but holds that, even if attainable, it is worthless, save when it becomes necessary for the acquisition of further knowledge.

It was not, obviously, Brouwer's ambition to construct a meaning-theory for the language of mathematics. On the contrary, he wanted to develop a manner of employing mathematical language which would be transparent of itself, and would therefore need no explicit theory to make it comprehensible. His critique of classical mathematics shows, however, what he demanded of a language for it to be comprehensible. It must stand up to critical scrutiny of its functioning; and the employment of mathematical language by the classical mathematicians failed this test. Such scrutiny does not merely survey the heterogeneous conventions governing the established practice of using the language, in particular, of framing definitions and setting out proofs. It also aims at a systematic means of ascribing *content* to the expressions and sentences of the language, in terms of which accepted modes of operating with it (including the rules of inference observed) can be justified, or, better, are evidently justified. We may describe this process, in Wittgensteinian terms, as that of gaining a clear view of how the language functions. We may also say that such a systematic ascription of content constitutes an implicit grasp of a meaning-theory for the language. The mere existence of a common practice in using it, a practice that can be learned and that incorporates a means of distinguishing conventionally correct uses from incorrect ones, did not, for Brouwer, guarantee that that practice was coherent. It is incoherent when there is disharmony between its component conventions, or, equivalently, when it cannot be rendered comprehensible by any systematic ascription of content—and this means, eventually, when it would be impossible to construct a meaning-theory that accorded with all features of the practice. We have seen that a practice may exist, and be learnable, but still open to criticism as failing to achieve the purpose that a linguistic practice should serve. That was precisely what Brouwer believed to be true of the practice of classical mathematics.

Holism denies that there is any such danger. Being the doctrine that any meaning-theory is inevitably circular, it repudiates the need for any coherent meaning-theory, and, with it, for any implicit grasp of the content of an individual utterance. For the holist, we ought not to strive to command a clear view of the workings of our language, because there is no clear view to be had. We have a haphazard assembly of conventions and rules, and there are no principles which govern our selection of them or render them any more appropriate than any others we might adopt. We should not seek to grasp the content of our sentences in any firmer way than by being competent speakers and hence knowing how to conform to the conventions governing ordinary linguistic exchange. This is, indeed, the condition in which, a large part of the time, we actually find ourselves. It is the condition we can describe by saying that we know what to say but do not know what we mean thereby: precisely the condition which gives rise to philosophical perplexity, and to which we strive to put an end by attaining a clear view. Holism in effect derides such strivings as an attempt to attain the unattainable. We are inexorably condemned to speak, to others and to ourselves, without knowing exactly what we mean, because the very conception of knowing what we mean, in this sense, is for the holist a mere illusion. As already remarked, there is no decisive refutation of this pessimism save by the successful construction of a compositional meaning-theory. But there is no reason, either, to embrace it before any good ground exists for doubting the feasibility of constructing one.

Inextricability

The term 'holism' has been applied to a number of distinct doctrines, connected by the mutual support they give to one another, but needing to be distinguished, nevertheless. This chapter ends with a brief glance at one that needs to be distinguished from holism proper, which I shall call the 'inextricability thesis'. Holism, as such, has nothing to do with the analytic/synthetic distinction. The Duhem-Quine thesis does, namely by denying that any sentence is in the strict sense analytic, or in the strict sense synthetic. Quine, in his famous article "Two Dogmas of Empiricism", caused much confusion by apparently condemning the concept of analyticity on the ground that it could be defined only in terms of one of a small circle of interdefinable terms. This led to much misplaced discussion about how far a sharp concept needs to be definable. In fact, although the article proceeded on this tack for a great part of its length, the celebrated picture, presented in the final section, of language as an articulated network on which experience impinges only at the periphery contains the apparatus for quite precise definitions of 'analytic' and 'synthetic': an analytic sentence will be one the assignment to which of the value *true* will be untouched by any admissible revision made in response to a recalcitrant experience; a synthetic sentence will be one the assignment to which of the value *true* will be overturned by any admissible revision made in response to certain possible experiences. The thesis of "Two Dogmas" is not that these concepts are incoherent or ill-defined but that they are without application: there are no sentences of either of the two kinds.

Subsequently, however, Quine has advanced the inextricability thesis, which *does* call into question the very coherence of the analytic/synthetic distinction. On the picture of sense which Frege had, the sense of a sentence determines by what means we *can* come to recognise it as true. In particular, therefore, it depends upon its sense whether it is a priori or a posteriori, analytic or synthetic. Whether or not a sentence *has been* recognised as true is, on this picture, in principle irrelevant to its sense; all that is determined by its sense is the manner in which it is *possible* so to recognise it. Hence, if a sentence not formerly recognised as true comes to be so recognised, it is in principle possible, on this picture, that it should retain the same sense that it had before. Its retention of that sense will be shown by the fact that we continue to justify it by that means by which we first came to recognise it as true.

The inextricability thesis states, conversely, that there is nothing in the use of a language, in the linguistic behaviour of the speakers, that will differentiate any one sentence generally accepted as true from any other so accepted, in respect of what is required to show that it is true. At any given time, a sentence not yet generally accepted as true may come to be so accepted in any one of a variety of ways, presumably depending upon its sense: on the basis of observation, as the conclusion of a chain of reasoning, supported or unsupported by observation, or simply by stipulation. Once it has come to be generally accepted, however, the manner in which this came about is a mere matter of history. Nothing whatever in the subsequent linguistic behaviour of the speakers will reveal any difference, in this regard, between it and any other sentence generally accepted as true.

It is natural to contrast the inextricability thesis with the Fregean picture as giving a dynamic rather than a static account of language: it does not merely describe the language as it is at some one time but gives an explanation of the way in which the senses of our words may alter. Though natural, however, this is not a happy way to state the contrast. A dynamic phonetics for example, may readily be contrasted with a static one: the static one merely tells you about the sounds employed in the language at any one time, the dynamic account adds to this some general laws about the way in which this phonetic system may be expected to change over time. But the notion of sense is not so clear-cut as that of sound. As soon as we adopt any systematic general principle governing the way an expression will come, in particular circumstances, to be used, that principle will come to be seen as part of the sense of the expression. Rather than say, therefore, that the inextricability thesis offers a dynamic, and not a static, account of meaning, it seems better to say that it views as not involving any change of meaning certain changes which, on the Fregean picture, would have to be regarded as changes in meaning not governed by any general law. A change of meaning occurs only when there is some change not previously provided for.

This observation seems reasonable enough until we begin to think how to implement it. To do so, we should have to describe the meanings of sentences in such a way that it could not be determined from the meaning of a sentence alone what is required to establish it as true, but only from the meaning together with the set of sentences generally accepted as true: the meaning of a sentence would have to be, or to yield, a function mapping any arbitrary finite set of sentences onto whatever would verify that sentence at any time at which the sentences generally accepted as true consisted just of those in that set. As stated, this applies only to sentences whose truth or falsity has not yet been generally established; further complications would be necessary to explain how those currently accepted as true can come to be rejected, and conversely. In fact it might seem contrary to the spirit of the thesis to suppose that this could ever happen; but, since it manifestly does, the thesis must be interpreted to allow for it.

Since it is hard to see how such a meaning-theory might be developed, it is better to fall back on regarding a theory incorporating the inextricability thesis as genuinely a dynamic one. So viewed, the meaning of a sentence would not be invariant under a change in the set of sentences generally accepted as true, but would directly determine what constituted a verification of it. The theory would differ from a static theory such as Frege's only in giving an account of the systematic shifts in meaning that would occur when any new sentence comes to be accepted as true, or any sentence ceases to be so accepted.

If we regard the inextricability thesis as at home within a dynamic meaning-theory, it plainly has nothing to do with holism. Such a meaning-theory could be compositional and treat the sentence as the fundamental unit; it would differ from other such theories only in having a dynamic component. If we take the thesis as at home in a static meaning-theory, we have something closely resembling holism of the Duhem-Quine variety; but, still, the fundamental unit would be the sentence, although its meaning would not be absolute but would be a function of the set of generally accepted sentences. The inextricability thesis, even when construed in the latter way, does not yet amount to a version of holism, however akin to it in spirit it may be, for it says something only about those sentences that have been generally accepted. By allowing a variety of different types of ground on which a sentence might be accepted in the first place, the thesis implicitly recognises that, relatively to the set of sentences currently accepted, a sentence not yet either accepted or rejected may have quite determinate verification-conditions. It therefore at most demands a fairly extensive complication of a compositional meaning-theory, not a theory of a totally different kind.

chapter 11

Proof-Theoretic Justifications of Logical Laws

Self-Justifying Rules

From a holistic standpoint, no justification of any logical law is either possible or needed. From that of a compositional meaning-theory, logical laws in general stand in need of justification; and such a justification can be given in terms of the semantics appropriate to the meaning-theory. This semantic justification will, in many cases, suffer from pragmatic circularity, although circularity of this kind will not impair its capacity to explain, in the light of that meaning-theory, what makes deductive inference possible and how the practice of engaging in deductive reasoning harmonises with the other features of linguistic practice. When the logical law under consideration is genuinely controversial, this will be because the meaning-theory, and in particular its semantic base, is questioned. In such a case, we shall seek, and frequently find, a semantic theory which permits of a justification that is not circular, even pragmatically; although the opponent of the law will reject *this* semantic theory also, he will at least be brought to recognise what is at issue. The same holds good for the criticism of a logical law. This, too, can be done by appeal to a semantic theory; and, when the law is one that has its supporters, and especially when it is currently in possession, we shall likewise seek a semantic theory which still allows a refutation of that law in the object-language even when it is taken as holding in the metalanguage.

Can there be a *proof-theoretic* justification of a logical law? We already know that there can, in the familiar process of deriving a given law from others, which we called a proof-theoretic justification of the first grade. This, however, as we remarked, supplies only a *relative* justification—one that assumes that certain other laws are valid. On reflection, it is evident that this must be true of *any* proof-theoretic justification: we cannot have a proof theory unless we have some means of proof. If, then, there is to be a general proof-theoretic procedure for justifying logical laws, uncontaminated by any ideas foreign to proof theory, there must be some logical laws that can be stipulated outright initially, without the need for justification, to serve as a base for the proof-theoretic justification of other laws. Although it is not true of logical laws generally that we are entitled simply to stipulate that they shall be treated as valid, there must be certain laws or systems of laws of which this holds good. Such laws will be 'self-justifying': we are entitled simply to stipulate that they shall be regarded as holding, because by so doing we fix, wholly or partly, the meanings of the logical constants that they govern, without thereby risking any conflict with the already given meanings of other expressions.

The Requirement of Harmony

It thus becomes important to enquire what form a logical law or set of logical laws must take if it is to be in this sense self-justifying. It is apparent that no set of logical laws, serving to provide a formalisation of some part of logic—sentential logic or first-order logic, say—that is even a candidate for being complete in the standard sense that all semantically valid laws are derivable from it, can qualify for being self-justifying. For such a set will certainly be unacceptable if it proves to be inconsistent, and probably also if it proves to have some less grave defect such as violating the requirement of harmony. It might, of course, be maintained that any such set should be regarded as self-justifying provided that it can be shown to be consistent and to lack any other defect which we wish to rule out. That was precisely the proposal made by Nuel Belnap in his brief but perceptive reply to Arthur Prior's critique, mentioned previously, of the thesis that we have the right to stipulate whatever logical laws we choose. Prior refuted that thesis by exhibiting a combination of introduction and elimination rules for an imaginary binary connective, each acceptable in themselves, that would allow the swift derivation of a contradiction. Belnap's reply was that we must impose certain conditions on the total set of logical laws we are stipulating to govern a logical constant. The first of these was harmony, a stronger requirement than consistency, but one which guarantees it. The second was uniqueness, which we may explain for the case of a binary connective, although the notion is quite general. Suppose that we have a set L of logical laws governing a connective $*$. L will be said to guarantee uniqueness if, for a new connective $\#$, we can derive from L and L' the equivalence of $\ulcorner A * B \urcorner$ and $\ulcorner A \# B \urcorner$, where L' is the set of laws obtained by replacing $*$ throughout L by $\#$. ($\ulcorner A * B \urcorner$ and $\ulcorner A \# B \urcorner$ will be said to be equivalent if each can be derived from the other.) The intuitive purpose of this requirement is obvious. We are entitled to stipulate a set of logical laws only if we thereby fix the meanings of the logical constants that they govern. If the set **L** did *not* guarantee uniqueness, * and # would, in an obvious sense, obey the same logical laws, even though, not being equivalent, they might bear different meanings; it would follow that **L** did *not* fully determine the meaning of the logical constant *.

Why should harmony be demanded, and what does it amount to in the context of logical laws? We have seen that harmony *within the language as a whole* is a precondition for the possibility of a compositional meaning-theory. As applied to a logical constant, say a connective *, this means that the canonical ways of establishing a statement ⌜**A** * **B**⌝ as true should match, and be matched by, the consequences which accepting that statement as true is canonically treated as having. There is no reason in principle, however, given the fact that * is a logical constant, why all the canonical grounds for, and all the canonical consequences of, such a statement should be logical in character; after all, we are as yet lacking an explication of 'logical constant'. When we are regarding certain logical laws governing * as self-justifying, however, we do so in the belief that, by stipulating them to hold, we determine the meaning of *. In this case, the canonical grounds for the truth of ⌜**A** * **B**⌝ will be given by the introduction rules governing it, and its canonical consequences will be drawn by means of the elimination rules governing it: it is therefore these that must be in harmony. The demand that the introduction rules and the elimination rules be in harmony is not reasonable in a general context, since it is not required in order to secure harmony in the language as a whole: but it is compelling when it is being maintained that the meaning of the logical constant in question can be completely determined by laying down the fundamental logical laws governing it.

What is it for the introduction rules and the elimination rules governing a logical constant to be in harmony? We saw that harmony, in the general sense, obtains between the verification-conditions or application-conditions of a given expression and the consequences of applying it when we cannot, by appealing to its conventionally accepted application-conditions and then invoking the conventional consequences of applying it, establish as true some statement which we should have had no other means of establishing: in other words, when the language is, in a transferred sense, a conservative extension of what remains of it when the given expression is deleted from its vocabulary. The analogue, within the restricted domain of logic, for an arbitrary logical constant **c**, is that it should not be possible, by first applying one of the introduction rules for **c** and then immediately drawing a consequence from the conclusion of that introduction rule by means of an elimination rule of which it is the major premiss, to derive from the premisses of the introduction rule a consequence that we could not otherwise have drawn. Let us call any part of a deductive inference where, for some logical constant **c**, a **c**-introduction rule is followed immediately by a **c**-elimination rule a 'local peak for **c**'. Then it is a requirement, for harmony to obtain between the introduction rules and elimination rules for **c**, that any local peak for **c** be capable of being levelled, that is, that there be a deductive path from the premisses of the introduction rule to the conclusion of the elimination rule without invoking the rules governing the constant **c**.

Examples are easily given. The standard introduction rule for '&', written in sequent notation, is:

$$\frac{\Gamma : A \qquad \Delta : B}{\Gamma, \Delta : A \ \& \ B}$$

where we use Γ and Δ to represent sets of sentences, and **A**, **B**, and **C** to represent single sentences. Since, in this chapter and the two following ones, introduction rules and elimination rules are our principal concern, it is more convenient to think of arguments as carried out exclusively in natural deduction form, even though we are compelled temporarily to narrow our conception of a rule of inference to those for which the conclusion depends on some or all of the hypotheses on which the premisses depend. We may therefore adopt the simpler notation:

$$\frac{A \qquad B}{A \ \& \ B}$$

for the &-introduction rule.

The standard elimination rules for '&', written in the same notation, are:

$$\frac{A \ \& \ B}{A} \qquad \frac{A \ \& \ B}{B}$$

If, in the course of a deduction, we apply the introduction rule, and then immediately one of the elimination rules, we obtain a part of our deduction of the following form:

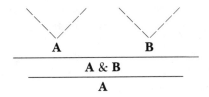

It is obvious that the detour through ⌜**A & B**⌝ was superfluous; we had already arrived at the conclusion **A**, dependent in its upper occurrence only on hypotheses on which its second occurrence depends.

Again, the standard introduction rules for 'v' are:

while the standard elimination rule is:

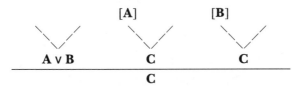

The square brackets indicate that the hypotheses **A** and **B**, on which the two upper occurrences of **C** depend, are discharged by the application of the rule, whose conclusion **C** will depend on those hypotheses other than **A** and **B** on which the two premisses **C** depend, together with those on which the major premiss ⌜**A v B**⌝ depends. If, in the course of a deduction, we follow an application of one of the introduction rules by an application of the elimination rule, that part of our deduction will have the following form:

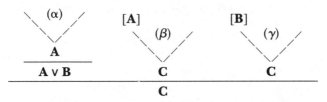

If we replace the initial premiss **A** of the subargument (β) for the left-hand upper occurrence of **C** by the subargument (α), and suppress the rest of the argument, we obtain:

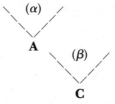

We thus have an argument for the conclusion **C** of the original argument, depending only on hypotheses on which it depended in that argument; as previously, we have avoided the detour through ⌜**A v B**⌝.

We may thus provisionally identify harmony between the introduction and elimination rules for a given logical constant with the possibility of carrying out this procedure, which we have called the levelling of local peaks. The procedure is the fundamental type of reduction step used in the process of normalising natural deduction proofs. This process was introduced by Dag Prawitz as an analogue of Gentzen's operation of eliminating applications of the cut rule in the sequent calculus. A normalised natural deduction proof is defined simply as one to which no further reduction step can be applied; such proofs have properties almost as nice as those of cut-free proofs in the sequent calculus. The other reduction steps are auxiliary, being principally concerned to rearrange the order in which the rules are applied, so that a proof in which a sentence is introduced by an introduction rule, and only later removed by means of an elimination rule in which it is the major premiss, can be transformed into one in which the elimination rule is applied immediately after the introduction rule to form a local peak. Normalisability implies that, for each logical constant **c**, the full language is a conservative extension of that obtained by omitting **c** from its vocabulary. For, if we have a proof whose final sequent does not contain **c**, any sentence containing **c** must first have been introduced by an introduction rule, and then eliminated by an elimination rule; hence, by normalisation, we can obtain a proof not involving that sentence. This, of course, implies relative consistency: if an arbitrary atomic sentence can be proved using the rules governing **c**, it could have been proved without using those rules.

The ease with which these auxiliary reduction steps can usually be carried out should not mislead us into believing them always to be possible; an example will be given later of a logic in which each logical constant is governed by harmonious introduction and elimination rules, but which, when the connective 'v' is added to it, subject to the usual rules, allows the construction of proofs in which the auxiliary reduction steps will not go through. In such a case, the enlarged theory is *not* a conservative extension of the original theory: we shall be able to derive sequents not containing 'v' which were not derivable in the theory lacking that connective. We ought, therefore, to distinguish between 'intrinsic harmony' and 'harmony in context', or 'total harmony'. We may continue to treat the eliminability of local peaks as a criterion for intrinsic harmony; this is a property solely of the rules governing the logical constant in question. For total harmony, however, we shall demand that the addition of that logical constant produce a conservative extension of the logical theory to which it is added. This notion is in a high degree relative to the context, that is, the base theory to which the addition is being made. For certainly the standard rules governing 'v' do not offer any obstacle, in intuitionistic logic or other familiar systems, to the execution of the auxiliary reduction steps.

Introduction Rules as Self-Justifying

Belnap's requirements were that the rules of inference governing a logical constant be in harmony, and that, collectively, they guarantee uniqueness. These two requirements may be sound; that is to say, it is plausible that self-justifying laws, taken together with the other laws that can be justified by appeal to them, must satisfy those requirements. At the same time, his proposal that any complete set of primitive laws governing a logical constant should be regarded as self-justifying, provided that it satisfies the requirements, violates the sense of the term 'self-justifying', as does the weaker proposal that we should require no more than consistency. Something may be called 'self-justifying' only if no proof is needed that it is in order; if, say, a proof of consistency is required, it cannot be self-justifying. It follows that, if any absolute justifications of logical laws are to be possible by purely proof-theoretic means, the procedure of justification must be stronger than those of the first grade; for proof-theoretic justifications of the first grade require, as a base, a *complete* set of primitive laws, if every valid law outside the base is to be within their scope. It is therefore essential to develop a characterisation that will allow us to recognise a set of logical laws as self-justifying by their very form. Nevertheless, it is more convenient to postpone this enquiry until we have seen what kind of proof-theoretic justification, stronger than those of the first grade, it is possible to give.

Gerhard Gentzen, who, by inventing both natural deduction and the sequent calculus, first taught us how logic should be formalised, gave a hint how to do this, remarking without elaboration that 'an introduction rule gives, so to say, a definition of the constant in question', by which he meant that it fixes its meaning, and that the elimination rule is, in the final analysis, no more than a consequence of this definition (*The Collected Papers of Gerhard Gentzen*, trans. and ed. M. E. Szabo, Amsterdam, 1969, p. 80). Plainly, the elimination rules are not consequences of the introduction rules in the straightforward sense of being derivable from them; Gentzen must therefore have had in mind some more powerful means of drawing consequences. He was also implicitly claiming that the introduction rules are, in our terminology, self-justifying.

Proof-Theoretic Justifications of the Second Grade

Prawitz, in a series of articles, beginning with "Towards a Foundation of a General Proof Theory" (*Logic, Methodology, and Philosophy of Science IV*, ed. P. Suppes et al., Amsterdam, 1973), and including that already cited ("On the Idea of a General Proof Theory", *Synthese*, vol. 27, 1974, pp. 63–77), has elaborated this suggestion and sought to make it precise. It is confusing to speak of the elimination rules as *consequences* of the introduction rules: it is better to speak of them as being *justified* by reference to them. As a first step towards explaining justifications of this kind, we may consider what I shall call 'proof-theoretic justifications of the second grade'. The method of exposition adopted here is slightly different from Prawitz's, because the aim is somewhat more general. Prawitz considers justifications in terms of the standard introduction rules for the standard logical constants, whereas our present aim is to achieve a quite general formulation for all conceivable logical constants, provided that they are governed by introduction rules of a restricted type yet to be specified.

A proof-theoretic justification of the first grade assumes, of the logical laws it takes as its base, only that they are valid. The new kind of justification will be more powerful; and so the assumption it makes concerning the introduction rules it takes as a base is correspondingly stronger, namely, that they are collectively in a certain sense *complete*. The view that the introduction rules are self-justifying because they fix the meanings of the logical constants has its home in a verificationist meaning-theory: the introduction rules for a constant **c** represent the direct or canonical means of establishing the truth of a sentence with principal operator **c**. A statement may frequently be established by *indirect* means, but to label certain means 'canonical' is to claim that, whenever we are justified in asserting the statement, we *could have* arrived at our entitlement to do so by those restricted means. The exact meaning of this 'could have' is a question for further discussion; but Prawitz expressly assumes that, if a statement whose principal operator is one of the logical constants in question can be established at all, it can be established by an argument ending with one of the stipulated introduction rules. It will be seen that this assumption is essential to the claim of his procedure actually to *justify* the logical laws to which it is applied.

Let us see how the assumption can be used to yield an intuitive justification of a logical law, say, a law of the kind that can be represented by a single sequent—that is, a rule of inference, most easily written without sequents, not involving the discharge of any hypothesis. The distributive law

$$\frac{A \ \& \ (B \lor C)}{(A \ \& \ B) \lor (A \ \& \ C)}$$

will do very well for this purpose. By the assumption, if we are in a position to assert the premiss, we could have arrived at it by means of an argument whose last step was an application of the &-introduction rule:

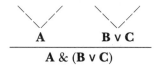

Applying the assumption a second time, we conclude that, if we were genuinely entitled to assert the second premiss, we could have arrived at it by means of an argument ending with one of the ∨-introduction rules, say with premiss **B**. We should then have an argument for the statement ⌜**A** & (**B** ∨ **C**)⌝ ending as follows:

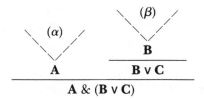

It is now evident that we can obtain a derivation of the conclusion ⌜(**A** & **B**) ∨ (**A** & **C**)⌝ of the distributive law from the two premisses **A** and **B** by appeal to the introduction rules alone. Hence, if we had a legitimate derivation of the premiss of the distributive law, we could obtain a legitimate derivation of its conclusion; and that serves as a justification of the law.

When the rule of inference in question is an elimination rule, the argument simply reduces to the levelling of local peaks, that is, to demonstrating intrinsic harmony with the introduction rules. We have already seen how to accomplish this both for '&' and for '∨': the justification procedure will be exactly that illustrated earlier for the levelling of a local peak. The difference lies only in the fact that, previously, we were *given* both the introduction and the elimination rules and had to show them to be in harmony, whereas now we are given only the introduction rules and are justifying other rules by reference to them. Our procedure has the effect that *any* elimination rule shown to be in harmony with the introduction rules is justifiable, and hence to be considered valid.

The strategy of proof-theoretic justifications of the second grade is that of all proof-theoretic justifications, namely, to show that we can dispense with the rule up for justification: if we have a valid argument for the premisses of a proposed application of it, we already have a valid argument, not appealing to that rule, for the conclusion. But the justification depends heavily upon what we may call the 'fundamental assumption': that, if we have a valid argument for a complex statement, we can construct a valid argument for it which finishes with an application of one of the introduction rules governing its principal operator. We must now give a precise description of this procedure; we may follow Prawitz in formulating it as a *definition* of a *valid argument,* relative to a given set of logical constants and a given set of introduction rules for them, considered as self-justifying and as satisfying the fundamental assumption.

We are for the time being considering an argument as being carried out in natural deduction fashion, as an array of sentences in tree form, together with a specification of the hypotheses on which each occurrence of a sentence rests. It should be noted that we are here thinking of actual arguments, whose lines are genuine sentences, rather than of argument-schemata, whose lines are formulas. Each initial sentence (one at a topmost node) will be taken to depend on itself alone. Every sentence other than the initial ones will depend on all, or on only some, of the assumptions on which the sentences at the nodes immediately above it depend; for the time being, we are not considering inferences that introduce new hypotheses into the antecedent. Initial sentences representing hypotheses subsequently discharged in the course of the argument will be shown enclosed in square brackets, as was done above for the rule of v-elimination. For an argument in general, we make no other restriction on the transitions involved, that is, on the rules of inference by which each step in the argument is taken. The *final conclusion* of the argument is the sentence associated with the lowest node; the *initial premisses* of the argument are the assumptions on which the final conclusion depends, namely those initial sentences not shown as enclosed in square brackets.

In this context, we shall take an atomic sentence to be one not containing any of the logical constants in the given set, and a complex sentence to be one that is not atomic in this sense. We assume that we are given certain rules of inference, which we recognise as valid, for deriving atomic sentences from one or more other atomic sentences; we may call these 'boundary rules'. We now define a 'canonical argument' to be one in which no initial premiss is a complex sentence (no complex sentence stands at a topmost node) and in which all the transitions are in accordance either with one of the boundary rules or with one of the given set of introduction rules. A canonical argument, as thus defined, is therefore by assumption valid, as expressed by Prawitz when he says that the introduction rules are 'valid by the very meaning of the logical constants'; in such an argument, all the initial premisses are atomic, and every complex sentence is derived by means of one of the given introduction rules. Given an arbitrary argument—whose initial premisses may of course be complex—we define a 'supplementation' of it to be the result of replacing any complex initial premiss by a canonical (sub)argument having that premiss as its final conclusion. We may then define an arbitrary argument to be 'valid' if we have an effective means of transforming any supplementation of it into a canonical argument with the same final conclusion and no new initial premisses.

Prawitz requires of a canonical argument only that its *last* step be in accordance with one of the given introduction rules; but this simplification is possible only because he confines himself to demonstrating the validity of the elimination rules. When we are concerned with that of an arbitrary rule of inference, we may have to apply the fundamental assumption to more than the premisses of that rule, as we saw with the distributive law; there we had to apply it also to one of the premisses of the introduction rule by means of which we were assuming that the premiss of the distributive law could be derived. Evidently, if the fundamental assumption is sound, and if none of the given introduction rules involves the discharge of a hypothesis, then any sentence we are entitled to assert can be derived by means of a canonical argument in the present sense; requiring the initial premisses of the argument up for validation to have been derived by a canonical argument guarantees that the fundamental assumption is applied as often as is necessary. The need to allow for the application of boundary rules is not as yet apparent but evidently can do no harm: they might be rules governing either non-logical expressions or logical constants not in the given set. If we say that we are canonically entitled to assert a sentence when we have a canonical argument for it, then our definition deems an argument valid when we can effectively show ourselves canonically entitled to assert the conclusion whenever we are canonically entitled to assert the premisses.

The foregoing definition specifies when an *argument* is to be considered valid, relatively to the given set of introduction rules. An 'argument', in the present context, is a deduction, in tree form, involving actual sentences. The definition does not in fact pay any attention to what goes on between the initial premisses and the final conclusion of the argument: we may therefore regard the procedure simply as a means of validating one-step arguments, that is, particular applications of rules of inference of the least complex kind, rules other than those which discharge hypotheses or introduce new hypotheses into the antecedent. The rule itself is not an argument but a *schema* for arguments; our definition therefore does not directly specify the condition for the validity of a rule. For rules of the least complex kind, it lies ready to hand how to do this: the rule is *valid* if we have an effective means of showing any application of it to be valid. We may take the distributive law as an example, as before. When we substitute any particular sentences, say **P**, **Q**, and **R**, for the schematic letters '**A**', '**B**', and '**C**' of the schema, we obtain a one-step argument. It is evident that we have a uniform method for converting any supplementation of such an argument into a canonical argument for the same conclusion.

What Is an Introduction Rule?

We need to generalise our procedure in order to take into account introduction rules which discharge hypotheses. Before doing so, however, we need to address the hitherto neglected question what formal properties an introduction rule should have to rate as self-justifying.

The terms 'introduction rule' and 'elimination rule' themselves may be explained in a very general way. A rule of inference may be called an introduction rule for a logical constant **c** if its conclusion is required to have **c** as principal operator; it may be called an elimination rule for **c** if one of its premisses is required to have **c** as principal operator, relative to which that will be the 'major premiss'. (When the rule is expressed as a schema for passing from one or more upper sequents to a bottom sequent, the 'conclusion' is the succedent of the bottom sequent, and the 'premisses' the succedents of the upper sequents.) On this definition, a rule can simultaneously be an introduction rule for one logical constant and an elimination rule for another, like the distributive law, or an introduction rule and an elimination rule for the same constant, like the law of transitivity for '→', or an elimination rule for two different constants, like *modus tollendo ponens;* we shall not, however, consider any such rule self-justifying.

Some terminology is required to distinguish rules of different kinds. We may continue to set aside the rules peculiar to the sequent calculus, in which a logical constant is introduced into the antecedent. For the rest, let us call a rule 'single-ended' if it is either an introduction rule but not an elimination rule, or an elimination rule but not an introduction rule. A rule of inference is of course expressible as a schema. Many logical constants may appear in any one *application* of the rule, but only a few will appear in the *schema* giving its general form, and we may say that these 'figure' in the rule. A rule may be called 'pure' if only one logical constant figures in it, and 'simple' if any logical constant figuring in it occurs as principal operator of the sentence. Thus the double negation rule (to infer **A** from ⌜not not **A**⌝) is pure and single-ended but not simple; *modus tollendo ponens* is simple and single-ended but not pure; and the transitivity law is pure and simple but not single-ended. We may call a rule 'sheer' if either it is an introduction rule for a logical constant that does not figure in any of the premisses or in a discharged hypothesis, or it is an elimination rule for one that does not figure in the conclusion or in a discharged hypothesis. Finally, we may call a rule 'oblique' if a logical constant figures in a hypothesis discharged by it, as in the rule

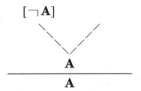

Rules that are not oblique may be called 'direct'.

The fundamental assumption is that, whenever we are entitled to assert a complex statement, we could have arrived at it by means of an argument terminating with at least one of the introduction rules governing its principal operator. Hence what is to be taken as determining the meaning of that logical constant is the *set* of introduction rules governing it as a whole. To determine the meaning of a logical constant, in a compositional meaning-theory, it is necessary and sufficient to determine that of a sentence of which that constant is the principal operator, relative to the meanings of the subsentences. Hence, what the introduction rules for a constant **c** are required collectively to do is to display all the canonical ways in which a sentence with principal operator **c** can be inferred. This might suggest that we should follow the example of Gentzen by restricting our rules, at least for constants other than negation, to those that are pure, simple, and single-ended. Reflection shows that this demand is exorbitant. An impure **c**-introduction rule will make the understanding of **c** depend on the prior understanding of the other logical constants figuring in the rule. Certainly we do not want such a relation of dependence to be cyclic; but there would be nothing in principle objectionable if we could so order the logical constants that the understanding of each depended only on the understanding of those preceding it in the ordering. Given such an ordering, we could not demand that each rule be simple, either. The introduction rules for **c** might individually provide for the derivation of sentences of different forms with **c** as principal operator, according to the other logical constants occurring in them: together they would provide for the derivation of *any* sentence with **c** as principal operator. For example, one might have different rules for ¬-introduction, according to the principal operator of the negated sentence: $\ulcorner\neg(\mathbf{A} \vee \mathbf{B})\urcorner$ would be stipulated to be derivable from $\ulcorner\neg\mathbf{A}\urcorner$ and $\ulcorner\neg\mathbf{B}\urcorner$; $\ulcorner\neg(\mathbf{A} \,\&\, \mathbf{B})\urcorner$ from $\ulcorner\neg\mathbf{A}\urcorner$ alone, and also from $\ulcorner\neg\mathbf{B}\urcorner$ alone; $\ulcorner\neg(\mathbf{A} \rightarrow \mathbf{B})\urcorner$ from **A** and $\ulcorner\neg\mathbf{B}\urcorner$; and $\ulcorner\neg\neg\mathbf{A}\urcorner$ from **A**. This particular example, natural as it is, is unconvincing, because it would be difficult to provide for the derivation of $\ulcorner\neg\mathbf{A}\urcorner$ with **A** atomic by means of a purely logical rule; but it suffices to show that the demand for simplicity is too strong: even the demand that the rule be single-ended is shown by this example to be excessive. We could not even require that every possible sentence with a constant **c** as principal operator be the conclusion of an application of one of the introduction rules for **c**. Suppose, for instance, that the introduction rules for negation fail to provide any means of deriving a sentence of the form $\ulcorner\neg(\mathbf{A} \rightarrow \mathbf{B})\urcorner$. According to the fundamental assumption, if we were entitled to assert $\ulcorner\neg(\mathbf{A} \rightarrow \mathbf{B})\urcorner$, we should be able to arrive at it by means of one of the introduction rules: since we could not do so, it would simply follow that we should never be in a position to assert $\ulcorner\neg(\mathbf{A} \rightarrow \mathbf{B})\urcorner$; and there is nothing to rule out the possibility that that was the result we wanted.

In fact, we need not bother even with an ordering of the logical constants by dependence of meaning. It is attractive to give explanations of the logical constants that are as uniform as possible, but the principle of compositionality in no way demands this; all that is essentially presupposed for the understanding of a complex sentence is the understanding of the subsentences. Hence the minimal demand we should make on an introduction rule intended to be self-justifying is that its form be such as to guarantee that, in any application of it, the conclusion will be of higher logical complexity than any of the premisses and than any discharged hypothesis. We may call this the 'complexity condition'. In practice, it is evident that there will be no loss of generality if we require the rule to be single-ended, since, for a premiss with the same principal operator as the conclusion, we may substitute the hypotheses from which that premiss could be derived by the relevant introduction rule. We may accordingly recognise as an introduction rule a single-ended rule satisfying the complexity condition.

Proof-Theoretic Justifications of the Third Grade

A proof-theoretic justification of the second grade will suffice to validate a rule of inference of the least complex kind—the antecedent of the conclusion being the union of the antecedents of the premisses—the logical constants figuring in which are '&', 'v', and the existential quantifier: for the standard introduction rules governing these constants involve neither free variables nor the discharge of hypotheses. To deal with introduction rules displaying one or other of these two features, and to make precise the method of validating other rules, we need a more general procedure of justification.

The standard introduction rule for the universal quantifier derives the quantified sentence $\ulcorner \forall x\, A(x) \urcorner$ from an open sentence $\ulcorner A(a) \urcorner$ containing a free variable a that does not occur in the conclusion $\ulcorner \forall x\, A(x) \urcorner$ or in any of the hypotheses on which $\ulcorner A(a) \urcorner$ depends. (We shall use the letters $a, b, c, \ldots$ for free variables, and $x, y, z, \ldots$ for bound ones, assuming the two classes to be disjoint.) We must therefore broaden our notion of an argument, including canonical arguments, to admit those containing some lines that are open sentences. We may continue to apply our fundamental assumption to all genuine (that is, closed) sentences: if we can assert a universally quantified sentence, we could have arrived at it by the foregoing introduction rule. But we cannot apply the assumption to open sentences. Suppose that we are entitled to assert $\ulcorner \forall x\, (A(x) \vee B(x)) \urcorner$. This could have been derived from the open sentence $\ulcorner A(a) \vee B(a) \urcorner$, where a does not occur in any of the hypotheses on which it depends. If, now, we assume that $\ulcorner A(a) \vee B(a) \urcorner$ could have been derived by v-introduction either from $\ulcorner A(a) \urcorner$ or from $\ulcorner B(a) \urcorner$, it will follow that we must be entitled to assert either $\ulcorner \forall x\, A(x) \urcorner$ or $\ulcorner \forall x\, B(x) \urcorner$ and hence, in either case, $\ulcorner \forall x\, A(x) \vee \forall x\, B(x) \urcorner$. We have thus given a justification of the patently invalid rule allowing the derivation of $\ulcorner \forall x\, A(x) \vee \forall x\, B(x) \urcorner$ from $\ulcorner \forall x\, (A(x) \vee B(x)) \urcorner$. The remedy is not to apply the fundamental assumption to open sentences.

The easiest way to handle free variables is to assume that the language contains a constant term for each element of the domain. Given an argument, we may take an *instance* of it to be an argument obtained from it by replacing each free variable occurring in its final conclusion or in any of its initial premisses by one and the same constant term, in each of its occurrences in the argument. The idea will then be to characterise an arbitrary argument as *valid* if we possess an effective means of converting any supplementation of an instance of it into a valid canonical argument. We need, however, to impose one further constraint upon an introduction rule for it to be self-justifying, namely, that if one or more of the premisses of an application of the rule contains a free variable, but the conclusion does not, that free variable should not occur in any of the hypotheses on which the conclusion depends. This condition, which is satisfied by the universal quantifier-introduction rule, is needed in order to guarantee that, if we are entitled to assert a closed sentence, it should be possible to derive it by means of the given introduction rules from closed initial premisses.

We shall no longer be able to define 'canonical argument' in such a way that a canonical argument is automatically valid, because we can place no general restriction upon the derivations of open sentences. A further reason appears when we consider rules that discharge hypotheses. The part of the argument that leads to a premiss of such a rule depending on the hypothesis to be discharged is called a 'subordinate deduction'; and it is impossible to demand that a subordinate deduction be capable of being framed so as to appeal only to introduction rules. For instance, from the initial premiss **A** the conclusion ⌜**B** & **C** → **A** & **B**⌝ can obviously be validly drawn. The most straightforward argument for this is

$$\frac{\dfrac{\quad}{\text{A}} \qquad \dfrac{[\textbf{B \& C}]}{\textbf{B}}}{\dfrac{\textbf{A \& B}}{\textbf{B \& C} \rightarrow \textbf{A \& B}}}$$

The conclusion is drawn by the standard introduction rule for '→'; but, in the subordinate deduction, there is no way of avoiding the appeal to the elimination rule for '&'. Hence, when the canonical argument involves an appeal to introduction rules that discharge one of the hypotheses of their premiss or premisses, we cannot place any restriction on the forms of the rules of inference appealed to in subordinate deductions. The result is a much more complicated procedure of justification, in that we now have simultaneously to define 'valid canonical argument' and 'valid (arbitrary) argument'.

Let us say that (an occurrence of) a sentence belongs to the 'main stem' of an argument if it, and every sentence intervening between it and the final conclusion, depend only on (some or all of the) initial premisses of the argument. We may then specify an argument to be *canonical* if:

(a) its final conclusion is a closed sentence;

(b) all its initial premisses are closed atomic sentences;

(c) every atomic sentence in the main stem is either an initial premiss or is derived by a boundary rule;

(d) every closed complex sentence in the main stem is derived by means of one of the given set of introduction rules.

This definition places no restrictions on the derivations of open sentences, such as the premiss of a universal quantifier-introduction rule, or of sentences not in the main stem, such as the premiss of an if-introduction rule. We may define the 'degree' of any argument to be the maximum number of logical constants occurring in any of its initial premisses or in its final conclusion. Any closed or open sentence occurring within an argument determines, in an obvious way, a 'subargument' of which it is the final conclusion; the initial premisses of that subargument will be the hypotheses on which, within the argument as a whole, that sentence depends. A subargument of an argument (α) will be said to be 'critical' if its conclusion stands, in (α), immediately above a closed sentence in the main stem of (α), but is itself either an open sentence or a closed sentence not in the main stem. A supplementation of an argument is to be essentially as before: it results from replacing every initial premiss by a *valid* canonical argument with that premiss as final conclusion.

It is important to notice that a sentence **A** standing immediately below the conclusion **C** of a critical subargument of a canonical argument must be of higher logical complexity than either the conclusion or the premisses of that subargument. This holds good of **C** because **A**, being a closed sentence in the main stem, must be derived by an application of one of the introduction rules, of which **C** must accordingly be one of the premisses; by the complexity condition on the introduction rules, **A** must be of higher logical complexity than any of its premisses. The premisses of the subargument must either be initial premisses of the entire argument, in which case they are atomic, or be hypotheses discharged by the introduction rule, in which case they must again be of lower logical complexity than **A**.

With this machinery, validity can be defined as follows. An arbitrary argument will be said to be 'valid' if we can effectively transform any supplementation of an instance of it into a valid canonical argument with the same final conclusion and initial premisses. A canonical argument will be said to be 'valid' just in case every critical subargument it contains is valid. The definition may be illuminated by some examples. Suppose that we want to demonstrate the validity of the argument

$$\frac{\dfrac{\dfrac{\forall x\,(\mathbf{A}(x) \vee \mathbf{B}(x))}{\mathbf{A}(a) \vee \mathbf{B}(a)}}{\mathbf{B}(a) \vee \mathbf{A}(a)}}{\forall x\,(\mathbf{B}(x) \vee \mathbf{A}(x))}$$

Since the initial premiss and final conclusion are both closed sentences, we have no need to form an instance of this argument. If we assume that we are entitled to assert the initial premiss, we must be able to provide a supplementation of the argument, which will take the form

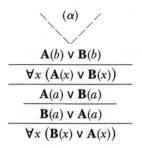

$$\frac{\mathbf{A}(b) \lor \mathbf{B}(b)}{\forall x \, (\mathbf{A}(x) \lor \mathbf{B}(x))}$$
$$\frac{\mathbf{A}(a) \lor \mathbf{B}(a)}{\mathbf{B}(a) \lor \mathbf{A}(a)}$$
$$\forall x \, (\mathbf{B}(x) \lor \mathbf{A}(x))$$

The initial premisses of the valid canonical argument (α), being closed, will not contain the free variable b; the assumption that such a supplementation is possible is based not only on the fundamental assumption but also on the condition for the applicability of the universal quantifier-introduction rule, namely, that the free variable occurs neither in the conclusion of the rule nor in any of the hypotheses on which it depends. Since everything down to the penultimate line of the supplemented argument constitutes a critical subargument, it is already a canonical argument by our definition. We have therefore to show it to be valid, which it will be if any instance (γ) of the critical subargument, say,

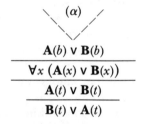

$$\frac{\mathbf{A}(b) \lor \mathbf{B}(b)}{\forall x \, (\mathbf{A}(x) \lor \mathbf{B}(x))}$$
$$\frac{\mathbf{A}(t) \lor \mathbf{B}(t)}{\mathbf{B}(t) \lor \mathbf{A}(t)}$$

is valid, no further supplementation being needed. Since (α) is a critical subargument, from closed atomic premisses, of the valid canonical argument for $\ulcorner \forall x \, (\mathbf{A}(x) \lor \mathbf{B}(x)) \urcorner$, we can find a valid canonical argument (β) from the same premisses for the instance of it obtained by replacing b by t; (β) will have the form

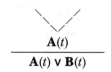

$$\frac{\mathbf{A}(t)}{\mathbf{A}(t) \lor \mathbf{B}(t)}$$

or else the corresponding form with $\ulcorner \mathbf{B}(t) \urcorner$ in place of $\ulcorner \mathbf{A}(t) \urcorner$. By replacing the conclusion of (β) with $\ulcorner \mathbf{B}(t) \vee \mathbf{A}(t) \urcorner$, we obtain a canonical argument with the same initial premisses and final conclusion as (γ), as desired. This completes the demonstration of the validity of our original argument.

Our definition does not allow us to validate the obviously invalid argument

$$\frac{\forall x \, (\mathbf{A}(x) \vee \mathbf{B}(x))}{\forall x \, \mathbf{A}(x) \vee \forall x \, \mathbf{B}(x)}$$

The penultimate line of a valid canonical argument for the premiss will have the form $\ulcorner \mathbf{A}(a) \vee \mathbf{B}(a) \urcorner$. Since all down to this line will be a critical subargument, it will be possible to obtain a valid canonical argument, from the same initial premisses, for $\ulcorner \mathbf{A}(t) \vee \mathbf{B}(t) \urcorner$, and hence for either $\ulcorner \mathbf{A}(t) \urcorner$ or $\ulcorner \mathbf{B}(t) \urcorner$; but that is no help towards obtaining a proof of $\ulcorner \forall x \, \mathbf{A}(x) \urcorner$ or of $\ulcorner \forall x \, \mathbf{B}(x) \urcorner$.

Our definitions escape circularity because, in order to judge the validity of a canonical argument of degree n, we need only to be able to recognise the validity of arbitrary arguments of degree $< n$, while, to judge the validity of an arbitrary argument of degree n, we need only to be able to recognise the validity of canonical arguments of degree $\leq n$. The former holds good in virtue of the remark made above about critical subarguments of a canonical argument; the latter because the validity of an arbitrary argument will depend on that of a canonical argument with the same conclusion and atomic premisses.

We may illustrate this by the easy argument from $\mathbf{A}$ to $\ulcorner \mathbf{B} \, \& \, \mathbf{C} \rightarrow \mathbf{A} \, \& \, \mathbf{B} \urcorner$ set out earlier. If we suppose $\mathbf{A}$ to be atomic, this is a canonical argument of degree 3, since the only sentences in the main stem are the final conclusion and the initial premiss $\mathbf{A}$, and the conclusion is derived by means of the appropriate introduction rule. It is therefore valid provided that its critical subargument

$$\frac{\mathbf{A} \qquad \dfrac{\mathbf{B} \, \& \, \mathbf{C}}{\mathbf{B}}}{\mathbf{A} \, \& \, \mathbf{B}}$$

is valid. This argument, of degree 1, is valid provided that a supplementation of it can be transformed into a valid canonical argument. If we suppose $\mathbf{B}$ and $\mathbf{C}$ to be atomic, a supplementation will take the form

$$\frac{\mathbf{A} \qquad \dfrac{\dfrac{\mathbf{B} \qquad \mathbf{C}}{\mathbf{B} \, \& \, \mathbf{C}}}{\mathbf{B}}}{\mathbf{A} \, \& \, \mathbf{B}}$$

This has a local peak which can be levelled, transforming it into the canonical argument of degree 1:

$$\frac{\textbf{A} \qquad \textbf{B}}{\textbf{A \& B}}$$

This is valid, because it contains no critical subarguments. We have thus provided a justification of the original argument, a proof-theoretic justification *of the third* (and highest) *grade*.

This gives us a comprehensive criterion for the validity of an arbitrary argument, relative to our introduction rules. In fact, our criterion takes no overt account of more than the initial premises and final conclusion of the argument: what comes between may help to supply us with the effective means of transformation that we need to show the argument valid, although these intervening lines play no explicit role in our criterion. We may therefore convert our criterion for the validity of a rule into one for the validity of a *sequent;* the sequent $A_1, \ldots, A_k : B$ will be valid if the one-step argument

$$\frac{\textbf{A}_1 \qquad \textbf{A}_2 \qquad \ldots \qquad \textbf{A}_k}{\textbf{B}}$$

is valid. A *rule* of the simplest kind, that involves no discharge of hypotheses (or introduction of new assumptions), may be represented by a schematic sequent, one whose antecedent is composed of formulas rather than sentences and whose consequent is a formula. As before, we may call such a rule valid if we have a means of showing any sequent resulting from the schematic sequent representing it by instantiation to be valid. A rule in general may be represented by a finite number of *base* schematic sequents, and a single *resultant* schematic sequent. (It would be confusing to call these the 'premisses' and 'conclusion' of the rule.) A rule so represented may be said to be valid if we have a means of showing, of any uniform instantiation of the schematic sequents, that if it renders the base sequents valid, it will render the resultant valid also.

chapter 12

The Fundamental Assumption

Is the Fundamental Assumption Plausible?

It is plain that proof-theoretic justification of the third grade is a powerful procedure. It has here been formulated so as to be applicable to any set of logical constants, governed by whatever introduction rules are chosen, provided only that they conform to the mild constraints we laid down. Given the usual introduction rules, it will certainly serve to justify all valid laws of first-order positive logic (the negation-free fragment of intuitionistic logic), a fact that can be verified by confirming that it validates all the standard elimination rules. It is recognisable as a *justification* procedure, however, only to the extent that the fundamental assumption is plausible: that must therefore be the next topic of our enquiry.

Evidently, the plausibility of the fundamental assumption is entirely relative to the logical constant in question and to the set of introduction rules being proposed as governing it. For instance, it would have no plausibility at all if applied to the modal operator '◊', regarded as subject to the sole introduction rule allowing an inference from **A** to ⌜◊ **A**⌝. If the fundamental assumption were taken to hold in this case, the converse inference could be validated, so that the operator '◊' would become quite nugatory; for, if a canonical derivation of ⌜◊ **A**⌝ must end by deriving it by means of the sole introduction rule, we must be able to give a canonical derivation of **A** whenever we can give one of ⌜◊ **A**⌝. We can therefore consider the fundamental assumption only on a case by case basis.

Disjunction

The problem is in part one of elucidating the 'could have' that occurs in the statement of the assumption. What does it mean to say that, if we are entitled to assert a statement of the form ⌜**A** or **B**⌝, we *could have* arrived at that position by applying one or other of the or-introduction rules? Plainly, this is untrue if applied to individual speakers.

I may be entitled to assert ⌜**A** or **B**⌝ because I was reliably so informed by someone in a position to know, but if he did not choose to tell me which alternative held good, *I* could not apply an or-introduction rule to arrive at that conclusion. Of course, the fundamental assumption is not intended to be understood so as to make this a counter-example to it, or else the most doctrinaire intuitionist would be unable to endorse it. We must distinguish between individual possession of a piece of information and our collective possession of it: *my* source may be the testimony of another, but *our* original source must stem from whoever first established the statement as true, say by observation. Here whatever witnesses we trust must be included among 'ourselves'. If an angel reveals that either the citizens of Nineveh will repent or the city will be destroyed, whoever accepts the revelation must include the angel among the community with whose collective information we are concerned. The testimony may derive from someone long dead: we may believe, on the authority of a contemporary chronicler, that Constantine either murdered his son or procured his murder; if so, the chronicler must rate, for this purpose, as a member of the community, which will include the dead as well as the living. The fundamental assumption, as applied to disjunctive statements, must thus be to the effect that whichever member of the community originally established the truth of such a statement could have arrived at its truth by the rule of or-introduction. To make this plausible, we must not only broaden the boundaries of the community to comprise the dead and, in so far as we can communicate with them and trust them, the non-human, but distinguish our past from our present selves; for memory must be treated in analogy with testimony. If, having been an eyewitness, I report that either Gertrude or Diana tore up her invitation card, but confess that I cannot remember which of them it was, my memory is delivering partial information to me, just as another informant might do. My observation at the time was the original source, the information I have retained being only a weakened consequence of that which I originally possessed.

None of this, however, concedes enough. This is evident from the fact that, without further concessions, the plausibility of the fundamental assumption will depend heavily on what we take to be the primitive predicates of the language. Should we construe 'is a child' as a disjunction of 'is a boy' and 'is a girl', or should we construe 'is a boy' as equivalent by definition to 'is a male child', and similarly for 'is a girl'? Under the former alternative, but not the latter, my seeing that a child was playing on the lawn, without being able to tell whether it was a boy or a girl, would appear a counter-example to the fundamental assumption; but, obviously, the choice is spurious. If we are to distinguish at all between defined and primitive expressions of natural language, the distinction must lie between those an understanding of which is characteristically mediated by knowing a verbal equivalent and those for which this is not so. On this criterion, 'child', 'boy', and 'girl' must all rank as primitive: they belong to a circle of expressions an understanding of any of which demands, but does not consist in, a knowledge of equivalences between each of them and expressions constructed from the others.

This requires an extension of our conception of 'boundary rules'. These were intended to take account of inferential connections between non-logical expressions and were restricted to inferences from atomic premisses to an atomic conclusion. Unless we are prepared to consider deductions as being carried out in a highly regimented version of natural language, in which the primitive predicates have been cut down to a minimum as in an axiomatised mathematical theory, we shall have to extend the notion of a boundary rule to allow the conclusion to be complex. When the conclusion is an open sentence, this will cause no difficulty, since the fundamental assumption will not be applied to it. When it is a closed sentence, however, we are left with an apparent counter-example to the fundamental assumption: if I know that there is a child playing on the lawn, I thereby know that either a boy or a girl is playing there, perhaps without knowing which, even though it is my own observation that constitutes the source of my knowledge. Likewise, if a boundary rule in the extended sense permits an inference from 'That is a child over there' to 'That is either a boy or a girl over there', the disjunctive conclusion was not arrived at by 'or'-introduction, and may well not have been able to be on the basis of the observation actually made.

Manifold other examples are independent of any linguistic question. Hardy may simply not have been able to hear whether Nelson said, 'Kismet, Hardy' or 'Kiss me, Hardy', though he heard him say one or the other: once we have the concept of disjunction, our perceptions themselves may assume an irremediably disjunctive form.

To interpret the fundamental assumption, then, we have to invoke the sense of 'could have' which was used earlier to characterise what may be called the minimal undeniable concession to realism demanded by the existence of deductive inference. The proof of the Königsberg bridge theorem provides an effective means so to carry out simultaneous observations to check whether the traveller crosses every bridge and to check whether he crosses any bridge more than once as to ensure that a positive result for the former will be accompanied by a positive result for the latter. We treat this as warranting us in asserting that some bridge was crossed at least twice, given that he was observed to have crossed them all, even though we cannot now observe him to have done so or recall specific observations to that effect. This can be explained only in terms of a certain conception of the condition for an assertion to be correct: namely, that a sufficient condition for its correctness is that there exist effective means by which, at the relevant time, someone appropriately situated *could have* converted observations that were actually made into a verification of the statement asserted. The resulting notion of truth, possessed by any statement that meets this minimal condition for being capable of being correctly asserted, is very far from being that of full-fledged realism. Full-fledged realism does not merely regard a statement as true if it could as a matter of fact have been verified at the relevant time by an appropriately situated observer and hold it to be determinate whether or not he could have done so: it goes much further, maintaining that truth attaches to statements that we have not and could not have verified. Nevertheless, even this spare notion of truth, far too lean to satisfy the realist, debars us from making the coarsest identification of a statement's being true with its having been verified: if we understood the concept of truth in so coarse a manner as that, we should be unable to countenance deductive argument at all.

It is the 'could have' that occurs here to which the fundamental assumption appeals. If I pass from saying, 'A child ran out of the house', to saying 'Either a boy or a girl ran out of the house', it may be said that I *could have* arrived at the latter statement by or-introduction—not on the basis that I was in fact in a position to assert either of the two disjoined statements 'A boy ran out of the house' and 'A girl ran out of the house', but on the strength of the fact that, given that I was entitled to make the statement I did make, I had an effective means available to me for putting myself in a position to make one or other of the disjoined statements. This explanation will force us to adopt a laxer criterion for the validity of an argument. The criterion given earlier was that we had a means to transform any supplementation of an instance of the argument into a valid canonical argument *with the same initial premisses and final conclusion.* If, however, there occurs in the given argument an application of a boundary rule of the extended kind, leading, say, from atomic premisses to a disjunction of atomic statements, the resultant canonical argument will not have the *same* initial premisses as the supplementation but will have new ones; the rationale will be that, if we can or could establish the initial premisses of the supplementation, then we can establish, or could have established, the new ones.

We are concerned with proof-theoretic justification, on the basis of rules of inference regarded as self-justifying inasmuch as they serve to determine the meanings of the logical constants they govern. The claim of the rules to be self-justifying itself depends upon the fundamental assumption, since, if it does not hold, the introduction rules cannot together exhaust the canonical means of establishing a statement with the logical constant in question as principal operator, and hence cannot suffice, in the framework of a verificationist meaning-theory, to fix the meaning of that constant. The fundamental assumption is even more essential to the claim of our procedure to *justify* other laws. Unsurprisingly, however, what underpin the fundamental assumption are considerations that are not themselves proof-theoretic but are in a broad sense semantic: we are driven to invoke some notion of *truth,* and so have not achieved a *purely* proof-theoretic justification procedure. Now, at first sight, the fundamental assumption, as applied to the connective 'or', cannot hold good for classical logic: for a classical logician, we know a priori that $\ulcorner$**A** or not **A**$\urcorner$ is true, although we may not know, or have any means of discovering, which of the disjuncts is true. But the principle that, if a disjunctive statement is true, one of the two disjuncts must be true, although not holding in certain semantic theories, is of very general validity; if the fundamental assumption, applied to 'or', is to reduce to this, it appears largely banal. It will reduce to this only if it is held that any true statement can be recognised as true by one suitably placed and, if necessary, with sufficient powers. A realist may believe that our powers are too restricted for us to be able to recognise the truth of every true statement, however well placed we are to do so; he must therefore interpret the fundamental assumption, applied to 'or', as meaning that one entitled to assert a disjunction could have recognised one or other disjunct as true if ideally placed to do so and endowed with the requisite powers of observation and intellect. But would not the content of the fundamental assumption then dwindle almost to nothing?

A response to this may be that, in interpreting the fundamental assumption, we have to construe the critical modality 'could have' in whatever way our meaning-theory makes appropriate to the validity of rules of inference. A realist believes that a valid rule is required to preserve a property of truth which may attach to a statement independently of *our* capacity to recognise that it attaches. If he is not to render his own position untenable, he must make this a principle of his meaning-theory: he must hold it to be integral to our understanding of our language that we conceive of our statements as determinately true or false, independently of our capacity to recognise them as such. He will therefore accept the fundamental assumption as holding for disjunction on a lax interpretation of 'could have' such as that suggested above. A verificationist will interpret it much more strictly, holding the criterion for valid inference to be that someone in a position to verify the premises was then in a position to verify the conclusion, by the means available to anyone with no more than ordinary powers; or even more strictly, in accordance with the principle sketched above, that there exists an effective procedure by which someone in a position to verify the premises could at that time have verified the conclusion. The choice between these interpretations is not a matter for logic but for the theory of meaning, just as the choice of a semantic theory is not a matter for logic but for the theory of meaning. Given a semantic theory, logic can determine whether a given formalisation is sound or complete; but whether or not the semantic theory is correct it is not for logic to say. Similarly, logic can determine, for a given set of introduction rules, whether some other set of logical laws can be justified by reference to them; but whether or not the fundamental assumption genuinely holds for those introduction rules, or, if so, under what interpretation, or whether that interpretation is the appropriate one, it is, again, not for logic to say. Proof-theoretic justifications form an interesting alternative to justifications in terms of semantic theories. Neither is autonomous, however: both depend on the defensibility of the meaning-theory within which each finds its proper habitat.

The general principles invoked by this response are sound, but it skirts one critical fact. It is exceedingly plausible that, on a verificationist meaning-theory, the correct logic will be intuitionistic; and we have noted that the standard introduction rules for 'and', 'or', 'if', and the two quantifiers will validate every intuitionistically valid rule involving these constants, where, by the nature of the case, we need to appeal only to those introduction rules governing the logical constants involved in the general formulation of the rule in question. On a realist meaning-theory, however, the correct logic will be classical; and there will be many classically valid laws involving those logical constants that cannot be validated by appeal to the introduction rules governing them, such as those expressed by the classically valid schemata

$$(A \to B) \lor (B \to A)$$

$$(A \to B) \lor A$$

$$((A \to B) \to A) \to A$$

This difference cannot be explained simply in terms of divergent interpretations of the fundamental assumption. The realist will indeed profess to accept the fundamental assumption, applied to disjunction, as exemplified in instances of the law of excluded middle, for example, provided that the assumption is interpreted in terms of his notion of truth as verifiability by an ideal observer. But the validity of laws like those cited above cannot be established by simply applying the fundamental assumption, first to sentences of the given form, and then to the subsentences resulting from its application, so as to obtain supplementations whose initial premisses are all atomic. The realist does not believe that even the ideal observer could establish every true complex statement built up by the binary sentential connectives from atomic premisses he had verified by observation; rather, he would need to invoke negations of atomic statements as well. The realist's basic principle, that, for every atomic statement, an ideal observer could verify either it or its negation, will *not* result from applying our fundamental assumption, however interpreted, to a negation-free statement; it is a distinct hypothesis that cannot be incorporated into the proof-theoretic justification procedure.

The fundamental assumption is capable of a great range of interpretations, according to how strictly we construe its critical phrase 'could have'. When applied to disjunction, it will be obviously false under the strictest possible understanding of that phrase, since no conventions can bar incomplete testimony or defective memories. Under a variety of interpretations that equate 'could have been verified' with 'is true', it will almost always be sound. A notorious exception will be any semantic theory for quantum-mechanical statements that denies the applicability to them of classical logic, but treats quantum logic as the strongest logic that holds good for them. The critical question, however, is not whether the fundamental assumption holds, but whether it is sufficient to ground the validity of all logical laws accepted as valid. Those laws remain invariant under considerable variation in the interpretation of the fundamental assumption, because it will still serve to validate them by the proof-theoretic justification procedure, without the need for further assumptions. When the strong realist interpretation is adopted, however, the situation changes: not all laws can any longer be validated by proof-theoretic means, because their validity depends not only on the fundamental assumption but on the further assumption of bivalence.

The intuitionistic theory of elementary arithmetic with only bounded quantification coincides with the classical theory, since all statements are decidable: so we may say that, for the intuitionist too, classical logic holds good in this limited domain. This conceals the fact that, while every instance of a classically valid schema is true for the intuitionist, it will not be a logical truth for him but will be only an arithmetical theorem, if it is not intuitionistically valid; it holds in virtue of the specific meanings of the arithmetical primitives, and not just of the logical constants. Should a thoroughgoing realist, who believes classical logic to be valid for statements of all kinds, say the same? The question appears absurd, because classical logic for him rests not on the particular meanings our statements happen to have but on the kind of meaning we can give to any statement we can frame: he may hold, for instance, that we can grasp only those propositions for which we can conceive of an ideal observer for whom they would be decidable. The question is, however, whether he must regard such a limitation on what we are capable of understanding or of expressing in our language as a *logical* constraint. The question cannot be answered until we can distinguish by some precise criterion logical notions and principles from non-logical ones. We are free to choose where to draw this line. If, like, Frege, we make 'topic-neutrality' our criterion, then classical logic will remain a strictly logical theory in its entirety; the same will hold if we treat as a logical constant or device any that serves to form complex sentences from simpler ones. It could, alternatively, be proposed to recognise as logical only those such operators and operations as could be completely characterised by self-justifying logical laws—that is, under the proposal we are considering, by introduction rules, under our proof-theoretic definition of the validity of general rules of inference. On such a criterion, the classical operators would not be *purely* logical constants. That is certainly not, in itself, a ground for rejecting classical logic: no edict requires us to use 'or' as a logical constant in this strict sense. It merely gives a sharper and a better grounded principle than we are accustomed to employ for distinguishing what properly belongs to logic from what does not.

The Conditional

The fundamental assumption, when applied to 'if', makes ⌜If **A**, then **B**⌝ assertible only when an enthymematic logical entailment holds between **A** and **B**, that is, when **A** in combination with arbitrarily many additional assertible premises logically entails **B**; the additional premises may include **B** itself, or may include ⌜Not **A**⌝. This is unquestionably a *conceivable* meaning for 'if'; but it is not the meaning we ordinarily attach to it, nor that which is attached to it in intuitionistic mathematics. If we do not presume bivalence, we cannot capture the intuitive meaning of 'if' truth-functionally, that is to say, in terms of the truth or falsity of antecedent and consequent, and hence not by any combination of 'and', 'or', and 'not'. ⌜If **A**, then **B**⌝ says less than ⌜Either not **A** or **B**⌝ and more than ⌜Not both **A** and not **B**⌝. Its fundamental meaning is more naturally regarded as comprised in the elimination rule *(modus ponens)* than in the introduction rule. ⌜If **A**, then **B**⌝

ranks as assertible whenever we have ground to be confident that we shall be entitled to assert **B** on any occasion on which we are entitled to assert **A**. Plainly, this happens far more often than when an enthymematic entailment holds. Given such an entailment, we may transform any proof of **A** into a proof of **B** by simply appending to the proof of **A** a proof of **B** from the hypothesis **A**; but intuitionists allow us to assert ⌜If **A**, then **B**⌝ whenever we have an effective method of transforming any proof of **A** into a proof of **B**, however complex the process of transformation. Outside mathematics, indicative conditionals, when not expressions of intention, are most often asserted on the basis, in whole or part, of experience, as when someone says, 'If you do business with him, he will find some way of cheating you'.

The falsity of the fundamental assumption, applied to 'if', does not necessarily invalidate the proof-theoretic justification procedure, however. We originally admitted, as occurring within deductive proofs of the kind with which we are concerned, boundary rules allowing the inference of an atomic conclusion from atomic premises: these were, of necessity, left unspecified. Our original intention was that the boundary rules should be deductively valid. If we now include among them principles of non-deductive (and therefore fallible) inference, this will have the effect that a 'valid' argument, even if canonical, may have true initial premises but a false final conclusion. It will obviously not affect the justification procedure, however, as a means of determining the validity of logical laws. Under the original, restricted notion of boundary rules, such non-deductive principles would correspond to those conditionals we should be willing to assert whose consequents are atomic sentences (closed or open) and whose antecedents are conjunctions of such sentences; let us call these 'basic conditionals'. Evidently, we frequently make conditional assertions whose antecedents or consequents are highly complex. It thus appears that, if we admit only those non-deductive boundary rules that have atomic conclusions, the legitimacy of the justification procedure will depend on how plausible it is that all such conditionals could be derived by logical deduction, finishing with an application of 'if'-introduction, from basic conditionals.

This hypothesis, unfortunately, cannot be sustained. The recalcitrant case is that of a disjunctive consequent. If you tell me, 'If you ask him for a loan, he will either refuse or make an outright gift to you', because you have never known him do anything else, you presumably know which he did on each occasion that you know about; but, since you do not know on what principle he elects to do one or the other, you are not in a position to make a more specific prediction.

We have, however, extended the scope of deductive boundary rules to allow some with complex conclusions, the premises continuing to be required to be atomic. Should we respond to our difficulty by admitting *non*-deductive boundary rules of this extended kind, with complex conclusions? That would put a great strain on the fundamental assumption as applied to those conclusions, since that assumption would still be required to hold good whenever the atomic hypotheses of the subargument were verified. Doubtless suitable restrictions on the non-deductive boundary rules could be framed; but it seems better to rely on the commonplace that an experientially based conditional will be asserted only as the tacit consequence of some generalised version of it, even though, in complicated circumstances, the proponent might be hard put to it to frame the relevant generalisation. We must therefore turn our attention to the universal quantifier—which we have in any case to consider—in the hope that it will bring with it a solution to our problem.

Universal Quantification

The application of the fundamental assumption to the existential quantifier obviously resembles its application to disjunction; but the universal quantifier, as ordinarily understood, appears not to fit that assumption at all, which amounts to saying that we are entitled to say that something holds of *everything* only when we can show that it must hold of *anything*. It seems highly doubtful that we can hit on a genuine sense in which anyone entitled to assert a universally quantified statement could have arrived at it from the corresponding free-variable statement. Intuitionists would agree. For them, a universally quantified mathematical statement has been proved when we have demonstrated an effective way of obtaining a proof of any given instance. How this can be done will depend on the domain being quantified over. In number theory, for example, the fundamental method is that of mathematical induction; but in all cases it must be allowed that the form of the proof, for a particular instance, may depend upon the instance, and need not take the simple form of replacing a free variable by a term for the element in question. The most natural view, for general contexts, is that our primitive understanding of 'all' is as extending over a finite, surveyable totality, as when a mother says to a child that all his fingernails are dirty, and that its extension over finite but unsurveyable totalities, and further over infinite ones, is arrived at by analogy with this primitive case.

If there is to be a defence of the appeal to the fundamental assumption, as applied to the universal quantifier, it therefore cannot rest upon its unqualified truth. It is intuitively natural to regard the meanings both of the disjunction operator and of the existential quantifier as determined by their introduction rules: the fundamental role of each is to give an 'incomplete communication' of some more specific truth. For the universal quantifier, however, as for the conditional, it is equally natural to take its meaning as encapsulated in the elimination rule. It is in connection with the consequences we draw from a universally quantified statement, not with our means of arriving at it, that it is correct to say that we can assert about *every* object in the relevant domain just those things we are prepared to assert about *any* such object. That is to say, something will serve us as a ground for asserting a universally quantified statement just in case we take it as entitling us to make that assertion about an arbitrary member of the domain. An enthymematic derivation of the free-variable statement— that is, a logical deduction of the assertion, as applied to an unspecified element, from premises established empirically or otherwise—is only one such ground. Inductive procedures form the most obvious alternative type.

A universal generalisation is sometimes based on purely deductive inference. From an open atomic sentence $\ulcorner \mathbf{F}(a) \urcorner$ we may deduce $\ulcorner \mathbf{G}(a) \urcorner$ by a boundary rule: by if-introduction and universal quantifier-introduction we then arrive at the quantified statement $\ulcorner \forall x \, (\mathbf{F}(x) \rightarrow \mathbf{G}(x)) \urcorner$. It is the evident fact that such methods will not yield all the universal statements we are willing to assert that has led to our doubts about the fundamental assumption. Does this fact show the fundamental assumption, as applied to the universal quantifier, to be false? That depends on a different point in its interpretation. If we take its content to be that we assert a universally quantified statement $\ulcorner \forall x \, \mathbf{A}(x) \urcorner$ only when we have a deductively valid derivation of the free-variable form $\ulcorner \mathbf{A}(a) \urcorner$ from established truths, then indeed it is manifestly false. For our purpose, however, we need not construe it in so strong a sense; it suffices for us that we can always regard the universally quantified statement as derived from the free-variable one, however the latter was arrived at. We can then allow some licence to the derivation of free-variable statements, because the validity of the subargument for a free-variable statement does not require us to be able to convert a supplementation of that subargument itself into a valid canonical argument; we need only be able so to convert a supplementation of an *instance* of the subargument, which is a much weaker condition. The question is, therefore, whether we can, within our framework, accommodate inductive inferences (in the sense of empirical induction) without so far disrupting that framework as to invalidate our proof-theoretic justification procedure.

A universal generalisation based on inspection of a surveyable totality rests, of course, on the knowledge that the elements $t_1, \ldots, t_n$ of the totality comprise all those objects satisfying the predicate $\mathbf{A}(\ )$ defining the totality. Such knowledge certainly requires that, for each i $(1 \leq i \leq n)$, we can give a proof of $\ulcorner\mathbf{A}(t_i)\urcorner$; we are here adopting the convention that t is a constant term denoting the object t. The further component can be expressed by the statement

$$\forall x \, (\mathbf{A}(x) \to x = t_1 \vee \ldots \vee x = t_n)$$

To avoid having to involve ourselves in a formal treatment of identity, let us instead conceive of it as a quasi-empirical rule of inference, allowing a passage from premises

$$\mathbf{B}(t_1) \quad \ldots \quad \mathbf{B}(t_n)$$

to the free-variable conclusion

$$\mathbf{A}(a) \to \mathbf{B}(a)$$

here neither $\mathbf{A}(\ )$ nor $\mathbf{B}(\ )$ is required to be atomic.

Something similar may be envisaged for inductive generalisations. We make a finite number of observations, the results of which may be broken down into a finite number of closed atomic statements. These, combined with premises $\ulcorner\mathbf{A}(t_i)\urcorner$, may lead to a finite number of conclusions $\ulcorner\mathbf{B}(t_1)\urcorner, \ldots, \ulcorner\mathbf{B}(t_n)\urcorner$ of the same form, where, again, for each i $(1 \leq i \leq n)$, we can give a valid argument for $\ulcorner\mathbf{A}(t_i)\urcorner$. We shall be prepared to generalise that $\mathbf{B}(\ )$ holds good of all the members of a totality if we regard $t_1, \ldots, t_n$ as constituting an adequately representative sample of it. Where $\mathbf{A}(\ )$ defines the totality, we may then assume that we have a rule of inductive inference allowing us to infer $\ulcorner\mathbf{A}(a) \to \mathbf{B}(a)\urcorner$ from the premises $\ulcorner\mathbf{B}(t_1)\urcorner, \ldots, \ulcorner\mathbf{B}(t_n)\urcorner$. This is, naturally, a highly cavalier way of describing inductive inference, which, in its sophisticated forms, involves assurance of total relevant available evidence, estimation of a priori probabilities, sampling methods, tests of statistical significance, and much else. That does not matter here: we are concerned not to analyse inductive inference but to defend our justification procedure from doubts that assail the fundamental assumption that underlies it. The tests of statistical significance, and so on, may therefore be viewed simply as conditions of application for the schema of inductive inference—that is, as criteria for the representativeness of the sample.

What *is* a representative sample? This must depend on the conclusions $\ulcorner\mathbf{B}(t_1)\urcorner, \ldots, \ulcorner\mathbf{B}(t_n)\urcorner$ we are aiming to generalise. We shall regard a sample as representative, relative to those conclusions, if we are confident that, if we were or had been suitably placed to observe any given object, we should be or have been able to make observations establishing either that it is not a member of the totality, or that, if it is, it satisfies **B**( ). This is not something we can hope to *prove:* our criteria for sound inductive inference are designed to ensure that, if the universe is sufficiently orderly, our confidence will be misplaced as seldom as possible. The orderliness of the universe of course requires that what appears random should usually *be* random.

Given an argument whose last step is an application of universal quantifier-introduction, and whose initial premisses are all atomic, our criterion for its validity is the possibility of transforming any instance of the subargument leading to the penultimate line $\ulcorner\mathbf{P}(a)\urcorner$ into a valid canonical argument. There has to be, in other words, an effective means of finding how a canonical verification of any instance of that free-variable statement can be or could have been obtained. Suppose, now, that $\ulcorner\mathbf{P}(a)\urcorner$ is of the form $\ulcorner\mathbf{A}(a) \rightarrow \mathbf{B}(a)\urcorner$, and has been obtained by the inductive inference rule from premisses $\ulcorner\mathbf{B}(t_1)\urcorner, \ldots, \ulcorner\mathbf{B}(t_n)\urcorner$. We have, for any instance $\ulcorner\mathbf{P}(s)\urcorner$, to find a valid canonical argument for it: and that involves finding a valid deduction of $\ulcorner\mathbf{B}(s)\urcorner$ from the hypothesis $\ulcorner\mathbf{A}(s)\urcorner$. If s is one of the terms $t_1, \ldots, t_n$, we already have an outright proof of $\ulcorner\mathbf{B}(s)\urcorner$. For the rest, we must allow for the fact that $t_1, \ldots, t_n$ are not logically guaranteed to have formed a genuinely representative sample of the totality, even if the formal conditions for a correct inductive inference were satisfied. If it is, the conditions stated above for a sample to be representative ensure that the required argument can be given, invoking only new observational premisses which we can obtain, or could have obtained, but no non-logical rule of inference. If we do not have a genuinely representative sample, we shall of course be unable to prove the argument valid; but that is as well, since there will be no sense in which it is.

A Summing Up

Our examination of the fundamental assumption has left it very shaky. As applied to the disjunction operator, we have had to interpret it quite broadly; the need for this exemplified a general feature of reasoning about empirical matters, namely, the pervasive decay of information. Unlike mathematical information, empirical information decays at two stages: in the process of acquisition, and in the course of retention and transmission. An attendant directing theatre-goers to different entrances according to the colours of their tickets might even register that a ticket was yellow or green, without registering which it was, if holders of tickets of either colour were to use the same entrance; even our observations are incomplete in the sense that we do not and cannot take in every detail of what is in our sensory fields. That information decays yet further in memory and in the process of being communicated is evident. In mathematics, any effective procedure remains eternally available to be executed; in the world of our experience, the opportunity for inspection and verification is fleeting.

Worse yet, as applied to the conditional and the universal quantifier, we have had to concede that the fundamental assumption is not literally true. The meaning neither of 'if' nor of the universal quantifier is completely determined by the introduction rule governing it: rather, that rule is, in each case, a specialisation to the realm of logic of a more general principle. In both cases, we recognise as legitimate grounds for assertion what does not guarantee the correctness of the assertion, being willing to believe, and to assert, much more than we have *conclusively* established. In both cases, the fundamental assumption can be maintained in the narrow sense that the last step in establishing a conditional or universally quantified statement as true can be taken to be an application of the introduction rule. In order to do this, however, appeal to non-deductive principles must be admitted into the subordinate deduction—the subargument to the consequent of the conditional from the antecedent as hypothesis in the one case, or to the free-variable statement in the other; and the meaning of 'if' or of the quantifier depends on what non-deductive principles are allowed. Accordingly, neither operator is a purely logical constant, judged from this standpoint. The full content of either, in empirical or even in mathematical contexts, cannot be expressed in purely logical terms. In a broader sense, therefore, the fundamental assumption fails for both operators.

Thus our problem has been to find a way to cordon off those operations, other than appeal to the introduction rule, leading to the assertion of a conditional or a universally quantified statement, so that the falsity of the fundamental assumption would not invalidate the proof-theoretic justification procedure that apparently depends on it. The admission of non-deductive principles of inference has entailed severe disadvantages. We have had to loosen our conception of a valid argument: by allowing an argument to invoke non-deductive rules, in order to arrive at universally quantified statements, we have had in effect to replace the notion of a valid argument by something like that of an admissible one, all this to ensure that all closed logically complex statements, if correctly arrived at, can be arrived at by an introduction rule. We have also had to permit the valid canonical argument for a supplementation of a given argument, which we want to show to be valid, to appeal to *new* atomic premisses, as long as we are in a position to feel assured that they will be, or would have been, available.

For all that, it is clear that, however urgent these matters are for one wishing to construct a verificationist meaning-theory reasonably faithful to our practice, they no more affect our estimation of the validity of logical rules of inference than the fact that we sometimes make faulty observations, and hence draw conclusions from false premisses. As already observed, our justification procedure will readily validate all the laws of first-order intuitionistic logic, at least of its negation-free fragment. Those laws are not going to be called into question by any uncertainties over the scope or status of the fundamental assumption, precisely because the classical logician will admit that assumption, interpreted in terms of an ideal observer. Nevertheless, we have seen that the fundamental assumption, even so interpreted, will not suffice to validate all the laws of classical logic by proof-theoretic means. That is not a condemnation of classical logic, since there is no a priori reason to assume that meanings of the logical constants can be wholly specified by any set of self-justifying laws. The proof-theoretic justification procedure itself is elegant; but, in vindicating its applicability to arguments within empirical discourse, we have had to exchange this elegance for an unattractive messiness. It remains that the laws that would hold good if our introduction rules really did completely determine the meanings of the logical constants, and if the fundamental assumption held literally and under its most straightforward interpretation, are just those that hold good when we allow both for the decay of information and for reliance on less than conclusive grounds for assertion. It is only if we begin with logical laws, like those of classical logic, which violate the fundamental assumption even before such allowance is made, that we shall be unable to justify those laws by our proof-theoretic procedure.

chapter 13

Stability

Elimination Rules

Intuitively, Gentzen's suggestion that the introduction rules be viewed as fixing the meanings of the logical constants has no more force than the converse suggestion, that they are fixed by the elimination rules; intuitive plausibility oscillates between these opposing suggestions as we move from one logical constant to another. Per Martin-Löf has, indeed, constructed an entire meaning-theory for the language of mathematics on the basis of the assumption that it is the elimination rules that determine meaning. The underlying idea is that the content of a statement is what you can *do* with it if you accept it—what difference learning that it is true will, or at least may, make to you. This is, of course, the guiding idea of a pragmatist meaning-theory. When applied to the logical constants, the immediate consequences of any logically complex statement are taken as drawn by means of an application of one of the relevant elimination rules.

This proposal opens up the possibility of an inverse justification procedure, operating in a downwards instead of an upwards direction. In taking the introduction rules as self-justifying, and as fixing the meanings of the logical constants, we saw them as displaying the canonical means of arriving at a complex statement from premises of lower complexity than it. Repetition of the derivation of complex statements by the introduction rules led to the notion of an entire canonical argument for a complex statement, from atomic initial premisses. Conversely, if we see the content of a statement as determined by its consequences, we may regard the elimination rules as self-justifying and as displaying the canonical means of drawing consequences from a complex statement, in the form of statements of lower complexity. By repetition, this leads to the notion of an entire canonical derivation of an atomic consequence from the given complex statement; that statement will form the head of a path in the proof-tree, leading to the atomic final conclusion, on which each statement except the last is the major premiss of an elimination rule, and each except the first the conclusion of such a rule. The justification procedure will depend upon an inverse fundamental assumption, namely, that any consequence of a given statement *can* be derived by means of an argument beginning with an application of one of the elimination rules governing the principal operator of that statement, in which the statement figures as the major premiss. This assumption is open to fewer intuitive objections than the fundamental assumption on which our original justification procedure rested. It is more plausible that we derive simpler consequences from complex statements only when those consequences follow logically than that we assert such statements only when they follow logically from simpler statements we have previously accepted.

The underlying principle of our former justification procedure was that an argument is valid if, whenever we can establish the premisses in a canonical manner, we can establish the conclusion in a canonical manner: more precisely stated, if we supplement the given argument by canonical derivations of its initial premisses, we can transform the whole into a canonical derivation of the final conclusion. The underlying principle of the inverse procedure will be that an argument is valid if any ultimate consequence that can be drawn in a canonical manner from the conclusion can already be drawn in a canonical manner from the premisses. What is meant by an 'ultimate' consequence? We envisaged a canonical means of establishing a statement as consisting in a canonical derivation of it from atomic initial premisses. A tacit presumption was that the procedure for establishing it would not *begin* with those premisses, which must have come from somewhere. All that would begin with those premisses would be the canonical argument: the means of establishing the premisses themselves would lie outside language, in the observations which the premisses reported. Likewise, a statement must ultimately have consequences in action. Just as the chain of grounds for a statement would lead upwards through less and less complex statements, and eventually to atomic statements and from them outside language to observations, so the chain of consequences of a statement will lead downwards, through less and less complex statements, and eventually to atomic statements and from them outside language to actions. This explanation involves a pretence that atomic statements have specific consequences for action independent of the subject's desires and other beliefs, which is patently not so: but this pretence, while it would need careful treatment by one constructing an entire pragmatist meaning-theory, may be skated over in a theory for determining the validity of logical laws, just as, in the theory under which it was the introduction rules that were taken as self-justifying, we paid no explicit attention to procedures of observation. It is clear that the consequences of accepting an atomic statement are more readily grasped than those of accepting a complex one; and the principle on which this downwards justification procedure is intended to work is that the consequences of a complex statement are all mediated by logical inference, in particular, by the elimination rules. If so, every consequence can be traced down to the acceptance of some atomic statement; and that is all we need to know for present purposes. Of course, a given complex statement may have many consequences, but these can all be regarded as separately derived. It is also apparent that, in general, the consequences of a given statement will flow not from it alone but from it together with ancillary premisses encapsulating information already available or beliefs already accepted; these will be represented by statements figuring as minor premisses in applications of the elimination rules.

It follows that, for a precise formulation of the downwards justification procedure, we must employ a notion of what, to avoid ambiguity, we may call a 'complementation' of an argument whose conclusion is logically complex: this will be effected by appending to the argument a canonical derivation from its conclusion of an atomic consequence, where the original conclusion is the first of a sequence of major premisses of successive applications of elimination rules leading from it to the atomic statement which ends the complementation. An argument will then be characterised as valid if any complementation of it can be transformed into an entire canonical argument with the same initial premisses and the same atomic final conclusion. A rule of inference (of the simplest kind) will, as before, be recognised as valid if we have a means of showing that any application of it is valid. When applied to the special case of an elimination rule, our original upwards justification procedure yielded the result that it would be valid just in case it was in harmony with the given set of introduction rules for the logical constant concerned. In just the same way, the new downwards justification procedure will yield the result that an introduction rule will be valid just in case it is in harmony with the given set of elimination rules for the logical constant concerned. The downwards justification procedure may be displayed as in many respects simply the mirror image of the original upwards one.

We shall admit as elimination rules governing a given logical constant only those that are single-ended. Furthermore, the rule can require only one of the premisses, in every application of the rule, to have the given constant as its principal operator; that premiss cannot depend on a hypothesis discharged by the rule. The premiss in question is the *major premiss* of the rule; any others there may be are minor premisses. There is an additional classification of elimination rules, which plays an important part in what follows. Some elimination rules, which we may call 'vertical' rules, have one or more minor premisses coinciding with the conclusion of the rule; these premisses, which may be called vertical premisses, must depend on hypotheses discharged by the rule (if they did not, the inference would be superfluous). Examples of vertical rules are the standard rules for v-elimination and ∃-elimination. We need not require that, as in those instances, all the minor premisses of a vertical rule be vertical. An elimination rule that is not vertical may be called 'reductive', and a minor premiss of an elimination rule, whether vertical or reductive, may be called 'horizontal' if it is not vertical. It would probably involve no loss of generality to assume that all the following must be (proper) subsentences of the major premisses of an elimination rule: any horizontal minor premiss; any hypothesis discharged by the rule (where an instance of a quantified sentence counts as a subsentence of it); and the conclusion of a reductive rule. In any case, we must require all elimination rules to satisfy a complexity condition, similar to that previously imposed on introduction rules: the conclusion, all minor premisses, and all hypotheses discharged by an application of the rule shall be of lower logical complexity than the major premiss. As the rules of v-elimination and ∃-elimination are ordinarily formulated, this constraint is not imposed on their minor premisses. This will not matter for our purposes, however, since, from the special cases of these rules subject to the constraint, we shall be able to justify the rules in their general form.

The Downwards Justification Procedure

As in the upwards case, we must consider justifications of the third grade. A canonical argument, this time, will be one which terminates in an atomic final conclusion, which as far as possible employs only inferences in accordance with the given set of elimination rules, together with a set, also given, of boundary rules for inferring atomic sentences from atomic sentences. In the upwards case, we found it possible to restrict canonical arguments to employing introduction rules and boundary rules only when the introduction rules were of certain limited forms; when they included rules allowing the discharge of hypotheses, it was no longer possible, so that a canonical argument was no longer automatically valid. The analogue holds good in the downwards case; but here what provides the obstacle is the presence of elimination rules with a horizontal minor premiss. The simplest example is the rule of →-elimination *(modus ponens)*. The last step in a canonical argument to the conclusion **B** from the initial premiss $\ulcorner(A \rightarrow A) \rightarrow B\urcorner$ will be an application of this rule, with the minor premiss $\ulcorner A \rightarrow A \urcorner$; but there is no way of deriving this minor premiss by the use of elimination rules alone.

In any argument, we may call the sentence on any line 'principal' if it is either the major premiss of an elimination rule or a premiss of a boundary rule, and the same holds good of every sentence on the path from it to the final conclusion. The argument as a whole may be called 'proper' if one of its initial premisses is principal. Further, we may call the occurrence of a sentence on some line of the argument 'placid' if neither it nor any sentence on the path from it to the final conclusion is a horizontal minor premiss of an elimination rule. With this machinery, we may define a canonical argument to be one such that

(i) its final conclusion is a closed atomic sentence;

(ii) its initial premisses are closed sentences;

(iii) it is proper;

(iv) the subargument for any placid vertical minor premiss of an elimination rule is proper.

A critical subargument of a canonical argument may be taken to be one which is not canonical and whose conclusion is a horizontal minor premiss of an elimination rule.

The validity of a canonical argument obviously depends on that of its critical subarguments. We shall define a canonical argument to be valid in the narrow sense if all its critical subarguments are valid and of lower degree than the argument as a whole. The notion of the degree of an argument remains the same as before. A canonical argument may be said to be valid in the broad sense if there exists an effective means of transforming it into a canonical argument, with the same initial premisses and final conclusion, which is valid in the narrow sense. The reason for this more complicated definition is the following. Where **A**, **B**, and **C** are atomic, the argument (α)

$$\frac{A \rightarrow B \qquad \dfrac{(A \rightarrow B) \rightarrow ((C \rightarrow C) \rightarrow A) \qquad A \rightarrow B}{A}}{B}$$

is canonical and of degree 4; it is also valid in the broad sense. However, its critical subargument (β)

$$\frac{(A \rightarrow B) \rightarrow ((C \rightarrow C) \rightarrow A) \qquad A \rightarrow B}{A}$$

is also of degree 4. If we made the validity of (α), in the narrow sense, depend directly upon the validity of (β), our definition of validity would not be a correct inductive definition. We can, however, transform (α) into (α')

$$\frac{\dfrac{(A \rightarrow B) \rightarrow ((C \rightarrow C) \rightarrow A) \qquad A \rightarrow B}{(C \rightarrow C) \rightarrow A} \qquad \dfrac{[C]}{C \rightarrow C}}{\dfrac{A \rightarrow B \qquad\qquad\qquad\qquad A}{B}}$$

The argument (α') is again canonical, and is valid in the narrow sense, since its only critical subargument is

$$\frac{[C]}{C \rightarrow C}$$

which is of degree 1. Such a transformation of an intuitively valid canonical argument will always be possible if the logic determined by the given set of elimination rules admits of a natural deduction formalisation that is subject to normalisability. The fundamental step in normalisation, the levelling of a local peak, will always be possible, since, in analogy with the downwards case, an introduction rule will be capable of being validated provided that it is in harmony with the corresponding elimination rules.

We have now to characterise the validity of an arbitrary argument. To do this, we need the notion of a *complementation* of an argument (α) with a closed final conclusion **A**. If **A** is atomic, (α) is its own complementation. If **A** is complex, a complementation of (α) is an argument (γ) obtained from (α) by replacing **A** by a canonical argument (β), valid in the narrow sense, of which **A** is a principal initial premiss. The complement (β) will in general have additional initial premisses which are not initial premisses of (α); this is because the minor premisses of the elimination rule to be applied to **A** may not be derivable from the hypotheses to be discharged by the rule, together with the initial premisses of (α). The argument (γ) will have the same atomic final conclusion as (β), and its initial premisses will be made up of those of (α) and those of (β). We must further require that the degree of (β)—and hence of (γ)—be no higher than that of (α). A horizontal minor premiss of the elimination rule to be applied to **A** will be of lower logical complexity than **A**, and, if it is not derivable from the initial premisses of (α), may without loss of generality be taken as an initial premiss of (β). Equally, a vertical minor premiss **C** of the elimination rule may without loss of generality be taken to be atomic. The hypothesis **B** discharged by the rule, on which **C** depends, must again be of lower complexity than **A**; it seems reasonable to assume that **C** will then be derivable from **B** together with an additional initial premiss of complexity no higher than **A** (for example, ⌜**B** → **C**⌝, if '→' is among the logical constants). Admittedly, this assumption slightly tarnishes the generality of the treatment; in practice, it will always be satisfied. An arbitrary argument may then be said to be valid if there is an effective method of finding, for any complementation of an instance of it, a canonical argument, valid in the narrow sense, with the same initial premisses and final conclusion.

This definition, too, may be illustrated by the distributive law. A complementation of the argument

$$\frac{\mathbf{A} \,\&\, (\mathbf{B} \lor \mathbf{C})}{(\mathbf{A} \,\&\, \mathbf{B}) \lor (\mathbf{A} \,\&\, \mathbf{C})}$$

may take the form

$$\frac{\dfrac{\mathbf{A} \,\&\, (\mathbf{B} \lor \mathbf{C})}{(\mathbf{A} \,\&\, \mathbf{B}) \lor (\mathbf{A} \,\&\, \mathbf{C})} \quad \dfrac{(\mathbf{A} \,\&\, \mathbf{B}) \to \mathbf{D} \quad [\mathbf{A} \,\&\, \mathbf{B}]}{\mathbf{D}} \quad \dfrac{(\mathbf{A} \,\&\, \mathbf{C}) \to \mathbf{D} \quad [\mathbf{A} \,\&\, \mathbf{C}]}{\mathbf{D}}}{\mathbf{D}}$$

where **D** is atomic. This will readily be seen to be convertible into a canonical argument, valid in the narrow sense, with the same initial premisses and the final conclusion **D**; the only critical subarguments of this canonical argument will be

$$\frac{\mathbf{A} \qquad \mathbf{B}}{\mathbf{A} \,\&\, \mathbf{B}}$$

and the analogue for **A** and **C**.

The validity of a sequent may simply be equated with that of a one-step argument. A rule of inference of the most general kind involves a transition from certain sequents, the bases of the rule, to another sequent—the resultant of the rule. Such a rule will be said to be valid if we can show that the resultant will be valid whenever the bases are. It is apparent that the claim made earlier holds good: given a set of elimination rules, an introduction rule can be justified by the downwards procedure just in case it is in harmony with the elimination rules.

The Requirement of Stability

Harmony between logical rules cannot, in general, be demanded: it can be demanded only when those rules are held completely to determine the meanings of the logical constants. It was, indeed, suggested as a (very strict) criterion for an operator's being a logical constant that its meaning is completely determined by the rules of inference governing it. But harmony between the two aspects of linguistic practice in general *can* be demanded. This applies to what we ordinarily regard as logical constants as to all other expressions: there must be harmony between what we conventionally acknowledge as grounds for asserting a complex statement with a given principal operator and the consequences we conventionally draw when we have accepted such a statement as true, even when some of these cannot be expressed logically. A little reflection shows that harmony is an excessively modest demand. If we adopt a verificationist view of meaning, the meaning of a statement is determined by what we acknowledge as grounds for asserting it. The fact that the consequences we conventionally draw from it are in harmony with these acknowledged grounds shows only that we draw no consequences its meaning does not entitle us to draw. It does not show that we fully exploit that meaning, that we are accustomed to draw all those consequences we should be entitled to draw. Conversely, if we adopt a pragmatist view of meaning, the meaning of a statement will be determined by the consequences we draw from it. If there is harmony between these conventional consequences and the grounds we admit for asserting it, this guarantees that we shall not assert it when its meaning does not justify our doing so, that we do not treat as a ground for it what would not warrant the consequences that we draw. It does not show that we should be willing to assert the statement whenever those consequences would be warranted, and hence whenever we should be entitled to do so. But such a balance is surely desirable, at least from either a verificationist or a pragmatist standpoint. The demand that such a condition be met goes beyond the requirement of harmony: we may call it 'stability'.

If logical laws are open to being justified proof-theoretically, then harmony must obtain at the purely logical level, between introduction and elimination rules. If we use an upwards justification procedure, harmony validates a putative elimination rule; if we use a downwards procedure, it validates a putative introduction rule. In either case, harmony is guaranteed between valid rules. But, to verify that stability obtains, we have to appeal to *both* justification procedures. Suppose that we adopt the downwards procedure, and start with a set $\mathscr{E}$ of elimination rules. By our procedure, we can determine which introduction rules are valid: say these form a set $\mathscr{I}$. Now, with respect to this set $\mathscr{I}$ of introduction rules, the upwards justification procedure is well-defined: so we can use it to determine which elimination rules are valid, according to the criteria of the upwards procedure. If we get back by this means to the set $\mathscr{E}$, or to some set interderivable with $\mathscr{E}$, in the ordinary sense, in the presence of $\mathcal{I}$, stability prevails; otherwise not. Here we are still relying on the downwards justification procedure as determinative of validity. We were not *given* the set $\mathcal{I}$, but found it: we still wished to know whether stability obtained between our self-justifying rules $\mathcal{E}$ and the introduction rules $\mathcal{I}$ they validated. We therefore could not rectify the situation by tampering with $\mathcal{I}$: we should have to change $\mathcal{E}$ into a set $\mathcal{E}'$ yielding a set $\mathcal{I}'$ of introduction rules stable in relation to it.

Obviously, if we had adopted the upwards justification procedure, with a set $\mathcal{I}$ of introduction rules as basis, we could perform the converse test for stability. First finding the set $\mathcal{E}$ of valid elimination rules, we could apply the downwards procedure to discover which introduction rules were validated by it. If we got back to the set $\mathcal{I}$, stability would obtain; otherwise not. If not, then, since the upwards procedure would be our actual criterion of validity, we should have to modify $\mathcal{I}$ until stability was attained.

Is there a real danger that stability will fail between a set $\mathcal{E}$ of elimination rules and a set $\mathcal{I}$ of introduction rules validated by it, or vice versa? There is. Let $\mathcal{E}$ be a set of elimination rules for just two logical constants, '&' and 'v': the rules for '&' are the usual ones, that for 'v' is the restricted v-elimination rule, allowing no collateral assumptions in the subordinate deductions of the two (equiform) minor premises of the rule. In sequent notation, this is

$$\frac{\Gamma : A \vee B \qquad A : C \qquad B : C}{\Gamma : C}$$

This rule, taken as the sole elimination rule for 'v', apparently confers on it a clear meaning: $\ulcorner A \vee B \urcorner$ is the conjunction (the greatest lower bound) of all the statements that follow logically both from **A** alone and from **B** alone. Now the standard v-introduction rules are obviously in harmony with the restricted v-elimination rule: they are therefore valid by the downwards justification procedure. The set $\mathcal{I}$ of introduction rules validated by $\mathcal{E}$ therefore consists of the standard introduction rules for '&' and 'v'. But, since the standard v-introduction rules and the standard v-elimination rule are in harmony, the set $\mathcal{E}'$ of rules validated by the upwards procedure, with $\mathcal{I}$ as base, includes the *unrestricted* v-elimination rule (and in fact consists of the standard elimination rules for '&' and 'v'). We do not have stability.

What this result shows is that the restricted v-elimination rule does not, of itself, confer a coherent use on the connective. For, at least if we make our use of it harmonious, that rule will compel us to admit grounds for asserting a disjunction that would justify our making more extensive inferences from it than the rule permits us to do. If meaning is use, then the rule by itself confers no intelligible meaning. To put it differently, a verificationist would interpret the connective in one way, a pragmatist in another. The verificationist would see the elimination rule as defective, whereas the pragmatist would see the introduction rule as sound; but stability obtains only when both would assign essentially the same meaning (characterised in different ways), and would therefore be disposed to acknowledge the same logical laws.

This is not to say that there is no meaning to be given to 'v' which would justify the restricted, but not the unrestricted, elimination rule, but to say only that this could not be determined by purely logical means. If only the restricted rule holds, 'v' must have a weaker meaning than if the unrestricted one were valid; so there ought to be some additional ground for asserting a disjunction. There thus might be some *empirical* ground upon which certain disjunctive statements were recognised as assertible, grounds with which the unrestricted rule was not in harmony; that rule would then be invalid and rightly treated as fallacious. Could the existence of such grounds restore stability in the language as a whole, though not in its purely logical part? If so, we should have a refutation of the pragmatist theory of meaning, since the restricted v-elimination rule affords no hint of what empirical grounds for a disjunctive statement there might be. More likely, there might be some compensatory non-logical principle for drawing consequences from certain disjunctive statements: and then, perhaps, overall stability might prevail.

A similar situation obtains for the restricted →-introduction rule, which allows no collateral assumptions in the deduction of the premiss of the rule:

$$\frac{\mathbf{A} : \mathbf{B}}{: \mathbf{A} \to \mathbf{B}}$$

The intuitive meaning seems again to be clear: $\ulcorner\mathbf{A} \to \mathbf{B}\urcorner$ is assertible if and only if **B** is logically entailed by **A** alone. But, if we start with this as our sole introduction rule, *modus ponens* is obviously in harmony with it and will be validated by the upwards procedure, while the unrestricted rule is in harmony with *modus ponens* and so will be validated by the downwards procedure with *modus ponens* as base. Again, the restricted introduction rule by itself confers no coherent use on '→'. Given it, we shall draw consequences from $\ulcorner\mathbf{A} \to \mathbf{B}\urcorner$ that we could also draw if it had a weaker meaning. The pragmatist will regard the introduction rule as defective, while the verificationist will merely lament that we cannot fully exploit the meaning we accord to conditionals. Once more, stability may yet obtain within the language, if the logical laws fail to characterise exhaustively the use we make of statements of the form $\ulcorner A \to B \urcorner$.

The restricted 'or'-elimination rule also illustrates another interesting phenomenon. The ordinary 'or'-introduction and 'or'-elimination rules are, of course, in harmony. Now suppose we have a logic with two logical constants, '&', governed by the usual introduction and elimination rules, and 'Ü', governed by the usual 'or'-introduction rules and the restricted 'or'-elimination rule. The distributive law will then not hold. Now imagine the language expanded by adding the binary connective 'v', governed by the usual 'or'-introduction rules and the unrestricted 'or'-elimination rule. We shall now be able to derive the distributive law for '&' and 'Ü' as follows:

			A & (B Ü C)		A & (B Ü C)	
A & (B Ü C)	[B]	[C]	A	[B]	A	[C]
B Ü C	B v C	B v C	A & B		A & C	
	B v C		(A & B) Ü (A & C)		(A & B) Ü (A & C)	
			(A & B) Ü (A & C)			

Thus the expanded language is not a conservative extension of the original one, despite the harmony between the introduction and elimination rules for the added connective 'v'. A disjunction operator subject only to the restricted elimination rule is unable to survive intact when brought into the presence of another disjunction operator for which the unrestricted rule holds; the originally weaker connective becomes equivalent to the newly introduced stronger one. The reason is that normalisation is impossible in the logic containing all three connectives. Although, in the above deduction, the connective 'v' is first introduced by two simultaneous applications of the v-introduction rule, and then eliminated by the v-elimination rule, an application of the Ü-elimination rule intervenes, and there is no way to rearrange the deduction so that the v-elimination rule is applied immediately after the v-introduction rule. Thus, although the v-introduction and v-elimination rules are intrinsically in harmony, they are not in total harmony in this context. Although this distinction was drawn in the preceding chapter, we have since proceeded as though intrinsic harmony was all that mattered; but it is total harmony that must prevail if the *point* of the requirement of harmony is to be attained, namely, that, for every logical constant, its addition to the fragment of the language containing only the other logical constants should produce a conservative extension of that fragment. We may conjecture that the problem is a minor one, however: that is, that intrinsic harmony implies total harmony in a context where stability prevails.

Negation

Negation requires special attention, not only because it is the 'not'-elimination rule alone that distinguishes classical from intuitionistic logic in a natural deduction formalisation. The introduction rule common to both is a version of *reductio ad absurdum:*

$$\frac{\neg A}{\neg A}$$

or, in sequent form,

$$\frac{\Gamma, A : \neg A}{\Gamma : \neg A}$$

The intuitionistic elimination rule is the *ex falso quodlibet:*

$$\frac{A \qquad \neg A}{B}$$

while the classical rule is the double negation law:

$$\frac{\neg \neg A}{A}$$

Plainly, the classical rule is not in harmony with the introduction rule. A local peak of the form

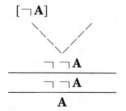

$$\frac{\neg \neg A}{\frac{\neg \neg A}{A}}$$

cannot be levelled. The usual rules for the other standard logical constants yield positive logic, that is, the negation-free fragment of intuitionistic logic. The addition of negation, subject to the classical rules, does not produce a conservative extension; rather, it enables us to derive the whole wide range of classical laws that do not involve negation but are intuitionistically invalid, such as

$$\frac{A \rightarrow B \vee C}{(A \rightarrow B) \vee (A \rightarrow C)}$$

and

$$\frac{(A \rightarrow B) \rightarrow A}{A}$$

Can the negation-introduction rule and the intuitionistic negation-elimination rule be said to be in harmony? A deduction containing the local peak

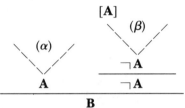

can be simplified to the form

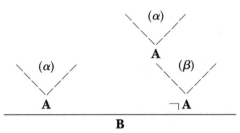

Here the application of the negation-introduction rule has been dispensed with, but that of the negation-elimination rule remains. The peak has been lowered, but *not* levelled, in that we have not found a way of arriving at the final conclusion **B** from the initial premises of the original argument without the use of the negation operator. This is of course due to the fact that the negation-introduction rule is not single-ended: when an application of it is removed, its negative premiss remains.

Thus the rule of negation-introduction cannot be regarded as justifying the weak rule of negation-elimination (henceforward the double negation rule will be left out of account); and, in any case, it cannot be regarded as a self-justifying introduction rule, since we required such rules to be single-ended. Of course, we expect to use negation-elimination only in subordinate deductions, since we feel assured of what we may label the 'principle of consistency', namely, that we can never rightly assert both **A** and ⌜ ¬ **A** ⌝. But we cannot appeal to this principle until we have shown it to follow from whatever rule or rules we have assumed completely to determine the meaning of the negation operator. In any case, we have to demonstrate the validity of subordinate deductions in a canonical argument, if we want to show the canonical argument valid, and this will involve considering a supplementation of the subordinate deduction as a complete independent argument: we cannot evade the difficulty by declaring that it could never be an independent argument.

The difficulty is serious, because negation appears a perfectly intelligible operator, and we need to establish the validity of fundamental arguments involving it such as *modus tollendo ponens*. What convinces us of the validity of *modus tollendo ponens* is the principle of consistency: if we can assert $\ulcorner \neg \mathbf{A} \urcorner$, and can also assert $\ulcorner \mathbf{A} \vee \mathbf{B} \urcorner$, as derived by $\vee$-introduction either from **A** or from **B**, it must, by the principle of consistency, have been derived from **B**. But this appeal to the principle of consistency is out of place in the context of proof-theoretic justification. Is negation unamenable to a justification procedure of this kind?

The position seems more favourable if we adopt a downwards justification procedure. If we are wanting to consider elimination rules as self-justifying, we shall need to restrict their applications to those whose conclusions are less complex than the premisses. This will involve no loss of generality for negation-elimination, however. We may even require the conclusion **B** to be atomic, since the general form of the rule, as yielding any specific sentence as conclusion, is derivable from this restricted form by the help of the rules governing other operators. We shall now find that the negation-introduction rule can indeed be validated. The reason is essentially that, if a consequence is drawn from $\ulcorner \neg \mathbf{A} \urcorner$ by negation-elimination, and $\ulcorner \neg \mathbf{A} \urcorner$ was derived by negation-introduction, the appeal to negation-introduction can be shown to be unnecessary, as was done above.

Does this show that a set of elimination rules including weak negation-elimination yields an unstable logic? The situation is not exactly parallel with that of the restricted $\vee$-elimination rule. That rule validated the standard $\vee$-introduction rules, which in turn validated a *stronger* $\vee$-elimination rule. The negation-elimination rule, by contrast, validates negation-introduction, which, however, *fails* to validate negation-elimination. This was a situation we did not envisage when we discussed stability.

The reason we did not envisage it is that harmony is a symmetrical relation, and we held that an introduction rule will validate an elimination rule, or vice versa, if and only if the two are intrinsically harmonious. The rules for negation are not in harmony by our criterion; so how does it come about that the elimination rule validates the introduction rule? Previously, we failed to envisage rules, like that of negation-elimination, whose conclusion bore no structural relation to any of the premisses. Suppose that there is just one elimination rule governing a certain form of statement, say R, and the rule takes the form

$$\frac{R \quad S}{T}$$

where S and T are related forms of statement. Typically, R will be the most general form of statement with a certain principal operator, which S and T will not be required to contain; but we need not assume that. (R might, for example, be of the form ⌜¬ ¬ **A**⌝, provided that there is no *general* elimination rule for '¬'.) Then the strongest introduction rule governing statements of the form R and in harmony with the elimination rule (thus validating it and validated by it) will take the form

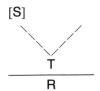

or so we should expect from first principles. This is exactly the relation in which the standard elimination and introduction rules for '→' stand to one another; but, when we apply this principle to the elimination rule for negation, taken as the sole such rule, we obtain as our introduction rule

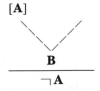

which is obviously wrong. The principle needs to be more exactly formulated. For each given statement of the form R, we need to consider all possible statements that can serve as the minor premiss of the elimination rule and all possible statements that can serve as its conclusion. When R has the form ⌜**A** → **B**⌝, there is only one possible minor premiss, **A**, and only one possible conclusion, **B**, and so the principle holds good. Otherwise, the introduction rule must have as many premisses as there are possible combinations of minor premisses and conclusions of applications of the elimination rule. In the case of the negation-elimination rule, when the major premiss is ⌜¬ **A**⌝, there is only one possible minor premiss, **A**; but the conclusion can be *any*

atomic sentence (supposing the rule restricted to yield an atomic conclusion). The corresponding form for the introduction rule is therefore the virtually infinitary, but single-ended, rule

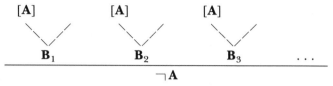

where the $\mathbf{B}_i$ run through all the atomic sentences of the language. If
we adopt this as our introduction rule for '$\neg$' and restrict the elimination rule to yield only atomic conclusions, the rules will be in harmony
and, moreover, stable.

This strongly suggests the well-known device of treating $\ulcorner \neg \mathbf{A} \urcorner$ as a
definitional abbreviation of $\ulcorner \mathbf{A} \to \perp \urcorner$, where $\perp$ is a constant sentence.
When this is done, the negation-introduction rule becomes derivable,
with the help of the introduction and elimination rules for '$\to$'. The
elimination rule also becomes derivable when we adopt as the elimination rule for '$\perp$'

$$\frac{\perp}{\mathbf{B}}$$

where $\mathbf{B}$, as before, may be restricted to be atomic. It is usual to impose
no introduction rule on '$\perp$'; the motivation for this is presumably the
principle of consistency, since if, for some sentence $\mathbf{A}$, both it and
$\ulcorner \neg \mathbf{A} \urcorner$ are assertible, then so will $\perp$ be, and conversely. From our previous discussion, however, it is plain that the appropriate introduction
rule is

$$\frac{\mathbf{B}_1 \quad \mathbf{B}_2 \quad \mathbf{B}_3 \quad \cdots}{\perp}$$

where the $\mathbf{B}_i$ are as before.

The constant sentence $\perp$ is no more problematic than the universal
quantifier: it is simply the conjunction of all atomic sentences. Negation, at least when subject to no more than the intuitionistic laws, is
therefore beyond the reach of the objections that some have tried to
bring against its intelligibility. It is, however, important to observe that
no appeal has been made to the principle of consistency, and that the
logical laws do not imply it. We may know our language to be such
that not every atomic statement can be true; but logic does not know
that. As far as it is concerned, they might form a consistent set, as they
are assumed to do in Wittgenstein's *Tractatus*. The principle of consistency is not a logical principle: logic does not require it, and no
logical laws could be framed that would entail it.

The consequence of this is that negation lacks a feature possessed by all other standard logical constants, which we may call 'invariance'. If the primitive vocabulary of a language *L* is embedded in a richer language *L'*, the negation-free sentences of *L* will translate homophonically, save possibly for some restrictions on the ranges of the quantifiers. That is, where **A** translates into **A'** and **B** into **B'**, ⌜**A & B**⌝ will translate into ⌜**A' & B'**⌝, and similarly for the other operators. Since *L'* has more atomic sentences than *L*, however, ⊥ will not translate homophonically; and hence ⌜¬**A**⌝, interpreted as, or at least equivalent to, ⌜**A** → ⊥⌝, will not translate into ⌜¬**A'**⌝ either. It is essentially for this reason that, while it is possible to prove a completeness theorem for the negation-free fragment of intuitionistic first-order logic, as was discovered simultaneously and independently by Harvey Friedman and myself, this cannot be done for the full system, as was originally shown by Kreisel.

Some Final Comments on Classical Negation

If the double negation rule were taken as the sole elimination rule for negation and the downwards justification procedure applied, it would of course validate the inverse rule

$$\frac{A}{\neg \neg A}$$

but would have the ridiculous result that this would be the *only* negation-introduction rule, and that hence there would be no grounds for asserting a negative statement other than a double negative. Obviously, the fundamental assumption of the downwards justification procedure—that every consequence of a given form of complex statement could be derived by means of one of the relevant elimination rules—is not intended to apply to negation. The double negation rule has to be taken in conjunction with the negation-introduction rule in order to recognise what consequences a classical logician regards a negative statement as having.

We may therefore think of the proper form of the classical negation-elimination rule as being the following:

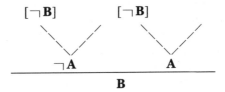

Under the usual rules, we should have, in order to reach the conclusion **B**, first to derive ⌜¬ ¬ **B**⌝ by negation-introduction, and then to apply the double negation rule. The above rule is, in our earlier terminology, oblique, that is, the schema contains a logical constant in hypotheses discharged by the rule; it is the first such rule we have seriously considered.

Should oblique rules be admitted as self-justifying, either as elimination rules (as here) or as introduction rules? We did not formally bar them; but reflection on the foregoing example will surely lead us to do so. For no way is apparent to formulate a corresponding introduction rule; it is certainly demonstrable that an upwards justification of the above rule, even if the conclusion is restricted to be atomic, is impossible from the standard introduction rule as base. Replacement of '¬', as primitive, by '⊥' in no way improves the situation; we obtain another oblique rule, as a form of ⊥-elimination:

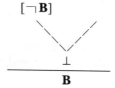

We may call this simply 'the classical ⊥-rule'.

It may be objected that not only the intuitionistic but also the classical natural deduction system is capable of normalisation, and that the laws of classical negation must therefore likewise be amenable to proof-theoretic justification. Now, in the usual case, the possibility of the principal normalisation step was our criterion for harmony between the introduction and elimination rules; and the fact that such harmony obtains demonstrates that the elimination rules are capable of an upwards justification with the introduction rules as base, and would likewise demonstrate that the introduction rules were capable of a downwards justification with the elimination rules as base. For instance, the possibility of a reduction step that cuts out an occurrence of an ∨-introduction whose conclusion is the major premiss of an ∨-elimination shows both the upwards validity of the ∨-elimination rule and the downwards validity of the ∨-introduction rule. Normalisation with respect to the classical ⊥-rule has an entirely different significance. To carry out a reduction step that removes applications of the classical ⊥-rule to obtain the major premiss of an elimination rule is to treat the ⊥-rule as a sort of introduction rule. When it is assumed in its general form, the conclusion not being required to be atomic, there is no restriction on the form of the conclusion; for that reason, it supplies one means by which a sentence of any form can be arrived at. If we rely on the upwards justification procedure but do not count the ⊥-rule as an introduction rule, the fundamental assumption cannot be taken to hold, and the procedure will lose its rationale. This is because no upwards justification of the ⊥-rule from the other introduction rules as base can be given, and, when it is taken as an elimination rule, no corresponding introduction rule can be found on the basis of which it could be justified. But, if we *do* regard the ⊥-rule as an introduction rule, we shall be unable to give an upwards justification of the elimination rules for disjunction and the existential quantifier. The reason is that the reduction step, applied (say) to an application of the ⊥-rule followed by an application of v-elimination, merely replaces that application of the v-elimination rule by another one (as it also replaces the application of the ⊥-rule by another one): it therefore does not provide a means of constructing a canonical argument for the conclusion. In this connection, we cannot restrict the ⊥-rule to have only atomic conclusions, since the new application of it will have as its conclusion the original conclusion **C** of the v-elimination, which may be of any complexity.

Thus suppose an application of v-elimination whose major premiss has been arrived at by the ⊥-rule. This will have the following form:

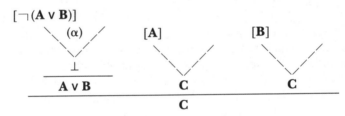

We may suppose this argument already to have atomic initial premisses. The reduction step transforms the argument into the following:

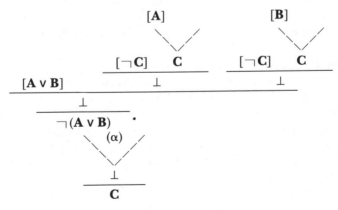

The new application of the ⊥-rule is the final step in the new form of the argument, so that that rule does not serve to introduce the major premiss of the new application of the v-elimination rule; but that rule is still used, and there exists no means of converting the argument into a valid canonical one.

This more detailed look at classical negation confirms what we had already concluded, that it is not amenable to any proof-theoretic justification procedure based on laws that may reasonably be regarded as self-justifying. That is not, of course, to say that the classical negation-operator cannot be intelligibly explained; it is only to say that it cannot be explained by simply enunciating the laws of classical logic. That it *can* be explained in some other way is open to some doubt. Attempted explanations rely always on the presumption that, knowing what it is for the condition for some statement to be true to obtain, in general independently of the possibility of recognising it to obtain, we thereby know what it is for it *not* to obtain; and this blatantly presupposes a prior understanding of classical negation. It almost seems that there is no way of attaining an understanding of the classical negation-operator if one does not have one already. That is a strong ground for suspicion that the supposed understanding is spurious.

Intuitionistic logic, however, has come out of our enquiry very well. We have seen it to be an illusion to suppose there to be any such thing as an explanation of a logical constant innocent of all general presuppositions about meaning. A logical law can rank as a legitimate subject for stipulation, without the need for further justification, only if it can be claimed at least partially to fix the meaning of the logical constants it governs simply by being stipulated to be valid. It can be claimed to do this only if the explanation of meaning it is alleged to give can be incorporated into some meaning-theory for the language as a whole. We have seen that introduction rules give some promise of finding such a home in a verificationist meaning-theory, and elimination rules one in a pragmatist theory. Logic as a whole can only be thought wholly to rest on stipulated, self-justifying laws if a satisfactory proof-theoretic justification procedure can be based on them which will validate all the logical laws we firmly regard as valid; and this in turn depends on the soundness of some version of the relevant fundamental assumption.

For all that, the laws of intuitionistic logic appear capable of being justified proof-theoretically by any of the procedures we have discussed; and this means that the meanings of the intuitionistic logical constants can be explained in a very direct way, without any apparatus of semantic theory, in terms of the use made of them in practice. Many—possibly most—people who have thought about the matter believe that meanings should be given to the logical constants which cannot be explained in this way, but can be explained only on the basis of some semantic theory at a certain remove from practice (if they can be explained at all). The great majority of those—adherents of classical logic—would recognise all the intuitionistic laws but would admit others not intuitionistically valid; a few, perhaps, while admitting no others, would balk at some of the intuitionistic laws; others, again, such as proponents of quantum logic, would reject some intuitionistic laws, while admitting some non-intuitionistic ones. All of these are likely to have to have recourse to semantic explanations. We took notice of the problem what metalanguage is to be used in giving a semantic explanation of a logic to one whose logic is different. A metalanguage whose underlying logic is intuitionistic now appears a good candidate for the role, since its logical constants can be understood, and its logical laws acknowledged, without appeal to any semantic theory and with only a very general meaning-theoretical background. If that is not *the* right logic, at least it may serve as a medium by means of which to discuss other logics.

chapter 14

Truth-Conditional Meaning-Theories

How Can Accepted Laws of Logic Be Criticised?

The proof-theoretic justification procedures do not easily lend themselves to methods of demonstrating the *in*validity of putative logical laws. Semantic theories are well adapted to doing so; but the interesting question is how anyone can set about criticising an *accepted* logical law. We may assume that the criticism does not take the form of producing a demonstrably strong counter-example—an instance of a putative rule of inference with obviously true premises and an obviously false conclusion—because, while that is a criticism everyone would accept, it is conceptually unproblematic. We may then be perplexed to explain how we ever came to think the rule to be valid, or to decide exactly which weaker rule we ought to replace it with; it remains that a strong counter-example provides an unchallengeable ground for rejecting the rule. Likewise, a paradox gives rise to conceptual problems, but there is nothing problematic about the fact of its doing so. A paradox is either a strong counter-example to a whole deductive argument, rather than to a single rule, the puzzle being at which step the error occurred; or it is an application of a rule of inference our confidence in the validity of which is exactly counterbalanced by our confidence that the premises of this application are true and the conclusion false. Weaken the confidence in the truth of the premises, or in the falsity of the conclusion, just a little, and you will have merely a surprising argument, that will be resolved by either accepting the conclusion or going back on our former acceptance of the premises without a thought of tampering with the logical laws. Our question is how anyone can raise objections to an accepted logical law *otherwise* than by the production of what is at least a paradox.

The objection is puzzling only if it is directed against a form of argument actually employed, rather than merely against an attempted formulation or formalisation of the arguments we use, as in the dispute over existential import in the Aristotelian logic. No argument ever actually advanced went astray because of inattention to the ambiguity about existential import. By contrast, the intuitionistic criticism of classical reasoning in mathematics is a critique of a practice: it alleges that classical mathematicians reason wrongly, not that logicians wrongly summarize their practice; and it does not posit that this incorrect reasoning could be put right by citing some true, though suppressed, premisses. It is with criticism of speakers' practice, not of logicians' systematisations, that we should be concerned.

With the question how it is possible to criticise an accepted logical law goes along the question how one can recommend a new system of logical laws. Any revision in the logical laws generally accepted involves a change in the meanings of at least some of the logical constants. People can argue fallaciously, but there can hardly be such a thing as a fallacy which one is required to commit if one is to be said to speak the language properly, one a training in which is an essential part of learning the language. It may be objected that this is just what intuitionists believe about mathematics as usually practised: the standard training in mathematical theorem-proving involves the inculcation, on their view, of invalid modes of reasoning. It is not, however, that intuitionists think that classical mathematicians understand the logical constants just as they do themselves, but simply make a mistake about what follows from what; still less do they suppose that classical mathematicians attach clear meanings to the logical constants under which the classical forms of argument really are valid. Rather, they think that classical mathematicians are under an illusion that they have a coherent understanding of the logical constants. For someone to commit a fallacy, and still be said to understand the logical constants in such a way that it really *is* a fallacy, it must be possible to convince him that it is a fallacy by perfectly ordinary means already provided for in the language as he uses it, for instance by the production of a strong counter-example. It is precisely when a mode of argument cannot be criticised by quite ordinary means that a rejection of it, or replacement of it by some different form of argument, will involve a change in the meanings of the logical constants. It is this case with which we are concerned.

Our fundamental logical laws are those which it is an essential part of our practice in speaking the language to observe. The view that a revision of them involves a change in the meanings of the logical constants is unshakable. This is so because it is impossible to deny either that the meanings of the logical constants determine the manner in which the truth of a complex sentence depends upon its constituents, or that the validity of a form of argument depends on whether it is so constructed that the truth of the premisses guarantees the truth of the conclusion. Hence, if we come to view as invalid a form of argument we had formerly considered valid, although there was no mistake that could have been pointed out by appeal to existing linguistic practice, we must have changed the way in which we take the truth-values of the premisses and conclusion to be determined in accordance with their structure; and this entails that we have changed the meanings of the logical constants.

By what means can anyone recommend the adoption of a new set of logical laws? Unlike the intuitionists, he might not even want to criticise the existing laws. Agreeing that, under the meanings currently attached to the logical constants, the laws generally accepted are valid, he might wish to introduce new meanings alongside the old ones and, correspondingly, new laws for use when these new meanings are invoked. More radically, he might wish to replace the existing laws by new ones. We have seen that he cannot do either simply by enunciating the new logical laws and expecting them to be self-explanatory.

Criticising a Semantic Theory

We saw that it is possible, without begging any questions, to criticise a putative logical law on the basis of some given semantic theory. But, if the law is both fundamental and generally accepted, the semantic theory cannot be completely faithful to existing practice. Why, then, is the result not merely a ground for rejecting that semantic theory in favour of one that validates all generally accepted laws?

If we know a semantic theory that does validate them, the laws can be criticised only by framing objections to that theory. A semantic theory may be criticised on two quite different grounds. It may be criticised as not being capable of being extended to a meaning-theory which accounts for existing linguistic practice, and as therefore not being the *right* semantic theory for the language we have. Alternatively, a semantic theory may be criticised on the ground that it cannot be extended to a coherent or workable meaning-theory at all; and since, by definition, a semantic theory can be so extended, this criticism amounts to saying that it is not, after all, a genuine semantic theory. It is a criticism of this second kind on which a criticism of a fundamental logical law must depend. The critic is professedly a revisionist, aiming to change existing practice. As long as any feature of existing linguistic practice has not been shown to be incoherent, it remains in possession, and we shall automatically opt for any meaning-theory that accords with it in preference to one that does not. The logical revisionist has no argument, unless he can show that no coherent meaning-theory is possible that would justify the logical law he wishes to reject; he must claim, on this ground, that existing practice is confused, and must be put in order again.

Two-Valued Semantics

What grounds can be given for holding a meaning-theory resting on some given semantic theory as base to be incoherent? We may answer this by example: the objections that can be raised to a meaning-theory based on the two-valued semantics. This type of meaning-theory is the most familiar to us, being that advocated by Frege, by Wittgenstein in the *Tractatus,* by Davidson, and by many other philosophers. It is often characterised as taking the meaning of a sentence to be given by its truth-conditions, but that is a somewhat misleading description, since it is possible to represent any compositional meaning-theory as treating the meaning of a sentence as determined by the condition for it to be true. What is intended is that, in such a meaning-theory, truth is not explained in terms of any other semantic notion. Rather, it is the central notion of the meaning-theory in the stronger of our two senses: the semantic value of a sentence consists simply in its being or not being true. Thus, in a meaning-theory of this type, truth is an irreducible notion, not explained in terms of any other notion, taken as more fundamental, but only in terms of its role in the theory as a whole and, in particular, by the connection established in the theory of force between the truth-conditions of a sentence and its actual use in the language. It is therefore natural to describe a meaning-theory of this kind as framed in terms of truth, as opposed to others framed in terms of verification or consequences.

Many-Valued Semantics

We may set aside objections telling in favour of replacing the two-valued semantic theory by some finitely many-valued one. What is characteristic of a meaning-theory based on the two-valued semantics—a truth-conditional meaning-theory, in the usual terminology—is that it takes the truth-value of a statement to attach to it determinately and objectively, independently of our knowledge or our capacity to know. According to such a meaning-theory, therefore, the meaning of a sentence is not, in general, given to us in terms of the means available to us for recognising it as true or as something we should be justified in asserting. Our understanding of the sentence consists, rather, in our knowing what has to hold for it to be true, independently of the knowledge how, if at all, we may recognise it as true or as false; we are assumed to have a concept of truth according to which we know the sentence to be determinately true or false. Our knowing how to recognise the sentence as true is *derived* from our understanding of it. Since this understanding consists in our grasp of its truth-conditions, we may, on occasion, grasp these well in advance of coming to know how it could be shown to be true (as in the example of the child's understanding of the statement that every positive integer is the sum of four squares). A meaning-theory which substitutes, for the two-valued semantics, a finitely many-valued one represents a very trivial variation on this: we have merely been provided with a slightly more complicated mechanism for determining the truth or otherwise of a complex sentence in accordance with its composition from the subsentences. In such a semantic theory, truth, as we have been using this notion, corresponds to having a designated value. If there are distinct designated values, these therefore represent different ways of being true, while the various undesignated values represent different ways of failing to be true; the distinctions between the various values are needed solely to explain how the truth of a complex sentence is determined in accordance with its composition. The essential conception of the way in which meaning is given remains the same: a grasp of the meaning of a sentence still involves an awareness that the sentence objectively possesses some determinate one of the finitely many statement-values, and it remains the case that our knowledge of what must hold for it to have any particular one of these is, in general, given independently of the means which we may have for recognising which of the different values it has. Hence the distinction between a meaning-theory based on the two-valued semantics and an n-valued one, for finite $n > 2$, is comparatively insignificant.

Wittgenstein

In his middle and later writings, Wittgenstein waged a protracted internal struggle against the truth-conditional meaning-theory he had espoused in the *Tractatus*. In the writings of the intuitionists, conclusions about the meanings of mathematical statements almost always appear as derived from metaphysical premises about the nature of mathematical reality; Wittgenstein, by contrast, criticised certain metaphysical views as pictures generated by incorrect models of meaning. My contention is that a theory of meaning does have metaphysical consequences, whether we downplay them as pictures or accord them the status of theses, but that we must attend to the meaning-theory first and construct our metaphysics in accordance with it, rather than first enunciating metaphysical assumptions and then attempting to draw from them conclusions about the theory of meaning.

The disadvantage of approaching these questions via Wittgenstein's writings is the relatively unsystematic character of his discussions. Though they are not as unsystematic as they might appear superficially, there does seem to be an ineradicable ambiguity in his attitude to whether or not it is possible to give a comprehensive and systematic meaning-theory for a natural language. His language-games are presented as complete miniature languages, of which a comprehensive description can be given from outside. If they are to have the interest they are represented as having— if, in particular, they are to be as illuminating about what it is for expressions of a language to have meaning as is apparently intended—such a description, though enormously more complicated, ought to be in principle possible for existing human languages. And yet Wittgenstein's whole practice appears to repudiate the very possibility of any systematic framework for such a description, without any reason being advanced for its impossibility. However this may be, he was undoubtedly personally uninterested in the construction of such a meaning-theory. It is therefore best to proceed simply by setting out a number of considerations that tell against a truth-conditional meaning-theory, some of them recognisably prompted by Wittgenstein's work, without engaging in any careful exegesis to determine how faithfully they represent his views.

Meaning and Knowledge

A truth-conditional meaning-theory violates the requirement that meaning be correlated with speakers' knowledge. According to the meaning-theory of the *Tractatus,* two sentences may have the same sense, because they partition logical space in exactly the same way, even though we may be unaware of their equivalence. In general, the *Tractatus* allows for no distinction of principle between analytic equivalence and identity of sense. Now, obviously, we do not actually know every analytic equivalence; if we did, most mathematical proofs would be superfluous. On the *Tractatus* theory, the sense of a sentence is determined by which combinations of states of affairs render it true, irrespective of how we recognise whether such a combination obtains or not. Hence, it is only in respect of a kind of ideal knowledge, not of our actual knowledge, that we may be said to know when two sentences have the same sense. The demand that meaning be correlative to speakers' knowledge requires, however, that if two expressions have the same sense, then anyone who understands them must know them to be equivalent.

This was Frege's principle of the transparency of sense, which may be rejected as far too strong. Frege held that the equivalence should be *immediately* obvious if the expressions really were synonymous; but the definition of numerical equality he made his own is certainly not immediately obvious, and it needs at least a moment's reflection to recognise the equivalence of 'are first cousins' and 'share a pair of grandparents'. Once reflection is allowed, the concept of synonymy becomes vague, for the line between 'recognisable as equivalent upon reflection' and 'recognisable as equivalent on the basis of an argument' is blurred. This does not weaken the present objection, however. If sense is to be correlative to knowledge, it must be *possible* for anyone who understands two synonymous expressions to come to recognise their equivalence without acquiring any new information. The *Tractatus* theory plainly does not allow for this possibility.

The natural reply is that the argument tells not against a truth-conditional meaning-theory in general but only against the very special form it assumed in the *Tractatus*. The argument, it may be said, merely shows the extent to which the *Tractatus* represents a retrogression from Frege's theory of meaning, one resulting from Wittgenstein's repudiation of the distinction between sense and reference as drawn by Frege. For Frege, the sense of an expression *was* a matter of speakers' knowledge, which is why it goes to determine the cognitive value of a sentence containing it. The only way we can interpret the notion of a truth-condition, on Frege's theory of meaning, is not as an objective range of combinations of possible states of affairs, a region in logical space, but as the *sense* of the sentence, which consists in a speaker's grasp of the way in which the sentence is determined as true, if it is true. If we employ a Fregean distinction between sense and reference, we shall not need to allow that two sentences have the same sense just because they are rendered true by the same combinations of states of affairs; for we shall regard it as part of the sense of the sentence how a certain combination of states of affairs, or range of such combinations, is given to us, that is, how we conceive of it. What is objectively the same combination may be given in different ways.

Truth and the Recognition of Truth

The reply is certainly cogent: the objector is surely right that, in rejecting Frege's distinction between sense and reference, or, rather, in transforming it, so that only a sentence could have sense and only a name could have reference, Wittgenstein took a long step backward.

Nevertheless, the point is not disposed of: it only needs reformulation. The proper form of the objection is that it is impossible to explain in terms of a truth-conditional meaning-theory how, in general, we can derive from the meaning of a sentence our knowledge of what counts as showing it to be true, or of when we are to recognise it as true. These are features of its use which depend upon its meaning. An adherent of a truth-conditional meaning-theory may, indeed, claim that it is possible for someone to know the meaning of a sentence without knowing how we are able to recognise it as true, as in the case of the child and the arithmetical proposition. What makes this possible is that our means of recognising the statement as true is not for him a *part* of its meaning; the meaning is not given to us in terms of that. It would, however, be intolerable to hold that, although the meaning of a sentence has been completely fixed, there remains room for us to choose what we propose to count as showing a statement made by means of it to be true. That, indeed, would be inconsistent with a purely truth-conditional meaning-theory, for it would involve that what constituted a means of showing the statement to be true *was* a part of the meaning of the sentence, although a part assigned in partial independence of the condition for its truth. The most that the adherent of a truth-conditional meaning-theory can allow is that we acknowledge something as showing a sentence to be true *in the light of* our grasp of its meaning—that, in deciding to take something as establishing its truth, we are responsible to its meaning, and are therefore right or wrong in so doing. It will follow that we are capable of overlooking some things we should be entitled to take as showing the sentence to be true and of mistaking certain things as doing so when in fact they do not.

This does not resolve the question, however. In so far as the meaning of a sentence is given independently of the means we have for recognising it as true, the question is how we are able to get back from the meaning, as so given, to what we are to count as showing it to be true. It is no answer to say that, in deciding what to count as showing that the sentence is true, we are responsible to its meaning as we have been given it: the problem is how we are able to exercise this responsibility. Frege's notion of sense does not resolve this problem; it merely pushes it back one stage. Let us suppose, for example, that the meaning of a proper name consists not merely in its having a certain referent but also in our grasping a sense which determines it as having that referent. Now, in what does our grasp of such a sense consist? If we say that it consists in an effective means, or ability, to recognise an object, when presented to us in a certain way, as the referent of the name, then, so far, we have not severed the truth-conditions of sentences in which the name occurs from our means of recognising them as true. That part of the procedure for determining the truth-value of such a sentence which consists in the identification of an object as the referent of the name will be an effective one. Hence, if there is to be any substance to the contention that our grasp of truth-conditions is independent of our means of recognising statements as true, it cannot be that the sense of every expression is to be explained after this model, that is, as consisting in the mastery of an effective means of determining the reference.

We must, therefore, allow that our grasp of the sense of a name may consist merely in the knowledge of the condition which an object has to satisfy for it to be the referent of that name, a condition whose satisfaction by any given object we may have no effective means of deciding. In view of the fact that we freely use names of objects inaccessible to us, for instance of people who have long since died, this may strike us as highly plausible. It remains, nevertheless, that the appeal to Frege's notion of sense has wholly failed to answer our original question.

It is natural to suppose that, in a verificationist meaning-theory, the sense of a proper name, say 'General Noriega', will consist in some effective means of identifying its bearer. The verification of an atomic statement, such as 'General Noriega snores', will then be dissectable into two subprocedures: the identification of an individual as the bearer of the name, and the verification that that individual satisfies the predicate. The model remains quite plausible when the predicate concerns the past. One could verify the statement, 'Henry Kissinger said, "I am discombobulated"', by first identifying the bearer of the name, and then recognising him as the same individual appearing on an old newsreel saying, 'I am discombobulated'. The verificationist does not have to maintain that all verifications of statements involving proper names have to proceed via the identifications of their bearers; he has to maintain only that such identifications are required for the *direct* or *canonical* verification of such a statement.

Even so understood, however, the model loses all plausibility when the bearer has long ceased to exist; and this casts doubt on cases in which the bearer still exists, but the predicate concerns relatively remote history. Even were Bertrand Russell still alive, that would surely make little difference to the verification of the statement, 'Russell frequently altered his philosophical views'. What would the identification of an aged individual as Bertrand Russell have to do with the truth of that statement? Still less can the fantasy of protracted survival have any bearing on the sense of names like 'Titian' or 'Hannibal'. A verificationist must, rather, allow that a canonical verification may have been possible only under conditions that can never be recreated (since the belief in the general resurrection does not apply to animals, ships, cities, and so on). As our study of proof-theoretic justifications of logical laws made clear, he has to admit as assertible statements for which we have an effective method of showing that they *could have* been verified, even if they can no longer be; this is the role in our linguistic practice that he must assign to the conception of a canonical verification.

The truth-conditional meaning-theorist has an entirely different conception. For him, the entire history of the universe, past and future, subsists in an eternal plenum of reality and *is* that reality to which our assertions relate. We pick out individual objects within this plenum by associating with the names we employ certain uniquely satisfiable conditions. Whether these conditions are expressible in purely general terms or have demonstrative components, and whether they do or do not themselves involve our use of the names with which they are associated, are questions of detail that do not affect the general conception. The condition we associate with a name, as that which must be satisfied by an object for it to be the referent, need not be one whose satisfaction by an arbitrary object we should have any effective means of deciding, however favourably placed: our use of the name is mediated solely by the knowledge that, objectively, the condition is satisfied by at most one object in the history of the universe, and our belief that it is satisfied by at least one. It therefore makes no difference to the truth-conditional theorist whether the object is presently accessible to us or not.

Our first reaction is thus confirmed: the truth-conditional theorist has no *special* problem about names of inaccessible objects. This leaves our original question untouched, however. Specialised to statements identifying an object as the bearer of a name, the original question was how we pass from a grasp of the sense of the name to a capacity to recognise an object as its bearer in favourable circumstances. If the sense is given by a non-effective condition for an object to be the bearer, our knowledge of that condition cannot consist in a means of recognising whatever object is the bearer. Moreover, our capacity to refer to inaccessible objects, and to judge statements about them to be true, generates a further, variant, question: what enables us to judge the truth of a statement involving the name of an object, when the identification of some object as the bearer of the name need play no part in our recognition of its truth?

The verificationist, provided that he can give a satisfactory account of the past tense in general, has an answer to this: our recognition of the truth of the statement is due to our possessing a means of showing that it could have been verified. But the truth-conditional theorist's conception of truth is not dependent on verifiability by any observer, however located in space and time. How can he connect our grasp of the conditions for the truth of our statements to the actual means we use to recognise them as true or as false, when, after all, he has been at such pains to sever them?

Basic Vocabulary

Explanations come to an end somewhere. There are a great many words for which we are able to state the condition for their application, including ones for which an explicit knowledge of this condition is required for an understanding of them. There are others for which it is possible to give an informative answer to the question how we recognise them as applying, although a speaker may know it only implicitly; if there is implicit knowledge, it may be brought to the surface. But this cannot go on for ever. Of necessity, there are words for which no informative statement of the conditions for their application is possible, and for which, therefore, an attempt to state those conditons will inevitably be circular. For these words, we cannot be said to recognise the presence of what they denote *by* anything—we just immediately recognise it. More exactly, that is what we must say if we think of understanding as consisting in a knowledge of the condition that must obtain if a sentence is to be true. Among such words, for example, are 'pain' and 'yellow': we can tell that someone comes from Scotland by his accent, we can tell that we are going to vomit by a characteristic feeling of nausea, but there is nothing by which we tell that we have a toothache or that the curtains are yellow. The same holds good for operations. We may be able to explain the rule for computing the factorial function $n!$ as consisting in multiplying together all the numbers from 2 to n, and we may be able to give the rule for multiplication tables; but we cannot give the rule for following the rule for multiplying in accordance with the multiplication tables (or, if we can, we cannot give the rule for following *that* rule).

I once remarked, in print, that, if Wittgenstein were right, communication would at every moment be in danger of breaking down. Saul Kripke commented to me, in private conversation, that communication *is* at every moment in danger of breaking down. The right thing to say, from a Wittgensteinian standpoint, is that communication is in no danger of breaking down, and that this is one of the things of which we are entitled to be sure, but that our assurance does not *rest* on anything. A rule for computing a function, say the factorial function, only determines the value of that function for all the infinitely many arguments if it reaches out to deal with all those cases to which we have not yet applied the rule. That, indeed, it does, since it is formulated in general terms. But that formulation reaches out to all those untried cases only in virtue of the meanings of the general terms, the fact that they too reach out to cases to which they have not yet been applied. And now we can ask again, 'How do *they* do that?' In so far as we can give a rule for their application, we can give the same answer as before, 'Because we have a general formulation'. Ultimately, however, we must come to some terms for whose application we have no general formulation: we learned the principle of their application just from being shown a finite number of cases, and then 'we knew how to go on'. So the determinateness of the original function rests, ultimately, on the determinateness of those terms, perhaps for basic operations like replacing one symbol by another, whose application is not given by any general formula. And what does their determinateness rest on?

If we regard meaning as given by truth-conditions, there will be certain sentences the conditions for whose truth we cannot state informatively, but can state only in a circular manner. What, then, is involved in attributing to a speaker a grasp of a condition of this kind? For words like 'pain' and 'yellow' it involves ascribing to him a faculty for immediate recognition of some object, quality, process, or event; for words for fundamental operations it involves ascribing to him an immediate grasp of a general principle. This capacity for immediate recognition, this immediate grasp of a principle, can be no further explained: in the former case, the speaker simply associates the name with the object (quality, etc.) which is immediately present to him, and which he is simply able to recognise whenever he encounters it; in the latter case, he simply associates the word with the principle, which he directly grasps without the mediation of a general formula. This association is the private ostensive definition. As long as the meaning of a sentence is thought of as given by a grasp of the condition for it to be true, the meanings of the most basic parts of our vocabulary can be thought of only as being conferred in this way, namely, by an immediate association, in the mind of the speaker, between the word and its referent, since there is nothing to mediate its reference.

This ascription of a capacity for immediate recognition, or for an immediate grasp of a principle, is idle, however. Not only does it explain nothing, but everything could go on in exactly the same way if the ascription were mistaken. If the speaker is supposed to be capable of recognising something, then it must also make sense to suppose that he misrecognises it; but, if we suppose that this is what happens— namely, that he repeatedly takes the same object or quality to be present, although it is, each time, a different one—our supposition has, in itself, no consequences. Likewise, if we suppose that someone who thinks he has got hold of a principle is in fact under an illusion and merely has the impression of doing the same thing every time, that supposition, in itself, alters nothing. What does make a difference, in many of these cases, is the fact of our agreement: the fact that, by and large, we call the same things 'yellow', the fact that we agree on the results of our computations.

What also matter are the external manifestations of perception. Consider, for instance, the orientation of the visual field. It may seem to us that the visual field comes to us like a picture labelled 'Top' and 'Bottom' or 'This Way Up'. What could be a more immediate feature of the visually given than location on the vertical axis? If someone is made to wear a pair of inverting spectacles, he will see everything the wrong way up: what is on the ground will appear to him at the top of his visual field, and conversely. But, now, if he continues to wear these spectacles over an extended period, he will gradually come to see things the right way up, as is shown by the fact that, when at last the spectacles are removed, everything looks upside down to him again. If the orientation of the visual field were part of the immediately given, one of the things which we immediately recognise, then this could only mean that his visual field gradually rotates. Obviously, it does not mean this. What, when he has become thoroughly accustomed to wearing the spectacles, his seeing things as being the right way up consists in is that he *raises* his head or his eyes to look at something physically at the upper border of his range of vision, *stoops* to catch a glass that he sees fall from the table, and so on. These are the manifestations of his seeing one thing as higher or lower than another; they are what his doing so *consists* in. Likewise, the fact that we, who wear no inverting spectacles, react in these ways to what we see, unless, as when we occasionally stand on our hands or hang by our feet, we take pains to inhibit these reactions, *constitutes* our seeing one thing as higher, another as lower, in the visual field. Presumably someone like an acrobat, who spends much of his time upside down, might be hard put to it to say whether in that state, he saw things the wrong way up or not: which *is* the top of his visual field?

If the truth-conditional account of meaning were right, then someone's immediate recognition of, say, a colour quality would serve to *explain* his agreement with other speakers; his immediate grasp of a rule that could not be formulated would *explain* the fact that the results of his computations agreed with those of others; his immediate recognition of an inner sensation would *explain* the manifestations of it in his behaviour. It would, however, be possible that these explanations were the wrong ones, that, for example, our perceptions of colour shifted from day to day, without our noticing, the changes in our perceptions being exactly balanced by our mistakes of memory, so that the agreement between the judgements of different speakers was not affected. The fact is not that such a hypothesis is improbable; it is, rather, that no explanatory hypothesis is called for. We shall say that someone knows the meaning of the word 'yellow' just in case his judgements of what is yellow agree, by and large, with those of others. If, then, we call this his 'capacity to recognise the colour', his having that capacity is not a hypothesis which serves to explain the agreement of his judgements with those made by others: the agreement is that in which his having that capacity consists. If the truth-conditional account of meaning were right, it would be possible that everything we agreed on as true was in fact false, and then what would be the connection between the meanings we attached to our sentences and our use of them?

Undecidable Statements

For reasons such as these, Wittgenstein came, in his middle period, to substitute the notion of the justification of an assertion for that of truth as the central notion of the theory of meaning: 'It is what is regarded as the justification of an assertion that constitutes the sense of the assertion' (*Philosophical Grammar*, I, §40). In giving an account of what justifies the assertion of a sentence, we escape the circularity inevitable at certain points in any attempt to state the condition for it to be true. The circularity is inevitable because the truth-conditional account involves construing the meanings of basic terms 'after the model of name and object', and also because it requires the truth or falsity of a sentence containing no reference to human activities to be represented as objectively determined by a reality that does not include those activities, whereas any comprehensive account of what justified an assertion made by uttering the sentence would have to mention facts relating to our employment of our common language.

There is, however, another area in which circularity infects attempts to state what has to hold for a sentence to be true. It has to do, not with the lowest levels of language, but with comparatively high levels. Wittgenstein was much less concerned with this topic than with that discussed in the previous section; but it is the most directly connected with the metaphysical issues concerning realism.

Our language contains many sentences for which we have no effective means, even in principle, of deciding whether statements made by means of them are true or false; let us label them 'undecidable sentences'. If it is assumed that truth is subject to the principle of bivalence—that every sentence is determinately either true or false—the language also contains sentences for which we have no ground for thinking that, if true, we must in principle be capable of being in a position to recognise them as true. The presence in our language of sentences of this latter kind is an inevitable result of a fundamental characteristic of a truth-conditional meaning-theory, that the meanings of our sentences are not given in terms of that by which we recognise them as true. Three features of our language may be singled out as especially responsible for the occurrence of undecidable sentences.

(i) Our capacity to refer to inaccessible regions of space-time, such as the past and the spatially remote.

(ii) The use of unbounded quantification over infinite totalities, for example, over all future time.

(iii) Our use of the subjunctive conditional. This is much more pervasive than appears on the surface, because it is involved in almost all 'operational' explanations of meaning. We understand a term for a property by reference to some test which would reveal the presence or absence of that property; but, since we interpret the term realistically, we assume that an ascription of that property to an object of an appropriate kind is objectively either true or false, independently of whether the test has been carried out or can any longer be. The rendering of the sentence ascribing the property to the object in terms of the test and its results therefore has to assume the form of a subjunctive, or actually counterfactual, conditional.

In what does a knowledge of the condition for a statement to be true consist, when that condition is not one we are capable of recognising as obtaining whenever it obtains, and may, in some cases, obtain although we are unable, even in principle, to recognise that it does? Sometimes this knowledge may be explicit; it will then unproblematically consist in our capacity to state the condition, in words our understanding of which is presupposed for our understanding of the sentence in question. It is evident that our understanding of sentences cannot always consist in explicit knowledge, however; in what, then, does our knowledge of the truth-condition of an undecidable sentence consist when it is not explicit? It is not possible that all undecidable sentences should be explicable by vocabulary drawn from the decidable fragment of our language. It can only be by means of specific linguistic devices— quantification over infinite totalities, the past tense, and the subjunctive conditional among them—that we import undecidability into the language, and the question is what constitutes our understanding of such devices, or, equivalently, of sentences involving them. Our knowledge of the truth-condition of an undecidable sentence cannot consist in an ability to recognise that condition as obtaining whenever it obtains, because, by hypothesis, we do not have that ability. Nor can it consist merely in our ability to recognise that condition as obtaining in those special cases in which such a recognition is possible: for the condition may obtain even when we cannot recognise it as obtaining. On the truth-conditional theory, a speaker's grasp of the meaning of the sentence consists in his awareness that that very condition is both sufficient and necessary for its truth. In the phrase to which exponents of the theory repeatedly resort, he knows what it is for it to be true. By the nature of the case, however, his grasp of the condition cannot be exhaustively manifested by the use he makes of the sentence.

The consequence is that, just as with Chomsky's unconscious 'cognition', the theory provides us with no conception of how a knowledge of the truth-condition is *delivered* to the speaker. Explicit knowledge can be delivered in verbal form; and we take the ability to apply it to particular situations as comprehended in the mastery of the language. The conception of knowledge which is not explicit remains opaque, by contrast, until it is explained in what mode it is delivered whenever it is to be applied, since, after all, the subject's application of it furnishes the only ground for ascribing possession of it to him. Such explanation is needed to take the place of that which can be given, for explicit knowledge, of the means by which the language mediates between the general principle and its application. That is what is wrong with the plea that a speaker manifests his knowing what it is for the sentence to be true precisely by adhering to linguistic practices, such as arguing in accordance with classical logic, that would be indefensible from a verificationist standpoint. The intuitionist claims that the classical mathematician cannot manifest the grasp he claims to have of what it is for a universally quantified statement to be true even when there is no proof of it. It is of no use for the classical mathematician to reply that he does so by reasoning on the assumption that the statement is determinately either true or false; we want to know what is the content of this assumption. For the truth-conditional theorist, the condition for the truth of a statement constitutes an indissoluble cognitive lump, which guides us but whose applications to particular cases cannot be dissected. This is a sure sign that the conception of the truth-condition transcending our capacity to recognise it, but not our capacity to grasp it, is a piece of mythology, fashioned, like the centaur, by gluing together incompatible features of actual things. It has all the properties of explicit knowledge, save only that it is not explicit. Once more, the truth-conditional meaning-theory involves ascribing to a speaker a piece of knowledge of which it is impossible to give an account. And this violates the principle that meaning is use, the requirement that a meaning-theory must say in what the knowledge which constitutes the understanding of an expression consists, in terms of the way in which it is manifested.

The Alternatives

The foregoing arguments have only been sketched; the purpose was not to review them comprehensively but merely to indicate the *kind* of argument that can be directed against a type of meaning-theory, as characterised by the semantic theory that serves it as a base. We have now to enquire what other type of meaning-theory should be adopted by one who finds these or similar arguments convincing.

The evident remedy is to replace truth, as the central notion of the meaning-theory, by some notion that can be wholly accounted for in terms of the use a speaker actually makes of the sentences of the language. We have already mentioned two candidates for the position: the acknowledged means of establishing a statement as true, and the consequences of accepting it as true. Probably all possible candidates are variants of one or other of these two. On the first, verificationist, option, the condition that determines the sense of the sentence, and in a grasp of which a speaker's understanding of it consists, is one that he *can* be taken as recognising whenever it obtains: there is therefore no problem about attributing to him a knowledge of that condition. The word 'establish' is misleading in two respects. First, it suggests that we can offer evidence or grounds for the truth of every statement we accept, which is notoriously not the case. Secondly, some statements resist being definitively established but are persistently defeasible. Different versions of verificationist meaning-theory will handle these matters in different ways; we may continue for convenience to use the word 'establish', while gesturing at a general formulation by saying that the relevant condition is that in which we are unquestionably entitled to assert the statement. What establishes a sentence as true, in this sense, will be of the most various kinds, according to the meaning of the sentence: some sentences can serve as reports of observation, others, such as mathematical statements, can be established only by argument that is independent of observation, and many will require both observation and some form of argument based on that observation. In all cases, however, it will be correct, according to a verificationist theory, to say that that in which an understanding of the sentence consists is an ability to recognise, whenever presented with it, whatever we take to count as establishing its truth. In calling this for short 'verification', we must bear in mind that verification is not to be taken, as on the classic positivist view, to consist in mere exposure to some sequence of sense experiences. On this understanding, the central notion of a meaning-theory of this type will be that of verification. That is to say, the central core of the meaning-theory will consist of an inductive specification, for each sentence of the language, of what is to constitute a verification of it, corresponding to the inductive specification, in a truth-conditional theory, of the condition for the truth of every sentence.

The core of the meaning-theory is not the whole. We saw that every meaning-theory, on pain of futility, must connect the meanings of the sentences, as specified by the core, with the actual practice of using them. In doing so, the theory must lay down the appropriate criterion for an assertion to be correct. We may call this the criterion for the truth of a statement: it is in this sense that every meaning-theory can be described as concerned to determine the condition for any statement to be true. The crucial difference is that in a 'truth-conditonal' theory, truth is a primitive notion of the theory, whereas, in theories of other types, it must be explained in terms of the central notion. We have seen that a verificationist theory cannot crudely identify the truth of a statement with its having been verified, on pain of being unable to recognise quite simple reasoning as valid. Rather, it must explain truth as attaching to a statement in some such way as that it does so when the statement either has or could have been verified. Whatever the correct formulation should be, the resulting notion of truth will not be subject to the principle of bivalence. It was precisely the observation that the language contains sentences for which we have no ground for assuming that they will, or even can, be either verified or falsified that provided one reason for overthrowing the truth-conditional meaning-theory.

Rejection of bivalence is not, in itself, rejection of classical logic. An adherent of a verificationist meaning-theory will inevitably reject a pure realist metaphysics. He must hold that reality is in some degree indeterminate, for we have no conception of reality save as that which renders true those true statements we can frame and those true thoughts we can entertain. If our statements and our thoughts are not all determinately either true or false, then reality itself is indeterminate; it has gaps, much as a novel has gaps, in that there are questions about the characters to which the novel provides no answers, and to which there therefore are no answers. I have heard it maintained that this is an atheistic doctrine, on the ground that God, not being subject to our limitations, must know of every proposition whether it is true or false, so that our inability to determine this should not lead a theist to doubt bivalence. This argument begs the question by assuming that every proposition *is* either true or false; God's omniscience involves that he knows every true proposition, but it says nothing about how many true propositions there are. Somewhat flippantly expressed, God does not speak our language; his thoughts are not as our thoughts.

The appeal to God's knowledge in no way serves to explain in what our knowledge of the conditions for our statements to be true consists, if there is no explanation of it without that appeal. The appeal *is* pertinent to the distinction between reality as it appears to us and as it is in itself. We do strive to come ever closer to grasping how it is in itself; but this phrase has no sustainable sense in an uncreated or self-creating universe. Just as there is no gap between the truth of a proposition and God's knowing it to be true, so the phrase 'how things are in themselves' has, in the end, no meaning distinct from 'how God apprehends them to be'. Save under this interpretation, the claim to have described the world as it is in itself—a description which will assume an ever more purely formal, mathematical character, as it is progressively emptied of terms whose meanings derive from our faculties of observation—has no intelligible content. But there is no reason why God, in creating the universe, should have filled in all the details, have provided answers to all conceivable questions, any more than a human artist—a painter or a novelist—is constrained to do so. The conception of a created but partially indeterminate universe is easier to grasp than that of an uncreated and partially indeterminate one.

A verificationist may be able to fashion a semantics of alternative worlds—alternative plenary descriptions of reality, relative to each of which bivalence holds—attributing to each speaker a conception of what it is for any given statement to be true in any one such world. If he interprets the logical constants as obeying the two-valued semantics relatively to each world, he will obtain a classical logic; but he may still identify assertibility (absolute truth) with truth in *all* worlds, so that bivalence will fail and reality will still have gaps. It is far more likely that he will adopt a semantic theory yielding a non-classical logic—quantum logic or, more probably, intuitionistic logic. In so far as classical logic may be considered to be in possession, he will be a revisionist; but, if his arguments against a truth-conditional meaning-theory are sound, and if he can find no way of reconciling his verificationist theory with a semantics whose valuation system is a Boolean algebra, he is in a strong position to demand revision. His semantic theory will necessarily be more complex than any of those proposed for intuitionistic mathematics, because empirical language differs from that of mathematics in a crucial respect. In mathematics, if a predicate or sentence is decidable, it remains decidable, whereas an empirical statement may be decidable now but become undecidable subsequently. Nevertheless, it is plausible that a semantic theory could be constructed for empirical statements that would yield standard intuitionistic logic. Under such a semantic theory, it will be impossible to *identify* any statements as being neither true nor false, just as, in intuitionistic mathematics, there are no statements identifiable as neither provable nor refutable: for to say of a statement that it was not true would be to declare that it could never have been verified, which is just to declare it false. Plainly, adoption of a revisionist meaning-theory, and hence of a non-realist metaphysics, would, in such a case, result in a significant change in linguistic practice.

A pragmatist meaning-theory, whose central notion is that of the consequences of a statement (the second of the 'candidates' discussed above), is less readily envisaged, principally because of the dependence of the consequences for a subject of accepting a statement as true upon his contingent purposes and wishes. There is, nevertheless, no reason to suppose that a suitable notion of consequences, independent of individual desire, cannot be disentangled and made the basis of a meaning-theory. If so, such a theory would have to employ the conception of a picture of reality. If you are told that the music shop is opposite the post office, this has no immediate consequences for you if you do not intend to buy a musical instrument or use the postal services; it merely fills in a detail of the mental map you use in getting around. This may prompt a suspicion that a pragmatist theory might collapse into a truth-conditional one, thereby vindicating the metaphysical realism which the truth-conditional theory supports. The suspicion is surely misplaced, however: a statement cannot have consequences for action, actual or potential, beyond the range within which we can obtain evidence for or against it.

A verificationist meaning-theory must be able to derive the consequences of a statement from its content as determined by what verifies it. Correspondingly, a pragmatist meaning-theory must be able to derive, from the content of a statement, as determined by its consequences, what is to count as verifying it. In both cases, the derivation will guarantee harmony within the language as a whole between the two aspects of linguistic practice, just as a proof-theoretic justification of logical laws, proceeding in either direction, guarantees harmony between introduction and elimination rules. There is, indeed, no assurance in advance that either type of theory will accord completely with our existing practice, since total harmony may not in fact obtain within that practice. In such a case, the construction of the meaning-theory will uncover a malfunction which we need to amend, and we shall aim to make the simplest adjustment possible.

It seems intrinsically reasonable to extend the demand for stability, as well as that for harmony, from the logical constants to the language as a whole. We can satisfy this demand only if we know how to construct both a verificationist and a pragmatist meaning-theory. Given a verificationist meaning-theory, we can derive what the consequences of our statements are to be. On the basis of these consequences, we can construct an alternative, pragmatist, meaning-theory. From this we can then derive what is to count as verifying any given statement: if there is stability, the verification-conditions thus derived will be the same as those with which we began. Conversely, we could start with a pragmatist meaning-theory, derive the corresponding verification-conditions, construct upon them a verificationist meaning-theory, and derive the consequences with which we started. Once more, we might not be able fully to accord with existing practice; but, again, this would be a criticism of the practice, which would require amendment, and not of the meaning-theories. If the demand for stability is acknowledged to be just, verificationist and pragmatist meaning-theories are not genuine rivals but complementary aspects of a single enterprise which alone can fully describe the working of that most profound of all human creations, language. That is why the verificationist has no cause to fear that the pragmatist will surreptitiously reintroduce the conception of truth-conditions that he has rejected. The verificationist has himself to treat, within his theory, of that notion of the consequences of a statement which the pragmatist makes his starting point. If, to vindicate his theory completely, he has to demonstrate stability, then he, too, must be able to construct a pragmatist meaning-theory. Should it really prove that, in order to attain an adequate account of consequences, we are necessarily driven back upon a fully realist conception of truth-conditions, then that was latent in the verificationist approach from the outset. The verificationist will then himself have discovered the true answer to the challenge he issued to the truth-conditional theorist. It is more probable that a workable account of consequences can be attained without retreating to the mythology of truth-conditions, and, if so, the pragmatist is no threat to the verificationist: the two of them are partners in the most ambitious of intellectual endeavours, to gain a clear view of the working of our language.

chapter 15

Realism and the Theory of Meaning

Reductionism, Weak and Strong

Salient examples of the type of metaphysical dispute discussed in the Introduction are: realism concerning the physical world versus phenomenalism; platonism in mathematics versus constructivism; realism concerning the future versus neutralism (the denial of truth-value to contingent statements about the future) and the corresponding though less frequent dispute concerning the past; scientific realism versus instrumentalism; and realism about mental states, events, and processes versus behaviourism. Quite obviously, these are all disputes concerning the correctness of a realistic interpretation of some class of statements, which we may call 'the disputed class'.

Now what is the dispute about? It is, in the first place, a dispute about what, in general, makes a statement of the disputed class true when it is true, that in virtue of which such a statement is true. The opponent of realism makes some claim to the effect that a statement of the disputed class, if true at all, must be true in virtue of such-and-such a kind of thing. A statement about the physical world, if true, must be true in virtue of actual or possible sense experiences; a mathematical statement, in virtue of the existence of a proof; a statement in the future tense, in virtue of present tendencies; a statement in the past tense, in virtue of memories, evidence, or other traces; a theoretical statement, in virtue of observations which confirm it and which it serves to explain; a statement about mental events in virtue of the agent's behaviour. What makes a statement true, that in virtue of which it is true, is a fact: but, to avoid appealing to an ontology of facts, we may say that, in each case, the opponent of realism is singling out some other class of statements, which we may label 'the reductive class', and saying that a statement of the disputed class, if true at all, must be true in virtue of the truth of one or more statements of the reductive class.

It is therefore obvious that opposition to realism always involves some weak form of reductionism. Full-blooded reductionism, however, embodies a thesis about translatability: it claims that the statements of one class can actually be translated into equivalent statements of another class. A rejection of realism, for some class of statements, need not involve espousing a full-blooded reductionism, for two reasons. First, it may be conceded that, for the truth of a statement of the disputed class, infinitely many statements of the reductive class will, in general, have to be true, and that, for any given statement of the disputed class, there will, in general, be infinitely many sets of statements of the reductive class the joint truth of which would render that statement true. There is therefore no guarantee that there exists in the language the means of expressing the infinite disjunction of infinite conjunctions that would, if expressible, render the statement of the disputed class in terms of the vocabulary of the reductive class.

Secondly, it is not integral to the thesis which the opponent of realism maintains that statements of the reductive class can be expressed in a vocabulary the understanding of which is independent of an understanding of the disputed class. Such a contention has indeed been part of the doctrines of instrumentalism and of behaviourism, and phenomenalists have historically gone in for a full-blooded reductionism as well. Consider neutralism about the future, by contrast. The neutralist maintains that future-tense statements cannot be considered to be rendered true or false by what is in fact going to happen, because he denies that there *is*, now, any one determinate future course of events; one version of neutralism concludes that the only admissible notion of truth for future-tense statements is that under which such a statement is true just in case it accords with present tendencies. How, then, do we characterise tendencies towards some given future event? Doubtless, we may get some way by talking about inductive evidence, confirmation of hypotheses, and the like; but we also have to take intentions for the future into account, and there seems no hope of characterising an intention otherwise than by what it is an intention to do. Even apart from intentions, there seems very little likelihood of our obtaining a systematic rule that associated with any future-tense statement those statements in the present tense which would record the existence of tendencies in that direction, a rule yielding an actual scheme of translation. The neutralist will be quite unperturbed by this—finding a translation is not integral to his purpose. He is interested in the kind of meanings possessed by future-tense sentences, but not in order to explain how we could do without them. He thinks, rather, that he can see a connection between what renders such a sentence true, under the only notion of truth he takes to be legitimate for such sentences, and the truth of certain statements in the present tense; whether these latter statements can or cannot be expressed without using future-tense sentences as constituents is all one to him.

Precisely analogous remarks apply to the rejection of realism concerning the past. Consider also constructivism as a philosophy of mathematics. The constructivist's original aperçu is that a proof is the *only* thing that can render a mathematical statement true. He disbelieves in an objective mathematical reality that renders each such statement determinately true or false, independently of our knowledge. It might then be asked whether there is some way of characterising what in general is demanded of a proof of, say, the Bolzano-Weierstrass theorem, without employing the vocabulary in terms of which that theorem is stated, 'real number', 'set', 'interval', and 'infinite'. The constructivist's primary contention does not wait on the answer to this question, however: it is neither proved correct by an affirmative answer, nor refuted by a negative one. An anti-realist position *may* be reductionist, in the full-blooded sense, but it *need not* be.

What of the realist? Is it integral to his position to reject the weakly reductionist claim made by his opponent? This is a matter of terminology, but it is more convenient to deny that a realist needs to reject that claim, and to distinguish varieties of realism according to whether it is rejected or not. When the word 'realist' is used in this way, a sophisticated realist may even be a full-blooded reductionist: one form of realism about mental states and events might admit the possibility of an actual translation of statements about such mental entities into statements of neurophysiology.

What Realism Is

What, then, *is* integral to a realist position? Meinong is sometimes described as an 'ultra-realist', on the score of his attitude to merely possible objects (and, indeed, to impossible ones), and he may be called a realist about possible objects. We cannot say that a realist about things of a certain category is one who believes that such things *exist*, for Meinong differentiated between actual and merely possible objects in that the former, but not the latter, existed; it is quite common for philosophers to distinguish, *within* reality, between those of its denizens which exist and those which only subsist, or are ideal, or the like. Meinong's realism consisted in his treating singular terms as always *denoting* objects—actual ones, merely possible ones, or even impossible ones.

There have been two escape routes from Meinongian realism on offer. One is the account of sentences of natural language containing empty terms (terms not denoting actual objects) proposed by Frege in his post-1890 writings. According to this, such terms do not denote anything; the sentences in which they occur express intelligible propositions (thoughts in Frege's terminology), but these propositions are neither true nor false. Frege was an archetypal realist, both about the physical universe and about mathematics; the whole drive of his philosophy was realist, and, in the Preface to his *Grundgesetze der Arithmetik*, he made a classic pronouncement of the realist faith, saying that the truth of a proposition has nothing to do with its being taken as true. It may therefore seem odd to cite him as an opponent of realism. That is because few realists would be disposed to accept Meinong's ultra-realism about possible objects; and Frege undoubtedly rejected that, although he downplayed even this deviation from realism by stigmatising the ability to form empty terms as a defect of natural language.

Frege's strategy of escape from Meinongian realism was to repudiate the principle of bivalence for propositions expressed in natural language. A quick review of the disputes over realism listed above serves to show that the principle of bivalence is a salient ingredient of realism. Russell, however, provided an escape route that necessitated no violation of bivalence. According to Russell's theory, there is a small category of logically proper names, which are guaranteed a denotation on pain of being meaningless, while all other apparent singular terms are explicit or disguised definite descriptions. Under Russell's celebrated analysis, a definite description is not a genuine singular term at all, nor even an integral semantic unit. When a sentence containing it is correctly analysed, it is seen as expressing a proposition either true or false in every case, but no longer containing any term, or even any distinguishable constituent, corresponding to the definite description.

This solution is obtained by not taking apparent singular terms at face value; since they are not really singular terms, the question of their denotation no longer arises. It is apparent from this example that realism cannot be characterised in purely metaphysical terms: it essentially involves the semantic notion of denotation, as well as the semantic notions of truth and falsity. Integral to any given version of realism are both the principle of bivalence for statements of the disputed class, and the interpretation of those statements at face value, that is to say, as genuinely having the semantic form that they appear on their surface to have. Rejection of either one of these will afford a means of repudiating realism and will constitute a form of anti-realism, however restrained, for statements of the disputed class.

It might be suspected that this example is atypical. It is true that certain doctrines to which the term 'realism' has been applied fit rather badly into the framework here proposed. One such is scholastic realism about universals, opposed by nominalism. Even more difficult to accommodate is realism about vagueness, the doctrine that there is vagueness in reality, not just in our words; vagueness is, of course, a feature quite different from indeterminacy. But Meinong's realism is atypical only in its lack of general appeal. A realist interpretation of number theory, for example, must certainly maintain bivalence for arithmetical statements. But it must also reject the 'nominalist' thesis that numerical terms do not denote, but that arithmetical sentences are to be reinterpreted so that no such terms appear in them (but only, say, numerically definite quantifiers of the general form 'There are n . . .'). Under such a reinterpretation, arithmetical sentences are *not* to be construed at face value.

We may thus characterise a realistic interpretation of a given class of statements as one which applies to them, in accordance with the structure they appear on the surface to have, the classical two-valued semantics, in particular treating the (apparent) singular terms occurring in them as denoting objects (elements of the relevant domain) and the statements themselves as being determinately true or false. This is a narrow understanding of the term 'realism', which classifies even finitely many-valued semantic theories as non-realist; they belong to a broader category of 'objectivist' theories by virtue of their assumption that every statement has a determinate one of the finitely many truth-values, independently of our knowledge. Such theories normally reject bivalence, because, equating the falsity of a statement with the truth of its negation, they do not regard it as being false whenever it is not true; but they maintain the weaker objectivist thesis that every statement is determinately either true or not true.

The versions of anti-realism listed above are all, however, characterised by a rejection of bivalence, and even of objectivism in the foregoing sense. Of all the features of classical semantics, it is the principle of bivalence that has the greatest metaphysical resonance. A weakly reductionist thesis is not, of course, essential to all non-realist doctrines, when 'realism' is understood in the present strict sense, but it is common to the forms of anti-realism on our list. A weakly reductionist thesis does not, however, of itself amount to a rejection of realism. The point at which the weak reductionist parts company with the realist will be that at which he says, 'For a given statement of the disputed class, there need not exist a statement of the reductive class which renders it either true or false', that is, when, on strength of his weakly reductionist view, he rejects the principle of bivalence for statements of the disputed class. He is here taking the falsity of a statement of the disputed class to consist in the truth of what is ordinarily regarded as its negation.

Such a step he is very likely to take. Unless one is a determinist, there is no reason why, for a given future event, there should now exist tendencies for it to happen or tendencies for it not to happen. The neutralist, who is usually not a determinist, will therefore be disposed to say that a future-tense statement need not be either true or false, as one who rejects a realistic view of the past will say about past-tense statements. Again, even on a platonist view, there is no a priori necessity that, for any mathematical statement, there should be a proof, which we are able to recognise as such, either of the statement or of its negation. The constructivist, too, will accordingly reject the principle of bivalence for mathematical statements. In the case of behaviourism, the point is not usually stressed very heavily, but it operates there also. Scratching is the obvious behavioural manifestation of itching, and, if one makes a very crude equation of having the sensation with exhibiting the behaviour, one may say, 'Either someone scratches or he does not; so either he has an itch or he does not'. No one is likely to be a behaviourist of so crude a kind, indeed; having an itch entails having an *impulse* to scratch, an impulse which one may inhibit. When it comes to more complicated mental phenomena, however, a behaviouristic account leads quite naturally to a rejection of bivalence. Suppose that someone has been perplexed how to end a short story that he is writing, and he tells you the following: 'I was, for once, thinking about something quite different, and suddenly it came to me how to end that story; but just at that moment the telephone rang (the universal modern visitor from Porlock), and, when I sat down again, it had completely gone from me'. Now what were the behavioural manifestations of his alleged inspiration? An incredulous but rapturous smile spread over his face, perhaps he muttered, 'That's it, that's *it*'—and he later gave you that report. Did he really see how to end the story, or he did merely have a momentary illusion of doing so? Perhaps he is someone who often has such flashes of inspiration, and perhaps, half the time, they turn out to be genuine and, the other half, ludicrous states of mental confusion. The immediate behavioural manifestations of a genuine and a spurious inspiration are exactly the same—so, if the manifestations are what makes a statement about the inspiration true, there need not be any fact of the matter as to whether that lost inspiration was genuine or spurious.

Naive Realism

If it is his rejection of the principle of bivalence that marks the reductionist's divergence from realism, then the realist may continue to be a realist, despite espousing even a full-blooded reductionism, as long as he continues to adhere to the principle of bivalence. Someone who identifies mental with neurophysiological events is likely to believe that it must be either true or false that a given neurophysiological event took place, and will presumably hold that the non-occurrence of a given mental event demands only the non-occurrence of the corresponding neurophysiological event, not the occurrence of any other. Thus central-state materialism is unlikely to lead to a repudiation of bivalence for statements about mental events. Nevertheless, a realist very often rejects even the weak reductionist thesis: this version of realism is that known as 'naive realism'.

The principle that, if a statement is true, there must be something in virtue of which it is true, is a regulative principle that can hardly be gainsaid. It is a regulative principle, in that nothing yet follows from it, taken by itself: it determines the form of what we shall say, not the content. Nothing substantial follows from it until it is laid down what sort of things count as rendering a given type of statement true. The realist can therefore hardly repudiate the question in virtue of what a statement of the disputed class is true, when it is true: but, since he rejects the reductionist thesis, he has no informative answer to it. He has, in fact, no *general* answer; and, for specific statements of the disputed class, he can give only a circular answer—that the continuum hypothesis, if true, will be true in virtue of there being no non-denumerable set of real numbers not of the power of the continuum, or that the statement, 'The Andromeda galaxy rotates', if true, is true in virtue of the rotation of the Andromeda galaxy. He need not return so lame an answer to *every* such question; he can, for example, say of a disjunctive statement that, if true, it is true in virtue of the truth of one or other disjunct. Nevertheless, he can only cite, as rendering true a specific statement of the disputed class, the truth of some one or more statements of that same class.

Let us say of a true statement that it is 'barely true' if there is no other statement or set of statements of which we can say that it is true in virtue of their truth. This formulation suffers both from appealing to a criterion of identity for statements and from reliance on the obscure, if compelling, notion of a statement's being true in virtue of the truth of another. One way of avoiding this would be to replace the predicate with one relating a class of statements. Thus we may call a class of statements 'irreducible' if there is no disjoint class such that a necessary and sufficient condition for the truth of any statement in the first class is that of some set of statements of the second class. It is then clear that any specific way of construing the notion of a statement's being true in virtue of the truth of other statements will require that *some* true statements be barely true; and the naive realist regards the true statements of the disputed class as barely true because he holds the disputed class to be irreducible.

Phenomenalism

Phenomenalists claimed material-object statements to be translatable into statements about sense-data, but they never suggested, on this ground, that material-object statements are not subject to bivalence. Indeed, A. J. Ayer maintained that the material-object language and the sense-datum language were simply equivalent alternative modes of expression neither of which was more fundamental than the other. He could hardly have made this suggestion if the phenomenalistic translation imposed a different logic on the material-object language. The phenomenalists thus appear after all to have been not anti-realists but sophisticated realists, according to our criteria. This would call our criteria into question, were it not that phenomenalism contained a strong drive against realism, as judged by those criteria.

The various disputes over realism may be distinguished according as subjunctive conditionals do or do not play a role in them. They play no role in discussions of realism about the future, nor of scientific realism in general. They usually play a role in all the other disputes. At a certain stage in the discussion, one or other disputant is liable to use a subjunctive conditional to explain the condition for the truth of certain statements of the disputed class: usually the opponent of realism, but sometimes the realist. Thus, in the example of the interrupted short story, the behaviourist would be likely to say, 'Though in the actual circumstances there was no behavioural difference between having a genuine and a spurious inspiration, to declare his inspiration genuine amounts to saying that, if he had not been interrupted, he would have gone on to write an ending to the story'. A behaviourist might even claim that to say that someone has an impulse to scratch means that he *would* scratch if he had no reason not to.

In the same way, the first step in the proposed phenomenalistic translation of material-object statements was to form a subjunctive conditional about what would be observed under certain conditions. Isaiah Berlin once wrote an article attacking phenomenalism on the ground that it involved the truth of a large number of counterfactual conditionals whose truth did not rest on that of any statements not involving the subjunctive conditional. Say a phenomenalist wishes to make a translation into sense-datum language of the statement, 'There is a star in the Andromeda galaxy with exactly nine planets'. His first step will be to form a subjunctive conditional about what we should observe were we to visit that galaxy and inspect all the stars in it. He will take the original statement to be equivalent to that subjunctive conditional, and its negation as equivalent to the opposite conditional, with the same antecedent and the contradictory consequent. Now, from a *realist* standpoint, if the original statement is true, its truth would be a compelling *ground* for the truth of the corresponding subjunctive conditional; and, if the statement is false, the truth of its negation would be a ground for the truth of the opposite conditional. In both cases, the relevant conditional would be true in virtue of the corresponding material-object statement. But the phenomenalist cannot say this: for him the truth of the material-object statement would not be a ground for the truth of the subjunctive conditional, since the latter is simply the analysed form of the former. Berlin's argument was that it is contrary to intuition to suppose that there is any true subjunctive conditional whose truth does not rest on that of some categorical statement. Phenomenalism appears to require this; hence it is false.

There was nothing amiss with Berlin's intuition. He was saying, in our terminology, that subjunctive conditionals cannot be *barely* true, or that the class of subjunctive conditionals is not irreducible; and he was surely right. But what made him think that the phenomenalist position demanded that there should be any such barely true subjunctive conditionals? Only the assumption of bivalence for material-object statements: if the statement about the Andromeda galaxy is either true or false, then since, according to the phenomenalist analysis, that statement and its negation turn out to be a pair of opposite subjunctive conditionals, one or other of that pair must be true. But, since there need be no actual observation we shall ever make (no actual sequence of sense experiences) that would give any ground for the one conditional or the other, it follows that there are barely true subjunctive conditionals, including counterfactual ones, and indeed a great many. It is apparent, however, that, if the phenomenalists accepted bivalence, and with it, classical logic, for material-object statements, they were simply thoughtless. They had no reason to accept it and every reason not to, namely, the principle that subjunctive conditionals cannot be barely true. If they had rejected bivalence for material-object statements, Berlin's argument against them could never have been framed.

The phenomenalists made two mistakes: not repudiating bivalence and maintaining a strong reductionist thesis. They were defeated not merely because they could not actually produce the translation but because there cannot be such a thing as a sense-datum language. The general estimation that it was their intention to oppose realism is surely right, but that intention miscarried. To realise it, a strong reductionist thesis was unnecessary. It would have done just as well to advance the weak reductionist thesis that, for a material-object state-ment to be true, there must be some observations that directly or indirectly support it. They could even have conceded that such obser-vations could be reported only by using the ordinary material-object vocabulary; the reductive class would then consist of statements to the effect that such-and-such observations had been made. Nevertheless, it was necessary for the phenomenalists to renounce bivalence, and the logical laws that depend on it, for material-object statements. Realism about the physical world scored too easy a victory: it had the wrong opponent. A reformed anti-realism might yet deprive it of the champion's title.

Disquotation

The correspondence theory of truth is often claimed as essential to realism. This is evidently false, since Frege was undoubtedly a realist but rejected the correspondence theory. The correspondence theory is also often confused with a truth-conditional meaning-theory, which is the natural extension of the classical two-valued semantic theory that we have taken as characteristic of realism. A properly constructed meaning-theory rightly seeks to characterise the concepts of truth and meaning simultaneously, whereas the correspondence theory took meaning as already given. It is an analogous mistake to regard the principle that, if a statement is true, there must be something in virtue of which it is true, as peculiar to realism. On the contrary, it is a regula-tive principle which all must accept.

An uninformative or disquotational explanation of that in which the truth of a statement consists, of some such form as, 'The truth of the statement "Mr. Callaghan urged the nation to break its solemn obliga-tions" consists in Mr. Callaghan's having urged the nation to break its solemn obligations', plays a curious double role in discussions of realism. On the one hand, it can be the expression of adherence to the redundancy theory of truth, or to the similar view that the whole ex-planation of the notion of truth is given by a Tarskian truth-definition. As we have seen, these views exclude the possibility of taking the notion of truth to have a significant role in a meaning-theory, and certainly of its being the central notion in the strong sense; they there-fore implicitly criticise the truth-conditional type of meaning-theory characteristic of realism. In Wittgenstein's later writings, citations of the equivalence thesis, that is, of Tarski's (T) schema, play just this role. On the other hand, it can also serve as a means of expressing the conviction that a certain class of statements is irreducible, and thus as an expression of adherence to a naive realist view of statements of that class. This is the role it serves in Putnam's article "Mathematics without Foundations" (*Journal of Philosophy,* vol. 64, 1967). (In this latter role, it would be better expressed by asking what makes the statement true rather than what its truth consists in, or, as Putnam does, what it means to say that it is true.) What makes it possible for the disquotational device thus to serve two masters is the fact that realism is the metaphysical counterpart of a truth-conditional meaning-theory, and a specification of an interpretation in the two-valued semantics can be formulated in the style of a Tarskian truth-definition. There is a great difference, however, between a complete truth-conditional meaning-theory and a truth-definition: for the former involves much more than merely specifying a semantic interpretation. The fundamental difference, as Davidson has observed, is one of objective: the truth-definition takes meanings as given, whereas the meaning-theory treats truth as a primitive theoretical term. Confusion between these two things, or a wavering from one to the other, will only befog discussion of issues concerning realism.

The Ancillary Use of Non-classical Logical Constants

When we oppose a realist interpretation of statements of a certain class to a non-realist one, we must take the realist as understanding the logical constants classically. Moreover, he must treat what would normally be taken to be the negation of a statement as genuinely being its negation. This does not mean that a realist is restricted to using the classical logical constants. A platonistic mathematician, for example, can still distinguish between constructive and non-constructive proofs, although his distinction will not be the same as that drawn by the constructivist; for whether he recognises a procedure as effective will depend upon whether he can prove that it will terminate, and he employs methods of proof unavailable to the constructivist. Markov's principle well illustrates this difference. Since the platonist can distinguish constructive proofs from non-constructive ones, he might find it convenient to introduce a constructive existential quantifier and a constructive disjunction operator alongside the classical ones. He would use the constructive existential quantifier only when he had a proof providing an effective means of finding an actual instance, and the constructive disjunction operator only when he had one from which he could determine one or other disjunct as true.

The realist may, then, employ logical constants not to be explained by means of the two-valued semantic theory. If he does, he will not be disposed to assert the principle of bivalence for the statements formed by means of them, and will thus not interpret *these* statements realistically. He nevertheless remains a realist in his metaphysics, because the non-classical operators he uses are superimposed upon the classical ones, which he still understands in accordance with the two-valued semantics. In particular, he may explain the non-classical operators by means of the classical ones. For instance, the classical mathematician cannot explain his notion of a constructive proof, and hence his use of the constructive logical constants, save by appeal to an existential statement, understood platonistically, that is, in terms of the truth-conditional meaning-theory: the existence of a number with a certain property, non-constructively proved, may guarantee the effectiveness of a certain procedure.

Even one who does not habitually use the classical logical constants in regular discourse, finding the non-classical ones of more practical use, may still qualify as having a realist metaphysics. This will show in his admitting the intelligibility of classical logical constants—in particular, that of classical negation—applied to statements of the given class, considered as subject to a two-valued semantic theory in which the strong principle of bivalence holds. This is the crucial question for realism about quantum mechanics. The mere use of quantum logic is not, in itself, inconsistent with realism: one repudiates realism only when one denies that the classical logical constants, understood in terms of the two-valued semantics, can be intelligibly applied to quantum-mechanical statements. Putnam did implicitly deny this in his article "Is Logic Empirical?" since he compared the replacement of classical by quantum logic with that of a Euclidean geometry (for physical space) by a Riemannian one. Once the latter replacement has been effected, one *cannot* mean by any expression what one formerly meant by 'straight line'; so, likewise, once quantum logic has been adopted, one can no longer introduce other operators to mean what, formerly, one meant by 'and' and 'or' and 'not'.

Anti-realist Meaning-Theories

What sort of meaning-theory for statements of the disputed class will the opponent of realism adopt? This depends crucially upon whether or not he puts a realistic interpretation upon statements of the reductive class. It will make a great difference, for example, whether or not the neutralist is willing to allow that every present-tense statement, unlike a future-tense one, is determinately either true or false (he probably is). It will make an equally great difference whether the opponent of platonism is willing to allow that a statement asserting the existence of a proof of a given mathematical statement is necessarily either true or false (he probably is not). It is important to note that the principle of bivalence, as applied to statements of the disputed class, regarded as integral to realism in respect of those statements, must be formulated as 'Every statement is either true or false', where falsity is equated with the truth of the negation, rather than in the weaker objectivist form, 'Every statement is either true or not true'. One who holds a mathematical statement to be true if and only if there is a proof of it, but who believes that there must either be or not be such a proof, will agree that every mathematical statement is either true or not true, but will not agree that it must be either true or false; and it is his refusal to agree to the latter that robs him of the title of a realist concerning mathematics.

Here we must think of the expression 'There exists a proof . . .' as being used tenselessly, rather than in the sense in which there has existed a proof that π is transcendental only since 1882. Someone who thinks the existence of a proof is required for the truth of a mathematical statement, but who accepts the principle of bivalence for statements of the form ⌜There exists an (intuitively valid) proof that **A**⌝, where these are construed tenselessly, holds a position different from that normally described as constructivist. A constructivist properly so called might choose to take the reductive class to consist of statements of the form ⌜There exists a proof that **A**⌝, where these are construed, this time, as significantly in the present tense; if so, he would presumably accept the principle of bivalence for *them*. This will result in his employing, for mathematical statements, a truth-predicate admitting tense inflections: on this mode of speaking, a mathematical statement may have been neither true nor false but have since become true. For what immediately follows, I wish to set temporarily on one side any such formulation of an anti-realist view: one, namely, that involves applying a significantly tensed truth-predicate to sentences not themselves admitting tense inflections, or to those with a non-indexical temporal reference; this will include any statement of an anti-realist view concerning the future or the past.

If the anti-realist interprets statements of the reductive class realistically, he will adopt a truth-conditional meaning-theory for them. He will also regard them as semantically prior to statements of the disputed class. His meaning-theory will specify the meanings of statements of the disputed class in a manner presupposing the meanings of those of the reductive class. It does not matter whether or not he thinks that statements of the reductive class can be framed in a vocabulary disjoint from that of the disputed class (save for the logical constants). Suppose that the disputed class is that of statements about the physical universe, and the anti-realist is not a phenomenalist but is of the reformed variety described above. Then he will agree that it is impossible to express the statement that some given material-object statement **A**, capable of being used as a report of observation, has been observed to hold, save by using the vocabulary of **A**. He may, however, believe that the statement ⌜It has been observed that **A**⌝ is determinately either true or false. He will then suppose that the meaning-theory has first to give a direct explanation of statements of such forms as ⌜I am observing that **A**⌝ and ⌜Jones observed that **A**⌝. This explanation will be by means of a truth-conditional account, but it will not represent the sentence **A** in the 'that'-clause as a genuine constituent of such a statement. He will believe, further, that material-object statements not used as reports of observation will have to be explained, but not by truth-conditional means, in terms of those recording the making of an observation.

If the anti-realist does not interpret the reductive class realistically, he may hold that there is some class of statements forming a reductive class for *it,* which we may call 'the second reductive class'. We can again ask whether he interprets the second reductive class realistically, and so on: eventually we may reach an *n*th reductive class which he does interpret realistically. Given that in no case are there variable truth-values (the truth-predicate is not significantly tensed), then, whether it is the first reductive class that is interpreted realistically or a later one, it is, in general principle, clear what his meaning-theory is going to look like. Although he does not adopt a truth-conditional meaning-theory for statements of the disputed class, nevertheless his meaning-theory is ultimately based on a conception of statements as having determinate, objective truth-values, independently of our knowledge, namely, the statements belonging to the last of the series of reductive classes. Even of statements of the disputed class, he will be prepared to say that they are, determinately, either true or not true, though not that they are determinately either true or false. He will not usually hold that a statement of the disputed class can be true independently of our *capacity* to know it to be true, since, typically, the reductive class will consist of statements of such a kind that, if true, we can know them to be true, and since, from the realist's standpoint, these statements represent our ordinary type of evidence for the truth of statements of the disputed class. He will nevertheless allow that they can be true independently of whether we *actually* have any means of knowing them to be true. Just because anti-realism of this type is based upon realism concerning another class of statements, it assumes a moderate, rather than a radical, form.

The most interesting form of anti-realism arises when the opponent of realism does not interpret statements of the reductive class realistically but proposes no second reductive class. For instance, a constructivist who takes the reductive class to consist of statements of the form ⌜There exists a proof that **A**⌝, construed as not significantly tensed, will not interpret such statements realistically; but he will not explain the failure of bivalence for them by citing some second class of statements forming a reductive class for them. At first sight, this is a counter-example to the foregoing characterisation of the form that a repudiation of realism, for some class of statements, always takes; but the counter-example is superficial. For it is not that the constructivist *could* not cite a class of statements, which he interprets realistically, the truth of one of which is required for the truth of a statement of his first reductive class; rather, he does not choose to put the matter in this way. He could say, for example, that what makes a statement ⌜There exists a proof that **A**⌝ true is the truth of some statement of the form ⌜We have constructed the proof **P** that **A**⌝. What differentiates this case from those we have been discussing is that this second reductive class consists of statements that are significantly tensed, and therefore have variable truth-values for a commonplace reason. This does not compel the constructivist to employ, for statements either of the disputed class or of the first reductive class, a truth-predicate admitting tense inflections, if he does not wish to. It does mean that he will not be prepared to say, of every statement of the disputed class, that it is determinately either true or not true, or that it may be true independently of our possessing the means of knowing it to be true. His anti-realism is thus of a radical, not a moderate, character.

We temporarily set aside cases in which the anti-realist proposes, for statements of the disputed class, a truth-predicate admitting tense inflections. These have essentially the same character. Such an anti-realist cannot accept, for statements of the disputed class, any notion of truth that attaches to those statements objectively and independently of our *changing* states of knowledge: he therefore has to develop a meaning-theory for them on the basis of some semantic theory into which time enters in an essential way. Although I listed disputes over realism concerning the physical universe, the past, and the future as separate metaphysical disputes, because they tend to arise out of distinguishable philosophical motivations, they must, ultimately, be treated together, just because statements about the physical world do involve reference to time. The problem concerning statements about the past should really be subsumed under that concerning statements about the spatio-temporally inaccessible; and this, in turn, cannot be treated in isolation, since what was spatio-temporally accessible may become inaccessible. An anti-realism about the physical world that takes the reductive class to consist of statements about what at some time has been or will be observed will, if statements of this reductive class are interpreted realistically, constitute only a moderate anti-realism. But, if statements of this reductive class are *not* interpreted realistically, or if the reductive class is taken to consist of significantly tensed statements about what has to date been observed, or is now known to have been observed, then we shall have a radical anti-realism about the physical universe.

A moderate anti-realism will require some semantic theory other than the two-valued one, which may sometimes still yield classical logic. A radical anti-realism, by contrast, will always demand some non-classical logic. The precise form of semantic theory required is a matter for detailed investigation, which will not be pursued here. We are fortunate in having one model, if as yet an imperfect one, for such semantic theories, in those that have been developed for intuitionistic mathematics; intuitionistic logic is surely an even better model for the logic that such a semantic theory will yield for statements of the disputed class. Wittgenstein, who became the most severe critic of a truth-conditional theory of meaning, refused to draw the consequence that our logic demands revision, partly because he placed an unwarranted prohibition upon philosophy's interfering with actual practice, and partly because he held that logical laws need no justification and fix the meanings of the logical constants without the need for further explanation or for the backing of a semantic theory. The intuitionists are so far the only anti-realists who have taken seriously the consequences for logic of their metaphysical and semantic—one should really say 'their metaphysico-semantic'—views, working out those consequences in detail. Quantum logic exemplifies the reverse phenomenon: there we have a still underdeveloped logic, with no good semantic theory to back it, and nothing as yet resembling a plausible metaphysics, which must necessarily be anti-realist. Plainly, we cannot expect that the semantic theories that serve the purposes of intuitionistic mathematics will be adequate to radically anti-realist interpretations of empirical propositions, because the language of mathematics has special features which other parts of language do not have. It remains quite likely that intuitionistic logic will prove appropriate for the task; but that cannot be determined without much arduous enquiry.

Metaphysics and the Theory of Meaning

A realist may argue that any form of radical anti-realism involves construing statements of the disputed class as containing a tacit reference to the present, in addition to any time reference they may explicitly carry, for the assertibility of a statement will always depend on the evidence currently available. A realist maintains a wide gap between the objective correctness of an assertion—its truth—and its subjective justification, the evidence possessed by the speaker. For the anti-realist, the gap is narrower: the question for him is whether he can make it sufficiently wide to admit a notion of objective truth which is not lost when our evidence decays and is not acquired for the first time when our information is obtained. Truth, so understood, would have to be explained as consisting in an objective possibility, for a suitably placed observer, of verifying the statement. If this explanation is to render truth a timeless attribute, it will have to be allowed that there either *is* or *is not* such a possibility, where the 'is' is tenseless and the 'or' is determinate; and now the anti-realist has shifted his position a good way in the direction of moderation. The realist's charge therefore appears well grounded, when directed at genuinely radical anti-realism; and some anti-realists, such as neutralists about the future, may be willing to admit it cheerfully. We already have in our language a use of the future tense which overtly refers to present tendencies, as in 'The marriage announced between X and Y will not now take place' (it was going to up to two days ago); so one type of neutralist will express his view as being that there is no other intelligible use of the future tense than this one. Another type will distinguish this use of the future tense from that in which a statement about the future is rendered true only by *irreversible* present tendencies, so that such a statement cannot change in truth-value but may *acquire* one. But, if the anti-realist acknowledges that statements of the disputed class carry this tacit reference to the present, there is no way of forcing him to concede that it should be made explicit, still less that, when it has been made explicit, it should be replaceable by references to other times. The demand for such a mode of expression is motivated by the realist assumption that every proposition should be formulable by a sentence that timelessly possesses whatever truth-value it has (or timelessly lacks one); but the anti-realist neither shares this assumption nor believes that it can be realised.

How, then, can such disputes be resolved? My contention is that all these metaphysical issues turn on questions about the correct meaning-theory for our language. We must not try to resolve the metaphysical questions first, and then construct a meaning-theory in the light of the answers. We should investigate how our language actually functions, and how we can construct a workable systematic description of how it functions; the answers to those questions will then determine the answers to the metaphysical ones. For the metaphysical questions are formulated in terms of the appropriate *picture* of the reality to which our statements relate: the picture of an objective disposition of matter within space-time, existing in supreme indifference to us and the way it impinges on us, as against the picture of a world of sense perceptions, out of which we construct the material universe as a representation of their complicated regularities; the picture of an ethereal realm of abstract entities, likewise existing objectively and independently of our knowledge, as against the picture of our creating mental structures which are objects of our understanding in a sense analogous to that in which fictional characters are objects of our imagination; the picture of the mind as a locus of immaterial transactions between immaterial entities, as against that of a human being as simply a material object that functions in a particularly complicated way, but *empty* within, so to speak; or the picture of a determinate and static four-dimensional reality, through which our consciousness travels, as against various pictures of a changing reality—a four-dimensional one which continually grows as the passage of time brings new states of affairs into being, reality consisting of present and past, but not future, states of affairs (cf. C. E. Broad, *Scientific Thought*, Chapter 2), or simply an ever-changing three-dimensional one, reality consisting only of what there is *at present*. Philosophers have perennially argued for particular pictures against their rivals. The realist argues that an independently existing material universe is the only hypothesis that explains the regularities in our experience. The idealist retorts by asking, with Berkeley, what content the belief in an autonomous realm of matter can have. It is, however, useless to carry on a debate in favour of one or other of these competing pictures as if they were rival hypotheses to be supported by evidence. What we need to do is to formulate theses which are no longer in pictorial language but which embody the intended applications of these pictures. If we do that, those theses will be found to be theses belonging to the theory of meaning, theses about the correct meaning-theory for statements of one or another kind. When we have resolved the issue about the correct meaning-theory, then we shall surely find that one or another of the rival pictures will force itself on us, unless it proves that we want to reject *all* the competing pictures.

What Is a Correct Meaning-Theory?

But how are we to decide what *is* the correct meaning-theory? Ultimately, the only test is the production, in sufficient detail to ensure that no further problems would arise, of the outline of a workable meaning-theory: its assessment as workable would depend upon a careful prior analysis of that practice in using our language which we acquire in the course of learning it. There is here an asymmetry between realist and anti-realist meaning-theories. With due allowance for the existence of non-truth-functional operators such as the subjunctive conditional, classical logic may be said to be in possession. Hence, as against a version of anti-realism demanding a non-classical logic, any meaning-theory that can be shown to be workable and that validates classical logic is to be preferred. To make it plausible that we should adopt a meaning-theory that requires a non-classical logic, and hence any embodying a radical anti-realism, we must not only show that meaning-theory to be reasonably workable but also make it probable that there can be no workable meaning-theory that validates classical logic, since the meaning-theory we are recommending demands a revision of our actual practice, instead of merely describing and explaining it.

What is meant by a 'workable' meaning-theory? Plainly, first, that it should accord with our practice, to the greatest extent that is possible. But, secondly, that it should enable us to explain in a non-circular manner, and without appeal to notions which presuppose a meaning-theory, and are not explained by the meaning-theory we are giving, what a speaker's grasp of the sense of any expression is. Which notions do presuppose a meaning-theory? Obviously those expressed by such words as 'true', 'assertion', 'denotes', and 'equivalent', but also those of propositional attitudes, like intention and, particularly, belief, at least except for the simplest kinds of intention and belief. The reason is that—save for the very simplest intentions and beliefs, such as those we ascribe, without excessive anthropomorphism, to dogs—it is unintelligible to ascribe to anybody the intentions and beliefs expressible by means of our language, without presupposing that he has a mastery of a language in which they can be expressed. He must at least grasp the relevant concepts; and these will include concepts the possession of which we know how to explain only in terms of the mastery of a language capable of expressing them. This appears to rule out any approach along the lines proposed by Paul Grice. It might be retorted that we can carry out the Gricean programme if we divide our task into suitable stages and our language into corresponding levels. We begin by giving a Gricean account of the first level of the language in terms of those intentions and beliefs which it does make sense to ascribe to one who has no language, having first explained what it is to have such a belief or such an intention. Next, we give a Gricean account of the second level in terms of those intentions and beliefs which it makes sense to ascribe to someone who has mastered the first level; and so on through all the levels. This stratified Gricean programme is unlikely to be feasible, however. As stated by Grice himself, the speaker's intention must be to convey precisely that belief expressed by his assertion; it is difficult to see how this could be replaced by an intention expressible in a lower level of language than the sentence uttered.

What is involved in giving a non-circular explanation of a speaker's grasp of the sense of an expression? This is the most critical question, to which much of this book has been directed towards giving a partial answer. The arguments reviewed in the last chapter were all aimed at showing that a truth-conditional meaning-theory must violate the requirement of non-circularity. As a very general formulation, to which everybody could agree, one might say that a circular explanation is any that invokes a capacity on the part of the speaker which cannot intelligibly be ascribed to him in advance of his knowing the language: it will require much philosophical discussion before we can determine the application of this highly general requirement. The more specific general principle here proposed has been that the explanation, while given in terms of what the speaker knows, must be filled out by an explicit account of that in which such knowledge consists. Such an account must be given in terms of how that knowledge is delivered to him, and hence how it is manifested in his observable linguistic and non-linguistic behaviour. This amounts to an interpretation of one component in Wittgenstein's slogan 'Meaning is use'. Even to be sure of the content of this principle, we have to look at how it is applied in particular arguments for or against a given type of meaning-theory. To make the issues a little sharper, we may end by considering what the realist's response might be to the last of the four arguments against a truth-conditional meaning-theory sketched in the previous chapter. This will be done in the spirit of Gaunilo's plea on behalf of the fool.

A Realist Rejoinder

The argument which the realist has to rebut is this: If the principle of bivalence holds, there will be sentences of our language that will be true even though we are not capable of knowing them to be true. It is impossible that, for every such sentence, a knowledge of the condition which must obtain for it to be true can be explained as explicit knowledge, that is, as an ability to *state* that condition in other words. But, since a knowledge of the condition for the truth of the sentence will transcend the capacities we have for recognising it as true in special cases, it follows that we cannot, without circularity, exhaustively explain, in terms of its actual manifestations, in what a knowledge of that condition consists.

There are three possible replies that the realist may make. First, he may agree that any knowledge that is ascribed by a meaning-theory to a speaker has to be explained, ultimately, in terms of how that knowledge is manifested. He may point out, however, that since the view taken by the radical anti-realist is a revisionist one, there *is* a feature of actual practice which may be taken as manifesting a knowledge of the truth-conditions of the sentences, namely, the practice of reasoning in accordance with the canons of classical logic.

This reply we have already rejected. It is implausible that the mere propensity to reason in accordance with the laws of classical logic should *constitute* a grasp of a notion of truth satisfying the principle of bivalence, though it might well give rise to an illusion that we had such a notion. Imagine, for example, that we had been subjected, since childhood, to a training in applying to counterfactual conditionals the laws of classical logic, construing the negation of a counterfactual as the opposite counterfactual. We should then be under a strong compulsion to do what we are often tempted to do now, namely, to suppose that any counterfactual must be determinately true or false independently of our knowledge, as when we wonder what would have happened if we had made some important decision in our lives otherwise than we did, in a frame of mind in which we submit to the illusion that there must be some definite answer, whether or not we can know it. But the fact that we reasoned in accordance with these classical laws would not show that we really had a realist notion of truth for counterfactual conditionals. This reply, on the part of the realist, generalises the thesis that any consistent set of logical laws serves to fix the meanings of the logical constants to the claim that they fix the meanings of the sentences to which those constants are applied.

If the first reply is unsuccessful, then the realist must, as a second reply, somehow repudiate the principle that we must be able to explain that knowledge in which our understanding of any expression consists by reference to its manifestations, although he will still agree that it is only by learning the use of an expression that we come to grasp its meaning. One way in which he may seek to rebut this principle is by emphasising the *theoretical* character of a meaning-theory. Within such a theory, we explain a speaker's understanding of an expression or sentence by ascribing to him a knowledge of some feature of it, or by viewing him as somehow associating some semantic item with it. But, the realist claims, we do not then need to explain in terms of his linguistic behaviour what it is for him to have this knowledge or make this association. In constructing a meaning-theory, we are not, he says, attempting to articulate the complex of practical abilities that make up the mastery of a language into its constituents, conceived of as isolable though interconnected practical abilities. All that we are aiming at, according to him, is what any theory attempts to provide—a picture which, taken as a whole, renders a complex phenomenon surveyable, even though there is no one-to-one correspondence between the details of the picture and the observable features of the phenomenon.

According to the first possible realist reply, acceptance of classical logical laws *constitutes* a grasp of a notion of truth for our statements which is subject to the strong principle of bivalence. According to this second reply, it does not constitute a grasp of such a notion of truth but, rather, *warrants the ascription* to a speaker of a grasp of that notion, without the need for further explanation or justification. This is the most sophisticated of the three realist replies here considered, but it, too, fails.

The theoretical character of a meaning-theory must indeed be respected: the concepts it employs are not answerable to their counterparts in everyday parlance but are justified and explained solely by their roles in the theory. But a meaning-theory should not be treated as an indissectable Duhemian whole. Although a scientific theory must account for a complex of phenomena, there is only *one* such complex for which it must account. A meaning-theory, by contrast, has not fulfilled its function if it merely provides an accurate conspectus of a single complex phenomenon, the use of a language within a community whose language it is; it has also to explain in what the understanding of the language by any individual member of the community consists. The language is indeed a social practice, and an individual's mastery of it is his ability to participate in that practice. But his understanding of what is said to him, and of what he himself says, is a conscious understanding: he does not merely react in accordance with the training he has received like one conforming to a post-hypnotic suggestion. For this reason, we must demand from the meaning-theory the capacity to explain what it is for an individual to understand a particular utterance, his own or someone else's. Very often it will be correct, as a first answer to the question of what constitutes such understanding, to say, 'He utters / hears the sentence, and he knows the language'. This reply is a counter to the idea which Husserl had, and which Wittgenstein repeatedly attacked, that there must be an inner mental process that accompanies the utterance or the act of listening and that constitutes the understanding. But, to understand the utterance, one need not know *all* the language; to maintain otherwise is to espouse holism. Indeed, one may misunderstand, or fail to understand at all, because one misunderstands, or does not know, a single word contained in the sentence. Mastery of a language must, therefore, be dissectable: it must be possible to say what part of the language a speaker must know if he is to be able to understand a given sentence or a given word, and what it is to have that knowledge. The meaning-theory will fail even to describe adequately the use of the language by the community if it resists such dissection, because it is a feature of the phenomenon that every speaker's mastery is partial and imperfect. Above all, the realist's second reply makes the mistake to which the anti-realist is more prone, of regarding mastery of a language as a *purely* practical ability. Since understanding is genuinely a form of knowledge, and not a single piece of knowledge but the knowledge of a great many distinct though interrelated items, a meaning-theory that merely feigns to ascribe knowledge to the speakers, but fails to explain in what the constituent pieces of knowledge consist, must be regarded as defective.

Third, and in a quite different spirit, the realist may contend that what is required for a grasp of the meanings of our expressions is not a mere aptitude in their use, or even a knowledge of the rules that govern that use, but the formation of the right mental conception of the principles underlying those rules. Use, he argues, does not constitute meaning, as it might if we were computers being programmed in one way rather than another. It *guides* us, as rational creatures, to select the intended mental representation from among different possible candidates. He admits that we learn the most primitive parts of language by connecting their use with our own actual capacities, for instance to effect an immediate recognition of certain unanalysable features of our sensory environment, to carry out more complex feats of recognition of observable features, and to perform computations. But, he claims, having mastered this lowest level of language, we proceed to higher levels by analogy. This means that we come to understand the condition for the truth of a higher-level sentence via a conception of an ability to determine their truth or falsity effectively and directly, an ability which we do not ourselves possess, but of which we conceive by analogy with those abilities we do have. For instance, having learned, by means of an effective procedure, the meaning of quantification over a finite and surveyable domain, we extend our understanding to quantification over an unsurveyable or even infinite domain, by appealing to a conception of what it would be to determine the truth or falsity of sentences involving such quantification by means analogous in principle to those we were taught to employ for small domains. In a similar way, without noticing that any step is being taken, we transfer our understanding of sentences referring to what is spatio-temporally accessible to those referring to the inaccessible; in so doing, we make a surreptitious appeal to the conception of an ability to determine, by inspection, the truth of a sentence of the new kind in the same general way as we determine the truth of one of the old kind. Such an ability comprises the capacity to view at will any region of space-time, so that all are accessible; but, according to this defence of realism, we can conceive of it by extension from the capacity to survey a small spatio-temporal region. Again, we understand statements about other people's mental states by appeal to the conception of a capacity to inspect the content of a mind, arrived at by analogy with our capacity to inspect the contents of our own minds. On this realist view, the behaviour of others is our *evidence* for ascribing certain mental states to them, but does not give the *meanings* of such ascriptions.

What prompts us to invoke such analogies, the realist maintains, is precisely our learning to apply the laws of classical logic, in particular the law of excluded middle, to mathematical statements, statements about the indefinite future, statements about the spatio-temporally inaccessible, statements about mental events, and the rest. We derive from this practice an awareness of the fact that we are meant to understand that what any such statement relates to, and either renders it true or renders it false, is *there* independently of our knowledge or means of knowledge. Now, the realist argues, for decidable statements—those statements, belonging to the most primitive part of language, for which we do have an effective method of determining their truth-value—the anti-realist's account is correct: our knowledge of that in which the truth of such a statement consists, of what makes it true, if it is true, really does lie in our knowledge of what it is to *perceive* or *recognise* that it is true. This, he claims, is why the circularity that arises, in these cases, from any attempt to *state* in words what renders such a statement true, when it is true, is harmless. Furthermore, he concedes the absurdity of supposing that a statement of any kind could be true if it was in principle impossible to know that it was true. The anti-realist's mistake, he thinks, is to apply this proposition in such a way that 'impossible' is taken to mean 'impossible *for us*'. Our spatio-temporal perspective is a quite particular one, and our observational and intellectual faculties are, contingently, limited, so that there is no reason to suppose that any true statement will be able to be known to be true by us. All that is necessary is that there could be a subject capable of knowing it, if only one with greater perceptual or cognitive powers than ours. Thus, for any statement, our knowledge of what has to hold for it to be true, which constitutes our understanding of it, will always consist in a conception of what would be involved in recognising it to be true in the most direct manner.

It follows that our knowledge of the truth-conditions of sentences whose truth we cannot or cannot always recognise directly as true, but must rely on indirect evidence or roundabout reasoning, will involve our forming, by analogy with our own faculties, the conception of a hypothetical being with superhuman powers. For us to be said to have such a conception, the powers in question must be conceived as extensions of ones we have, that is, by genuine analogy, such as the power to inspect each member of a set in a finite time, even if the set is denumerably infinite. It would not do to attribute to such a hypothetical being the power to recognise counterfactual reality (the truth or falsity of counterfactual conditionals) directly, unless we were given some account of what such a power would be like; perhaps the possible-worlds picture, when construed realistically, is intended to do just that.

According to this third reply, the practice of using classical forms of argument neither *constitutes* our grasping a notion of truth satisfying the principle of bivalence, nor merely *warrants the ascription* to us of a grasp of such a notion; rather, the practice *prompts* us to form that notion. It is scarcely surprising that realists who offer this argument, or have it in the back of their minds, are anxious to stress what they take to be the contingent character of our lack of those superhuman powers which would make all our statements decidable: thus Russell spoke of our inability to perform infinitely many tasks in a finite time as 'a mere medical impossibility'. Of the three realist replies, the first is certainly the weakest, the second, the strongest debating position, and the third, that which has in practice the strongest appeal. As a psychological analysis of the kind of philosophical reflections that incline us, including those who are not practising philosophers, to adopt realistic interpretations of our sentences, it could not be better. As a reasoned defence of realism, however, it is far from cogent.

How can we give meaning to our expressions by reference to operations which are only analogically described, which so far as we know are not carried out, and which are in principle impossible for us? Suppose there really were a being of whom we had good reason to believe that he did perform one of these operations: say a being twelve feet high, of majestic but not quite human figure, living at the top of a mountain, and having lived there as long as the records stretch back. Twice a week, at fixed times, he will converse with any who make their way up the mountain, and, on one of these two days, will answer questions in first-order arithmetic. He discourages people from regarding him as a god, and explains that he is able to perform infinitely many computations in a finite time, since he can speed up his calculations without limit. Whenever a question has been asked to which the answer was already known, his answer has always agreed with ours, save in one case, when an error was subsequently discovered in a hitherto accepted proof. We ask him to perform the calculations on paper for us, say, for whether there are infinitely many twin primes. He explains that that would need an infinite amount of paper, and that, in any case, there is an upper bound to the speed of his external bodily movements; nevertheless, he will, by elementary methods, determine for us which numbers are prime among those less than one million, speeding up as he goes along in a convergent geometrical series, provided that we provide him with sufficient writing materials. As far as we can see until everything becomes a blur, and as much farther as is revealed by the slow-motion camera, he speeds up his calculations as he had said; and when the paper is carted away and laboriously examined, the calculations prove correct.

There are still objections that might be brought against his story; but suppose that we accept it, and therefore henceforth accept any answers that he gives. Wittgenstein would say that we had accepted a new criterion for the truth of statements involving unbounded arithmetical quantifiers, but let us not raise any question along those lines. In the light of various agreements between what he does and what we have hitherto been doing, and of certain evidence in support of his account of himself, we accept that his answers are correct. Now, how does that fantasy help to explain the meanings that, as things are, we attach to arithmetical statements? The realist may say that, if there were such a being, he would be able to decide the truth or falsity of every statement of elementary arithmetic, and his answers would be correct according to the meanings we now give to such statements. But, even if we accept that claim, why does that give us grounds for thinking that, as we now understand arithmetical statements, each such statement must, determinately, be either true or false?

The realist will answer that, if there were such a being he would determine the statement either as true or as false; and what we *mean* by saying of an arithmetical statement that it is true is that, if there were such a being, he would determine it as true. This, however, is just the same fallacy that is always committed by realists whenever they devise an argument for realism that appeals to counterfactuals. From the fact that, if there were such a being, he would determine the statement either as true or as false, it does *not* follow that either it is the case that, if there were such a being, he would determine it as true, or, if there were such a being, he would determine it as false. If we assume from the outset that the statement *is* determinately either true or false, then it does follow: but this was just what the realist was supposed to be proving. An appeal to counterfactuals, considered as the equivalents of statements of a certain form, never succeeds in yielding a reason to interpret the latter statements realistically, to accept the principle of bivalence for them. For we shall always need, in order to make out the argument, to assume that one or other of certain pairs of opposite counterfactuals must be true; and the only reason we could have to assume this is that we have already decided on a realistic interpretation of the statements in question, those the truth and falsity of which are being equated with the truth of one or other opposite counterfactual.

If there really were such a superhuman arithmetician, and if he were known to be immortal, and if he undertook to answer any question put to him, then we could legitimately reason classically within elementary number theory. It would not matter whether, for a given arithmetical proposition, we considered it *already* determinate what answer the oracle would give to the question whether or not it was true: we should have an effective means, albeit non-mathematical in character, for deciding the question whenever we chose to employ it; anything demonstrated to follow both from the truth of the proposition and from its falsity could therefore be definitively established. But that would not be because we can *conceive* of the superhuman being; it would be because he existed and would answer our questions. If he were not certain to reply, his abilities would not justify our employment of classical reasoning; still less can they do so while he remains hypothetical.

An appeal to hypothetical beings is of no help to us in giving an account of the meaning *we* attach to the sentences of *our* language. Nor is an appeal to analogy of the kind made in this third realist reply. The notion of analogy has a role to play in the theory of meaning. The application to the very large or the very small of predicates first learned in application to objects we can perceive as a whole can hardly be explained without it. But the analogies that the realist draws, if he gives a reply of the third form to the anti-realist, are of the useless kind that Wittgenstein caricatured in his example of its being five o'clock on the sun; when asked what that means, one says, 'Well, it means that it is on the sun just the same as it is here when it is five o'clock here'.

God's Omniscience

Can a theist resist the realist's argument? When we approach the issue from the side of metaphysics, theism seems a natural ally of realism. For reality must be as God apprehends it; and his knowledge of it guarantees that it is as it is, independently of how it appears to us or of whether we know it or can know it. But, when we approach from the side of the theory of meaning, the matter appears differently: for we are concerned with the meanings *we* confer on *our* words in virtue of *our* use of them; and how can divine knowledge bear on those? And yet the theist can hardly fault the realist's appeal to the conception of a being with superhuman abilities on the score that it is merely hypothetical, for he believes that there is a being whose cognitive capacities are unbounded. The question is whether the realist can justify his ascription to *us* of an association with each of our statements of a truth-condition which determinately either obtains or does not obtain by an appeal to God's omniscience.

Even an intuitionist is compelled to appeal to the hypothetical outcome of procedures we cannot in practice carry out because of their length, although they are composed of steps each of which we know how to take. He treats as decidable, and hence as satisfying the law of excluded middle, a mathematical statement that would be decided by such a procedure if it could be carried out; the fact that it cannot be is, for him, a contingent feature of human limitations, of no mathematical significance. If we can derive a proposition both from such a statement and from its negation, he views us as entitled to assert that proposition, since we could 'in principle' give a canonical proof of it. To do so, we should have to decide the truth or falsity of the statement, which we could 'in principle' do. The thought that makes this attitude plausible is that it must be determinate what the outcome of the decision procedure would be, were it to be carried out by one not subject to our limitations, since it is finite and composed of steps each of which is fully determinate.

Now, must not the theist say something similar about the statement that there are infinitely many prime pairs? Granted, God's thoughts are not as our thoughts, but that seems beside the point; we are concerned not with divine concepts but with God's knowledge of truths involving human concepts, truths in which there is no indefiniteness since the concept of a prime number is quite definite, being fixed by a decision procedure. Since primality is decidable, the statement that any particular natural number is prime must be determinately either true or false, since the decision procedure, if applied to that number, would have a determinate outcome. If we deny this, we shall be forced to repudiate the relatively liberal intuitionist criterion for decidability and be driven back into strict finitism, a doctrine that involves admitting infinite sequences with finite upper bounds on the number of their terms, and that is very dubiously coherent. But then if God knows everything, he must know, of every natural number, whether or not it is prime: must he not therefore know whether there is a largest prime pair?

The reasoning appears very compelling; in fact, there could be no purer example of the question-begging processes of thought which reinforce our inborn attraction to realism. There is no reason to construe God's knowledge of a proposition as requiring his eternal concentration upon it, any more than your knowing your own name involves your incessantly repeating it to yourself; something is known if it is available for use as it is needed. The realist assumes that, if God knows every prime number, he must *thereby* know whether or not there are infinitely many prime pairs; but the transition from the determinacy of the infinitely many instances to that of the (doubly) quantified statement was precisely what he was trying to establish, so that he is at just this point begging the question. The constructivist allows that it is determinate, for every natural number, whether it is prime or composite; he denies that it follows that the proposition that there are infinitely many prime pairs is determinately either true or false. The realist cannot prove that it does follow by simply assuming it, even when he makes a detour via God's knowledge of mathematical truths. It no more follows that God must know whether there are infinitely many prime pairs from knowing every prime number than it follows that a calculating prodigy can say whether there are infinitely many prime pairs from being able to say straight off, of any number, however large, whether it is prime or composite.

God indeed knows everything: so, if we are capable of proving that there are, or that there are not, infinitely many prime pairs, or even if we should be capable of proving one or the other if we could decide all propositions decidable in principle, God may be supposed to know it. That does not vindicate the realist's claim that he must know one or the other *from* knowing, of each number, whether it is prime or not. That would follow only if we assume that the infinitely many individual propositions to the effect that a particular number is prime together determine the proposition about prime pairs as true or as false. That, however, is just the question at issue. The realist wishes to attribute to us an understanding of the quantifiers as operators yielding a statement whose truth-value is jointly determined by the individual instances, independently of our means for recognising it as true or as false. When the domain is infinite, his opponent denies that we can understand them in any such way: even should an angel inform him that God understands them in that way, he would still deny that *we* can; this would then really be a case of our being unable to understand the thoughts of the Almighty. We want to know whether God either knows, of the proposition *we* express by saying that there are infinitely many prime pairs, that it is true, or knows that it is false. It is irrelevant to remark that he knows the truth or falsity of some related proposition that we cannot understand. The realist contends that they are the same proposition; but that, again, is the question at issue.

The anti-realist may even be disposed to doubt the angel: if an infinite process is one which it makes no sense to speak of as having been completed, then it makes no sense to speak of God's completing such a process, either. Our objection to the fantasy of the superhuman arithmetician was that he did not exist; a stronger objection is that, since he completes infinite tasks and uses their outcome to evaluate quantified propositions, he *could* not exist. It is a persistent illusion that, from the premiss that God knows everything, it can be deduced that he knows whether any given proposition is true or false—that is, that he either knows that it is true or knows that it is false, and that his omniscience therefore entails that the proposition *is* either true or false. On the contrary, its being either true or false is required as a further premiss in order to deduce from his omniscience that he knows, in the sense stated, whether it is true or false.

Index

algebraic characterisation of logic, 18, 40, 45, 81–82
analytical philosophy, 1–4, 18–19, 111–112
anti-realism, 4, 9–12, 16, 331, 334–339; global, 16; radical, 336–338
Aquinas, St. Thomas, 233
Aristotle, 2
assertion, 114–115, 117, 121, 165–166, 172, 174
assertoric content, 48, 114–115
Augustine of Hippo, St., 6
Austin, J. L., 44–45, 120
awareness, 97–100
axiom of choice, 191, 201
Ayer, A. J., 7, 329

behaviourism, 322–323, 327
Belnap, N., 246, 251
Berkeley, G., 339
Berlin, I., 329–330
Beth trees, 26–27, 34–35, 37, 41, 55, 65, 152–154, 203
Birkhoff, G., 9
bivalence, 9–10, 74–75, 318, 325–328, 330, 334, 336, 342
Broad, C. E., 339
Brouwer, L. E. J., 9, 239–241

central notion of a meaning-theory, 32–33, 162–164, 317
Chomsky, N., 97, 316
circularity, 200–204, 314
classical semantics, 25, 31, 35–38, 60, 304
completeness, 22; of intuitionistic logic, 27, 296
complexity condition, 258, 283

compositionality, 221–225
conditionals, 171–174, 272–274; counter-factual, 181–183, 206–208, 217, 342, 347; subjunctive, 315, 319–330
conservative extension, 217–220
constructivism in mathematics, 5, 9, 12, 177–179, 192, 302, 322, 327, 332, 333, 335–336
cut elimination, 250
cut property, 42, 44

Davidson, D., 22, 65, 102, 103, 108–110, 112, 116, 119–120, 304, 332
designated truth-values, 34–35
'determinately', 75–80
dialects, 86–87
distributive law, 9–10, 252–253, 286, 290
Duhem, P., 225–226, 231–232, 234–238, 242, 244, 343

elimination rules, 251–253, 256, 280–281, 287–290
Evans, G., 3–4, 222
excluded middle, 9, 17, 191, 345
existential import, 17, 301–302

falsity, 49
finite model property, 42
force (of an utterance), 114–121
Frege, G., 2–3, 12, 18, 24–25, 30, 38, 65, 102, 114–116, 119, 121–122, 123–126, 130–138, 140, 141–151, 195–199, 209, 224, 239–240, 244, 272, 304, 306–308, 324–325, 331
Friedman, H., 296
fundamental assumption, 254, 265–279, 281

Geach, P., 141–144, 147
Gentzen, G., 41, 250, 251, 257, 280
Gödel, K., 27, 197
Goodman, N. D., 27
Grice, P., 340

Hare, R. M., 115
harmony, 215–220, 246–251, 286–287, 290, 320
Harrop, R., 42
Hegel, G. W. F., 2
Heyting's explanations of the logical constants, 26, 29, 34, 58, 177, 227
Hintikka's games-theoretic semantics, 34, 157–159
holism, 212, 221–244
Husserl, E., 343

idiolects, 86–88, 105–106
imperatives, 114–118
inconsistency, 209–210, 214–215
ingredient sense, 48
instrumentalism, 5–6, 323–324
interpretation, 20; by replacement, 23–24; internal, 27–29, 31–32, 56–60; programmatic, 32, 36, 57, 60, 72–73; semantic, 24, 36, 57, 60, 72–73
introduction rules, 251–252, 256–258, 270, 280, 287–290
intuitionistic logic, 9, 16, 41, 43, 270, 299–300, 319, 337

justification of logical laws, 22–23, 162–163, 184–199, 200–215, 244–264, 301–304

Kant, I., 6, 199
Kitcher, P., 240
knowledge: *de re,* 132; explicit, 96–97; implicit, 95–96; manifestation of, 104–105; of a language, 93–95, 102–103, 306–307; of a proposition, 70–71, 109–110, 112. *See also* meaning
knowledge-what, 126–131
Kreisel, G., 27
Kripke, S., 48, 72, 88, 311
Kripke trees (models), 26, 34–35, 41, 45, 55

Lewis, C. I., 7
Lindenbaum algebra, 42–44
local peak, 248–250

Locke, J., 11
logical constants, 54–55, 215–217, 247, 272, 278, 287, 302, 332–333
Łukasiewicz's three-valued logic, 39, 46–47, 49–50

Markov's principle, 27
Martin, R. L., 72
Martin-Löf, P., 280
meaning, 21, 195; and knowledge, 83, 93–105; of words and of sentences, 100–103, 224
meaning-theory, 18, 22, 32–33, 61–62, 66, 72, 92, 103, 107–113, 138–140, 148–151, 162–164, 280, 333–335, 337–341, 342–344; modest, 107–113, 135–136; pragmatist, 102, 211–214, 216, 217, 229–230, 280, 287, 289, 320–321; verificationist, 102, 211–214, 216–217, 229–230, 252, 269–270, 287, 289, 309–310, 317–321
Meinong, A., 324–326
metaphysics, 4–18, 66, 170, 325, 333, 337–339
Mill, J. S., 5, 176
model theory, 23

negation, 291–299, 333
neutralist view of the future, 7, 323–324, 333, 338
Nijmegen school, 152–154
normalisation, 250, 297

omniscience, 318–319, 348–351
optatives, 114–115
or-elimination, restricted, 205–207, 217, 288–289, 290, 293
orthomodular lattices, 42, 45–46

phenomenalism, 4–5, 10, 323–324, 329–331
place-names, 85–86
platonism in mathematics, 5, 12, 322, 327, 332–333
positivism, logical, 10
possible worlds, 154–157
Prawitz, D., 200–201, 250, 252, 254–255
principle of consistency, 292–293, 295
Prior, A., 209, 246
priority of language over thought, 3–4

probability, 50–51
proof-theoretic justification-procedure: downwards, 280–288; upwards, 252–264, 265–279, 287–288
propositional attitudes, 65, 88
Putnam, H., 66, 83–85, 332, 333

quantum logic, 9–10, 16, 42, 55, 206, 271, 319, 333, 337
quantum mechanics, 6, 13, 271, 333
questions, 114–117
Quine, W. V. O., 65, 104, 133, 208–209, 211, 230–232, 236–238, 242–244

realism, 4–19, 181–183, 268, 271, 314–315, 321, 322–351; about mental states, 322; about the external world, 4–5, 322; about time, 6–8, 322, 336–337; moral, 6; naive, 327–329; scientific, 5–6, 322
reductionism, 322–324, 330–331
reference, 24–25, 123–127, 130–133, 135–136, 142–148, 308–309
relativised truth-values, 34, 169
requests, 118–119
rules of inference: direct, 257; oblique, 257, 297; pure, 257; reductive, 283; sheer, 257; simple, 257; single-ended, 256; vertical, 283. *See also* elimination rules; introduction rules
Russell, B., 133, 197, 325, 346

semantic theory, 18, 25, 31–35, 61–62, 81–82, 107, 124–125, 138–140, 148–157, 224, 270, 303–305; skeletal, 151–157
semantic value, 24, 30–31, 35, 122–126
sense, 114, 122–126, 130–133, 135–138, 141–148, 306–307
sequents, 40–41, 185–188
social character of language, 83–88
soundness, 22
Spinoza, B., 11
stability, 280–300, 320–321
statement-values, 30–31

Stenius, E., 115
straightforward stipulations, 25–26, 35–39, 57, 107; absolutely, 25; relatively, 26
subjectivism in ethics, 6
syntax, 25, 30, 33

Tarski, A., 52, 67, 157, 195–196, 203, 209. *See also* Tarski's schema; truth-definition/truth-theory
Tarski's schema, 39, 52–53, 62–65, 67–69, 70–72, 107, 166, 170–171, 331–332
theory of constructions, 27
theory of meaning, 20, 22, 112, 158, 270, 337–339
time, 6–7
tone, 121–122
truth, 20, 32–33, 40–47, 49, 51–54, 67–69, 113, 157–164, 165–183, 271, 308, 338
truth-conditions, 21, 161–163, 171, 305–316, 330–332, 341–348
truth-definition/truth-theory, 22, 63–65, 66–69, 70–72, 107–108, 331–332

understanding, 83–84, 86, 91, 93–105, 124, 206–208

vagueness, 73–74
validity, 20, 40–44, 175–183, 192–194; in terms of ordering, 43–44; in terms of truth, 41
van Dalen, D., 28
von Neumann, J., 9

Waismann, F., 116
Whitehead, A. N., 197
Wiggins, D., 38
Wittgenstein, L., 10, 13, 89, 93, 109–110, 163–164, 209, 211, 217, 219, 305–306, 311, 314, 331–332, 337, 341, 343, 347, 348; *Tractatus*, 102, 149, 295, 304, 305–307
Wodehouse, P. G., 94
Woodruff, P., 72